PRAISE FOR *URBAN LOGISTICS*

'*Urban Logistics* will give you a competitive edge. It is rooted in the real-world experiences of leaders who are at the top of their game, sharing lessons learned from some of the most complex cities around the world.' **Stacey D Hodge, former Director, Office of Freight Mobility, New York City Department of Transportation, USA**

'This book provides a powerful and topical set of authoritative chapters that address the rapidly changing scene of urban logistics, covering complexity, heterogeneity, innovation in delivery systems and technological advances. It provides a welcome addition to the international research in this growing area of transport and, as such, will be of interest to those involved in management, policy and innovation.' **David Banister, Emeritus Professor of Transport Studies and Senior Research Fellow, University of Oxford, UK**

'Management and regulation of urban freight transport is becoming increasingly important for operators, customers and policymakers. In spite of the importance of the subject, there is still a dearth of research, analysis and evaluations. This book will be useful for policymakers and for anyone needing to get a broad overview of this crucial and fast-moving field.' **Jonas Eliasson, Director, Stockholm City Transportation Administration, Sweden**

Urban Logistics

Management, policy and innovation in a rapidly changing environment

Edited by
Michael Browne, Sönke Behrends,
Johan Woxenius, Genevieve Giuliano
and José Holguín-Veras

KoganPage

First published in Great Britain and the United States in 2019 by Kogan Page Limited

2nd Floor, 45 Gee Street
London EC1V 3RS
United Kingdom

c/o Martin P Hill Consulting
122 W 27th St, 10th Floor
New York NY 10001
USA

4737/23 Ansari Road
Daryaganj
New Delhi 110002
India

www.koganpage.com

Hardback 978 0 7494 8777 5
Paperback 978 0 7494 7871 1
eBook 978 0 7494 7872 8

British Library Cataloguing-in-Publication Data

A CIP record for this book is available from the British Library.

Library of Congress Cataloging-in-Publication Data

Names: Browne, Michael, 1955-
Title: Urban logistics : management, policy and innovation in a rapidly changing environment / Edited by Michael Browne, Sonke Behrends, Johan Woxenius, Genevieve Giuliano and Jose Holguin-Veras.
Description: London ; New York : Kogan Page Limited, 2019. | Includes bibliographical references and index.
Identifiers: LCCN 2018044366 (print) | LCCN 2018049184 (ebook) | ISBN 9780749478728 (Ebook) | ISBN 9780749487775 (hbk : alk. paper) | ISBN 9780749478711 (pbk : alk. paper) | ISBN 9780749478728 (ebk)
Subjects: LCSH: Urban transportation–Planning. | Freight and freightage–Planning.
Classification: LCC HE305 (ebook) | LCC HE305 .U6837 2019 (print) | DDC 388.4068/4–dc23

Typeset by Integra Software Services Pvt. Ltd., Pondicherry
Print production managed by Jellyfish
Printed and bound by Ashford Colour Press Ltd.

CONTENTS

ABOUT THE EDITORS

Michael Browne was appointed professor at the University of Gothenburg in 2015. His main research focus is on urban logistics and he provides academic leadership in the Urban Freight Platform, a University of Gothenburg and Chalmers initiative supported by the Volvo Research and Education Foundations (VREF). He is also a member of the VREF Center of Excellence for Sustainable Urban Freight Systems (CoE-SUFS) led by Rensselaer Polytechnic Institute. He is committed to engaging practitioners and policymakers with the research community on all aspects of logistics impacting on future urban goods transport. Before his appointment in Gothenburg he was at the University of Westminster in London for 25 years and he continues to chair the Central London Freight Quality Partnership. He is a visiting professor at the University Paris II (Panthéon-Assas) and the University of Southampton.

Sönke Behrends is a senior researcher at IVL Swedish Environmental Research Institute. He has worked as the operational manager of the Urban Freight Platform, an initiative at the University of Gothenburg and Chalmers University of Technology supported by the Volvo Research and Education Foundations (VREF), since it was established in 2014. His primary research interest is to advance the understanding of the interaction between logistics, transport and land use in an urban context and to develop solutions to improve the sustainability of urban logistics operations. His expertise is in impact assessment of logistics measures, urban freight planning and city logistics. Sönke received a master's degree and PhD in industrial engineering from Chalmers University of Technology, and a master's degree in transport engineering from Leibniz University of Hannover.

Johan Woxenius has been Professor of Maritime Transport Management and Logistics at the University of Gothenburg since 2008. He received the degrees of MSc (Industrial engineering), PhD and associate professor/docent at Chalmers University of Technology. He leads the university's part of the research centres Lighthouse (maritime), Northern LEAD (logistics) and the Area of Advance Transport, all run together with Chalmers. He is Topic Area Manager for B Freight, including the special interest group

Urban Goods Movement, for the World Conference on Transport Research Society. His main research field is maritime and intermodal freight transport and the research covers sustainability, industrial organization, production systems, traffic designs and information systems. Increasingly, he engages in urban freight research. Johan is a member of the Royal Swedish Academy of Engineering Sciences.

Genevieve Giuliano is the Margaret and John Ferraro Chair in Effective Local Government in the Sol Price School of Public Policy, University of Southern California, and Director of the METRANS joint USC and California State University Long Beach Transportation Center. Her research focus areas include relationships between land use and transportation, transportation policy analysis and information technology applications in transportation. Her current research includes examination of relationships between land use and freight flows, spatial analysis of freight activity location and analysis of markets for zero and low emissions trucks. She has published over 170 papers, and has received many awards, most recently the Walter Isard Award for Distinguished Scholarship in Regional Science. She is the Director of the Volvo Research and Education Foundations Center of Excellence MetroFreight.

José Holguín-Veras is the WH Hart Professor of Civil and Environmental Engineering at the Rensselaer Polytechnic Institute, and the Director of the VREF Center of Excellence for Sustainable Urban Freight Systems. He is the recipient of numerous awards, including the 2013 White House's Transportation Champion of Change Award, 2001 National Science Foundation's CAREER Award, and the 1996 Milton Pikarsky Memorial Award. His research interests are in the areas of freight transportation modelling and economics, and humanitarian logistics. He is one of the most widely published and cited freight researchers in the world. He received his PhD from the University of Texas at Austin in 1996; an MSc from the Universidad Central de Venezuela in 1984; and a BSc from the Universidad Autónoma de Santo Domingo in 1982.

ABOUT THE CONTRIBUTORS

Julian Allen is a Senior Research Fellow at the University of Westminster, where he is involved in research and teaching activities relating to freight transport and logistics. His research interests include urban freight transport operations, the role of transport and land-use policy in reducing the negative impacts of logistics operations, developments in retailing and its relationship with logistics and transportation systems, and the history of freight transport. He is currently working on two major projects funded by the UK Engineering and Physical Sciences Research Council: Freight Traffic Control 2050 (www.ftc2050.com) and the Centre for Sustainable Road Freight (http://www.csrf.ac.uk/). He is also carrying out research as part of the Volvo Research Foundations Center of Excellence in Sustainable Urban Freight Systems (https://www.coe-sufs.org/).

Alena Brettmo is a PhD student at the University of Gothenburg, conducting her research within the field of urban freight, focusing on different stakeholders and decision-making processes, considering different aspects such as behaviour of stakeholders, relations between them and managing of their resources, power and influence distribution, perception and attitudes towards urban freight, as well as finding the ways to make it more sustainable. Alena is a part of Gothenburg Urban Freight Platform, a working group within Northern LEAD, supported by VREF. Alena comes from Belarus and prior to her doctoral studies she was awarded her master's degree in Logistics and Transport Management at the University of Gothenburg. She has also been working as a purchaser in a big Swedish automotive company.

Shama Campbell is a graduate student at Rensselaer Polytechnic Institute (RPI) in Troy, NY pursuing a PhD in Transportation Engineering. She has received a BS in Computer Science and an MS in Transportation from South Carolina State University. She has also earned an ME in Transportation Engineering while at RPI. Her research interests include transportation planning, freight systems and sustainable transportation systems. Shama has been a part of various technical publications and significant research projects as a part of the Center for Infrastructure, Transportation and the Environment (CITE) and the VREF Center of Excellence for Sustainable Urban Freight Systems hosted at RPI.

Elise Caspersen is Research Economist in the fields of Freight Transport and Logistics at the Norwegian Institute of Transport Economics (TOI). Her primary research interest is on the interdependency between freight transport and cities. As of January 2016, she is also a PhD student at the Norwegian University of Life Science. Her PhD project concentrates on data access and data use when analysing urban freight transport in municipalities and regions. She has an MSc in Economics from the Norwegian University of Science and Technology.

Tom Cherrett is a Professor in Logistics and Transport Management within the Transportation Research Group at the University of Southampton. He teaches transport planning, freight and passenger systems and construction management to masters and undergraduate students. His research interests cover: 1) Core goods distribution (things that we buy) and how retail logistics can be made more efficient within and between our urban areas but particularly over the last mile; and 2) The use of technology and operational systems in both forward and reverse logistics to enable customers and employees to better share and use data. He has over 130 journal and conference papers published and is a Chartered Member of the Institute of Logistics and Transport.

Laetitia Dablanc is Director of Research at the French Institute of Science for Transport (IFSTTAR, University of Paris-East) and a member of MetroFreight, a VREF Center of Excellence in urban freight research. She is a part-time visiting professor at the University of Gothenburg. Her areas of research are freight transportation planning, freight and the environment, urban freight and logistics. She received a PhD in transportation planning from Ecole des Ponts-ParisTech, and a master's degree in city and regional planning from Cornell University. She was initially trained in policy analysis and economics at Science Po Paris.

Trilce Encarnación is a PhD student in Transportation Engineering at the VREF Center of Excellence for Sustainable Urban Freight Systems at Rensselaer Polytechnic Institute. Her research interests are in the areas of sustainable freight transportation and humanitarian logistics; she has authored papers and participated in several projects in these topics. She obtained a BS in Systems Engineering from the Pontificia Universidad Católica Madre y Maestra in the Dominican Republic, an MS in Scientific Computing at the University of Puerto Rico at Mayaguez and an ME in

Industrial and Management Engineering from RPI. She is an ENO Fellow and winner of the SAS INFORMS Analytics Scholar Competition.

Carlos A González-Calderón is an Associate Professor of Transportation Engineering at the Universidad Nacional de Colombia at Medellín. He received his BS (2004) in Civil Engineering and MS (2007) in Transportation Engineering from Universidad Nacional de Colombia at Medellín; and his ME (2010) and PhD (2014) in Transportation Engineering from Rensselaer Polytechnic Institute in Troy, NY. He has strong theoretical foundations and practical experience in transportation. His research focus includes freight transportation, freight modelling and economics, sustainable transportation systems and transportation planning. He has played a role in multiple research projects funded by the National Science Foundation, the US Department of Transportation, the National Cooperative Freight Research Program, the World Bank and the Inter-American Development Bank, among others.

Jesús González-Feliu is Assistant Professor in Industrial Engineering at Ecole Nationale Supérieure des Mines de Saint Etienne (EMSE) and member of EVS-PIESO. He obtained his master's degree in Civil Engineering and Urban Planning in 2003 at INSA Lyon (France) and a PhD in Computer and Systems Sciences – Operations Research in 2008 at Politecnico di Torino (Italy). His PhD thesis focused on urban freight distribution solutions and two-stage vehicle routing problems. He joined CNRS (French National Centre of Scientific Research) in 2008 for a post-doctoral position, and in December 2011 he became research engineer in data production and analysis. He joined EMSE in October 2014 where he combines teaching and research, mainly related to urban logistics and collaborative systems. His research interests include urban logistics planning and policy, freight demand modelling, scenario assessment, decision support systems, vehicle routing optimization, sustainable supply chain management and collaborative logistics.

Adeline Heitz is a researcher at the French Institute of Science for Transport (IFSTTAR, University of Paris-East). Her areas of research are urban planning, urban logistics, public policies in metropolitan areas and mobility of freight and passengers. She received a PhD in urban planning and geography from University of Paris-East, a master's degree in urban planning and bachelor's degrees in law and geography from Panthéon-Sorbonne-Paris University.

Bram Kin acquired the degree of Master of Science in Comparative International Politics at the University of Leuven. He is a research associate at the MOBI – Mobility, Logistics and Automotive technology research group of Professor Dr Cathy Macharis at the Vrije Universiteit Brussel. His PhD focuses on alternative ways to improve the efficiency and sustainability of fragmented last mile deliveries to small, independent retailers in European and global (mega) cities.

Philippe Lebeau is postdoctoral research and teaching assistant at the Vrije Universiteit Brussel. After graduating from a Master in Management Sciences and a Master in Transport Management, he joined the research group MOBI, an interdisciplinary group focusing on sustainable logistics and mobility. There he developed his PhD on the electrification of city logistics under the supervision of Professor Dr Cathy Macharis and Professor Dr Joeri Van Mierlo. After his PhD, he experienced the logistics sector by joining Decathlon Logistics before coming back to the academic world in 2018. His expertise fields are in sustainable logistics, electric vehicles, urban freight transport in Brussels, Discrete Event Simulation, Total Cost of Ownership, Conjoint Based Choice and Multi-Criteria Multi-Actor analysis.

Maria Lindholm defended her PhD thesis 'Enabling sustainable development of urban freight from a local authority perspective' in January 2013 at Chalmers University of Technology in Gothenburg, at the division of Logistics and Transportation. She has performed research in the area of sustainable urban freight transport, transport policy and the interaction between local authorities and transport operators, including Freight Quality Partnerships (FQPs). The research was based on several qualitative studies during seven years from 2005 to 2012. Interview studies, questionnaire surveys and workshops have been held in several north European countries, including Sweden, United Kingdom, Germany, the Netherlands, Poland and Lithuania. Both local authorities and freight stakeholders have been involved as respondents in the studies. Since then Maria has been chairing the Gothenburg Freight Quality Partnership. Maria is now working as research coordinator and project manager at CLOSER/Lindholmen Science Park AB. Maria coordinates CLOSER's research partner contacts, the network for young researchers and the Round table for urban mobility.

Greger Lundesjö having gained an MSc in Industrial Engineering worked for Swedish Company BT Systems and later the Swiss company Swisslog in senior roles in Sweden and the United Kingdom. His focus was on logistics automation for clients in retail and manufacturing. In 2004 Greger became an independent consultant but also worked as an associate to the consultancy The Logistics Business. Here Greger developed an expertise in construction logistics, applying the logistics thinking from other sectors in the construction industry. A major part of his work has been with WRAP (the Waste and Resources Action Programme) focusing on reducing the industry's environmental impact through efficient logistics. For WRAP he has produced several reports including 'Using Construction Consolidation Centres to Reduce Construction Waste and Carbon Emissions'. In 2015 his edited book *Supply Chain Management and Logistics in Construction* was published.

Cathy Macharis is Professor at the Vrije Universiteit Brussel. Her research group MOBI (Mobility, Logistics and Automotive Technology – http://mobi.vub.ac.be/) is an interdisciplinary group focusing on sustainable logistics, electric and hybrid vehicles and urban mobility. Her research focuses on how to include stakeholders within decision and evaluation processes in the field of transport and mobility. She has been involved in several regional, national and European research projects dealing with topics such as the implementation of innovative concepts for city distribution, assessment of policy measures in the field of logistics and sustainable mobility, development of a multi-actor multi-criteria analysis framework, etc. She published several books and wrote more than 100 papers. She is Chair of Brussels Mobility Commission and vice-chair of Nectar (Network on European Communications and Transport Activities Research).

Olof Moen is Senior Research Fellow in transport geography at the University of Gothenburg and a logistics consultant, where he is involved in research and consulting activities relating to logistics, digital transport planning and new business models in freight transport, in both the private sector and in local government. For the last 10 years he has been involved in developing the procurement process of Swedish municipalities and the concept of co-distribution of goods based on action research. He is the author of books, reports and articles on the subject in collaboration with the Swedish Transport Administration and the Swedish Association of Local Authorities and Regions, as well as Director of R&D in the newly government funded National Centre of Municipal Co-distribution of Goods (https://www.kosava.se).

Eleonora Morganti is currently senior research fellow in urban freight and food logistics at the Institute for Transport Studies, at the University of Leeds. Prior to this, she spent four years in Paris as researcher at the Ecoles des Ponts and at the French Institute for Transport. She received her PhD on Policies for Sustainable Development at the University of Bologna in Italy. Her research combines aspects related to urban freight policies, low-carbon transport and food logistics. Her current focus is on e-commerce logistics and consumers' purchasing behaviours.

Anna Pernestål Brenden is Director of the Integrated Transport Research Lab (ITRL) at KTH Royal Institute of Technology (Sweden). Dr Pernestål Brenden received her MSc in Engineering Physics from Uppsala University (Sweden) and her PhD in Systems Engineering from Linköping University (Sweden). Dr Pernestål Brenden has led several innovation projects in the transport industry, both road and rail, for more than 15 years before joining ITRL in 2016. She has been involved in multiple projects related to urban transport and mobility. Her research focuses on the implementation and impact of novel technical concepts in the transport system.

Maja Piecyk is a Reader in Logistics at the University of Westminster. She is a Deputy Director of the Centre for Sustainable Road Freight, an EPSRC-funded research centre between Westminster, Heriot-Watt and Cambridge universities (http://www.csrf.ac.uk/). She has also led a number of research projects focusing on the environmental performance and sustainability of freight transport operations. Much of her current work centres on the optimization of supply chain networks, GHG auditing of businesses and forecasting of long-term trends in energy demand and environmental impacts of logistics. Maja is a Chartered Member of the Chartered Institute of Logistics and Transport (UK), and a Fellow of the Higher Education Academy.

Marzena Piotrowska is a Research Associate at the University of Westminster. Her primary research interests are focused on city logistics, urban freight consolidation and transport policy. Marzena has been involved in a number of research projects looking at various aspects of freight transport and logistics operations, including urban goods distribution, rail freight and modal shift. The majority of her current research work centres on the role of urban freight consolidation facilities in supporting sustainable city logistics. Marzena is also responsible for leading the MSc programme in Logistics and Supply Chain Management.

Nicolas Raimbault is a postdoctoral researcher at Luxembourg Institute of Socio-Economic Research where he is working on urban social geography and urban governance, and especially investigating the urban and social impacts of logistics activities development. He completed his PhD in urban planning in 2014 at the University of Paris-East. His PhD thesis deals with the governance of logistics development in the Greater Paris Region and in the inland corridor of the port of Rotterdam in the Netherlands. His current research analyses the transformations of blue-collar places and their governance in the dual context of the rise of logistics blue-collar jobs and the fall of manufacturing jobs in European and North American urban regions. He also received a master's degree in regional and urban affairs from Sciences-Po Paris.

Diana G Ramírez-Ríos is a PhD student in Transportation Engineering and Research Assistant at the VREF Center of Excellence for Sustainable Urban Freight Systems at Rensselaer Polytechnic Institute. Her areas of research are Urban Freight and Disaster Response Logistics. Her recent work includes freight trip generation modelling, behavioural modelling in freight transportation, last mile delivery trends, and disaster response supply chain modelling. She is an ENO fellow and Colciencias Scholar by the Governor of the Atlantico in 2015. She obtained her BS-MS in Industrial Engineering at Universidad del Norte in Barranquilla, Colombia.

Carlos Rivera-González is a civil engineer with a master's degree focused on Transportation Engineering. Currently he is a PhD student in Transportation Engineering at Rensselaer Polytechnic Institute, and Research Assistant at the VREF Center of Excellence for Sustainable Urban Freight Systems and the Center for Infrastructure, Transportation and Environment (CITE). He is a member of the Albany Young Professionals in Transportation. His interests lie in sustainable urban freight, supply chain and operations, land use modelling, freight transportation modelling, transport and city economics, and new technologies.

Jean-Paul Rodrigue has been a professor at Hofstra University, New York since 1999. His research interests mainly cover the fields of transportation and economics as they relate to logistics and global freight distribution. Specific topics over which he has published extensively involve maritime transport systems and logistics, global supply chains, gateways and transport corridors. Dr Rodrigue developed a widely used online reference source about transportation, The Geography of Transport Systems, now in its fourth edition. He is a lead member of the PortEconomics.eu initiative regrouping the world's leading maritime transport academics and performs advisory and consulting assignments for international organizations and corporations. Between 2011 and 2016, Dr Rodrigue sat on the World

Economic Forum Global Agenda Council on the Future of Manufacturing. In 2013, the US Secretary of Transportation appointed Dr Rodrigue to sit on the Advisory Board of the US Merchant Marine Academy at Kings Point, a position he held until 2018.

Iván Sánchez-Díaz is Senior Lecturer at the Division of Service Management and Logistics at Chalmers University of Technology (Sweden), where he is part of the Urban Freight Platform funded by the VREF. Dr Sánchez-Díaz received his BS in Civil Engineering from the Universidad del Norte (Colombia); and he received his MSc and PhD in Transportation Engineering from the Rensselaer Polytechnic Institute (New York). Dr Sánchez-Díaz has been involved in multiple projects related to freight demand modelling, freight policy and innovations in the United States and in Sweden. He is an expert in urban freight transportation policy and modelling; his research involves econometric analyses, behavioural modelling and analytical modelling.

Renato da Silva Lima has been Associate Professor in Logistics and Transportation at the Federal University of Itajuba (UNIFEI), Brazil, since 2003, where he leads the LogTranS – Centre for Logistics, Transportation and Sustainability. Since 2007 he has also been fellow of research productivity at the Brazilian National Council for Scientific and Technological Development (CNPq). His research interests are in the areas of freight transportation modelling and simulation, and reverse logistics. He received his PhD in Transportation Engineering from the University of São Paulo, Brazil, in 2003, and was Visiting Scholar at University of Minho, Portugal, in 2006 and Rensselaer Polytechnic Institute (RPI) in 2018.

Eiichi Taniguchi is Professor Emeritus of Transport and Logistics in the Resilience Research Unit, Kyoto University, Japan. His research centres on City Logistics and urban freight transport modelling focusing on stochastic and dynamic vehicle routing and scheduling with time windows, multi-agent simulation considering behaviour of stakeholders who are involved in urban freight transport. Recently his research covers the health and security issues including humanitarian logistics after catastrophic disasters, and home healthcare problems in an ageing society. He has published more than 200 academic papers and 10 books. As the president of Institute for City Logistics since 1999, he has organized nine International Conferences on City Logistics in various venues in the world. He has been actively involved in collaborative research in international organizations including the Organisation for Economic Co-operation and Development, the World Conference on Transport Research Society, the Transportation Research Board and the World Road Association.

Russell Thompson is an Associate Professor in Transport Engineering in the Department of Infrastructure Engineering at the University of Melbourne in Australia. His research areas are urban freight, resilient transport systems and intelligent transport systems. He has over 15 years of experience in urban freight research. Russell has been involved in a number of local and international studies relating to urban freight, including the European Union's Best Urban Freight Solutions (BESTUFS) project and the OECD report on urban distribution. Russell was a founding Director and has been the Vice President of the Institute for City Logistics based in Kyoto since 1999. He is also a team leader within the VREF Center of Excellence in Sustainable Urban Freight Systems. Russell has published over 10 books and 50 refereed publications in the field of urban freight. He is currently involved in a number of projects involving hyperconnected city logistics.

Jeffrey Wojtowicz is a senior research engineer at the Center for Infrastructure, Transportation and the Environment (CITE) at Rensselaer Polytechnic Institute (RPI) in Troy, NY. He is also the Assistant Director of Administration at the Volvo Research and Educational Foundations Center of Excellence for Sustainable Urban Freight Systems (VREF CoE-SUFS). He received his BS in Civil and Environmental Engineering and his MS in Transportation Engineering from RPI. His research interests include freight systems, intelligent transportation systems, traffic modelling and emergency response from planned special events and traffic incident management. In addition to his work at CITE he also has an extensive working knowledge of the trucking industry; since an early age Jeff has been actively involved with a family trucking business that has been in operation for over 85 years. As time permits he still drives truck, works as a mechanic and assists with other operational components of the business.

FOREWORD

Urban logistics is a challenge today, and it will be far more challenging in the future, with growing demand for the delivery of goods and services, and intense competition for street space among cars, vans, public transport, cyclists and pedestrians. Making better use of the capacity available for urban freight and finding smarter solutions to sharing space in cities is becoming increasingly important.

The Volvo Research and Educational Foundations (VREF) recognizes the importance of urban freight and logistics as one of the themes within the overall programme it supports concerned with 'Future Urban Transport – How to deal with complexity (FUT)'. VREF started the FUT theme Urban Freight in 2012 with a symposium to consider Urban Freight for Liveable Cities, followed in 2013 by the long-term support to two international Centres of Excellence: CoE MetroFreight and CoE Sustainable Urban Freight Systems (SUFS). In 2014 the network of centres was extended with support for the Gothenburg Urban Freight Platform. It is noteworthy that some of the speakers and participants at the 2012 symposium feature as authors within this book – but what is also highly encouraging is to see new names coming forward to take part in this increasingly dynamic field.

The problems experienced by those providing logistics services in urban areas are not well understood. Transportation professionals, urban planners and policymakers lack comprehensive understanding, robust data and common terminologies, all of which have major implications for the management of individual urban freight systems as well as the larger global freight network. The VREF theme Urban Freight has helped to play a key role in addressing this critical knowledge gap and leading efforts to raise the profile of goods movement in planning and policy arenas. Research on urban freight and logistics has grown considerably during the past five years with an increase in contributions from around the world and the developments of research from a wide variety of disciplines. This is important because the nature of urban logistics and freight transport problems requires multidisciplinary approaches.

Freight transport and logistics in cities tend to respond effectively to economic requirements but are also major contributors to social and environmental impacts, particularly to congestion and local air quality and noise. Urban freight activities often result in conflicts between economic and social/environmental priorities. Addressing such conflicts and trade-offs in urban freight transport requires change and innovation in the public and private sectors.

The chapters in this book address a wide range of topical and important issues. The initiatives discussed here are based on solid research by leading experts in their fields. The book goes beyond the presentation of research and illustrates how research can be translated into actions for change and improvement. This fits very well with the VREF philosophy to inspire, initiate and support research and educational activities promoting sustainable transport for fair access in urban areas. We aim to nurture processes of change and transformative capacity in city authorities as well as in businesses. The book contains important insights that are relevant to all stakeholders involved in urban logistics from both the public and private sectors.

Some aspects of urban logistics are contextual in the sense that regulation, consumer demand, business practice and physical conditions differ between continents, countries and cities. To address this, the VREF Urban Freight theme funding is internationally distributed. Authors from 16 countries in five continents living in a wide range of cities contributed chapters adding to the empirical richness of the book.

This book is a timely and exciting contribution to the important field of urban freight and logistics. As the chair of the VREF board I welcome this book and believe that it will mark a further major step in supporting changes and improvements in tackling urban logistics and freight transport challenges.

Torbjörn Holmström
Chairman of the Board
Volvo Research and Educational Foundations (VREF)

PART ONE
Setting the scene

Introduction to urban logistics 01

MICHAEL BROWNE, SÖNKE BEHRENDS AND JOHAN WOXENIUS

Introduction

More than half the world's population now lives in urban areas, with much higher levels observed in advanced economies. Metropolitan areas propel economic growth, act as sources, sinks and gateways in the global trade network, and drive technological, business and social innovations. The vitality of cities is critical to the success of national economies and in some political areas, the influence of mayors matches that of ministers at the national governance level. Consider that: the top 600 cities in the world produce about 60 per cent of the global Gross Domestic Product (Dobbs *et al*, 2011); and 80 per cent of the total cargo transported in the United States (US) has its origin or destination at one of the country's top 100 metropolitan areas (Tomer and Kane, 2014). Without modern supply chains – the circulatory systems of metropolitan areas – urban and national economies would collapse. Yet, major challenges threaten the performance of supply chains and the quality of life in metropolitan areas, including the combined effects of climate change, rising urban congestion, the health impacts of pollution, the emergence of megaregions, the surge of e-commerce fulfilment deliveries, social concerns for temporarily employed staff and already high last mile delivery costs.

Efficient logistics are critical to sustaining both the quality of life and vitality of metropolitan areas. In developed countries, the freight-intensive sectors of the economy – where the production and consumption of freight is a central component of the activity (eg manufacturing, construction, accommodation and food) – represent about half of commercial establishments and employment. Service-intensive sectors – where the primary business function is one of service (eg finance, education) – represent the other half (Holguín-Veras *et al*, 2018). Both sectors need supplies brought in and shipments sent out, though in different amounts; the bulk of the freight and freight-trips are generated by the freight-intensive-sectors. In developing countries – which depend heavily on economic activities such as agriculture, mining, manufacturing – supply chain activity is even more important, as the freight-intensive sectors represent a significant part of the economy. Essentially, the performance of logistics directly impacts more than half the economy in metropolitan areas, and indirectly affects the rest (Holguín-Veras *et al*, 2018). Increasing the efficiency and sustainability of freight is crucial to both economic and environmental goals.

However, alongside these positive features are problems of environmental externalities. Urban freight is a substantial contributor to these problems accounting for 30 to 40 per cent of urban transport-related CO_2 emissions and nearly 50 per cent of particulate emissions. Urban freight activities also create problems for local communities (noise, community severance, impacts on safety) and are in competition for scarce infrastructure capacity. Yet efficient urban freight systems can be seen as vital to the wellbeing of urban areas as freight activity is a physical expression of the economy; failing to take account of the importance of freight flows can result in economic and commercial problems.

Challenging goals are being set in terms of future developments for urban freight. For example, the EU 2011 Transport White Paper established a specific urban goal related to freight transport stating the need for 'a strategy for near-zero-emission urban logistics' by 2030 (European Commission, 2011).

Public-sector agencies often focus commuting and other passenger transport flows over freight, despite the obvious importance of freight activity. They are generally uninformed about the role freight systems play in the economy, and the role that they could play in fostering urban freight sustainability assuming that the private sector supplies efficient logistics services. Agencies lack the models and tools to understand freight in its context and its place within complex economic, environmental and technological systems. Quite frequently, freight activity is perceived as something detrimental: something to be managed or curtailed. Advancing towards sustainable economies requires a holistic transformation in the ways in which supplies are produced, distributed and consumed. The chief goal is to maximize the beneficial economic effects associated with the production and consumption of goods, while minimizing, or eliminating, the negative impacts produced by the resulting freight traffic. Greater global collaboration and research translated into practice are essential to advancing freight sustainability solutions.

Significantly growing interest in urban logistics and freight transport systems

The urban freight transport and distribution considerations of national governments and city authorities have traditionally tended to take place as a reaction to problems, usually arising from complaints made by residents and other road users. Most authorities with an urban remit have not developed coherent freight transport policies to the same extent that they have their public transport policies. Although the European Commission has actively promoted the development of Sustainable Urban Mobility Plans (SUMPs) covering both passenger and freight transport, the focus of these plans has traditionally been on passenger transport (eg passenger cars and public transport). However, this has begun to change over the last 10 to 15 years with growing interest in the logistics of collection and delivery services in town and city centres on the part of the various tiers of government both from the perspective of its importance economically and in terms of its impact on urban environmental sustainability.

For example, there are a growing number of research initiatives aimed at developing the concept of Sustainable Urban Logistics Plans (SULPs) and implementing them in cities (eg the EU project ENCLOSE and the NORSULP project in Norway). In the United Kingdom local authorities have been encouraged by central government to focus greater attention on freight transport and to include consideration of urban distribution and its sustainability in their Local Transport Plans over the last decade. The Department for Transport also encouraged local authorities to include freight initiatives and especially Freight Quality Partnerships (FQPs) in their local transport plans.

Research on the issue of moving freight in urban areas has developed in line with the increased attention from businesses and local authorities. As for other research fields, the scope, focus and terminology develop over time. One simplistic interpretation of the development is that researchers first addressed how to replenish high street retail shops, often using the term City Logistics. Widening the geographical scope from the city centre to the whole urban area and emphasizing all flows of materials and effects of freight vehicle traffic, Urban Goods Movement was then increasingly used by researchers. Nowadays, the terms Urban Freight and Urban Logistics seem to dominate in names of conferences or sessions, article titles and keywords. The breadth of the research topics is currently truly wide as a result of more researchers, consultants and practitioners being engaged in analysing the phenomenon of physical flows within the built environment. Consequently, publishing international research into urban freight transport has also increased since the late 1990s (for recent examples see Dablanc, 2009; Giuliano *et al*, 2013; Gonzalez-Feliu *et al* (ed), 2013; Rhodes *et al*, 2012; Taniguchi and Thompson, 2012; Vaghi and Percoco, 2011; Holguín-Veras *et al*, 2011).

Research projects about urban logistics and freight transport have taken place over the last 15 to 20 years assessing urban freight requirements and strategies, exploring the feasibility of new logistics equipment, developing intelligent transport systems, investigating the opportunities for increasing the sustainability of operations and achieving modal shift, and demonstrating new technologies, equipment and operations. An example from Europe is interesting. The EC-funded Best Urban Freight Solutions (BESTUFS) thematic network was formed in 2000 and continued until 2008. The main objective of BESTUFS was to identify, describe and disseminate information on best practices, success criteria and bottlenecks of urban freight transport solutions. Furthermore, BESTUFS aimed to maintain and expand an open European network between urban freight experts, user groups/associations, ongoing projects, the relevant European Commission Directorates and representatives of national, regional and local transport administrations and transport operators.

Topics addressed at BESTUFS workshops included vehicle access and parking regulations, urban goods vehicle design, e-commerce and last mile solutions, non-road modes for urban distribution, road pricing, urban consolidation centres, public–private partnerships in urban goods transport, night delivery, ITS in urban goods transport and urban waste logistics. The initiative received considerable attention from practitioners as well as from researchers, and all information was made publicly available via the website (BESTUFS, 2008). Continuing with European funded projects, the project entitled 'Transferability of Urban Logistics Concepts and Practices from a World Wide Perspective' (TURBLOG) took place between 2009 and 2011 and aimed to carry out the same goals as BESTUFS but at a global scale, especially with reference to Latin America (TURBLOG, 2010). The 'Sustainable Urban Goods Logistics Achieved by Regional and Local Policies' (SUGAR) project, which was completed in 2011, aimed by means of interregional cooperation to improve the effectiveness of urban freight transport policies by promoting the exchange, discussion and transfer of policy experience, knowledge and good practice. A best practice guide to urban freight policies was one output of the project (SUGAR, 2011). The 'Best Practice Factory for Freight Transport' (BESTFACT) project continued to collect and share information about urban logistics (2012 to 2016). More recent projects have focused on specific issues such as electric freight vehicles (FREVUE) or on new ways to approach innovation by means of living labs in cities (CITYLAB). The outputs of these projects and the strengthened research networks have certainly contributed to the increased scale of urban logistics research.

Comparing with other streams of freight transport research, urban freight researchers were rather early to organize scientific communities and conferences. Urban Freight Movements was one of the first Special Interest Groups within the World Conference on Transport Research Society (launched in 1995) and SIG B4 assembles a significant number of researchers at the tri-annual conferences. The bi-annual International Conference on City Logistics was launched in Cairns in 1999 and has been pivotal in creating an international city logistics research community. In the United States, the Standing Committee on Urban Freight Transportation (AT025) of the Transportation Research Board (TRB) serves as a link between researchers and practitioners and it increasingly attracts international attendance at the annual TRB conferences.

The first EU–US urban freight research symposium bringing together academics and practitioners from both continents took place in 2013. This was jointly funded by the European Commission, the US Department of Transportation and the TRB (Transportation Research Board, 2013). Since then the European Union and the United States have worked on continuing and strengthening these links and a special focus has been placed on the idea of twinning EU and US urban freight and logistics projects.

The METRANS Transportation Center organized and hosted the first Annual National Urban Freight Conference in North America in 2006. This brought together North American researchers and practitioners to consider urban freight in a specialist conference setting for the first time and has continued to grow and extend its international reach since then with the conference in 2017 attracting over 230 participants (METRANS, 2018).

There have also been several important national initiatives. One example is the Institute for City Logistics (ICL), established in Kyoto, Japan, in 1999. The Institute is a centre of excellence for research and development in city logistics and urban freight transport, bringing together academics and practitioners to exchange knowledge, experience and information through conferences and short courses (Institute for City Logistics, 2018).

The Volvo Research and Educational Foundations (VREF) initiative on Urban Freight supports targeted research and outreach with the goal of creating a strong international professional network that can influence government and industry decision-making. The initiative originally began at a symposium held in 2012, Urban Freight for Livable Cities, and has since developed into a much broader effort to consider the challenges and opportunities that currently face urban freight transport and logistics. Following the symposium, VREF launched two international Centres of Excellence (CoEs) in 2013, MetroFreight led by the METRANS Transportation Center in Los Angeles, California, and Sustainable Urban Freight Systems (SUFS) led by Rensselaer Polytechnic Institute in Troy, New York, as well as an additional research centre in 2014, the Urban Freight Platform (UFP) in Gothenburg, Sweden. Each centre works with a number of global partners to further their research and professional networks (more details are contained in Figure 1.1 (and www.vref.se/).

All the chapters in this edited book have been written by researchers with strong links to partners in one or more of the three VREF centres.

The complexity and heterogeneity of urban logistics activities

Urban logistics is a complex field with a wide range of stakeholders. This complexity and the heterogeneity of activities (range of vehicles used, the products carried and the variety found in city size, form and governance) make it challenging to identify simple solutions to problems. One example is the diverse regulatory approaches to vehicles above and below 3.5 tonnes gross vehicle weight. Indeed, the range of vehicles used in urban freight is very wide ranging from couriers delivering on foot or by bicycle, through the use of cargo cycles (powered and not powered) and so on through vans to small trucks and then to large trucks used especially in operations such as some phases of construction.

This heterogeneity extends to the products moved (which also require different transport options in many cases). Letter and parcel delivery, for example, is organized in an entirely different way to construction logistics and waste collection. Temperature controlled products delivered to supermarkets need a physical chain very different from that applying to catering supplies delivered to offices – yet both are dealing with food products.

Discussion of urban freight and research into the subject has tended to be dominated by considerations that concern the urban centre – ie the denser core of the city. This is not always the case but the majority of research has focused on the more central areas within cities. In addition, there has been a

Figure 1.1 VREF research initiative centres and partners

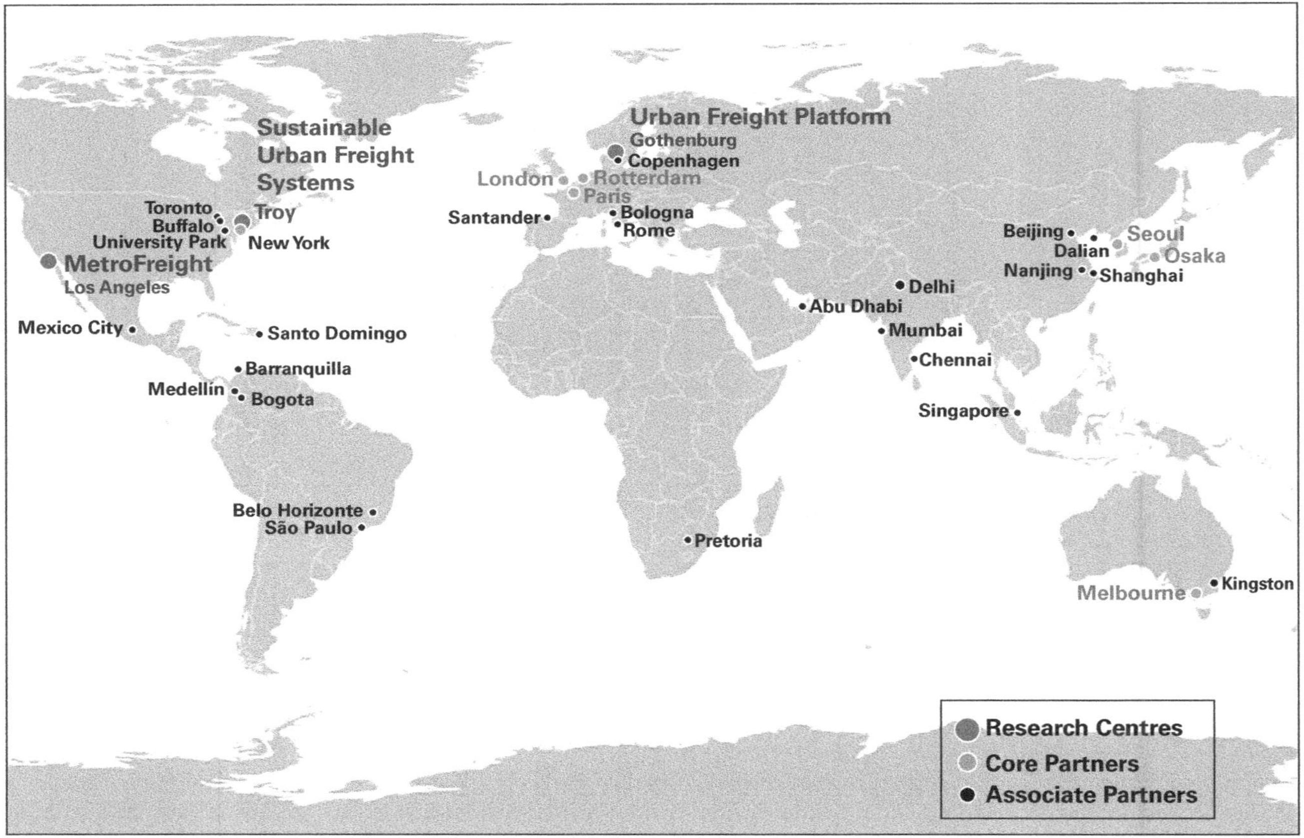

lot of attention paid to retail chains in terms of work on urban freight. This is understandable because the retail sector is typically a very important part of the economic activity of the city familiar and close to the citizens in their role as consumers. However, in terms of trip generation it may be less relevant to focus on retailing (especially on large and organized retail chains). For example, the fragmented nature of much last mile activity delivering to offices and small business means that the number of trips generated here is often very high and yet remains rather poorly understood. There are signs that this perspective is developing quite rapidly. Recent research would seem to be much stronger in dealing with the variety of sectors that are important in the city.

In the same way, the focus on increased understanding about trip generation is helping to refine the insights into the activity resulting from different land use categories. Allied to this there seems to be a strong surge of interest in the scope to develop better analytical approaches to the use of loading spaces (in terms of understanding use and availability and also looking at pricing options). Just as classifying interventions in urban freight is challenging, so it is likely to be the case that researchers and also city authorities adopt a variety of classifications relating to freight sectors (or segments).

While the urban centre has been a strong focus there are recent studies that have looked at trends in logistics towards the edge of the city. A project being carried out in Sweden on this topic is designed to investigate the socio-economic potential of a streamlined suburban logistics for freight transport, through dynamic prioritization, and to prepare for a full-scale demonstration (Lindkvist *et al*, 2018).

The regional dimension is also increasingly recognized, as the evolution of global supply chains resulted in a concentration of logistics activities in fewer ports and gateways. The urban context in which these gateways are embedded is a critical factor for global and regional distribution networks. Major urban freight hubs around the world face spatial constraints due to their need to intensify and expand within already constrained and crowded land use arrangements. Additional friction arises from an increasing geographical imbalance between economic benefits and environmental impacts that global distribution networks generate.

Can contextual urban freight research results be transferred to other cities?

Cities are complex environments where many structures are not used in the way they were originally intended. Therefore, many systems including urban logistics have to adapt to these demands. The complexity of cities also gives rise to a debate about the extent to which problems (and their possible solution) may be considered context-specific. This leads to questions about how initiatives should be scaled up to gain greater traction in dealing with challenges now and in the future. The organization CIVITAS proposed six categories of measures that they argued were likely to be relevant to many cities (CIVITAS, 2015). However, they noted that 'each city needs a different set of measures'.

At a detailed level, it is likely that many initiatives are context-specific and that the way they are applied will vary considerably between one city and another (as will the impacts). However, this has made it very difficult to achieve scalability and transferability with some of the findings from pilot projects and demonstrations. The idea that all the solutions can only apply in a narrow range of circumstances leads to a 'not invented here' problem and also acts as a brake on the uptake of new approaches and ideas. The roadmap created by ALICE/ERTRAC pointed at some actions to improve the uptake of initiatives and project results (ALICE/ERTRAC, 2015):

- In assessing urban logistics in cities, it is recommended to develop urban freight KPIs and assessment models.
- There is a need to develop a framework for data collection to properly analyse urban freight movements in cities and their impact.

The need to better understand the impact of public policies on urban freight is mentioned. Here there could also be a role for tools and models in order to provide deeper insights into how different policies can be combined and the consequences of this action.

The roadmap also commented on the importance of business models to address the question of uptake of initiatives and the scale and speed of improvements in the urban freight system. The argument behind this is that without a strong business model projects will often run for a limited time and will not continue much beyond the funding period.

The implications of technology innovation

Technological innovation affecting urban freight transport includes digitalization, for example the internet of things (important in terms of connected objects) and big data. These developments are already established and starting to have impacts or at least implications in the field of urban freight. For example, the internet of things and the ability to deal with very large data flows provide opportunities for new ways to think about a diverse range of initiatives, from customer service to new ways to regulate urban freight.

Traceable (and therefore trackable) physical objects (goods) mean transparency of the supply network to the final customer at every step. This extra control is also potentially important when considering the vehicle as it opens up new possibilities in urban freight regulation. There will be scope for more flexible and customized regulation of city access, which today is limited to relatively coarse measures such as environmental zones and time slots for access and loading and unloading zones.

In the longer term, there will be the development of other technologies that could have an impact on urban freight movements. A potential innovation that has received attention for both personal mobility and goods movement concerns autonomous vehicles. While most attention has focused on autonomous cars there have also been some initiatives that are relevant to freight movements. At present, most attention in the freight sector concerned with autonomous vehicles has focused on longer distance and regional movements (eg platooning for larger trucks) in contrast to electrification that is first implemented over shorter, often urban, distances. However, the technology development for cars will be relevant for urban deliveries. There are some issues that are the same as for autonomous cars – for example, legal questions concerning liability and safety for other road users. However, there are some differences – for example, the issue of theft of the goods and also the challenge of the last few metres of the delivery (handling questions etc). Nevertheless, some trials of small (and slow-moving) autonomous delivery vehicles that could be used to make deliveries in urban areas have received attention as well as automated waste collection trucks. Furthermore, it has been suggested that drones could play a role in urban freight and there has been much interest in initiatives by Amazon to patent certain drone-related services, although the support for this idea is not universal (for example McKinnon, 2015).

There are reasons for optimism in future developments in this field. There has been a dramatic increase in research at all levels in the past 5 to10 years. Many more researchers are entering this area in universities and they come from a wide range of backgrounds, which is excellent. In addition, there has been growing engagement and stronger links between research, authorities and private sector companies. This is extremely important for finding better ways to resolve complex problems in urban logistics. In the next 15 years there will be continued progress in urban logistics with some cities successfully reducing emissions externalities and where the urban logistics system functions much more efficiently than it does today. However, there will be some big challenges in terms of the rapid level of global urbanization. There have been many positive developments in the past few years but it is very important to keep the momentum going. It is essential to increase the engagement of city authorities and regional and national governments in urban logistics and the related freight transport systems. At the moment some cities show leadership in this field and it is essential that many more join them. It is to be hoped that this book will make a contribution to these developments.

Outline for the book

The 16 chapters have been grouped into three parts. This chapter opens Part One: 'Setting the scene', and the remaining chapters provide essential information about urban logistics and freight transport. In addition, they raise relevant issues about the scale and scope of urban logistics activities.

Chapter 2, 'Metropolitan economies and the generation of freight and service activity: an international perspective', establishes a solid base for the arguments presented in the book. José Holguín-Veras, Diana G Ramírez-Ríos, Trilce Encarnación, Jesús González-Feliu, Elise Caspersen, Carlos Rivera-González, Carlos A González-Calderón and Renato da Silva Lima consider 11 cities and identify key features that influence freight and service trip activity. The complex patterns show that there are both similarities and differences between cities according to economic wealth and developments and city size. The importance of various economic sectors in freight and service trip generation is also clearly explained.

The following chapter 'Urban logistics: the regional dimension' widens the perspective beyond the city itself analysing how the city and the metropolitan region interact. Genevieve Giuliano discusses the link to global trade and highlights the steps that can be taken to improve efficiency and to reduce pollution of freight transport. She develops these arguments based on a wide range of research activity that has been carried out as part of the VREF urban freight initiative mentioned above. The arguments and examples all have a relevance to policymakers, practitioners and researchers involved in these debates.

Chapter 4 'Urban planning policies for logistics facilities: a comparison between US metropolitan areas and the Paris region' deepens the discussion on urban and regional interactions and focuses on the role of planning in the context of urban logistics property – distribution centres, terminals and inner-city hubs. Nicolas Raimbault, Adeline Heitz and Laetitia Dablanc develop this theme by means of two contrasting case studies from the United States and Europe. They clearly demonstrate that urban planning approaches and regulation have found it hard to adapt to the speed of change in urban logistics. They also point at important issues that now need to be addressed in many cities.

As mentioned, many urban logistics and freight studies have concentrated on the core of the city. But cities are far more complicated and different logistics needs can be found according to density and other features. The chapter by Sönke Behrends and Jean-Paul Rodrigue 'The dualism of urban freight distribution: city vs suburban logistics' addresses this question. In this chapter they highlight the way in which city density plays a central role in the efficiency of urban logistics. They also demonstrate the interactions with urban planning and personal mobility, which is an important theme that is now developing in urban logistics research.

The first part of the book closes with Chapter 6 'Port cities and urban logistics' where the historically strong link between ports and cities is addressed by Michael Browne and Johan Woxenius. They identify some important trends that are relevant to many cities around the world including a high proportion of transit traffic, concentration of heavy industry and distribution centres as well as large-scale construction, reclamation of land from the sea and renewing city centres when port terminals move out. They provide a focus for this by considering the case of Gothenburg.

Part Two of this book, 'Urban logistics diversity', connects with the complexity and heterogeneity of urban logistics. In addition, it addresses the rise of important developments such as e-commerce. Given the vast range of urban logistics activities it is not possible to cover all topics in depth within an edited book. Nevertheless, the five chapters in Part Two provide essential insights into topics as diverse as food and construction logistics. Additional themes such as the scope to shift delivery times are also addressed.

Chapter 7 'The logistics of parcel delivery: current operations and challenges facing the UK market' is based on ongoing research from London. Here Julian Allen, Tom Cherrett, Maja Piecyk and Marzena Piotrowska address some of the dramatic changes in parcel deliveries. They consider the range of different approaches that are now found and also identify the problems resulting from increased urban activity and congestion. New opportunities for rethinking the way this sector functions are discussed.

Following the insights into the parcel industry the following chapter 'E-commerce trends and implications for urban logistics' takes an in-depth look at this major change in commercial and consumer behaviour and the implications for urban logistics and freight transport. The growing significance of e-commerce flows in cities is a topic of major concern to planners responsible for urban design and urban transport systems. The profound changes that have already started and are continuing are discussed in detail by Laetitia Dablanc, building on a wealth of examples.

Chapter 9 'Food and urban logistics: a fast-changing sector with significant policy and business implications' draws on experiences from Europe and South America. The focus in this chapter by Eleonora Morganti concerns the inextricable link between urban food systems and the logistics in cities. The importance of a wide range of food outlets including shops, restaurants and so on is addressed. The chapter also covers the way in which food logistics and its sustainability are changing in response to the many developments in technology and consumer demand patterns.

Construction activities are ever-present in cities and create major complications for traffic flows. The challenge of construction logistics and supply chain management has been the subject of a book published in 2015 by Kogan Page (Lundesjö, 2015). One of the chapters from that book written by Greger Lundesjö has been slightly edited and used to illustrate present opportunities for improvement. Chapter 10 'Consolidation centres in construction logistics' highlights the scope for consolidation but also points out that achieving a coordinated approach among the many stakeholders (many with different subgoals) can be problematical and time-consuming. This topic is receiving more attention with many projects being carried out in various countries and cities.

The important scope to shift the time of day of deliveries has been established by a major initiative in New York led by the VREF centre SUFS. This has inspired other cities and research groups to test the idea and explore the scope for change. In Chapter 11, 'The socio-economic effects of off-peak hour deliveries in Stockholm: a case study', Sönke Behrends, Iván Sánchez-Díaz and Anna Pernestål Brenden look at what has happened in Stockholm and consider the challenges of such an initiative in terms of the evaluation required and the need for better data.

Part Three: 'Making change happen' builds on the first two parts with a focus on how change can be influenced in the field of urban logistics. The five chapters take several different perspectives.

This part opens with Chapter 12 'Stakeholder engagement and partnerships for improved urban logistics'. Here Michael Browne, Alena Brettmo and Maria Lindholm build on ongoing work that has addressed questions of the various approaches to engaging stakeholders and the important question of what works and what does not work.

The following chapter discusses 'Multi-actor multi-criteria analysis as a tool to involve urban logistics stakeholders'. This approach to understanding urban logistics problems and the relevance of various options for change has been developed strongly by the research team at the Vrije Universiteit Brussel. In this chapter Cathy Macharis, Bram Kin and Philippe Lebeau explain the MAMCA approach through a series of examples where the technique has been used.

The scope to change delivery times to the off hours was discussed in Chapter 11 in the context of Stockholm. Chapter 14 'Off-hour deliveries: the importance of outreach and proper planning' illustrates how transferring research into practice needs to follow a structured and well thought out approach. Jeff Wojtowicz, Shama Campbell and José Holguín-Veras use the successful New York initiative in which they have been key players to explain what needs to be done if the lessons from research are to end up informing stakeholders and changing urban logistics behaviour.

The importance of the receivers of goods (retailers and other commercial and public sector organizations) has received much more attention in recent years. One way that they can influence urban freight delivery operations is through their procurement management. In Chapter 15 'The procurement process: a key to improved urban logistics efficiency', Olof Moen presents a fascinating argument concerning the need to focus more strongly on the power of receivers in the supply chain, arguing that procurement strategies have major implications for urban logistics activities. The chapter also contains two case studies of successful implementations.

In the concluding Chapter 16 'Future developments in modelling and information' attention turns to some important recent and forthcoming developments. Eiichi Taniguchi and Russell Thompson argue that we need to consider a wide range of initiatives if we are to find strong analytical techniques to support better decision-making by multiple actors with multiple objectives. The chapter ranges across a number of themes including advanced information systems for collecting and sharing data and public–private partnerships.

References

ALICE/ERTRAC (2015) Urban freight research roadmap, Brussels

BESTUFS (2008) Bestufs.net [Online] http://www.bestufs.net

CIVITAS (2015) [accessed 15 July 2018] Smart Choices for Cities. Making Urban Freight Logistics More Sustainable [Online] http://civitas.eu/sites/default/files/civ_pol-an5_urban_web.pdf

Dablanc, L (2009) *Freight Transport for Development Toolkit: Urban freight*, World Bank [Online] http://siteresources.worldbank.org/EXTURBANTRANSPORT/Resources/341448-1269891107889/urban_freight.pdf

Dobbs, R *et al* (2011) *Urban World: Mapping the economic power of cities*, McKinsey Global Institute, pp 1–49

European Commission (2011) European Commission's White Paper 'Roadmap to a Single European Transport Area – Towards a Competitive and Resource-efficient Transport System' (Com 144 Final of 28 March 2011)

Giuliano, G, O'Brien, T, Dablanc, L and Holliday, K (2013) *Synthesis of Freight Research in Urban Transportation Planning*, National Cooperative Freight Research Program Report 23, Transportation Research Board [Online] http://www.trb.org/Publications/Blurbs/168987.aspx

González-Feliu, J, Semet, F and Routhier, JL (ed) (2013) *Sustainable Urban Logistics: Concepts, methods and information systems*, Springer, Heidelberg

Holguín-Veras, J, Ozbay, K, Kornhauser, AL, Brom, M, Iyer, S, Yushimito, W, Ukkusuri, S, Allen, B and Silas, M (2011) Overall Impacts of Off-Hour Delivery Programs in the New York City Metropolitan Area, *Transportation Research Record*, **2238** (2011), pp 68–76

Holguín-Veras, J, Ramirez-Rios, D, Kalahasthi, L, Campbell, S, González-Calderón, C and Wojtowicz, J (2018) *Quantification of Freight and Service Activity Trends in Cities*, Transportation Research Board 97th Annual Meeting, Washington DC

Institute for City Logistics (ICL) (2018) Institute for City Logistics [Online] http://www.citylogistics.org/

Lindkvist, H *et al* (2018) [accessed 15 July 2018] *Ring Road Logistics – efficient use of infrastructure*, Göteborg: CLOSER [Online] https://closer.lindholmen.se/projekt-closer/kringfartslogistik

Lundesjo, G (ed) (2015) *Supply Chain Management and Logistics in Construction: Delivering tomorrow's built environment*. Kogan Page, London

McKinnon, A (2015) Postscript Chapter, in *Green Logistics: Improving the Environmental Sustainability of Logistics*, 3rd edn, ed A McKinnon, M Browne, M Piecyk and A Whiteing, Kogan Page, London

METRANS (2018) Personal communication with METRANS representatives, 4 September 2018

Rhodes, S, Berndt, M, Bingham, P, Bryan, J, Cherrett, T, Plumeau, P and Weisbrod, R (2012) *Guidebook for Understanding Urban Goods Movement*, National Cooperative Freight Research Program Report 14, Transportation Research Board [Online] http://www.trb.org/Publications/Blurbs/166828.aspx

Taniguchi, E and Thompson, R (ed) (2012) Seventh International Conference on City Logistics, *Procedia – Social and Behavioral Sciences*, **39**, pp 1–858 [Online] http://www.sciencedirect.com/science/journal/18770428/39

Tomer, A and Kane, J (2014) *Mapping Freight: The highly concentrated nature of goods trade in the United States*, p 38, Brookings, Washington, DC

Transportation Research Board (2013) City Logistics Research: A trans-atlantic perspective final program, EU–US Transportation Research

Symposium No 1, 30–31 May [Online] http://onlinepubs.trb.org/onlinepubs/conf/2013/2013UrbanFreight/PreliminaryProgram.pdf

TURBLOG (2010) Transferability of urban logistics concepts and practices from a world wide perspective, Deliverable 1: 'A worldwide overview on urban logistic interventions and data collection techniques'

Vaghi, C and Percoco, M (2011) *City Logistics in Italy: Success factors and environmental performance,* in C Macharis and S Melo, *City Distribution and Urban Freight Transport. Multiple Perspectives*, Edward Elgar, pp 151–75

Metropolitan economies and the generation of freight and service activity 02

An international perspective

JOSÉ HOLGUÍN-VERAS, DIANA G RAMÍREZ-RÍOS, TRILCE ENCARNACIÓN, JESÚS GONZÁLEZ-FELIU, ELISE CASPERSEN, CARLOS RIVERA-GONZÁLEZ, CARLOS A GONZÁLEZ-CALDERÓN AND RENATO DA SILVA LIMA

Introduction

Global urbanization has been growing rapidly in the past six decades. In the 1950s, less than one-third of the world's population lived in urban settlements. In 2014, this had scaled up to 54 per cent of the population, and the trend is expected to continue. By 2050, the world is expected to be 34 per cent rural and 66 per cent urban, the opposite of what it was in the mid-20th century (United Nations, 2014). With increasing urbanization, cities face numerous challenges, particularly in regard to the movement of goods in and out of city centres. These challenges will grow as cities do, and as the demand for goods and services are concentrated in urban areas, producing numerous externalities. Congestion, pollution, noise and safety are just some of the issues that cities must contend with on a daily basis in relation to trucks and other vehicles that carry freight. Service activity also contributes to daily vehicle trips in and out of urban centres. An example would be plumbing repair trucks that service both city offices and residents. All service-related vehicles add, in smaller proportions, to the commercial vehicle traffic present in city centres. Estimates from cities across the United States show that service trips represent only 10 per cent of total freight trips generated (Holguín-Veras *et al*, 2018c); but in terms of parking needs, the effects may be larger. Studies show that service vehicles stay longer in parking spots, limiting curb space for freight vehicles (Campbell *et al*, 2017).

Understanding urban economies and how these relate to urban freight and service activity is imperative to addressing the key challenges faced in city logistics. Policymakers will need, as a key indicator of this activity, accurate quantification of commercial vehicles that carry freight and services on a daily basis. Yet, data related to the count of trucks, semi-trailers and tractor-trailers may be limited, or unavailable at a city or metropolitan level. At this level, data on the number of trips taken by vans, sport utility vehicles (SUVs), crossovers and small vehicles, which represents approximately 90 per cent of all urban deliveries in some US metropolitan areas (Bronzini, 2008), is rarely available.

The main goal of this chapter is to put in the hands of the transportation community a cogent characterization of urban economies and the freight and service activity (FSA) they generate. Doing so will help transportation planners and decision-makers to understand the interconnections between the economy and FSA, and to gain an idea about the magnitude of the latter. In doing so, the chapter exploits a series of generation models of FSA that have been developed in multiple countries.

To pursue this goal, the authors selected a number of metropolitan areas of different sizes and from countries in different income ranges, analysed key economic data and generated estimates for FSA at some of these urban centres. The models used correspond to New York and Albany, United States (Holguín-Veras *et al*, 2017a), Oslo (Caspersen, 2018) and Medellín (González-Calderón *et al*, 2018). Other cities where the models are available were included as well, as with Paris and Lyon (France), for which models have been built from a national rather than city-based database (González-Feliu *et al*, 2016). The estimates provide a sense of the number of freight and service-related commercial vehicles moving daily in the areas considered, and result in FSA rates that can be transferred to other cities where no empirical estimates are available.

The chapter is divided as follows: the first two sections provide a brief overview of the selection of the metropolitan areas, and the data and models used to develop the analysis. The third section provides an initial analysis of the urban economies, followed by an in-depth analysis of those economies by industry sector. The subsequent sections provide the estimates of freight and service generation, and their relationship to urban economies for a subset of metropolitan areas, where FSA rates are provided and analysed.

Metropolitan areas selected for the analyses

For the analyses of urban and metropolitan economies and their implications regarding FSA, a selection of metropolitan areas around the world was developed. These urban areas belong to countries with different income ranges located on a number of continents. Based on the United Nations 2015 ranking for urban agglomerations and metropolitan areas that exceed 300,000 in population (United Nations, 2014), the selection was developed for three different classes: Class I, with populations between 6 and 22 million; Class II, with populations between 2 and 6 million; and Class III, with populations of less than 2 million. Each class size includes at least a metropolitan area from a high-income country and a middle-upper income country, as defined by United Nations (2014). Table 2.1 shows the selected metropolitan areas and their classifications, followed by a brief description of each region represented.

São Paulo, Brazil

The metropolitan area of São Paulo (RMSP) is Brazil's largest, with 21 million inhabitants, distributed over 39 municipalities and 7,947 square kilometres (IBGE, 2017). It is the fourth largest urban agglomeration in the world, and concentrates nearly 18 per cent of Brazil's total GDP in its important industrial and commercial complexes (Brookings, 2012). The latest statistics show that there were over 7 million jobs in nearly 450 thousand establishments in RMSP (Brazilian Ministry of Labour, 2016). The RMSP concentrates diversified and specialized services with special highlights in the areas of communications, culture, education, health, transportation and gastronomy. Additionally, it is an important centre for business tourism in Latin America, as well as for numerous multinational companies.

New York, United States

The New York City metropolitan area is the largest in the United States, and includes the cities of Newark and Jersey, and neighbouring counties

Table 2.1 Metropolitan areas selected for the analyses

Metropolitan Areas	Population	Area (in km²)	Density (Pop/km²)	Country's Income	GDP per capita (in USD)	Number of Establishments	Total Employment
Class I: From 6 to 22M inhabitants							
São Paulo, Brazil	21,391,624	7,947	2,692	Upper-Middle	$ 16,650.00	436,424	6,174,605
New York, USA	20,153,634	21,483	938	High	$ 70,758.00	575,333	8,285,112
Paris, France	7,020,210	762	9,213	High	$ 96,845.28	676,090	3,788,321
Class II: From 2 to 6M inhabitants							
Phoenix, USA	4,661,537	37,723	124	High	$ 43,602.00	94,568	1,671,907
Medellín, Colombia	3,777,099	1,157	3,263	Upper-Middle	$ 8,489.00	117,514	1,762,895
Puebla, Mexico	2,941,988	2,392	1,230	Upper-Middle	$ 5,131.55	134,928	1,049,807
Class III: Fewer than 2M inhabitants							
Barranquilla, Colombia	1,991,000	520	3,829	Upper-Middle	$ 6,140.15	49,874	911,529
Lyon, France	1,370,678	534	2,567	High	$ 45,554.71	105,377	618,205
Oslo, Norway	1,570,000	8,894	177	High	$ 82,040.00	72,263	763,503
Santiago, Dominican Republic	577,000	524	1,101	Upper-Middle	$ 12,626.00	9,541	485,037

NOTE Establishment refers to a place of business, which could be local or a branch location of a larger business.

located in the three states of New York, New Jersey and Pennsylvania, with 21 million inhabitants and extending 21,483 square kilometres. It reported a GDP per capita of US $70,758 in 2016, a growth of 1.04 per cent from the first statistic recorded in 2001 (US Bureau of Economic Analysis, 2017). The latest statistics show that the number of non-agricultural jobs in the region is over 8 million (US Bureau of Labor Statistics, 2016). It is an important financial centre and host to many national and international headquarters, particularly in the technology, real estate and insurance sectors. Also known as the 'capital of the world', the city receives an estimated 59.7 million tourists each year (McGeehan, 2016), with very active food and accommodation sectors.

Paris, France

The metropolis of Greater Paris – which refers to the administrative multi-town structure within the Île-de-France region – includes the city of Paris and the departments located in the 'inner ring' of the region: Haut-de-Seine, Seine-Saint-Denis and Val-de-Marne. It has more than 7 million inhabitants, covers 762 square kilometres (Institut National de la Statistique et des Etudes Economiques-INSEE, 2018) and generates a GDP per capita of 97 thousand euros (Eurostat, 2018). It has total employment of 4 million and more than 600 thousand establishments in 2016 for the metropolis of Greater Paris (Institut National de la Statistique et des Etudes Economiques – INSEE, 2018). It is a smaller area within the most populated urban area in France, the Île-de-France region, with more than 12 million inhabitants (Île-de-France, 2018). The main economic activities are retailing and services – excluding public administration, but including transport and logistics (CCI Paris Île-de-France, 2017).

Phoenix, United States

Phoenix is the largest city of the state of Arizona and a major economic centre of the southwestern United States. The metropolitan area includes the city of Phoenix plus the cities of Mesa and Scottsdale, spans 37,725 square kilometres, and is home to 4.7 million inhabitants (US Bureau of Labor Statistics, 2016). The most recent GDP per capita measured for the Phoenix metro area (AZ) was US $43,602 in 2016, slightly lower than the one reported in 2001 (US Bureau of Economic Analysis, 2017). Employment, on the other hand, has grown faster than the national rate for the past five years, reporting over 1.6 million employees and nearly 95 thousand establishments

(US Census Bureau, 2017; US Census Bureau, 2016). The city boasts a healthy job market with large aerospace and defence companies, as well as a growing market of technological companies, all attracted to Phoenix's lower cost of living compared with other metropolitan areas in the west.

Medellín (Valle de Aburrá), Colombia

Medellín is the second largest city in Colombia after its capital, Bogotá. Its metropolitan area includes nine neighbouring urban areas, known as the Valle de Aburrá metropolitan area. Its area extends to 1,157 kilometres, with a total of 3.8 million inhabitants. The data collected shows a total employment of more than 1.7 million (Área Metropolitana del Valle de Aburrá *et al*, 2012), and its metropolitan area makes the second highest contribution to the country's GDP, with nearly US $8,500 per capita (Camara de Comercio de Medellín Para Antioquia, 2017). It is an important industrial urban area considering its manufacturing activity, and its international trade is also very active, with an international airport that handles a huge percentage of Colombia's imports and exports for different industry sectors, particularly the floriculture sector.

Puebla-Tlaxcala, Mexico

The metropolitan area of Puebla-Tlaxcala is the fourth largest in Mexico, with a total population of 2.9 million, according to the 2015 census (Instituto Nacional de Estadistica y Geografia – INEGI, 2018). The city of Puebla, its urban core, represents almost 50 per cent of the population of the entire metropolis, and it reported a GDP per capita of US $5,131 (Les Ateliers, 2012). The metropolitan area is composed of 38 municipalities (Consejo Nacional de Planeacion, 2010). The metropolitan area reported an employment of 1 million, and 135,000 establishments (Instituto Nacional de Estadistica y Geografia – INEGI, 2018). Puebla's economy was historically known for its industrial corridors, which have slowly been replaced by service sectors. This shift, so highly concentrated in its core city, has been accompanied by a reduction of economic activity (Puebla Online, 2018).

Barranquilla, Colombia

Barranquilla is the fourth largest city in Colombia, and the second largest in the Caribbean Basin after Miami, Florida. Its metropolitan area includes the city of Barranquilla and the municipalities of Puerto Colombia, Soledad, Malambo and Galapa (US Commercial Service and Amcham Colombia, 2015). It has nearly 2 million inhabitants, and extends 520 square kilometres (El Heraldo, 2017). In 2016, it reported over 900 thousand employees and a GDP per capita of USD $6,140 (Departamento Administrativo Nacional de Estadistica – DANE, 2018). It has been acknowledged as Colombia's Golden Gate Way due to its important maritime and river ports, which receive 60 per cent of the metal and 40 per cent of the steel consumed in Colombia (US Commercial Service and Amcham Colombia, 2015). Barranquilla is a dynamic industrial and commercial activity centre, with important sectors such as metal-mechanics, logistics, energy and business services (PROCOLOMBIA, 2018).

Lyon, France

The Grand Lyon Metropolis is the second largest metropolitan area in France. It includes 59 municipalities, has a surface area of about 538 square kilometres and counted 1.3 million inhabitants in 2014 (La Métropole de Lyon, 2018). It has a GDP per capita of 43,300 euros, occupying the 13th place among European cities (Le Progrès, 2018). The most recent data collected reported more than 600,000 employees and 100,000 establishments (Institut National de la Statistique et des Etudes Economiques – INSEE, 2018). The main industrial sectors are chemistry/environment and pharmaceutical production, digital and image industries and automotive manufacturing (Grand Lyon Economie, 2017).

Oslo (Greater Oslo region), Norway

Oslo is the capital of Norway, and the country's economic and governmental centre, as well as a traffic and cultural hub. The Greater Oslo region includes Oslo and another 45 surrounding municipalities that are both economically and socially connected to Oslo, covering an area of 8,894 square kilometres (Statistics Norway, 2018a). The region was home to 1.57 million people in 2015, which is approximately 30 per cent of Norway's population (Statistics Norway, 2018b) – and was one of Europe's fastest growing in the last decade (Eurostat, 2017). Over 200,000 establishments and nearly 900,000 employees were registered in the region in 2015, of which approximately half were registered in the city of Oslo (Statistics Norway, 2018a).

Santiago, Dominican Republic

Santiago is the second largest city in the Dominican Republic, with a population of 577,000 and an area of 524 square kilometres. Employment in Santiago has grown significantly in the past decade, as a result of the country's economic growth, with more than 450,000 employees reported in 2016, and a GDP per capita of US $12,626 (Banco Central de la República Dominicana, 2018). The city is located in a fertile region, the Cibao Valley, where cacao, coffee, tobacco, rice and other agricultural export products are grown. The city's main economic activities are processing the region's agricultural products, as well as manufacturing tobacco products, pharmaceuticals, furniture and leather goods (Oficina Nacional de Estadistica – ONE, 2018).

Data and models

Data collected

This section describes the data collected to analyse the economies of the selected metropolitan areas. The data used for the analyses consist of the counts of establishments and employment per industry sector. The main source of these data is listed in Table 2.2.

All datasets contain, for the entire metropolitan area, employment and establishment totals, and by industry sector. Given that the industry sectors were different among countries, a cross-referencing of these to the North American Industry Classification System (NAICS) had to be developed as part of the study. As Table 2.2 also highlights, some of the data were obtained from the census of establishments and business records in the respective Chambers of Commerce, while others were obtained from reports produced or estimates developed from secondary sources. The latter were used only if no primary data were available.

Freight and service generation models

To assess the magnitude of FSA in cities, the authors applied state-of-the-art models to estimate daily freight and service vehicle trips in selected metropolitan areas. Freight Trip Generation (FTG) models were used for daily freight trips, which include daily freight trips produced and attracted to the establishment. Service Trip Generation (STA) models were used to estimate service trips. The limited data available from the service sector only captures Service Trip Attraction (STA), but not Service Trip Production.

Table 2.2 Sources of data for selected metropolitan areas

Metropolitan Area(s)	Source
São Paulo, Brazil	Instituto Brasileiro de Geografia e Estatística (IGBE 2017)
New York, USA	US Census Bureau (2016; 2017)
Paris, France	Institut national de la statistique et des études économiques (2013)
Phoenix, USA	US Census Bureau (2016; 2017)
Medellín, Colombia	Area Metropolitana del valle de Aburra et al (2012)
Puebla, Mexico	Instituto Nacional de Estadistica y Geografia – INEGI (2018)
Barranquilla, Colombia	Dane (2015)
Lyon, France	Grand Lyon Economique (2017)
Oslo, Norway	Statistics Norway (2018)
Santiago, Dominican Republic	Oficina Nacional de Estadistica – ONE (2018)

The FTG models are available for the following geographical areas: New York and Albany (United States), Paris and Lyon (France), Medellín (Colombia) and Oslo (Norway). The STA models are available for New York and Albany (United States). These were linear and nonlinear Ordinary Least Square (OLS) models, as a function of industry type and employment, as shown in Equations 1 and 2, respectively. In the case where the values were reported per week, respective values per day were calculated, assuming that the firm operates for an average of 5.5 days per week.

Linear model:

$$f(E) = \alpha + \beta * E \tag{1}$$

Non-linear model:

$$f(E) = \alpha * E^{\beta} \tag{2}$$

Where f stands for FTG or STA. The nonlinear model in Equation 2 is a result of natural log transformation of dependent and independent variables, as given below in Equation 3:

$$\ln(f) = A + \beta * \ln(E) \tag{3}$$

Also for the nonlinear model, the log transformation bias is corrected by considering Mean Squared Error (S^2) in the calculation of α, as given in Equation 4, where 'exp' represents exponential function (Newman, 1993).

$$\alpha = \exp\left(\frac{S^2}{2} + A\right) \quad (4)$$

Table 2.3 shows the summary of the models available.

Table 2.3 Functional forms available for freight activity in the cities

Metropolitan Area(s)	Functional Forms Available	Freight Deliveries Received	Freight Shipments Sent	FTG	STA
New York, USA	Linear	x	x		x
	Non-linear	x	x		x
Paris and Lyon, France	Linear			x	
Medellín, Colombia	Constant	x	x		
Oslo, Norway	Non-linear			x	

A brief description of the models used to estimate freight and service trips for the analysis is provided below.

FTG models for the United States

Freight Trip Generation (FTG) and Service Trip Attraction (STA) models were developed from survey data collected from establishments located in the New York City metropolitan area, and the New York State Capital District (ie Albany, NY and surrounding cities), as part of research funded by the National Cooperative Highway Research Program and the National Cooperative Freight Research Program (Holguín-Veras *et al*, 2017a). These establishment-level models are solely based on employment, and were developed by industry sector, based on the North American Industry Classification System (NAICS). Specifically, these are estimates for daily shipments sent, and deliveries received, at a two-digit level NAICS for the two US cities mentioned. FTG is the result of the total of daily shipments and deliveries, under the assumption that one freight shipment sent equals one freight trip produced, and one freight delivery received equals one freight trip attracted.

The models were implemented in the Freight and Service Activity Generation Software (Holguín-Veras *et al*, 2017b), where an aggregation procedure was developed to automatically generate the estimates for any city in the United States, using as input the Census Business Patterns (CBP) database. Through the software, models have been successfully applied to a number of large cities in the United States (Holguín-Veras *et al*, 2018c).

FTG models for France

The FTG models for France are based on the work of González-Feliu *et al* (2016) and Sánchez-Díaz *et al* (2016). Data collected from the French surveys on urban goods (Ambrosini *et al*, 2010) were used to propose a set of models integrating a statistical analysis (mainly dispersion), and the FTG framework from Holguín-Veras *et al* (2011) and Holguín-Veras *et al* (2013). The authors examined different levels of aggregation and functional forms. The models are structured in 26 categories, where results from the most robust model were identified by Sánchez-Díaz *et al* (2016) in terms of both prediction capacity and heterogeneity caption.

FTG models for Medellín

The FTG models for Medellín were estimated using survey data collected in 2011–12. The surveys were conducted in 2,947 establishments in the urban area (González-Calderón *et al*, 2018). The FTG models were estimated by industry sector. The estimates developed consist of daily shipments (production) and deliveries (attraction) at a two-digit level based on the International Standard Industrial Classification of All Economic Activities (ISIC). The estimates are for both FIS and SIS commercial establishments. Similar to the models for New York City and Albany, the estimates for FTG assume that one freight shipment sent equals one freight vehicle trip produced, and that one freight delivery received equals one freight vehicle trip attracted.

FTG models for Oslo

The FTG models for Oslo were developed using survey data collected from establishments in Groruddalen, an urban area in the eastern part of Oslo, Norway. It covers four of Oslo's boroughs, and a wide spectrum of commercial and private activities. The survey was conducted in 2016, and inquired about the number of freight and service vehicles moving to and from the surveyed establishments during a typical week, as well as establishment-specific characteristics (Caspersen, 2018). Resulting models were similar to the NCFRP 25 FTG models, except only non-linear models were estimated, as this relationship was the most suitable fit for the data, as explained in Caspersen (2018).

Metropolitan economies

To start the analyses of metropolitan economies, it is crucial to get a global picture of the economic activity in metropolitan areas. To develop the analysis, the authors observed key economic data (ie GDP, employment and establishments) from the selected metropolitan areas. This section highlights the relationship between population, economic indicators (ie GDP per capita) and the size of the economic activity (establishments and employment) at each metropolitan area.

To understand where these metropolitan areas stand in terms of population and economic activity, a ranking was developed for each of the cities, as shown in Table 2.4. The first three cities in the population ranking are some of the largest cities in the world. In the Americas, for instance, São Paulo is the second highest after Mexico City. New York follows as third highest, and is the largest metropolitan area in the United States. These same cities are the top three in the establishments and employment rankings, clearly corroborating what Kötter and Friesecke (2009) mentioned about these cities being the centres and junctions of the global economy.

Based on population ranking, the metropolitan areas that follow are not as large, but fall in the category of cities where a significant proportion of the world's population live. In 2016, 1.7 billion people (23 per cent of the planet's population) lived in a city with fewer than one million inhabitants (United Nations, 2016). Also, as shown in Table 2.4, some of these cities fall naturally in order of employment as well, which suggests that there is a correlation between employment and population size. In terms of establishment numbers, less populated cities such as Lyon have climbed up in ranking. A larger number of establishments are very common in the French context, where cities have a large proportion of small single-employee establishments. Santiago is the smallest of all the cities, but belongs to the category of cities that are expected to increase most rapidly in the next decade, according to the United Nations (2016) report. Also, as expected, it is the smallest in terms of establishments and employment.

In terms of income, GDP per capita clearly separates the cities belonging to high-income countries – ie France, Norway and the United States – and the cities belonging to the middle-upper income countries – ie Brazil, Dominican Republic, Colombia and Mexico. There seems to be no clear connection between income and intensity of economic activity, as initially observed by the rankings of number of establishments and employment. Nevertheless, these GDP rankings were important to understand the level of

Table 2.4 Ranking of metropolitan areas

Rank	Population	GDP per capita (in USD)	Establishments	Employment
1	São Paulo, Brazil	Paris, France	Paris, France	New York, USA
2	New York, USA	Oslo, Norway	New York, USA	São Paulo, Brazil
3	Paris, France	New York, USA	São Paulo, Brazil	Paris, France
4	Phoenix, USA	Lyon, France	Puebla, Mexico	Medellín, Colombia
5	Medellín, Colombia	Phoenix, USA	Medellín, Colombia	Phoenix, USA
6	Puebla, Mexico	São Paulo, Brazil	Lyon, France	Puebla, Mexico
7	Barranquilla, Colombia	Santiago, Dominican Rep	Phoenix, USA	Barranquilla, Colombia
8	Oslo, Norway	Medellín, Colombia	Oslo, Norway	Oslo, Norway
9	Lyon, France	Barranquilla, Colombia	Barranquilla, Colombia	Lyon, France
10	Santiago, Dominican Rep	Puebla, Mexico	Santiago, Dominican Rep	Santiago, Dominican Rep

investment that can be made in these cities, particularly in terms of business improvements and the revitalization of city centres.

To understand the relationship of population and economic activity, as evidenced by the rankings of the metropolitan areas analysed, plots for the logarithm of the population with the logarithm of number of establishments and employment were developed, as shown in Figures 2.1 and 2.2, respectively. The number of establishments per city has a linear relationship with population, regardless of the level of economic development of the city. As seen in Figure 2.1, all cities show that as population increases, the number of establishments also increases. In the middle-upper income cities, the number of establishments per person ranges from 0.01 to 0.04, while high-income economies show a range of establishments per person of from 0.02 to 0.09. The lowest result for this ratio in high-income economies is for Phoenix, in the United States, and the largest value reported is for

Figure 2.1 Number of establishments and population per city

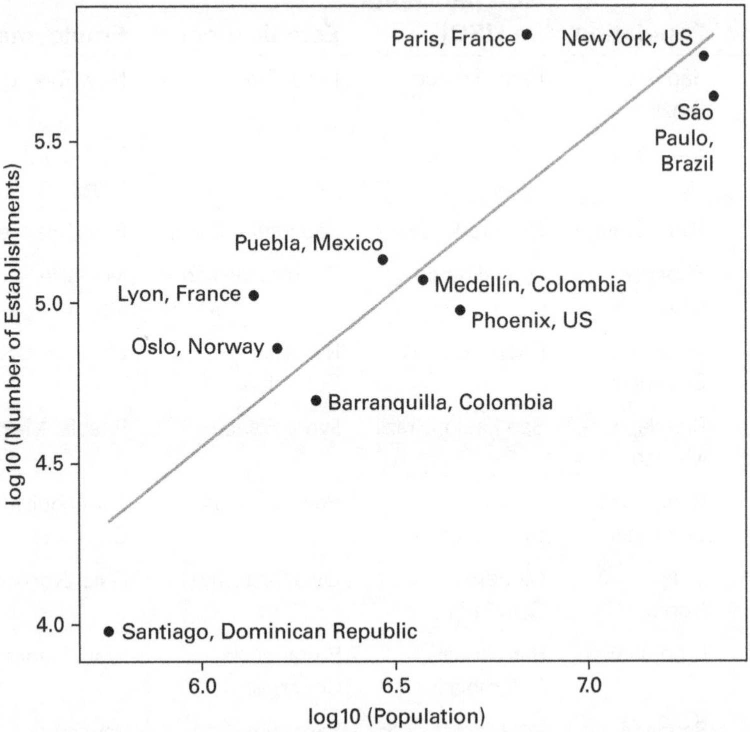

Paris, France. The difference between these cases is due to the types of businesses located in these urban areas. Paris and Lyon have a large number of small micro-enterprises, which significantly increases the number of establishments per person, while a greater concentration of large businesses reduces this ratio. The relationship between population and employment shows less variability, and does not exhibit significant outliers, as shown in Figure 2.2. Here, the same correlation is shown between establishments and population. With a median number of jobs per inhabitant of 0.41, these employment numbers reflect the high levels of economic activity concentrated in the metropolitan areas.

Understanding that there exists a correlation in the size of the economic activity with the size of the city can provide city planners with tools to assess the challenges involved in the movement of goods and services to city centres. For instance, more populous cities will have higher demands for freight and services than a smaller city, thus face a more critical situation. Further sections will expand on these opportunities, where estimates for freight and service are compared among cities of different sizes and urban economies.

Figure 2.2 Employment and population per city

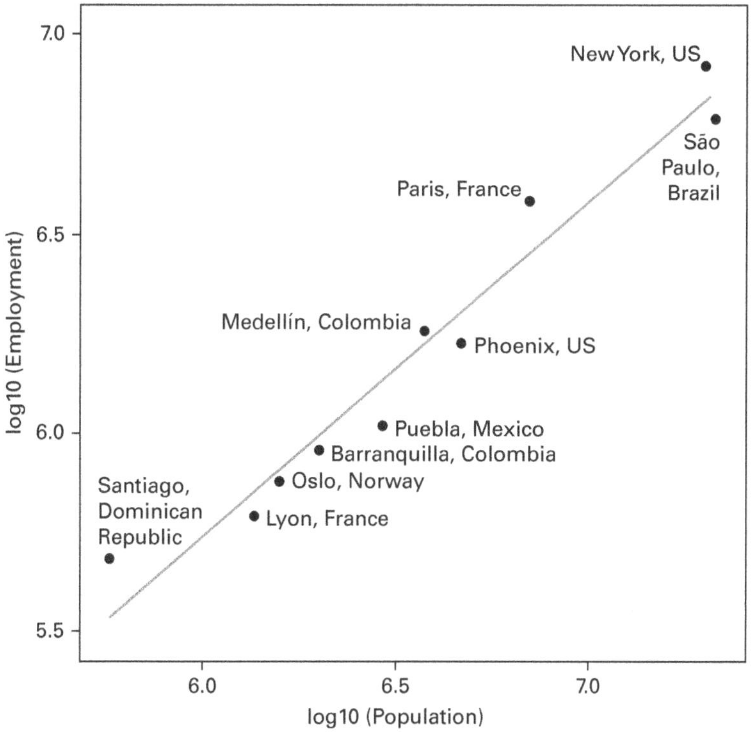

Freight and service intensive sectors

To grasp the intensity of freight and service activity (FSA), it is essential to get a better understanding of those sectors that generate the most freight traffic, and those that generate the most service traffic. Industry sectors were classified as Freight Intensive Sectors (FIS) or Service Intensive Sectors (SIS). The FIS are those industry sectors for which the production and consumption of freight is an important component of their economic activities. The SIS are those sectors where the provision of services is the primary activity. Table 2.5 shows the resulting classification of the sectors, based on the North American Industry Classification System (NAICS).

As shown, FIS do not just consist of warehouses and manufacturing facilities. Restaurants, hotels and retail stores also consume freight on a daily basis. Moreover, the proportion of economic activity in the FIS accounts for half of all of the economic activity. Previous research done on the metropolitan and micropolitan areas of the United States

Table 2.5 Classification of industry sectors based on FSA

NAICS	Freight Intensive Sectors (FIS)	NAICS	Service Intensive Sectors (SIS)
11	Agriculture, Forestry, Fishing, Hunting	51	Information
21	Mining, Quarrying, Oil/Gas…	52	Finance and Insurance
22	Utilities	53	Real Estate and Rental and Leasing
23	Construction	54	Professional, Scientific, Tech Services
31–33	Manufacturing	55	Management of Companies
42	Wholesale Trade	56	Administrative, Support, Waste Management
44–45	Retail Trade	61	Educational Services
48–49	Transportation and Warehousing	62	Healthcare and Social Assistance
72	Accommodation and Food Services	71	Arts, Entertainment and Recreation
		81	Other Services
		92	Public Administration

has determined that 45 per cent of all commercial establishments are accounted for in FIS, and 50 per cent of employment is generated in FIS (Holguín-Veras *et al*, 2018a). This implies that efficiency or inefficiencies encountered in the movement of goods in these sectors will have a direct impact on half of the economy, and an indirect impact on the other half. It is also worth mentioning that these previous studies found that Transportation and Warehousing accounts for only 2.8 per cent of commercial establishments, and 3.6 per cent of employment in the United States, while 30–35 per cent of employment is concentrated in the Retail and Wholesale businesses. This suggests that city centres least likely to have warehouses or manufacturing facilities are still receiving a lot of freight traffic, given the daily deliveries produced and shipments received in restaurants, hotels and retail stores.

The SIS, on the other hand, consists of all businesses that offer as their primary activity a given service or range of services to their customers. Banks, insurance companies, healthcare facilities, computer service enterprises, attorney offices, management consulting firms, plumbing repair companies and cable services are all examples of service-oriented businesses. Even though the intensity of freight is not as pronounced for these establishments as it is with FIS, service activity does have a significant impact on passenger and commercial vehicle traffic. On the passenger side, SIS includes the daily commuting of employees to these businesses, and on the commercial side, SIS involves vehicles that are required to get to establishments to perform a given service. The latter has important implications for urban logistics, particularly parking, as these vehicles typically spend extended periods of time at an establishment while performing a service. Thus, taking into account the number of service vehicles operating on a daily basis is essential for accurate city planning.

To understand the impact of FIS and SIS, total establishments and employment were obtained by industry sector for some of the metropolitan areas of analyses, as shown in Tables 2.6 and 2.7.

Freight Intensive Sectors

The first section of Table 2.6 shows that the percentage of establishments in FIS is significantly lower in metropolitan areas from high-income countries, where these represent typically half or below half of all establishments. In the middle-high income countries, FIS represents the majority of the establishments. This is the case of São Paulo (Brazil), Medellín (Colombia) and Puebla (Mexico), where FIS establishments represent 69, 70, and 74 per cent of the total, respectively. With regards to FIS employment, the case is similar. For instance, Medellín shows 52 per cent of employment in these sectors, and Puebla (Mexico) shows an employment of 81 per cent of the total. Table 2.6 also shows another interesting pattern regarding the estimates in different geographical areas. In European cities, for instance, the average employment per establishment is significantly lower than it is in cities in the United States. This was discussed earlier, for in French cities, as the data shows, there is a higher proportion of smaller establishments, where the average employment per establishment is 5 to 6. This is also reflected in Oslo, which has an average of 8 employees per establishment. In the United States, the value varies between 12 and 20 employees per establishment. As population increases in the high-income countries, the number of establishments per resident increases. In the case of medium-high income cities, there is a consistent pattern of employment per resident. As population decreases, the number of employees per 1,000 residents generally increases.

Table 2.6 also shows a breakdown by industry sector belonging to FIS, where some interesting patterns are observed. The percentage of establishments for the consumer-oriented sectors, such as Retail Trade (NAICS 44–45), Wholesale Trade (NAICS 42), and Food and Accommodation Services (NAICS 72), represents a large proportion of the FIS, where the percentage of establishments and employments ranges from 44 to 80 per cent. Particularly in the high-income cities, the Construction (NAICS 23) sector is also highly represented, as it accounts for 20 to 30 per cent of all establishments in FIS, and 12 to 20 per cent of all employment in FIS. In the middle-high income cities there is a higher representation of the Manufacturing (NAICS 31–33) sector, and a lower representation of Construction (NAICS 23) establishments. In Medellín, for example, the Manufacturing sector is 16 per cent of the total, while in Phoenix this sector is only 8 per cent of the total. In the Construction sector, the opposite holds true. In Medellín, Construction is only 6 per cent, while in Phoenix it is 21 per cent of the total establishments.

Service Intensive Sectors

When analysing the breakdown by SIS, as observed in Table 2.7, there are additional patterns that are worth noting. The share of establishments generated by these sectors ranges from 40 to 66 per cent in all metropolitan areas, with the exception of Puebla (Mexico), where the representation of establishments in SIS is much lower. The share of employment generated by SIS sectors ranges from 45 to 68 per cent, with the exception of Puebla (Mexico) and Barranquilla (Colombia) with a share of 19 and 34 per cent of all employment in SIS, respectively.

With respect to those sectors that generate a significant share of the jobs in urban areas in SIS, there is the Healthcare and Social Assistance (NAICS 62) sector, which is very well represented in some countries but not as well represented in other countries. For cities in the United States, in particular, this sector represents 30 per cent of all employment registered in SIS. This is not the case for the cities in France, where the Healthcare sector accounts for only 10 to 12 per cent of the employment in SIS. In the Colombian cities, this percentage is much lower, as it represents only 7 to 8 per cent of the employment in SIS.

Other industry sectors belonging to SIS are also well represented across metropolitan areas, particularly those that are related to technological services and sales. The Real Estate (NAICS 53) sector is particularly important in the French cities, as it represents almost half of

Table 2.6 Establishments and employment by FIS

NAICS	Description	São Paulo, Brazil	New York, USA	Paris, France	Phoenix, USA	Medellín, Colombia	Puebla, Mexico	Barranquilla, Colombia	Lyon, France	Oslo, Norway	Santiago, Dominican Republic
					Establishments						
23	Construction	7%	20%	27%	21%	6%	1%	12%	28%	19%	7%
31–33	Manufacturing	15%	6%	8%	8%	16%	17%	13%	11%	16%	18%
42	Wholesale Trade	8%	15%	16%	13%	11%	4%	13%	15%	14%	15%
44–45	Retail Trade	46%	32%	13%	31%	40%	61%	42%	16%	22%	43%
48–49	Transportation and Warehousing	5%	6%	18%	6%	7%	1%	7%	13%	19%	4%
72	Accommodation and Food Services	19%	21%	18%	21%	14%	16%	9%	17%	8%	10%
Number of Establishments (FIS)		301,327	250,209	227,995	37,216	82,667	99,774	29,547	35,572	39,049	5,279
Number of Establishments (Total)		436,424	575,333	676,090	94,568	117,514	134,928	49,874	105,377	72,263	9,541
% FIS Establishments of Total		69%	43%	34%	39%	70%	74%	59%	34%	54%	55%
					Employment						
23	Construction	9%	12%	16%	14%	16%	2%	15%	14%	21%	7%
31–33	Manufacturing	25%	10%	15%	13%	24%	13%	24%	27%	23%	18%
42	Wholesale Trade	9%	14%	16%	10%	12%	4%	10%	14%	18%	15%

(continued)

Table 2.6 *(Continued)*

NAICS	Description	São Paulo, Brazil	New York, USA	Paris, France	Phoenix, USA	Medellín, Colombia	Puebla, Mexico	Barranquilla, Colombia	Lyon, France	Oslo, Norway	Santiago, Dominican Republic
44–45	Retail Trade	28%	29%	11%	28%	19%	71%	33%	10%	9%	43%
48–49	Transportation and Warehousing	8%	10%	18%	9%	8%	2%	10%	16%	14%	4%
72	Accommodation and Food Services	21%	23%	24%	25%	7%	7%	7%	18%	10%	10%
Employment (FIS)		3,692,120	3,234,208	1,223,215	781,065	910,914	847,033	600,962	231,690	309,636	268,369
Employment (Total)		6,174,605	8,285,112	3,788,321	1,671,907	1,762,895	1,049,807	911,529	618,205	763,503	485,037
% FIS Employment of Total		60%	39%	32%	47%	52%	81%	66%	37%	41%	55%
Rates											
Establishments (FIS) per 1000 residents		14.09	12.42	32.48	7.98	21.89	36.56	14.84	25.95	24.87	9.15
Employment (FIS) per 1000 residents		172.60	160.48	174.24	167.56	241.17	310.41	301.84	169.03	197.22	465.11
Average Employment per Establishment (FIS)		12.25	12.93	5.37	20.99	11.02	8.49	20.34	6.51	7.93	50.84

all establishments in SIS. In terms of employment, the percentage is much lower, which suggests that most of these establishments are composed of single-person employees. The Professional and Technical (NAICS 54) sector is also very well represented in the majority of metropolitan areas, and represents 20 to 38 per cent of all establishments, and 13 to 28 per cent of all employment in SIS.

Freight and service activity

This section presents the estimates for freight and service trips in metropolitan areas in different parts of the world. To accomplish this, the authors selected metropolitan areas where FTG and/or STA models have been estimated, as explained above. The estimation of daily freight and service trips in the metropolitan areas of New York (United States), Paris (France), Medellín (Colombia), Lyon (France) and Oslo (Norway) were estimated directly from their models, as explained in previous sections. The metropolitan area of Phoenix (United States) used the New York and Albany (United States) models.

Table 2.8 shows the resulting estimates of FSA, together with the total population, number of establishments and employment. In addition, the authors decided to include a series of rates that express either FTG or STA as unit rates of population, number of establishments and employment. These rates provide a pragmatic and very useful mechanism to produce order-of-magnitude estimates of FSA for cities and metropolitan areas for which only approximate estimates are needed, or there are no trip generation models, or the input data are not available. An analyst would only need to decide which metropolitan area from Table 2.8 provides the best match for the area under study, and then apply the selected rates to the population, number of establishments or employment.

As observed, the magnitude of FSA is evidenced by how large the city is in regards to the population and employment indicators. A large city like New York, which reports over 500,000 establishments and 8 million employees, generates approximately 2 million freight trips, and 150,000 service trips daily. For a smaller city, such as Oslo, these numbers are reduced to 110,000 daily freight trips generated, and 14,000 daily service trips attracted.

The estimates also show that in some cities, the amount of freight and service generated is much higher when compared to another city of similar size. The city of Paris, with 7 million residents, shows 2.2 million freight trips generated, and approximately 130 service trips attracted; as compared

Table 2.7 Establishments and employment by SIS

NAICS	Description	São Paulo, Brazil	New York, USA	Paris, France	Phoenix, USA	Medellín, Colombia	Puebla, Mexico	Barranquilla, Colombia	Lyon, France	Oslo, Norway	Santiago, Dominican Republic
						Establishments					
51	Information	5%	4%	5%	3%	7%	1%	5%	3%	5%	3%
52	Finance and Insurance	7%	9%	8%	12%	13%	5%	9%	8%	3%	8%
53	Real Estate	26%	11%	48%	12%	5%	6%	2%	50%	11%	8%
54	Prof and Technical Services	34%	22%	2%	23%	27%	4%	23%	3%	38%	22%
55	Management of Companies	0%	1%	0%	1%	2%	0%	1%	0%	0%	0%
56	Administrative and Waste Mgmt	1%	9%	0%	10%	15%	9%	11%	1%	10%	7%
61	Education Services	8%	3%	3%	3%	3%	7%	3%	3%	5%	6%
62	Health Care and Social Assistance	16%	19%	2%	21%	7%	16%	7%	3%	12%	19%
71	Entertainment	3%	4%	4%	2%	4%	2%	3%	1%	4%	5%
81	Other Services	0%	19%	29%	13%	18%	50%	36%	28%	12%	22%
Number of establishments (SIS)		135,097	325,124	448,096	57,352	34,847	35,154	20,327	69,805	33,214	4,262
% SIS Establishments of Total		31%	57%	66%	61%	30%	26%	41%	66%	46%	45%

					Employment						
51	Information	6%	6%	9%	4%	5%	3%	9%	8%	7%	3%
52	Finance and Insurance	10%	12%	12%	14%	9%	6%	5%	7%	5%	8%
53	Real Estate	23%	4%	12%	4%	2%	4%	2%	9%	3%	8%
54	Prof and Technical Services	29%	15%	3%	13%	13%	2%	22%	5%	28%	22%
55	Management of Companies	0%	5%	0%	5%	1%	0%	1%	0%	0%	0%
56	Administrative and Waste Mgmt	2%	9%	15%	16%	56%	13%	11%	20%	14%	7%
61	Education Services	11%	7%	8%	5%	1%	25%	3%	13%	12%	6%
62	Health Care and Social Assistance	16%	30%	10%	27%	8%	16%	7%	12%	22%	19%
71	Entertainment	3%	4%	4%	4%	1%	2%	3%	1%	3%	5%
81	Other Services	0%	8%	26%	7%	4%	30%	37%	25%	6%	22%
Employment (SIS)		2,482,485	5,050,904	2,565,106	890,842	851,981	202,774	310,567	386,515	453,867	216,668
%SIS Employment of Total		40%	61%	68%	53%	48%	19%	34%	63%	59%	45%
					Rates						
Establishments (SIS) per 1000 residents		6.32	16.13	63.83	12.30	9.23	12.88	10.21	50.93	21.16	7.39
Employment (SIS) per 1000 residents		116.05	250.62	365.39	191.10	225.56	74.31	155.99	281.99	289.09	375.51
Average Employment per Establishment (SIS)		18.38	15.54	5.72	15.53	24.45	5.77	15.28	5.54	13.66	50.84

Table 2.8 Key statistics per metropolitan area

Description	New York, USA	Paris, France*	Phoenix, USA	Medellín, Colombia	Lyon, France*	Oslo, Norway
Estimates of Freight and Service Activity (FSA)						
FTG (FIS)	1,924,153	2,221,769	336,115	214,082	357,125	110,462
Freight Shipments (FIS)	1,031,160	1,199,755	157,355	117,139	192,847	52,249
Freight Deliveries (FIS)	892,993	1,022,014	178,760	96,943	164,277	58,214
STA (SIS)	152,758	131,472	34,522	18,750	11,565	14,343
Key Socio-Economic Descriptors						
Population	20,153,634	7,020,210	4,661,537	3,777,099	1,370,678	1,570,000
Area (in km²)	21,482.85	762.00	37,723.28	1,157.39	534.00	8,894.00
Density (pop per km²)	938.13	9,212.87	123.57	3,263.46	2,566.81	176.52
GDP per capita (in USD)	$ 70,758.00	$ 96,845.28	$ 43,602.00	$ 8,489.00	$ 45,554.71	$ 82,040.00
Establishments	575,333	676,090	94,568	117,514	105,377	72,263
Employment	8,285,112	3,788,321	1,671,907	1,762,895	618,205	763,503
FSA Rates						
FTG per establishment	3.344	3.286	3.554	1.822	3.389	1.529
STA per establishment	0.266	0.194	0.365	0.160	0.110	0.198
FTG per employment	0.232	0.586	0.201	0.121	0.578	0.145
STA per employment	0.018	0.035	0.021	0.011	0.019	0.019
FTG per 1,000 residents	95.474	316.482	72.104	56.679	260.546	70.358
STA per 1,000 residents	7.580	18.728	7.406	4.964	8.437	9.135

*Data collected from these metropolitan areas include a significant number of small micro-enterprises, which increases the number of establishments per person to New York – a city double the size of Paris – which generates approximately 2 million freight trips and 150 service trips. This difference is due to the increased number of establishments obtained from Paris' database, which increases the number of freight and service trips substantially. Even so, both megacities coincide with an average of 3.3 daily trips per establishment. Another example is the city of Lyon, which shows 3.4 daily freight trips per establishment. This rate is much higher than the one obtained in Oslo, which generates nearly 1.5 daily freight trips per establishment.

Different freight rates are also observed among cities with varied income levels. The case of Medellín is an example of this, where FSA is underrepresented in lower income countries. Medellín shows the lowest freight trips per establishment, approximately 1.8, and 57 daily freight trips per 1,000 residents. A city of similar size, Phoenix, shows a higher proportion of freight activity, with 3.5 freight trips per establishment, and 72 freight trips per 1,000 residents.

Freight activity for Freight Intensive Sectors

To illustrate the importance of freight in metropolitan areas, estimates of daily freight trips were analysed at each FIS, as shown in Table 2.9, where, in the largest metropolitan areas, total daily freight trips in FIS range from 1.9 to 2.2 million, which translates to approximately 80 to 110 daily trips per 1,000 residents. If internet deliveries are included, using the e-commerce freight rates of 0.12 per resident estimated by the authors using the National Household Transportation Survey, this indicator could climb to 200 daily trips per 1,000 residents. With respect to individual industry sectors, cities like Paris have a unique share of establishments, as they have a large share from intermediaries in the supply chain, as observed by the Wholesale Trade (NAICS 42), and Transportation and Warehousing (NAICS 48–49) sectors. These sectors generate approximately 15 daily freight trips per establishment. New York City displays a slightly different pattern, as their larger share of freight trips comes from the local and consumer-oriented establishments, such as Retail Trade (NAICS 44–45) and Wholesale Trade (NAICS 42). Both sectors generate approximately 9 daily freight trips per establishment.

The medium to large cities, as observed from the estimates for Phoenix (United States) and Medellín (Colombia), show similar patterns to each other in terms of daily freight trips in their FIS. The total daily trips are approximately 45–50 per 1,000 residents. They both have Retail Trade (NAICS 44–45) as the industry sector with the highest share of trips. They display

Table 2.9 FTG for selected metropolitan areas in FIS

NAICS	Description	New York, USA	Paris, France	Phoenix, USA	Medellín, Colombia	Lyon, France	Oslo, Norway
		Freight Trip Generation					
23	Construction	8.8%	19.0%	10.5%	5.4%	18.7%	16.3%
31-33	Manufacturing	7.9%	8.0%	10.7%	10.8%	11.7%	7.4%
42	Wholesale Trade	20.3%	27.2%	15.9%	5.8%	26.2%	19.1%
44-45	Retail Trade	35.5%	8.1%	40.4%	67.8%	9.7%	18.9%
48-49	Transportation and Warehousing	14.2%	24.7%	6.1%	3.8%	22.2%	30.5%
72	Accommodation and Food Services	13.3%	13.0%	16.5%	6.5%	11.5%	7.8%
Total Freight Trip Generation (FIS)		1,924,153	2,221,769	336,115	214,082	357,125	110,462
		Internet Deliveries					
Population		20,153,634	7,020,210	4,661,537	3,777,099	1,370,678	1,570,000
Internet Deliveries (Ratio=0.12)		2,418,436	842,425	559,384	453,252	164,481	188,400
Total FTG Daily Trips (incl online deliveries)		4,342,589	3,064,194	895,499	667,334	521,606	298,862
		Freight Trip Rates					
Daily FTG per 1000 residents		95.474	316.482	72.104	56.679	260.546	70.358
Daily FTG per 1000 residents (incl online deliveries)		215.474	436.482	192.104	176.679	380.546	190.358
Daily FTG per Establishment		3.344	3.286	3.554	1.822	3.389	1.529
Daily FTG per Employment		0.232	0.586	0.201	0.121	0.578	0.145

some differences in their freight patterns in other industry sectors. In the case of Phoenix, the FIS sectors that generate the highest freight trips include other consumer-oriented sectors, such as the Wholesale Trade (NAICS 42) and Accommodation and Food Services (NAICS 72). Together, all three sectors generate approximately 10 trips per establishment. For Medellín, the second place is occupied by the Manufacturing (NAICS 31–33) sector, which is common in a city that hosts 20 per cent of the largest companies in Colombia, particularly the largest textile manufacturers. Both Retail Trade (NAICS 44–45) and Manufacturing (NAICS 31–33) generate approximately 3.6 daily freight trips per establishment in Medellín.

The smaller metropolitan areas also produce a significant amount of daily freight trips, approximately 110,000 to 350,000. Even though less populated, these cities display higher freight rates than the larger cities (ie Phoenix and Medellín), most likely due to the higher economic activity observed in these smaller cities. In both Lyon and Oslo the value ranges between 80 to 180 daily freight trips per 1,000 residents. If internet deliveries are included, these values could surpass the 200 daily FTG per 1,000 residents estimated for megacities. In terms of the top freight generators, both cities have Wholesale Trade (NAICS 42) and Modal Transportation and Warehousing (NAICS 48–49) at the top, with a cumulative share of 50 per cent of all freight trips in the FIS, and a rate per establishment of 17 daily trips for Lyon and 4 daily trips for Oslo.

Service activity for Service Intensive Sectors

To illustrate the importance of service in metropolitan areas, estimates of daily service trips were analysed at each SIS, as shown in Table 2.10. The total estimates for daily service trips within SIS vary across metropolitan areas, as shown in Table 2.10. Larger metropolitan areas, such as New York and Paris, have much higher estimates for STA; typically more than 130,000 service trips on a daily basis. The smaller metropolitan areas show much lower estimates for STA, around 14,000 daily trips. For the majority of cities, service trips typically represent between 4 and 13 per cent of all freight trips. Yet these numbers should not be underestimated, as these trips contribute significantly to the lack of parking in city centres, as service vehicles stay for prolonged periods of time, preventing other commercial vehicles (ie delivery trucks) from parking and/or unloading supplies (Holguín-Veras *et al*, 2018b).

Total daily service trip rates vary across countries. In the cities belonging to the United States, these were approximately 7 daily STA per 1,000

Table 2.10 STA for selected metropolitan areas

NAICS	Description	New York, USA	Paris, France	Phoenix, USA	Medellín, Colombia	Lyon, France	Oslo, Norway
		Service Trip Attraction					
51	Information	6.3%	13.0%	2.7%	7.6%	2.9%	2.8%
52	Finance and Insurance	8.0%	11.4%	17.5%	20.5%	9.9%	3.1%
53	Real Estate	0.1%	0.2%	0.1%	0.1%	20.4%	2.0%
54	Professional and Technical Services	0.5%	0.1%	15.0%	19.8%	7.5%	44.3%
55	Management of Companies	1.0%	0.0%	1.1%	1.5%	0.0%	0.1%
56	Administrative and Waste Management	7.7%	0.7%	5.0%	8.3%	0.5%	4.5%
61	Education Services	0.7%	0.4%	1.9%	2.5%	13.1%	14.3%
62	Healthcare and Social Assistance	45.9%	6.7%	41.9%	15.1%	9.1%	18.8%
71	Entertainment	7.1%	11.9%	2.8%	5.7%	1.7%	2.9%
81	Other Services (except Public Admin)	22.7%	55.6%	12.0%	18.9%	35.0%	7.3%
Service Trip Attraction (SIS)		152,758	131,472	34,522	18,750	13,708	14,343
Freight Trip Generation (FIS)		1,924,153	2,221,769	336,115	214,082	357,125	110,462
% Service Trips of Freight Trips		8%	6%	10%	9%	4%	13%
		Service Trip Rates					
Daily STA (SIS) per 1,000 residents		7.580	18.728	7.406	4.964	10.001	9.135
Daily STA (SIS) per Establishment		0.266	0.194	0.365	0.160	0.110	0.198
Daily STA (SIS) per Employment		0.018	0.035	0.021	0.011	0.019	0.019

residents. In the case of the Colombian city, Medellín, this number was much lower, approximately 4 daily STA per 1,000 residents. In the capital of Norway, the rate is 9 daily STA per 1,000 residents. In the case of France, this rate varies, as Paris shows 19 daily STA, while Lyon estimates 10 daily STA per 1,000 residents.

In the individual industry sectors that belong to SIS, it seems that the larger proportion of service trips belongs to the Healthcare and Social Assistance (NAICS 62) sector. In the US cities, 40 per cent of all service trips typically relate to this sector. In the European cities, approximately 20 per cent of all service trips are within this sector. Yet, in the city of a lower income country (ie Medellín) the proportion is lower, as this sector accounts for 15 per cent of the total STA. The only exception is Oslo, which has Professional and Technical Services (NAICS 54) as its largest generator of service trips, representing 44 per cent of total STA.

Besides the Other Services (NAICS 81) sector – which occupies second place in most of the cities analysed – the second most important sector varies across cities. In the medium-sized cities, Phoenix and Medellín, the Finance and Insurance (NAICS 52) sector accounts for approximately 20 per cent of all service trips. New York also has this sector as the second most important, but it represents only 8 per cent of all service activity in the city. For Lyon, the Real Estate (NAICS 53) sector is the second most important. In Oslo, the second most important is the Healthcare and Social Assistance (NAICS 62) sector, followed by the Education Services (NAICS 61) sector.

Conclusions

This chapter provides an international comparison of metropolitan areas and the relationship of their economic activity to the freight and service generated in these areas. Metropolitan areas in a range of population sizes, income levels and economic development were selected among countries in Europe and the Americas. The general analyses developed show that growing urban areas are economic powerhouses, which contribute to a large share of the country's economic activity. The chapter also evaluated the contribution of establishments by industry sector to the urban economies, and their connection to FSA. Breaking down the analysis between FIS and SIS provides a better understanding of how urban economies are directly related to the generation of freight and service vehicle trips.

The bulk of the analysis focuses on how the size, income and economic activity affect the cities' FSA. Cities that are among the largest in the world, such as New York and Paris, are generating millions of daily freight trips, and hundreds of thousands of daily service trips. Smaller cities (eg Oslo, Norway) are also generating a huge amount of daily freight trips, but the magnitude is only a fraction of the total generated in larger cities. Further, lower income cities show less daily freight activity, but these numbers may merely be underestimates of the freight trips generated from all the informal jobs that are not reported in official databases. Service activity is less critical in smaller cities, but should not be ignored, as it has important implications for city planning for parking and parking facilities, as service trip vehicles occupy parking for longer periods of time.

The analyses reveal that a series of FSA rates provide a very consistent picture of freight and service activity in metropolitan areas: the freight trip generation per establishments (freight trips/establishment-day) ranges between 1.53 (Oslo, Norway) and 3.55 (Phoenix, United States); the service trip attraction per establishment (service trips/establishment-day) ranges from 0.16 (Medellín, Colombia) to 0.37 (Phoenix, United States); the freight trip generation per employment (freight trips/employee-day) ranges between 0.12 (Medellín, Colombia) and 0.23 (New York, United States); the service trip attraction per employment (service trips/employee-day) ranges from 0.01 (Medellín, Colombia) to 0.02 (Phoenix, United States); the freight trip generation per 1,000 residents per day (freight trips/1,000 residents-day) ranges between 56.68 (Medellín, Colombia) and 95.47 (New York, United States); while the service trip attraction per 1,000 residents per day (service trips/1,000 residents-day) ranges from 4.96 (Medellín, Colombia) to 9.14 (Oslo, Norway). Due to the overestimation of FSA in the French cities, the authors decided not to include them in these ranges.

These analyses are just the beginning of what should be a much deeper discussion about urban economies and FSA across the world. The results provide city planners and practitioners with international FSA rates that must be carefully applied as references for cities where no data on commercial vehicle traffic are available.

References

Ambrosini C, Patier D and Routhier JL (2010), Urban freight establishment and tour based surveys for policy oriented modelling, *Procedia-Social and Behavioral Sciences*, 2, pp 6013–26

Área Metropolitana del Valle de Aburrá, Municipio de Medellín and Universidad Nacional de Colombia Sede Medellín (2012) Encuesta Origen Destino de

Hogares y de Carga para el Valle de Aburrá, *Medellín: Área Metropolitana del Valle de Aburrá*, p 289

Banco Central de la República Dominicana (2018) *Variables Macroeconomicas* [Online] https://www.bancentral.gov.do/

Brazilian Ministry of Labour (2016) *Establishments and Jobs by Sub-Sector of Economic Activity* [Online] http://infocidade.prefeitura.sp.gov.br/

Bronzini, MS (2008) Relationships between land use and freight and commercial truck traffic in metropolitan areas, *Special Report 298: Driving and the Built Environment*, Transportation Research Board and the Division on Engineering and Physical Sciences, pp 1–16

Brookings (2012) *São Paulo Metropolitan Area Profile* [Online] https://www.brookings.edu/wp-content/uploads/2016/07/Sao-Paulo-1.pdf

Camara de Comercio de Medellín Para Antioquia (2017) Perfil Socioeconomico de Medellín y el Valle de Aburrá, *Informes – Estudios Economicos*, pp 1–32

Campbell, S, Holguín-Veras, J, Ramírez-Ríos, D *et al* (2017) Freight and service parking needs and the role of demand management, Submitted to *European Transport Research Review*

Caspersen, E (2018) An explorative approach to freight trip attraction in an industrial urban area, in *City Logistics 3: Towards Sustainable and Liveable Cities*, ed E Taniguchi and RG Thompson, pp 249–66, Wiley, London

CCI Paris Île-de-France (2017) Chiffres-Clés de la Région Île-de-France, Paris, France, pp 1–68

Consejo Nacional de Planeacion (2010) *Delimitacion de las Zonas Metropolitanas de Mexico 2010* [Online] http://www.conapo.gob.mx/en/CONAPO/Zonas_metropolitanas_2010

Departamento Administrativo Nacional de Estadistica – DANE (2018) COLOMBIA – Encuesta de Microestablecimientos – MICRO – 2012–16

El Heraldo (2017) *Área Metropolitana, 'Quiénes Somos?'A Dónde vamos?* [Online] https://www.elheraldo.co/barranquilla/area-metropolitana-quienes-somos-donde-vamos-371423

Eurostat (2017) *Statistics on European Cities* [Online] http://ec.europa.eu/eurostat/statistics-explained/index.php/Statistics_on_European_cities

Eurostat (2018) GDP per Capita in 276 EU Regions

González-Calderón, CA, Sánchez-Díaz, I, Sarmiento-Ordosgoitia, I *et al* (2018) Characterization and analysis of metropolitan freight patterns in Medellín, Colombia, *European Transport Research Review*, **10**, pp 1–11

González-Feliu, J, Sánchez-Díaz, I and Ambrosini, C (2016) Aggregation Level, Variability and Linear Hypotheses for Urban Delivery Generation Models, *Transportation Research Board 95th Annual Meeting*, Washington DC

Grand Lyon Economie (2017) *Chiffres-clés du Grand Lyon: L'économie du Grand Lyon en Chiffres* [Online] http://www.economie.grandlyon.com/chiffres-cles-donnees-economiques-metropole-de-lyon-49.html

Holguín-Veras, J, Jaller, M, Destro, L *et al* (2011) Freight generation, freight trip generation, and perils of using constant trip rates, *Transportation Research Record: Journal of the Transportation Research Board,* **2224**, pp 68–81

Holguín-Veras, J, Sánchez-Díaz, I, Lawson, C *et al* (2013) Transferability of freight trip generation models, *Transport Research Record,* **2379**, pp 1–8

Holguín-Veras, J, Lawson, C, Wang, C *et al* (2017a) NCFRP Report 37: Using Commodity Flow Survey Microdata to Estimate the Generation of Freight, Freight Trip Generation, and Service Trips: Guidebook, *NCHRP/NCFRP,* Transportation Research Board, Washington DC

Holguín-Veras, J, Ramírez-Ríos, D and Wojtowicz, J (2017b) *Freight and Service Activity Generation Software* [Online] http://54.200.164.152/home

Holguín-Veras, J, Campbell, S, González-Calderón, CA *et al* (2018a) Importance and potential applications of freight and service activity models, in *City Logistics 1: New Opportunities and Challenges,* ed E Taniguchi and RG Thompson RG, pp 45–63, ISTE Ltd and John Wiley & Sons, Inc

Holguín-Veras, J, Campbell, S, González-Calderón, CA *et al* (2018b) Service Trip Attraction in Commercial Establishments, Submitted for publication

Holguín-Veras, J, Ramírez-Ríos, D, Kalahasthi, L *et al* (2018c) Quantification of Freight and Service Activity Trends in Cities, *Transportation Research Board 97th Annual Meeting,* Washington DC

IBGE (2017) Population Estimates for the Brazilian Municipalities and Federation Units on July 1, 2017 [Online] https://ww2.ibge.gov.br/english/estatistica/populacao/estimativa2017/default.shtm

Île-de-France (2018) La Région [Online] https://www.iledefrance.fr/region

Institut National de la Statistique et des Etudes Economiques – INSEE (2018) Paris Official Statistics

Instituto Nacional de Estadistica y Geografia – INEGI (2018) Puebla-Tlaxcala: Metropolitan Area in Mexico [Online] http://www.citypopulation.info/php/mexico-metro.php?cid=A34

Kötter, T and Friesecke, F (2009) *Developing Urban Indicators for Managing Mega Cities*, World Bank

La Métropole de Lyon (2018) 59 Communes [Online] https://www.grandlyon.com/metropole/59-communes.html

Le Progrès (2018) C'est, en Pourcentage, la Part du Produit Intérieur Brut (PIB) de la Nouvelle Région [Online] http://www.leprogres.fr/lyon/2015/11/30/c-est-en-pourcentage-la-part-du-produit-interieur-brut-(pib)-de-la-nouvelle-region

Les Ateliers (2012) Documento de Analysis – Puebla y Su Zona Metropolitana, pp 1–151

McGeehan, P (2016) Record Number of Tourists Visited New York City in 2015, and More Are Expected This Year, *The New York Times* [Online] http://www.nytimes.com/2016/03/09/nyregion/record-number-of-tourists-visited-new-york-city-in-2015-and-more-are-expected-this-year.html

Newman, MC (1993) Regression analysis of log-transformed data: statistical bias and its correction, *Environmental Toxicology and Chemistry,* **12**, pp 1129–33

Oficina Nacional de Estadistica – ONE (2018) *Directorio de Empresas y Establecimientos (DEE)* [Online] https://www.one.gob.do/censos/directorio-de-empresas-y-establecimientos

PROCOLOMBIA (2018) *Investment Opportunities in Barranquilla – Atlántico* [Online] http://www.investincolombia.com.co/regional-information/barranquilla.html

Puebla Online (2018) *PIB por Habitante en Puebla, Apenas de 101 Mil Pesos al Año: INEGI* [Online] http://www.pueblaonline.com.mx/2017/portal/index.php/estado/item/61925-pib-por-habitante-en-puebla-apenas-de-101-mil-pesos-al-ano-inegi#.W0Zf8NJKiUl

Sánchez-Díaz, I, González-Feliu, J and Ambrosini, C (2016) Assessing the Implications of Aggregating Data by Activity-Based Categories for Urban Freight Trip Generation Modeling, *6th International Conference in Information Systems, Logistics and Supply Chain (ILS 2016),* Bordeaux, France

Statistics Norway (2018a) *Establishments* [Online] https://www.ssb.no/en/virksomheter-foretak-og-regnskap/statistikker/bedrifter/aa

Statistics Norway (2018b) *Population and population changes* [Online] https://www.ssb.no/en/beftett

United Nations (2014) *World Urbanization Prospects: The 2014 Revision,* Department of Economic and Social Affairs, Population Division, pp 1–517

United Nations (2016) The World's Cities in 2016 – Data Booklet, *ST/ESA/SER.A/392,* Department of Economic and Social Affairs, Population Division, pp 1–26

US Bureau of Economic Analysis (2017) *Gross Domestic Product by Metropolitan Area, 2016* [Online] https://www.bea.gov/newsreleases/regional/gdp_metro/gdp_metro_newsrelease.htm

US Bureau of Labor Statistics (2016) New York Area Economic Summary

US Census Bureau (2016) 2012 Commodity Flow Survey (CFS) Public Use Microdata (PUM) File: Data Users Guide, pp 1–19

US Census Bureau (2017) *2012 CFS Public Use Microdata File* [Online] https://www.census.gov/econ/cfs/pums.html

US Commercial Service and Amcham Colombia (2015) Barranquilla Open to Business

Urban logistics 03

The regional dimension

GENEVIEVE GIULIANO

Introduction

Global cities are the nodes of the global economy for both virtual and physical flows. Not only are they the financial and knowledge centres of the global economy; they are also the gateways for international trade. The largest cities function as logistics hubs in the global freight network. They are also centres of dense population and employment that generate supply and demand for consumption goods. These local and global flows influence and are influenced by city structure. Seaports and airports are among the most critical trade facilities of the global city; their freight and passenger flows affect the location of warehouses, hotels and housing. This chapter focuses on urban logistics in the context of the global supply chain.

Freight in metropolitan areas

Metropolitan freight activity may be described as of two main types: freight related to local supply or demand, and freight related to national or international trade. Globalization has increased as a result of transport and communications technology as well as trade liberalization policies (Dicken, 2007). Production supply chains have become more complex as producers seek out comparative advantage opportunities around the world.

Goods production processes – spatially fragmented but temporally integrated – connect countries and cities into 'global production networks' demanding cost-efficient and timely flow of goods (Leinbach and Capineri, 2007). This has resulted in consistent growth in cross-border trade for the last several decades. In the United States, total imports grew by 92 per cent from 2000 to 2017 while total exports grew by 98 per cent (US Census, 2018).

Large metropolitan areas are the major nodes of the global production network, containing the largest ports, airports and intermodal facilities. In the United States, 87 per cent of total exports come from metropolitan areas, defined as places with a population of over 50,000. In addition, the top 40 metro areas accounted for 68 per cent of total exports in 2017 (US Census, 2018). The top five, Houston, New York, Los Angeles, Seattle-Tacoma and Chicago, accounted for 27 per cent of total exports. The concentration of trade in large metro areas means concentrated demand on the rail and highway systems. Rodrigue (2004) notes that gateway cities are usually located in 'mega-urban regions' through which logistics functions are geographically and functionally integrated at the local, regional and global level. These regions developed historically as points of trade. With large and concentrated populations and economic activity, they generate much of the trade demand and provide the array of expertise for managing global supply chains.

The second type of freight activity is associated with the supply and demand of the local population: the 'last mile' delivery or pickup of imports/exports, and the intra-metropolitan trade of commodities (local production and consumption). Freight related to local supply and demand is also increasing due to longer and more complex supply chains, increasing velocity within supply chains (eg just-in-time practices), the rise of e-commerce, and overall per capita income, population and employment growth. Increased freight activity at the metropolitan level results in increased truck trips and vehicle miles travelled. The remainder of this chapter addresses the impacts of regional flows on metropolitan areas and discusses strategies for managing these impacts.

How trade affects cities

Cities that serve as trade nodes have an additional layer of freight and logistics demand, because they serve both local and non-local supply and demand. Table 3.1 gives an example. Using commodity flow data by metropolitan region, we calculate per capita flows by value for domestic and international flows in four California regions: Los Angeles, San Francisco, San Diego and Sacramento. We use the per capita measure because the regions vary greatly in size. Domestic flow is any flow with its origin/destination in the United States. It can be seen that domestic flow per capita is relatively consistent across the regions, ranging from about US $35,000 to $41,000. In contrast, international flow per capita is much higher for

Table 3.1 Commodity flow intensity by metro region

Metro Area	Domestic Flow/capita (US $)	International Flow/capita (US $)
Los Angeles	35,331	17,036
San Francisco	37,725	18,196
San Diego	37,564	4,992
Sacramento	41,013	3,450

SOURCE Giuliano *et al*, 2015, calculated from 2007 Commodity Flow Survey

Los Angeles and San Francisco – both well-known international trade centres – than for the other metro regions. Although about half the value is domestic flow, international trade clearly adds significantly to freight demand within the region. With more freight demand comes more impacts, including congestion, air pollution and growing numbers of warehouse and distribution facilities.

Congestion

Regional flows contribute to congestion throughout the metropolitan area, not just in the city core. Ports, airports, intermodal facilities and warehouse clusters all serve as heavy truck attractors, concentrating congestion, emissions, noise and conflicts with passenger traffic. Highways linking these facilities have heavy truck concentrations. Trucks, especially combination trucks, disproportionately contribute to traffic congestion, due to different performance characteristics (eg slower acceleration and deceleration, larger turning radius, etc). High volumes of rail freight traffic impose congestion at rail crossings and conflict with passenger rail services.

What is the impact of freight activity on metropolitan areas? In 2016, the Fixing America's Surface Transportation (FAST) Act included a requirement that each state consider congestion or delays caused by the freight industry and develop mitigation measures to address these problems. We developed the concept of 'freight impact area' to identify places with high levels of freight-related congestion (Giuliano *et al*, 2018). We define a freight impact area as a severely congested roadway corridor with high volumes of trucks. While most existing studies generate estimates of congestion experienced by freight, we stress the role of freight in producing general traffic delays.

We measure freight impact areas based on road links. An impact area could be a combination of continuous (linked) segments with different physical configurations (number of lanes, etc). When identifying them, we focus on the most congested period of time during a day – PM peak hours. The significance of freight impact areas depends on both the severity of congestion and the volume of trucks. We therefore use total peak hour delay as our measure of impact. Total peak hour delay is the combined delay of both passenger cars and trucks. We then rank the impact areas by total delay. We use the Los Angeles region as an example.

Table 3.2 gives descriptive statistics for the top 15 freight impact areas on the National Highway System (Giuliano *et al*, 2018). The impact areas range from very short to quite long (almost 10 miles). Total delay varies a great deal, with a maximum of nearly 12,000 vehicle hours of delay. All of the impact areas have higher than average heavy truck shares. Figure 3.1 shows the impact areas on a map. The inset box identifies the top 15 in rank order. They are located on the well-known freight corridors of the region: I-10, SR 60, I-710 and I-5.

Together the top 15 account for 53,615 hours of vehicle delay each PM peak period. Over the course of a year, the delay would be about 14 million vehicle hours – substantial by any standard. We do not know how much delay there would be without any trucks, hence we cannot attribute all the delay to the presence of trucks. Nevertheless, we can say that congested locations with high proportions of trucks are associated with significant delays for both passengers and trucks.

Table 3.2 Descriptive statistics of key variables of the top 15 freight impact areas on the National Highway System in the Los Angeles region

	Average	Minimum	Maximum
Length (mile)	2.24	0.11	9.95
Average Total Volume per Direction, PM Peak	43,241	32,529	61,762
Average Truck Volume per Direction, PM Peak	3,252	2,594	4,062
Average Share of Trucks	8.00%	4.38%	10.85%
Congestion Speed (mile/hour)	18.61	8.10	29.93
Total Peak Hour All-vehicle Delay (vehicle hours)	3,574.3	344.0	11,741.6
Total Peak Hour Freight Delay (truck hours)	285.0	20.4	1,103.7

Figure 3.1 Top 15 highway freight impact areas, Los Angeles region

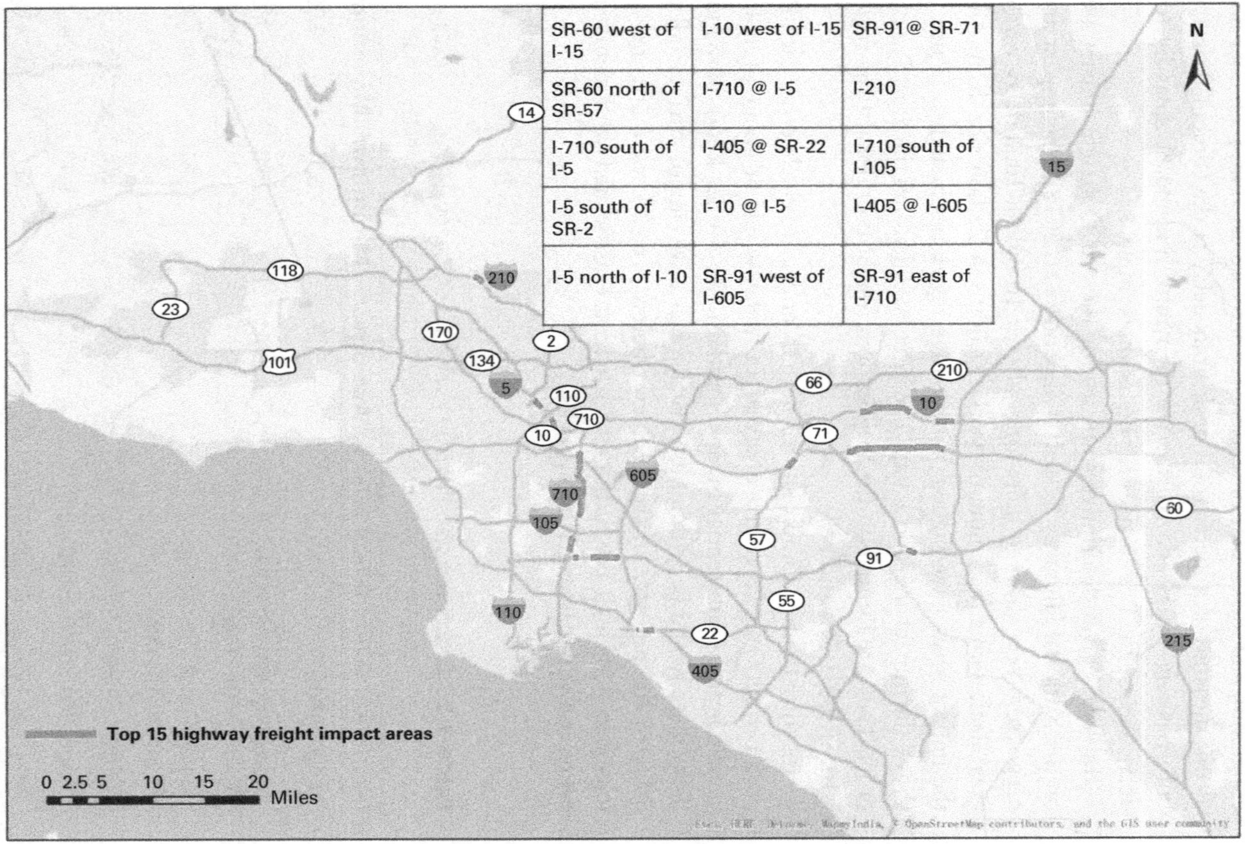

SR-60 west of I-15
I-10 west of I-15
SR-91@ SR-71
SR-60 north of SR-57
I-710 @ I-5
I-210
I-710 south of I-5
I-405 @ SR-22
I-710 south of I-105
I-5 south of SR-2
I-10 @ I-5
I-405 @ I-605
I-5 north of I-10
SR-91 west of I-605
SR-91 east of I-710
N
Top 15 highway freight impact areas
0 2.5 5 10 15 20
Miles

Table 3.3 Air pollutant emissions, transport and truck shares, United States, 2016

	NOX	VOC	PM10*	PM2.5*
Total (1,000 tons)	11,310	16,459	2,440	1,658
Transport Share	59.7%	22.4%	18.9%	19.4%
Truck Share of Transport	34.3%	N/A	28.6%	N/A

*Excludes fugitive dust and wildfires

SOURCE Calculated from US Environmental Protection Agency, Air Pollutants Emissions Trend Data, 2018

Air pollution

Trucks account for a significant share of air toxics and greenhouse gases. Table 3.3 gives emissions data for NOX, VOC, PM10 and PM2.5 for the United States. The transport sector accounts for nearly 60 per cent of NOX and 22 per cent of VOC, the precursors to smog and ozone. Trucks account for about one-third of the transport share. Due primarily to regulation of engines and fuels, emissions of all air toxics have declined steadily since 2000. However, trade facilities remain 'hot spots' due to the intensity of truck and rail traffic.

In the United States, the transportation sector accounts for 27 per cent of greenhouse gases, second only to industry (Figure 3.2). Within the on-road transportation sector, freight accounts for 23 per cent of all GHGs, and light duty vehicles (passenger transport) account for 60 per cent. The

Figure 3.2 Greenhouse gases by source, United States, 2014

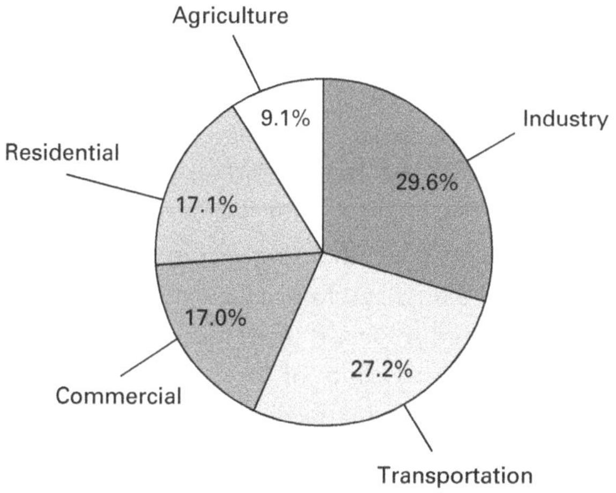

SOURCE Calculated from US Environmental Protection Agency, Air Pollutants Emissions Trend Data, 2018

Figure 3.3 Transportation GHG emission shares by source

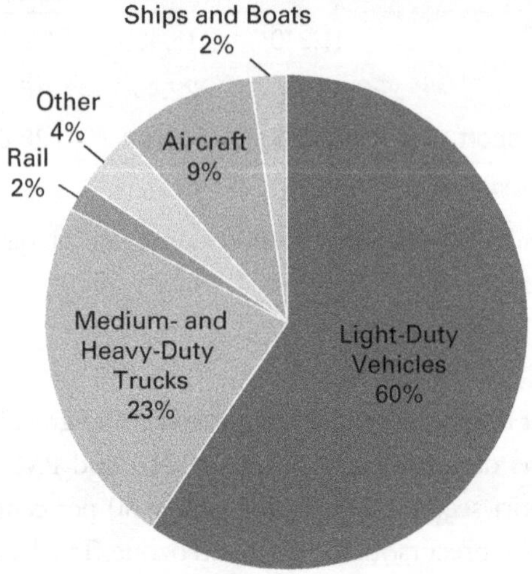

SOURCE US Environmental Protection Agency, 2018

remainder come from air, rail and water vessels (Figure 3.3). Within the freight sector, energy consumption depends on speed and load. Thus air transport is the most energy intensive, followed by trucking, rail and water. Trucking is about 1.5 times as energy intensive as rail when measured as BTU consumed per vehicle mile and freight car mile respectively (US Department of Transportation, 2018).

Warehousing and distribution facilities

Significant changes have taken place in the warehousing industry during the last decade. First, warehousing facilities are increasingly specialized in new services including transshipping, packaging, labelling, inventory management and so forth (Akman and Baynal, 2014). They serve a wide range of customers, and also cooperate with 3PL logistics providers, trucking and freight forwarders. Second, warehousing facilities serve more geographically dispersed markets (Hesse and Rodrigue, 2004) and respond to demand from regional markets and resources (Hesse, 2007). Therefore they do not have to remain in the close vicinity of local customers. Third, in spite of increased congestion, warehousing facilities make more frequent deliveries as retail businesses become more dependent on warehousing services (Hesse and Rodrigue, 2004) to reduce inventory and save on rent costs. Fourth, the scale of warehousing and distribution has increased due to automation and high-volume product flows. As the size of warehousing facilities increases, so do the sizes of land parcels they consume (Andreoli, Goodchild and Vitasek, 2010). More recently, increases in e-commerce and consumer demand for instant deliveries are creating demand for close-in distribution or fulfilment centres, but these trends have not reduced demand for large-scale warehousing. Rather, distribution chains are changing.

Over the past decade warehousing and distribution activity has increased faster than the general economy. For example, warehousing and distribution employment in California increased by 31 per cent between 2003 and 2013, while overall state employment grew by just 3 per cent over the same period (Giuliano and Kang, 2018).

The environment in which warehousing facilities operate is changing as well. First, transportation access has improved over the past decades (Giuliano, 2017). Convenient access to freeway and railroads is available in many locations in the major metropolitan areas. Second, land is getting more and more expensive, and industries that can afford high land rent occupy the land in the city cores. The warehousing industry becomes less competitive in obtaining space in those areas (Giuliano and Kang, 2018).

Decentralization

The result of increased warehousing activity, scale and demand has been the decentralization of warehouse and distribution facilities as documented by studies of Atlanta, Los Angeles and Chicago (Dablanc and Ross, 2012; Dablanc *et al*, 2014; Goodchild and Dubie, 2016), as well as studies of metropolitan areas in Sweden, the United Kingdom and Japan (Heitz *et al*, 2018; Allen *et al*, 2012; Sakai *et al*, 2015). Kang (2017) conducted a study of warehouse location in the 48 largest US metropolitan areas, from 2003 to 2013. He found the following: 1) for all 48 metro areas, warehousing decentralized by an average of 1.06 miles, measured as the average distance of all warehouse establishments to the CBD; 2) large warehouses (those with 100 or more workers) decentralized more than smaller warehouses (fewer than 100 workers); and 3) large warehouses decentralized more in large metro areas. The difference in trend between smaller and larger metro areas is shown in Figure 3.4. Population is in log form and decentralization is miles – the change in average distance from the CBD from 2003 to 2013. The darker grey dots are metro areas with a population of less than 2.2 million; the lighter grey dots are metro areas with a population of more than 2.2 million. There is no discernible trend among the smaller metro areas, but there is a positive trend of decentralization and metro area size

Figure 3.4 Scatterplot of warehouse decentralization and 2000 metro population

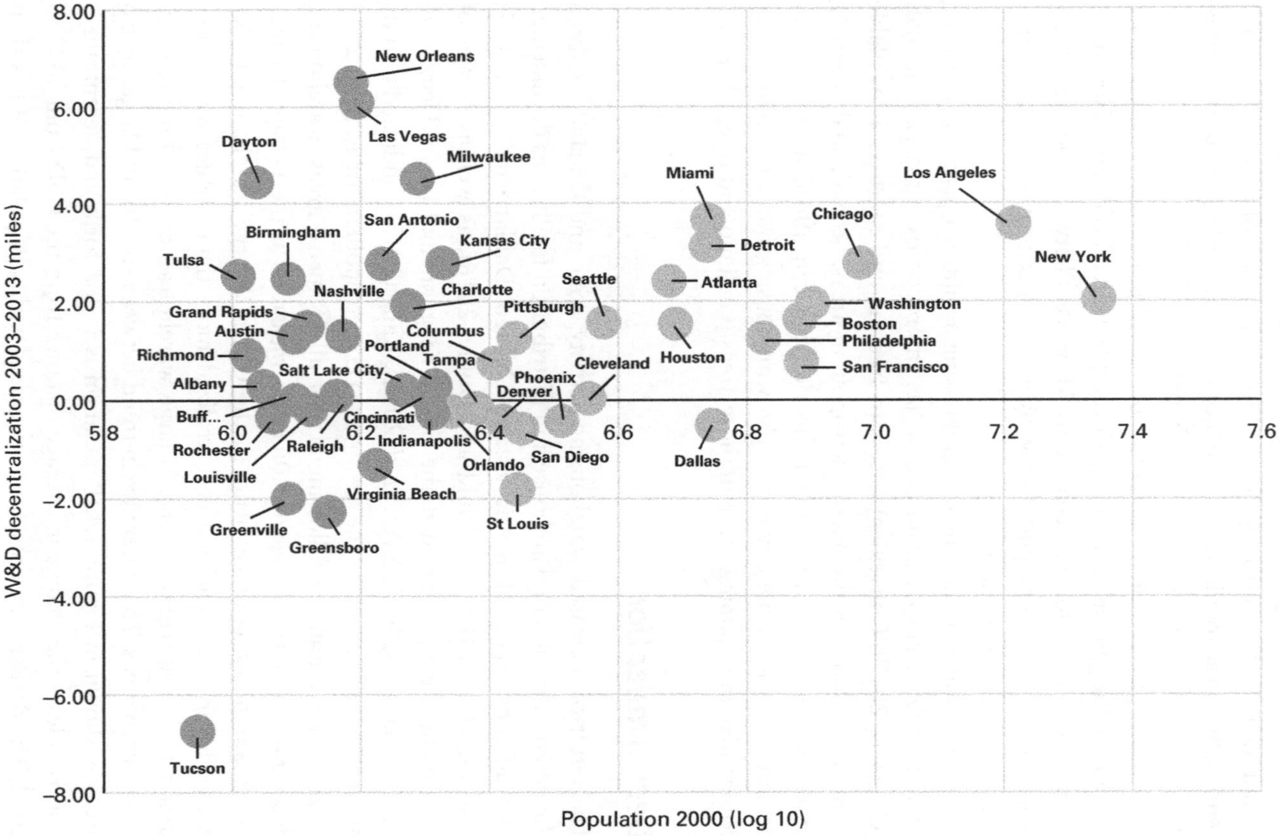

SOURCE Kang, 2017

among the larger metro areas. Note also that warehousing centralized in many metro areas over the period.

Kang then estimated statistical models to explain decentralization. He found that the density gradient, a proxy for the land price gradient, had the largest impact on decentralization in large metro areas. That is, the slower density declined with distance from the centre, the more warehousing decentralized in the search for lower rents. Peak density and changes in the number of large warehouses had almost half the effect size. Decentralization in small metro areas was most influenced by freight flow, measured as tons of domestic shipments to and from the metro area. That is, warehousing in smaller metro areas with a larger share of regional trade were more likely to decentralize. These results are highly consistent with our understanding of the dynamics of trade node cities.

Environmental justice

Another aspect of changing warehouse location is environmental justice. Warehousing facilities and truck activities generate negative impacts on local communities including land use and landscape changes, air pollution (Dablanc, 2013), noise, pavement damage (Dong *et al*, 2014; Cidell, 2015) and traffic safety threats. These impacts have grown with the expansion of the logistics industry. Their spatial distribution is uneven due to two dynamics: warehouse firm location choice and the housing location choice of a disadvantaged population. The environmental justice literature offers three possible explanations (Mohai and Saha, 2007; Mohai *et al*, 2009). First, warehouse developers prefer places with cheap land and low-wage labour, and these places are often where poor or minority people are concentrated. Second, disadvantaged populations are less politically empowered, and hence less able to prevent the development of locally undesirable land uses. Third, public policies and the housing market have been less supportive to poor and minority residents, making their housing choices more difficult and constrained.

Giuliano and Yuan (2017) conducted a study of the four largest metropolitan areas in California to test whether warehousing is more likely to be located near disadvantaged neighbourhoods. The metro areas include Los Angeles, San Francisco, San Diego and Sacramento. Although the urban contexts in the four regions are different, results are generally consistent. The results confirm that transport access, industrial linkages and economic attributes of a given zone are closely associated with warehousing activity. With these variables controlled, our analysis shows that warehouses

Figure 3.5 Location of warehouses and minority populations, a) Los Angeles and b) San Francisco

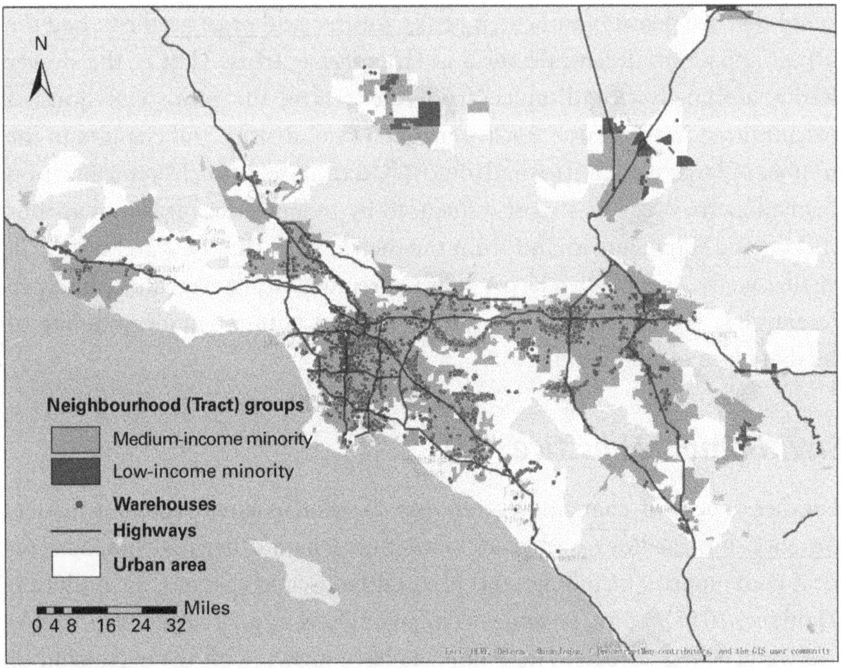

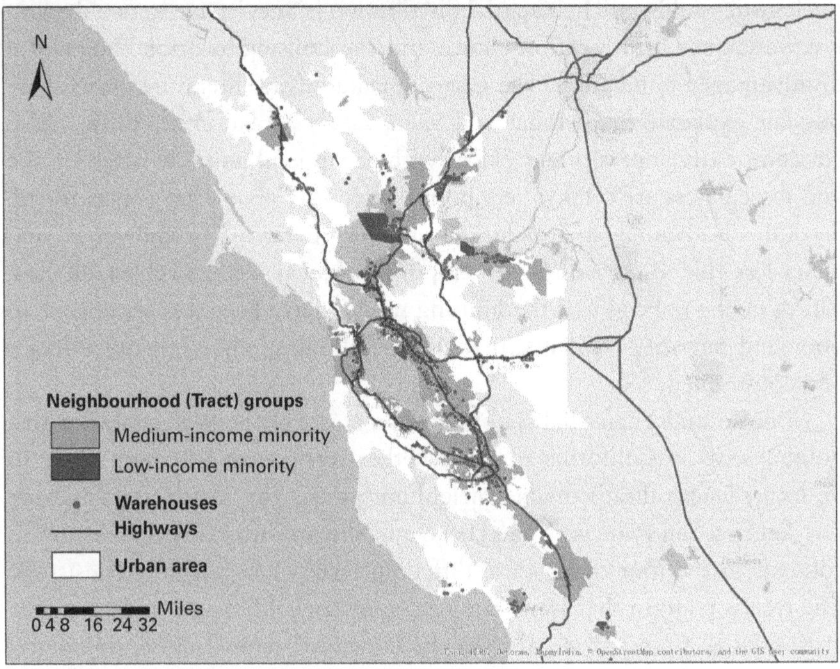

SOURCE Giuliano and Yuan, 2017

and distribution centres are disproportionately located in medium-income minority neighbourhoods. Low-income minority neighbourhoods in general do not have a higher concentration of warehousing development than medium-income minority neighbourhoods. Our findings may be partly explained by the location preferences of the warehousing industry. Low-income neighbourhoods are not necessarily located in areas with adequate land availability, transport access and labour force access. Results are mapped for Los Angeles and San Francisco in Figures 3.5a and 3.5b. The grey dots are warehouses, and the light and dark shading maps medium- and low-income minority populations.

Yuan (2018) extended this work to explore the causal relationship: do warehouses seek out minority populations, or do minority populations locate near warehouses? The argument for the latter is lower land prices; lower income or minority populations trade off the negative impacts for lower housing prices. Yuan found that warehouses seek out minority populations, indicating that warehouse location, at least in four Californian cities, is an environmental justice problem.

Managing trade related freight and its impacts

What are metropolitan areas doing to manage trade related urban freight and its impacts? In this section we focus on current and near-term strategies. In the long term, connected and automated vehicles, new technologies for moving freight (drones, underground tube systems) and new technologies of production (eg 3D printing) will restructure the global and local logistics systems in ways that are currently unpredictable.

There are an almost infinite number of possible strategies for mitigating freight impacts. We provide a broad array of examples, but by no means an exhaustive list. Our selected strategies are described in detail below and then evaluated based on the following four criteria: cost, effectiveness in reducing truck-related congestion, co-benefits, technical difficulty and implementation feasibility. Cost includes capital costs, maintenance costs and other costs incurred in the implementation of each strategy. Co-benefits refer to benefits other than freight congestion alleviation such as safety or emissions reductions. Technical difficulty considers whether the required technologies exist or are expected to exist within a five-year time frame, and whether design or construction involves technical challenges.

Implementation feasibility considers institutional supports and barriers, public perceptions and industry perspectives. We use a simple metric of high, medium and low for each criterion. Our evaluation is based on our research, policy experience and professional judgement. We organize our discussion into groups of strategies: infrastructure, efficiency, air pollution and public policy.

Infrastructure

Infrastructure strategies include various types of capital investments in new or rehabilitated structures.

Truck-only lanes

Truck-only lanes are highway lanes designated for the use of trucks. The main purpose of such lanes is to separate trucks from other mixed-flow traffic to reduce the impacts of truck flows on passenger traffic and enhance safety (California Department of Transportation, nd). Truck-only lanes can provide additional capacity for truck traffic, allow for tolling and provide a protected facility for truck platooning. In spite of these advantages, truck-only lanes are seldom built, as their disadvantages are equally significant. The construction of truck-only lanes is very costly given the high standards of road surface needed for accommodating heavy truck movement (Fischer, Ahanotu and Waliszewski, 2003). Second, right of way (ROW) availability is limited, especially in dense urban areas. Third, there is no consensus on who should pay for the high costs of truck-only lanes/highways (Forkenbrock and March, 2005). Finally, some question the effectiveness of truck-only lanes, since they would be underutilized during off-peak hours (Fischer, Ahanotu and Waliszewski, 2003; De Palma, Kilani and Lindsey, 2008). Truck-only lanes may be justified only in very high-volume truck corridors (Forkenbrock and March, 2005).

Railroad grade separations

Railroad grade separations are an effective way to reduce the impacts of freight rail on arterial traffic by eliminating at-grade conflicts between rail and vehicular traffic. Roads with grade separation allow traffic to move with no interruptions from freight rail movement, reducing traffic delays and risk of accidents (Gitelman *et al*, 2006). Railroad grade separations tend to be space-intensive and costly, because of the costs of building bridges or tunnelling under the rail right of way. Grade separations are widely recognized as an effective strategy for mitigating the impacts of high-volume train corridors. US examples may be found in Washington, California and Illinois.

The main problems with grade separations are financial. Railroads are generally unwilling to pay for the separations because they provide no benefit to the railroad. The public views grade separations as the responsibility of the railroads, because the trains are the cause of delay and accidents on the street system. Further, there is typically no dedicated fund for grade separations.

Expand highway capacity

Expanded highway capacity allows for a larger volume of all vehicles, thus reducing traffic delays that may result from heavy truck flows. Additional highway lanes can potentially be used as toll lanes. If toll lanes are reserved for passenger vehicles, the shift of passenger vehicles out of general purpose lanes would free up capacity for trucks.

The main challenges for adding highway capacity include lack of right of way, cost and the possibility of latent demand generating more overall travel (eg Noland, 2001), especially in already congested metropolitan areas. Adding more highway capacity without tolls is a potential problem, as any induced traffic would counter GHG reduction goals.

Table 3.4 Qualitative assessment of infrastructure improvement strategies

Strategy / Criterion	INFRASTRUCTURE IMPROVEMENTS				
	Truck-only lanes, bypass facilities	**Railroad grade separations**	**Expand highway capacity**	**On-dock rail**	**Inland ports**
Cost	High	Medium	High	Medium	High
Effectiveness	High	High	High	High	Low
Co-benefits	High (safety)	High (safety)	Medium	High (emissions)	Medium
Technical difficulty	Medium	Medium	Medium	High	High
Implementation feasibility	Low	Medium	Low	High	Medium

On-dock rail

On-dock rail allows for cargo to be transferred directly from ship to rail or rail to ship. If rail does not extend to the docks, rail shipments must be transferred via truck, adding both time and cost to the transaction. On-dock rail makes rail shipping more efficient, hence increasing mode share. The Prince Rupert Port (Canada) was designed to function almost exclusively as a direct ship to rail operation. Non-local cargo moves directly from ship to rail or rail to ship, greatly reducing drayage activity. The main challenge for on-dock rail is space. Many terminals do not have enough area to be able to retrofit on-dock rail.

Inland ports

The purpose of an inland port is to move cargo away from the port and provide secondary services at the inland port location in order to reduce congestion at the port and address land availability problems (Rodrigue and Notteboom, 2012). An inland port is in part an outsourcing of port functions and in part a logistics services centre, providing logistics services such as consolidation, transloading, packaging or secondary manufacturing (Rodrigue *et al*, 2010). Cargo is moved between the port and inland port by short haul rail to reduce truck trips.

Inland ports have been widely implemented in Europe, but are rare in the United States. In Europe, inland ports are developed (and funded) by terminal operators and port authorities. In the United States, rail operators and real estate developers are the project promoters. In addition, US short haul rail is not cost competitive with trucks at distances of less than 400–500 miles.

Our assessment of infrastructure strategies is summarized in Table 3.4. Shaded rows indicate that the scale is reversed: high cost and high technical difficulty are less preferred.

Efficiency improvements

There are many possibilities for efficiency improvements that would reduce truck VMT and hence contribute to congestion reduction.

Freight advanced traffic management systems

Freight advanced traffic management systems (F-ATMS) integrate ITS technologies including two-way communication, location and tracking devices, electronic data interchange, and advanced planning and operation decision support systems (Crainic, Gendreau and Potvin, 2009). With these technologies, freight traffic management systems collect data from stakeholders and provide advice on better routing and time scheduling. These systems can produce society-wide benefits including reduced traffic delays, and increased supply chain efficiency. They would also help to reduce emissions and other impacts on neighbouring communities, reduce energy consumption and increase safety.

One example of F-ATMS is the Freight Advanced Traveler Information System (FRATIS), supported by the US Federal Highway Administration. It has been demonstrated in several states. Test results in Memphis showed that the programme reduced the number of bobtail trips (ie empty-return loads) by 10 per cent, terminal queue times by 20 per cent, travel times by 15 per cent, fuel consumption by 5 per cent and the level of criteria pollutants and GHG by 5 per cent (Jensen, Fayez and DeSantis, 2015).

Despite the potential, there are challenges to large-scale adoption and implementation. First, reliable funding sources need to be identified to cover the high capital and maintenance costs of such systems. Second, private firms must be willing to participate, and participation means sharing proprietary data. Over time, technology development should solve this problem by developing ways to anonymize data, screen out critical data and improve data security. Third, a scaled-up system requires a designated system operator and participation of all the relevant state and local agencies. The institutional structure of such a system has yet to be identified.

Integrated freight load information systems

A key tool for achieving coordination across the supply chain is integrated information systems. An integrated freight load information system is one where the status (location, contents, origin and destination) of every shipment is known to all relevant supply chain participants. Efficient data sharing ensures stakeholders within the system the ability to monitor and operate different elements of the supply chain in consistent steps, and respond to adjustments quickly and effectively. In response to demands for more efficient supply chains, there is evidence that greater supply chain coordination is now occurring at all levels. In the case of port-related supply chains, for example, steamship lines now coordinate vessel stowage of individual containers at the port of origin and port of departure to expedite unloading and processing (Mongelluzzo, 2016).

At present, a system to track cargo from end to end exists; however, it exists in a piecemeal fashion and in most cases has yet to be stitched together.

Though these systems have greatly increased the efficiency of some links of the supply chain, they are not fully integrated and are developing in (mostly incompatible) pieces.

There are a number of implementation challenges for an integrated freight load information system: the need for an institutional structure in place to lead the development of such a system and manage its operation; a source of long-term funding; the need to address existing proprietary software and data security.

Freight priority traffic management

In areas with large volumes of truck traffic, a traffic management system that gives priority to trucks can result in net reductions in delay for all traffic. Truck priority reduces the frequency of acceleration and deceleration for trucks. Because heavy trucks have much slower acceleration and deceleration rates than autos or light trucks, they impose delay on the upstream traffic. Reducing truck delay therefore reduces total delay when truck volumes comprise a large share of the total traffic. A recent simulation modelling study found that freight signal priority (FSP) reduces travel delay of freight vehicles by up to 26 per cent (Kari *et al*, 2014).

Freight signal priority (FSP) requires Vehicle-Infrastructure Integration (VII), so that signal timing can be adjusted in real time in response to approaching traffic and instructions can be communicated to vehicles (eg to reduce speed and avoid a stop). The success of FSP relies on support from both the public and private sectors. Public funding is needed to install, operate and maintain the system. The logistics industry would need to invest in instrumenting the truck fleet. To date, no freight priority traffic management system has yet been deployed.

Cargo matching services

Cargo matching refers to allocating transport resources (drivers, vehicles, routing, etc) to efficiently achieve cargo movement in the freight network (Nieberding, Apfelstädt and Dashkovskiy, 2017; Cohn *et al*, 2007). Currently, the common practice is to transport empty containers back to the terminals, where they are picked up by the next user. These non-revenue generating trips increase truck VMT. Examples of cargo matching services include matching empty containers with cargo, first come first take pickups (an arriving truck picks up the first available load, rather than a specific load), and developing platforms to match available chassis with containers.

The challenges to implementing effective cargo matching services include having a sufficient volume to allow for efficient matches, the required sharing of proprietary information and stakeholder collaboration.

Smart truck parking

Smart truck parking includes a variety of strategies such as providing information on available spaces along the trucker's route and allowing advance reservation of spaces. As the truck fleet diversifies, smart truck parking systems could provide information on alternative fuel or charging stations. Many private Intelligent Truck Parking services are emerging. As in the case of freight load information systems, these are proprietary systems with different (and incompatible) software and information infrastructures. In order to be as effective as possible, a smart parking system must be statewide or nationwide and use common technology. Integrated smart parking requires a common information and technology platform so that truckers would need only one 'app' to access all parking options, public or private.

Terminal appointment systems

Terminal appointment systems assign time windows for drayage cargo pickups and drop-offs. They are intended to reduce truck queuing, increase the velocity of container movement and reduce container dwell time. The basic system has an information platform that informs shippers of container, chassis and space availability. Shippers select a time window for the transaction, and a truck is dispatched to arrive during the time window. Potential benefits of appointment systems include more efficient use of terminal space, equipment and labour; time savings for drayage truckers; and reduced terminal congestion (Morais and Lord, 2006; Huynh and Walton, 2008; Namboothiri and Erera, 2008; Huynh, 2009; Zhao and Goodchild, 2013).

There are many appointment systems operating around the world, but there is only one port-wide system. Vancouver established its appointment system in 1999 (Morais and Lord, 2006). A port-wide appointment system operates across all terminals using a single information platform, and thus has the most potential for efficiency improvements.

There are some significant implementation challenges for a port-wide system: 1) terminal operators and shippers/truckers have different objectives for an appointment system; 2) a port-wide system requires common infrastructure and operational practices, but terminals have different infrastructure and operating practices; 3) unreliability of truck travel times due to heavy regional congestion would affect appointment system efficiency.

Truck platooning

If trucks could operate with a shorter following distance in high truck-volume corridors, it would be possible to increase truck throughput. Truck platoons take advantage of communications technology to set common speeds and headways among several trucks travelling in the same direction. The technology and communications requirements of platoons can vary. In the simplest case, dynamic cruise control and communications between vehicles can facilitate platooning of two or three vehicles. A more automated system, with self-driving trucks, would require both vehicle-to-vehicle and vehicle-to-infrastructure communications. Truck platoons could increase the capacity of roads, reduce traffic congestion and fuel consumption, shorten travel time and improve traffic safety.

The major downsides of the technology include the high costs of developing the highway infrastructure, as near-term platooning would require a separate right of way to avoid the problems of other traffic entering the platoon. Truck platooning has been studied and tested in the United States and Europe, but is not yet commercially available.

The potential for widespread, full-scale platooning remains uncertain. Truck platoons make sense in high-density, longer distance corridors; we do not yet know the extent of this market. The technology is less challenging in a protected environment, meaning truck-only lanes; however, such lanes can be financially justified only in the highest density corridors. Without a protected right of way, truck platoons face many challenges, including the entry of other vehicles into the platoon, how drivers would or could respond to the equivalent of a 'train of trucks' on a highway, and how access and egress to/from the highway is to be managed (Table 3.5).

Emissions reduction

One of the most critical impacts of urban logistics is air pollution. Air toxics affect human health, and greenhouse emissions are driving climate change. We give three examples of emissions reduction strategies.

Low emissions standards

Countries around the world have emissions standards based on the health effect of specific pollutants. Emissions and fuel standards are among the most successful public policies in reducing emissions. Figure 3.6 gives the US example. The first national emissions standard was established in 1973. Over the years, standards have become more stringent and have expanded

Table 3.5 Qualitative assessment of efficiency improvement strategies

Strategy / Criterion	EFFICIENCY IMPROVEMENTS						
	Freight advanced traffic management systems	**Integrated freight load information systems**	**Freight priority traffic management**	**Cargo matching services**	**Smart truck parking**	**Terminal appointment systems**	**Auto truck platoon**
Cost	Medium	Low	High	Low	Low	Low	High
Effectiveness	High	High	Medium	Medium	High	High	Medium
Co-benefits	High (emissions)	Medium	Medium	High (cost savings)	Medium	High (emissions)	Medium
Technological difficulty	Medium	Medium	High	Low	Low	Low	Medium
Implementation feasibility	Medium	Medium	Medium	High	High	High	Medium

Figure 3.6 Trends in US highway vehicle emissions

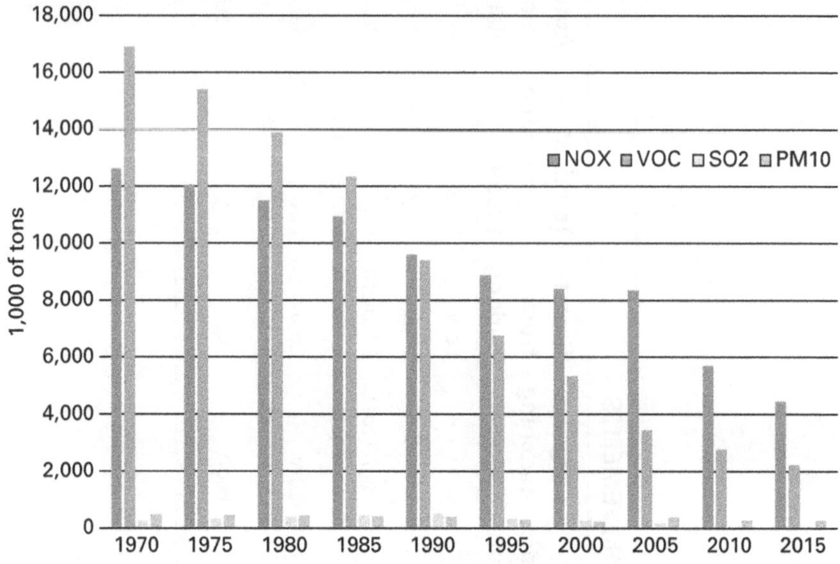

to new pollutants, most recently PM2.5. Sulphur dioxide (SO_2) has been nearly eliminated with the requirement of low sulphur fuel. Emissions of all four pollutants have declined dramatically, despite total vehicle miles travelled increasing from 1.1 to 3 trillion over the same period (Federal Highway Administration, 2013).

National emissions standards have several advantages. Standards set a target that must be met, hence benefits of the policy can be predicted. Enforcement is relatively straightforward via random testing. Regulatory standards tend to be more politically acceptable than tax or pricing strategies. All vehicle manufacturers face the same requirements, and the costs of compliance tend to be hidden. Finally, standards are often used as technology forcing mechanisms. Standards that cannot be met with current technology may be imposed to accelerate technological development.

Zero emission heavy-duty trucks

Substantial progress has been made in recent years on zero emission light-duty vehicles, mainly passenger cars. Most zero emission vehicles are battery electric. Range is increasing and fast-charging technology is reducing the time burden of refuelling. Nevertheless, market penetration is quite small in most countries. In the United States, electric vehicle sales constitute about 1 per cent of total sales in 2016, with more than half of those sales in California (EVAdoption, 2018). The highest penetration of EVs is in Norway; almost 30 per cent of new car purchases were EVs. Next highest is The Netherlands at about 7 per cent. Norway offers a wide variety of incentives including exemptions from taxes and tolls, free parking and access to public transit lanes (Pressman 2017).

Much less progress is being made on zero emission heavy-duty trucks (HDTs). The fundamental problem is energy density; to power a heavy truck carrying a load, the battery itself must be very large and weigh several thousand pounds. Even with a large battery, range is limited; current battery electric heavy-duty trucks (BEHDTs) have a range of 100–150 miles, compared to around 500 miles for conventional diesel HDTs.

The International Energy Agency generates forecasts of future energy demand. IEA estimates a 'Modern Truck' 2050 scenario for freight vehicles. It assumes vehicle efficiency improvements starting immediately and being pushed for more than several decades, systemic logistic and operations improvements in freight movement, and support for alternative fuels and technologies that enable their use. The Modern Truck scenario is predicted to require 45 per cent less energy for transport needs compared to the reference scenario. This scenario predicts high uptake of electric light commercial vehicles, and high uptake of hybrid and electric medium-freight vehicles, in both urban and non-urban settings. In the heavy vehicle category, it projects high uptake of catenary-enabled electric heavy-freight vehicles, but not BEHDTs (IEA, 2017).

Shift to more energy efficient modes

As noted earlier, the faster modes (air and truck) are less energy efficient than slower modes (rail and water). Thus one strategy for reducing pollutants is to shift freight to more energy efficient modes. Strategies typically focus on shifting truck traffic to rail, or rail traffic to water. Examples of shifting from truck to rail include use of short haul rail to inland ports or to near-city distribution and consolidation centres. Short haul rail for inland port deliveries exists in many countries of Europe. Studies of short haul rail show that total CO_2 emissions for a given set of shipments are much lower for rail than for trucking. For example, an intermodal rail container service in Scotland hauls cargo between intermodal facilities 43 miles apart. Given the level of shipments, using rail rather than trucks results in less than half the amount of CO_2 emissions on an annual basis (Department for Transport, 2010). However, short haul rail is often not financially competitive with truck, because of the high fixed costs of rail transport. Thus many

Table 3.6 Qualitative assessment of emissions reduction strategies

Criterion \ Strategy	EMISSIONS REDUCTIONS		
	Low emissions standards	**Zero emission HDTs**	**Shift to more energy efficient modes**
Cost	Medium	High	Medium
Effectiveness	High	Low	Medium
Co-benefits	High	Low	Medium
Technical difficulty	Medium	High	Medium
Implementation feasibility	High	Medium	Medium

short haul systems must be subsidized. Examples of shifting from truck or rail to water include short sea shipping or river barge shipping. Shifting from truck to water is difficult because of the greater travel time required of water transport. In addition, the 'last mile' must always be via truck (or some type of cargo vehicle), adding time and additional costs to the delivery (Table 3.6).

Public policy

Public policy has enormous influence on the transportation sector through the provision of infrastructure, the level of fuel taxes and fees, fuel and emission regulations, size and weight limits, hours of service, and a host of other policies. In this section, we identify policies that could have a significant effect on freight flows.

Truck and passenger VMT tax

A vehicle tax based on miles travelled provides a direct incentive for more efficient travel. A VMT tax has many benefits: 1) it would reduce VMT, all else equal; 2) it would generate new revenue transportation improvements, including support for alternative fuel vehicles. A VMT tax could be structured to reflect the greater damage trucks impose on highway infrastructure, or to compensate for environmental damages. With VII technology, a variable VMT tax is possible; the rate could be increased on congested facilities.

The implementation of a VMT tax could be challenging given the complicated system of charging the tax and other issues including privacy protection. However, the main challenge is political opposition in many countries. Distance-based fees for heavy trucks have been widely adopted in Europe, but not in the United States. Distance based fees for passenger travel have been tested, but no ongoing programme exists. Oregon was the first state in the United States to conduct pilot projects for passenger vehicles. As of this writing, the VMT tax is offered as a voluntary programme through the Oregon state DOT. The pilot programmes have been aimed at showing that concerns such as privacy and data security or incurring overall higher taxes can be addressed. However, to date, no universal VMT tax exists.

Truck lane tolls

The purpose of applying tolls to truck lanes would be to fund their construction. Tolls are typically used for two reasons: to manage congestion, or to provide a source of revenue. Newly built truck-only lanes are unlikely to be congested, and high tolls would divert traffic to other routes, unless a region-wide pricing system existed. Thus, truck-only toll lanes would be likely to have low tolls, which would contribute some revenue, but not enough to cover construction costs. The challenge would be to determine the level of potential demand and sensitivity to toll rates. Truck-only lanes would separate truck and general traffic, provide added capacity, and be likely to increase safety in corridors with very high truck volumes. However, as with any single-use facility, truck toll lanes would require a high level of demand to be justified.

Port cargo or gate tolls

A cargo or gate toll charges a fee for any cargo entering or exiting the port. Gate tolls may be used to shift demand to off-peak hours or days, or to raise funds for port improvements, for example to provide funding for a port-wide appointment system or to cover the costs of extended operating hours. Ports and terminal operators compete with one another on price, reliability and speed. They have no incentive to impose fees unless they result in an offsetting advantage, such as shorter dwell time for ships or shorter cargo delivery times.

The only existing gate fee programmes in the United States are in California, at the ports of Los Angeles, Long Beach and Oakland. In all cases the fee was imposed to spread out demand and reduce congestion at the ports. Oakland charges a flat fee of US $30 per TEU (twenty-foot equivalent container). The PierPass programme operates at the ports of Los Angeles and Long Beach. The programme charges US $71 per TEU for imports or exports arriving during weekdays. In late 2018 PierPass will shift to a flat-fee programme combined with a terminal appointment system (PierPass, 2018).

Table 3.7 Qualitative assessment of policy strategies

Criterion \ Strategy	POLICY STRATEGIES			
	Truck and passenger VMT tax	**Truck lane tolls**	**Port cargo or gate tolls**	**Turn time limits**
Cost	Low	Low	Low	Low
Effectiveness	High	Low	High	High
Co-benefits	High (emissions, safety)	Medium	Medium	Medium
Technical difficulty	High	Medium	Low	Medium
Implementation feasibility	Low	Low	Medium	Medium

Turn time limits

A turn time limit sets the maximum time a drayage truck may spend completing one transaction (eg cargo pickup or drop-off) at a terminal. If the truck takes longer than the maximum time, the terminal operator is fined. The purpose of a turn time limit is to incentivize terminal operators to reduce the waiting time (and associated air pollution) of drayage truckers. Terminal operators seek to optimize their operations, but have no incentive to minimize turn times for drayage truckers if doing so does not benefit the terminal. The Port of Vancouver instituted a turn time limit in 2014 in response to heavy congestion and long turn times at the terminals. Monthly statistics for each terminal are compiled, and terminals are charged for any trips exceeding the maximum. The revenues are distributed to the drayage truck operators. The programme has been effective in reducing truck turn times.

A turn time limit requires extensive reporting on the part of the terminal operators, and setting the appropriate limit is complicated. Moreover, terminal operators would oppose such fines (Table 3.7).

Conclusions

This chapter has described the role of global trade in urban logistics. Global cities are the gateways and hubs for international trade. They are centres of demand, production and management of the global economy. Trade adds another layer of freight demand in these cities. Imports and exports, warehousing and distribution, secondary processing and logistics management contribute to complex freight flows within, through, into and out of the city.

We discussed some of the major impacts of trade related freight and presented some potential solutions for reducing impacts, including infrastructure improvements, efficiency improvements, air pollution mitigation and policy strategies. Our overview demonstrates that there are many possibilities for addressing freight impacts. Some present challenges for implementation, but all provide insights on how the regional portion of urban logistics can be better managed.

References

Akman, G and Baynal, K (2014) Logistics service provider selection through an integrated fuzzy multicriteria decision making approach, *Journal of Industrial Engineering*, v 2014, ID 794918 [Online] http://dx.doi.org/10.1155/2014/794918

Allen, J, Browne, M and Cherrett, T (2012) Investigating relationships between road freight transport, facility location, logistics management and urban form, *Journal of Transport Geography*, **24**, pp 45–57

Andreoli, D, Goodchild, A and Vitasek, K (2010) The rise of mega distribution centres and the impact on logistical uncertainty, *Transportation Letters*, **2** (2), pp 75–88

California Department of Transportation (nd) Truck-Only Lanes [Online] http://www.dot.ca.gov/trafficops/trucks/truck-only-lanes.html

Cidell, J (2015) Distribution centers as distributed places: mobility, infrastructure and truck traffic, in *Cargomobilities: Moving Materials in a Global Age*, ed T Birtchnell, S Savitzky and J Urry, Routledge, New York

Cohn, A, Root, S, Wang, A and Mohr, D (2007) Integration of the load-matching and routing problem with equipment balancing for small package carriers, *Transportation Science*, **41** (2), pp 238–52

Crainic, TG, Gendreau, M and Potvin, JY (2009) Intelligent freight-transportation systems: Assessment and the contribution of operations research, *Transportation Research Part C: Emerging Technologies*, **17** (6), pp 541–57

Dablanc, L and Ross, C (2012) Atlanta: A Mega Logistics Center in the Piedmont Atlantic Megaregion (PAM), *Journal of Transport Geography*, **24**, pp 432–42

Dablanc, L (2013) City logistics, in *The SAGE Handbook of Transport Studies*, ed JP Rodrigue, T Notteboom and J Shaw, SAGE, London

Dablanc, L, Ogilvie, S and Goodchild, A (2014) Logistics sprawl: differential warehousing development patterns in Los Angeles, California, and Seattle,

Washington, *Transportation Research Record: Journal of the Transportation Research Board*, **2410**, pp 105–12

De Palma, A, Kilani, M and Lindsey, R (2008) The merits of separating cars and trucks, *Journal of Urban Economics*, **64** (2), pp 340–61

Department for Transport (2010) [accessed 17 July 2018] *Short Haul Rail Freight on Track for Profits in Scotland* [Online] https://www.transport.gov.scot/media/14380/short_haul_rail_freight_on_track_for_profits_in_scotland.pdf

Dicken, P (2007) *Global Shift: Mapping the changing contours of the world economy*, 5th edn, SAGE Publications, London

Dong, Q, Huang, B, Shu, X, Zhou, C and Maxwell, J (2014) Use of finite element analysis and fatigue failure model to estimate costs of pavement damage caused by heavy vehicles, *Transportation Research Record: Journal of the Transportation Research Board,* **2455**, pp 54–62

EVAdoption (2018) [accessed 16 July 2018] EV Market Share [Online] http://evadoption.com/ev-market-share/

Federal Highway Administration (2013) [accessed 17 July 2018] Public Road Mileage – VMT – Lane Miles 1920–2013, Chart VMT-421C [Online] https://www.fhwa.dot.gov/policyinformation/statistics/2013/vmt421c.cfm

Fischer, M, Ahanotu, D and Waliszewski, J (2003) Planning truck-only lanes: emerging lessons from the Southern California Experience, *Transportation Research Record: Journal of the Transportation Research Board*, **1833**, pp 73–78

Forkenbrock, DJ and March, J (2005) Issues in the financing of truck-only lanes, *Public Roads*, **69** (2)

Gitelman, V, Hakkert, AS, Doveh, E and Cohen, A (2006) Screening tools for considering grade separation at rail-highway crossings, *Journal of Transportation Engineering*, **132** (1), pp 52–59

Giuliano, G (2017) Land use impacts of transportation investments – highway and transit, in *The Geography of Urban Transportation*, ed G Giuliano and S Hanson, Guilford Press, New York

Giuliano, G and Yuan, Q (2017) Location of Warehouses and Environmental Justice, Report 16-1.1g, Los Angeles: MetroFreight Center of Excellence, University of Southern California [Online] https://www.metrans.org/sites/default/files/research-project/MF%201.1g_Location%20of%20warehouses%20and%20environmental%20justice_Final%20Report_021618.pdf

Giuliano, G and Kang, S (2018) Spatial dynamics of the logistics industry: evidence from California, *Journal of Transport Geography*, forthcoming

Giuliano, G, Showalter, C, Yuan, Q and Zhang, R (2018) Managing the Impacts of Freight in California, *National Center for Sustainable Transportation Research Report*, University of California, Davis

Giuliano, G, Kang, S, Yuan, Q and Hutson, N (2015) The Freight Landscape: Using Secondary Data to Describe Metropolitan Freight Flows, *Report METRANS UTC 1-1B*, METRANS Transportation Center, University of Southern California, Los Angeles

Giuliano, G, Kang, S, Hutson, N and Yuan, Q (2018) Material flows in the global city, in *Urban Empires: Cities as global rulers in the new urban world*, ed E Glaeser, K Kourtit and P Nijkamp, Routledge, Abingdon

Goodchild, A, and Dubie, M (2016) Logistics sprawl in Chicago, Illinois, Presented at 14th World Conference on Transport Research, Shanghai, China

Heitz, A and Dablanc, L (2015) Logistics spatial patterns in Paris: rise of Paris Basin as logistics megaregion, *Transportation Research Record: Journal of the Transportation Research Board*, **2477**, pp 76–84

Heitz, A, Dablanc, L, Olsson, J, Sánchez-Díaz, I and Woxenius, J (2018) Spatial patterns of logistics facilities in Gothenburg, Sweden, *Journal of Transport Geography*, DOI: 10.1016/j.jtrangeo.2018.03.005

Hesse, M (2007) The System of Flows and the Restructuring of Space Elements of a Geography of Distribution (Das System der Ströme und die Re-Strukturierung des Raumes. Elemente einer Geographie der Distribution), *Erdkunde*, pp 1–12

Hesse, M and Rodrigue, J-P (2004) The transport geography of logistics and freight distribution, *Journal of Transport Geography*, **12** (3), pp 171–84

Huynh, N (2009) Reducing Truck Turn Times at Marine Terminals with Appointment Scheduling, in Proceedings of Transportation Research Board 09, Washington

Huynh, N and Walton, CM (2008) Robust scheduling of truck arrivals at marine container terminals, *Journal of Transportation Engineering*, **134** (8), pp 347–53

International Energy Agency (2017) The Future of Trucks – Implications for Energy and the Environment, Np, 2017 [Online] 11 September 2017

Jensen, M, Fayez, S and DeSantis, S (2015) Los Angeles – Gateway Freight Advanced Traveler Information System – Demonstration Team Final Report. FHWA-JPO-14-197 [Online] http://ntl.bts.gov/lib/54000/54800/54838/FHWA-JPO-14-197_la_dtfr.pdf

Kang, S (2017) Unraveling Decentralization of Warehouses and Distribution Centers: Three Essays, Dissertation, PhD in Urban Planning and Development, University of Southern California

Kari, D, Wu, G and Barth, M (2014) Eco-Friendly Freight Signal Priority using connected vehicle technology: A multi-agent systems approach, Proceedings of the 2014 IEEE Intelligent Vehicles

Leinbach, T and Capineri, C (2007) *Globalized Freight Transport: Intermodality, e-commerce, logistics and sustainability*, Edward Elgar, Cheltenham

Mohai, P, Pellow, D and Timmons Roberts, J (2009) Environmental justice, *Annual Review of Environment and Resources*, **34**, pp 405–30

Mohai, P and Saha, R (2007) Racial inequality in the distribution of hazardous waste: a national-level reassessment, *Social Problems*, **54** (3), pp 343–70

Mongelluzzo, B (2016) US ports investing billions to expand operations to improve efficiency, *Journal of Commerce* [Online] http://www.joc.com/port-news/usports/us-ports- investing-billions-expand-operations-improve-efficiency_20160107.html

Morais, P and Lord, E (2006) Terminal appointment system study (No TP 14570E), A report prepared for Transportation Development Centre of Transport Canada by Roche Ltée, Groupe-conseil and Levelton Consultants Ltd [Online] https://www.tc.gc.ca/media/documents/policy/14570e.pdf

Namboothiri, R and Erera, A (2008) Planning local container drayage operations given a port access appointment system, *Transportation Research Part E: Logistics and Transportation Review*, **44** (2), pp 185–202

Nieberding, B, Apfelstädt, A and Dashkovskiy, S (2017) Cycles as a Solving Strategy for Matching Problems in Cooperative Full Truckload Networks, *IFAC-PapersOnLine*, **50** (1), pp 7941–46

Noland, R (2001) Relationships between highway capacity and induced vehicle travel, *Transportation Research Part A*, **35**, pp 47–72

PierPass Inc (2018) Revised PierPass OffPeak System Start Expected in Fourth Quarter, [Online] https://www.pierpass.org/news/revised-pierpass-offpeak-system-start-expected-in-fourth-quarter/

Pressman, M (2017) [accessed 17 July 2018] These Countries Are Leading the Way to an Electric Vehicle Revolution, *EVANNEX* [Online] https://evannex.com/blogs/news/here-comes-the-electric-vehicle-revolution

Rodrigue, JP (2004) Freight, gateways and mega-urban regions: the logistical integration of the Bostwash Corridor, *Tijdschrift voor economische en sociale geografie*, **95** (2), pp 147–61

Rodrigue, JP and Notteboom, T (2012) Dry ports in European and North American intermodal rail systems: two of a kind? *Research in Transportation Business & Management*, **5**, pp 4–15

Rodrigue, JP, Debrie, J, Fremont, A and Gouvernal, E (2010) Functions and actors of inland ports: European and North American dynamics, *Journal of Transport Geography*, **18** (4), pp 519–29

Sakai, T, Kawamura, K and Hyodo, T (2015) Locational dynamics of logistics facilities: evidence from Tokyo, *Journal of Transport Geography*, **46**, pp 10–19

US Census (2018) Foreign Trade Statistics 2018 [Online] https://www.census.gov/foreign-trade/data/index.html

US Department of Transportation (2018) Freight Facts and Figures 2017 [Online] https://www.bts.gov/sites/bts.dot.gov/files/docs/FFF_2017_Full_June2018revision.pdf

US Environmental Protection Agency (2018) Fast Facts: US Transportation Sector Greenhouse Gas Emissions 1990–2016, Report EPA-420-F-18-013, USEPA, Office of Transportation and Air Quality [Online] https://www.epa.gov/greenvehicles/fast-facts-transportation-greenhouse-gas-emissions

Yuan, Q (2018) Environmental justice in warehousing location: state of the art, *Journal of Planning Literature,* pp 1–12, DOI: 10.1177/0885412217753841

Zhao, W and Goodchild, A (2013) Using the truck appointment system to improve yard efficiency in container terminals, *Maritime Economics & Logistics*, **15**, pp 101–19

Urban planning policies for logistics facilities 04

A comparison between US metropolitan areas and the Paris region

NICOLAS RAIMBAULT, ADELINE HEITZ
AND LAETITIA DABLANC

Introduction[1]

The development of logistics activities and flows entails the construction of thousands of warehouses, distribution centres and terminals in large urban regions (Dablanc and Frémont, 2015). Thus, logistics exposes urban regions to new challenges concerning economic and social development (location of firms and jobs), sustainability (freight flows generated by logistics sites, land consumption), and urban development and regional governance (Hesse, 2008; Hall and Hesse, 2013).

Against this background, recent research has documented the spatial patterns of logistics industry geography in Europe and North America towards more and more concentration into major urban areas but also decentralization within them; that is to say 'logistics sprawl' (Dablanc and Andriankaja, 2010; Dablanc and Ross, 2012). The literature highlights also the primary role played by municipalities and local communities in the regulation of logistics land uses, the lack of regional coordination and vision and, within this context, the increasing power of the logistics real estate industry in terms of selection of logistics locations and the definition of the features of logistics buildings (Hesse, 2004; Cidell, 2011; Dablanc and Ross, 2012; Raimbault, 2016, 2017). In this context, logistics activities are organized by forces located outside local areas and meet the requirements of economic players in terms of location choice, employment, schedules and delivery frequencies and vehicle types.

This chapter aims at analysing how logistics development and subsequent governance arrangements fit within regional and urban planning policies, and especially within spatial planning frameworks. Two urban regions are observed: Paris, France and Atlanta, United States. Can public interventions lead to the emergence of dedicated planning policies for logistics facilities? If so, what is their effectiveness?

Planning logistics facilities at regional and local scales is a strategic area of public policy, because of its connection with economic, environmental and social issues. Planning these facilities includes influencing their location via land use zoning, developing new transport infrastructures or optimizing freight flows to reduce pollution and CO_2 emission. Planning logistics sites also refers to the means used for this purpose. It first corresponds to the regulatory management of logistics land uses and warehouse development, including zoning and building permissions. The second aspect relies on the implementation of specific freight and logistics projects by public authorities, including public infrastructure or real estate experimental projects.

Planning logistics facilities refers also to different scales: national, regional and local. At the local scale, the literature and the practitioners often refer to 'urban logistics' to describe the organization of freight flows and logistics infrastructures located in denser parts of metropolitan areas. In this chapter, we will use this specific designation for planning urban logistics in these urban spaces.

In order to cover the different dimensions of planning logistics facilities at regional and local scales, the chapter is organized in the following sections. The second section analyses how spatial and transportation planning policies take into account logistics issues in US metropolitan areas. The third section proposes a comparison with the regional planning framework of the Paris region. In the fourth section, freight villages, innovative planning and real estate experimental policies in the Paris region are studied. The last section focuses on the regulation of logistics land uses and warehouse development in the suburbs of Paris and Atlanta.

Planning logistics buildings and freight activities in US metropolitan areas

In the United States, spatial and transportation planning are essentially local. Municipalities are responsible for land use plans. Transportation planning is a 'bottom up' process, with municipalities, counties and other sub-regional levels of governments proposing projects that eventually become part of the regional transportation plan (Giuliano, 2007).

This very local and fragmented situation is more pronounced in the United States than in Europe (Gordon and Richardson, 2001; Cox, 2004). 'In the US case, what is striking is the relative absence of an explicit urban and regional planning policy implemented by more central branches of the state, either federal or at the individual state level' (Cox, 2004, p 253).

This context makes spatial planning extremely difficult to apply to logistics issues in US cities. A representative from the Atlanta Regional Commission confirmed this by saying in 2008: 'we are an MPO,[2] we know we have to promote a better planning of freight facilities in Atlanta, but land use decisions come from the local level. All we can do is advise that freight activities are a necessary part of the metropolitan economy and municipalities should be careful in not rejecting them' (2008 interview with Caroline Marshall, in Dablanc and Ross, 2012).

Focusing on regional and metropolitan spatial planning documents, this section presents the emergence of spatial planning approaches dedicated to logistics issues within land use and transportation planning in the United States. It analyses the case of Atlanta in this perspective.

Logistics in land use planning

Industrial land use zoning holds a special place in the history of American cities. A landmark decision by the Supreme Court in 1926, *Euclid vs Ambler*, recognized that economic activities, and especially manufacturing ones, do have impacts on the whole metropolitan area and that a community had the right, within its regular legal powers, to regulate them in order to decrease potentially negative impacts. Zoning to prevent industrial development, and by extension zoning in general, has been authorized since then, changing the fate of planning practice in the United States. In other legal decisions, more favourable to industrial uses, economic development has been repeatedly considered a 'public purpose', legitimating policies of eminent domain (the confiscation of private properties for public use with 'just compensation' in the sense of the Fifth Amendment to the Constitution).[3]

In today's US metropolitan areas, industrial activities often come down to logistics activities (De Lara, 2013). Logistics activities, among all economic activities, tend to go the farthest out in suburban areas, where they are sometimes the first industrial activities these suburban communities are confronted with. In this context, the implementation of industrial land use planning by local governments constitutes the main regulatory management of logistics land uses and warehouse development. It could support the development of logistics activities or, on the contrary, prevent them.

Several authors see logistics and industrial planning as a bad idea *per se*. According to Bogart (2006), the very essence of industrial zoning today is only a way for homeowners to avoid undesirable land uses locating nearby, 'since business activities became more footloose [can be located anywhere] as a result of trucks'. For Lee and Gordon (2007), repeated recommendations for regional public zoning and regulation are useless, regional intervention is both undesirable and unattainable, and cities should find other ways (other than planning for a specific ideal urban form) to mitigate congestion and other externalities. For other authors, logistics land use zoning is an option but can actually be damaging to cities. Hills and Schleicher (2010)[4] argue that non-cumulative zoning, that is zoning that does not allow the accumulation of uses less noxious than industry in manufacturing zones, actually prevents urban areas from developing much more useful uses than manufacturing. Because transport costs have fallen, the authors do not see any rationale to justify this kind of protection of industrial land uses in urban areas, which *de facto* act as a subsidy resulting in cheap land prices for manufacturing. This last argument probably disregards one – major – rationale of protecting manufacturing and logistics land uses, which is the prevention of increased freight transport distances, and parallel impacts, within urban regions (see below).

Freight in transportation planning

The Intermodal Surface Transportation Efficiency Act (ISTEA) of 1991 introduced a comprehensive and intermodal approach to the funding and implementation of transportation projects, with new planning requirements. Freight transportation was specifically identified as one of the planning targets. In ISTEA, 'for the first time (…), freight transport and freight facility location were factors to be considered by metropolitan planning organizations as they developed their long and short range transportation plans and programmes' (Czerniak *et al*, 2000). ISTEA started a new process where freight was to be integrated into state and metropolitan transportation planning.

Following ISTEA, freight planning has experienced slow but effective progress. For the first time at this level (ie at Federal level and with an extended outreach to local practitioners and experts), the 2011 *Freight Facility Location Selection: A Guide for Public Officials* provided a comprehensive set of recommendations to local governments regarding the integration of freight facilities. The overall purpose of the guidelines is 'to provide insight on location decisions for freight facilities and suggest best practices for transportation, land use, economic development, and regional partnerships to public sector agencies and officials considering and responding to freight facility development and location decisions.'

Interestingly, what the guidebook insists on is the support that public agencies can and should provide in order to retain and develop logistics activities. The document displays an impressive list of the different instruments that can be used: 'Public sector assistance in the forms of tax credits, grants, low-cost loans, training programmes, utility discounts and infrastructure development can address specific location shortcomings and is often used to close the gap between a location and its competition.'

Eventually, while land use zoning tends to give local communities the possibility to plan their industrial development, transportation planning documents insist on the importance of local support for logistics sites development.

The slow emergence of logistics and freight plans

The reduction of transportation-based CO_2 emissions via land use and planning policies has been an important focus of discussion and practice, notably via 'smart growth' and sustainable transportation strategies. This paradigm leads some metropolitan planning organizations to tackle logistics issues in their regional plan and strategy. As an example, Atlanta has been one the most active metropolitan areas to introduce land use and community impact elements in its regional freight plan and strategy as early as in the 2000s. A freight advisory task force was established in 2003 by ARC[5] and several freight studies were made. A Freight Improvement Program of more than US $75 million was set aside for the 2014–17 period (with 80 per cent of funds coming from federal programmes).

States do not emphasize freight in their transportation plans despite an increasing number of freight studies. Some of the freight studies have resulted in the reorganization of project ranking processes, seemingly pushing freight projects higher on the states' agenda. Rail freight is mentioned in several states as an important investment issue. The State of Georgia promotes freight and logistics issues in a seemingly active manner. A Statewide Freight Plan 2005–35 was prepared in 2006–07 in parallel with the state's Transportation Plan by Cambridge Systematics, subsequently updated (Georgia Statewide Freight and Logistics plan 2010–2050). The plan ensures that 'Georgia's transportation system is in balance with the demand for freight and logistics'. Other states are now involved in making freight plans: 2014 California Freight Mobility Plan; 2014 (and 2017 update) Washington State Freight and Goods Transportation System (FGTS).

In 2011, the San Diego Association of Governments (SANDAG) became the first urban region of California to adopt a Sustainable Communities Strategy as a mandatory component of its Regional Transportation Plan under SB 375, California's anti-sprawl law. In this document,[6] the first page reads that 'The SCS must demonstrate how the development patterns and the transportation network, policies and programmes can work together to achieve the greenhouse gas (GHG) emission reduction targets for cars and light trucks that will be established by the California Air Resources Board.' Further down the document, a Goods Movement Strategy (GMS) is developed producing 'a menu of projects that reflects the needs of the region and balances freight benefits with sustainability needs'. Although most of the freight strategy consists of a list of improvement projects in facilities such as intermodal facilities, ports and highways, two actions were directly related to freight land uses, and they involved local jurisdictions:

> Update the SANDAG Regional Comprehensive Plan (RCP) to include policies, programmes, and guidelines to integrate goods movement land uses and facilities, with minimal impact to adjacent communities.
>
> Support and provide assistance for the update of local general plans to identify the long-term needs of moving goods, industrial warehousing infrastructure, and connectors to the regional freight network. Coordinate this effort with economic studies and RCP updates.

Planning logistics facilities and freight activities in the Paris region

As in the United States, French municipalities benefit from extensive political powers vis-à-vis metropolitan and regional authorities, especially in terms of land use planning and building permits. However, France was one of the first European countries to take freight transport and logistics issues into account in the various urban and regional planning documents. It leads to the progressive inclusion of logistics issues in the Paris region master plan.

Logistics in transportation and metropolitan planning

In 1982 and 1996 (when they became mandatory), two national Acts gave a mandate to French metropolitan authorities, and to the Paris region (the Île-de-France), when drawing up their urban transport plans (known as PDU) 'to deal with the transport of goods and deliveries while rationalizing the supply conditions of the metropolitan area in order to maintain commercial and craft activities' (Orientation Act for Inland Transport). More recently, the Modernization of Territorial Public Action and the Affirmation of Metropolitan Governments Act of 2014 (known as the 'MAPAM Act') strengthened and broadened the missions of metropolitan transportation planning agencies, today called 'Mobility Organizing Authorities'. On logistics, these authorities may go as far as organizing a public service of urban freight and logistics, 'in order to reduce urban congestion and pollution and nuisances affecting the environment', and in the case of 'unsuitability of private initiative for this purpose'.

However, the implementation of these plans often remains a local matter. The municipalities – rarely the metropolitan or intermunicipal authorities[7] – decide on zoning and urban planning rules. Building permits are granted, on the basis of land use plans. In the Paris region, municipalities are very numerous (1,276, with an average surface area of less than 10 square kilometres). This means that building permits are decided by very local governments that are often poorly equipped in terms of logistics and freight expertise. Metropolitan governments, for their part, are responsible for another kind of planning document: the 'territorial coherence plans' (SCOT). The SCOT constitutes 'intermunicipal strategic planning at the scale of a large intermunicipal area or urban area, within the framework of a sustainable development project'. One of its roles is to strengthen the links between transport and land use planning policies with a general objective of managing passenger mobility and goods flows. The document relies on the metropolitan transport plan (PDU) for the implementation of practical logistics policies.

Île-de-France region is the only French region regulated by a regional master plan (known as SDRIF), functioning as a SCOT at the regional scale, and by a coherent transport plan, the PDUIF.

Regional planning and logistics in the Paris region

The master plan for the Île-de-France region (SDRIF) sets the main guidelines in terms of the location of residential areas, economic activities and infrastructures; it is a binding document, for some of its provisions, for local urban planning documents. The inclusion of freight in the SDRIF has been very incremental. In 1965, the regional master plan, after having recalled the importance of freight transport and assessed its future growth, made rapid reference to the 'ongoing studies relating to road terminals and transit centres' (which will give rise to the two freight villages of Garonor and Sogaris).[8] When the master plan was revised in 1976, freight was not specifically mentioned. The 1994 SDRIF, on the contrary, devoted a chapter to the 'freight transport network'. One of its goals was to 'enable the establishment of a coherent network of multimodal logistics zones to meet the very high demand noted in this sector' (p 16).

The 1994 SDRIF was replaced by a new master plan in 2013. A chapter entitled 'Optimizing metropolitan logistics' identifies the major multimodal sites and specifies those that need to be preserved or created, in connection with major rail corridors. A map, dedicated to logistics activities in the inner areas, identifies rail and port sites that should be preserved for urban logistics. It is actually in a sub-chapter in a completely different part of the SDRIF that proposals relating to the daily logistical functions can be found. The section 'Renewing and densifying business areas, particularly for small and medium-sized firms and the craft sector' (in a section on 'Re-establising the dynamism of the Île-de-France economy') emphasizes the need to support a mix of uses of activities, including logistics, in dense areas. The text is accompanied by a thematic map that indicates where to 'renew, densify and organize the supply of industrial areas', logistics not being specifically mentioned on the map.

The SDRIF proposes to polarize logistics and industrial activities around 20 sites, well distributed throughout the region. However, it should be noted that SDRIF deals with logistics by road mode only in the case of the outer suburbs.

One part of the SDRIF is legally binding: the 'general destination map of the different parts of the regional space'. The local land use zoning must be compatible with this map, which mainly distinguishes between areas that can be urbanized and areas that are protected from urbanization. The different logistics sites listed above are represented in this map. The map institutionalizes the objective of preservation of several terminals and warehousing zones in the dense areas, even though they can be located in areas of current urban redevelopments.

Will this attempt, via the SDRIF, to propose the concentration of logistics functions in a certain number of clusters suffer the fate of the previous regional plans? These had illustrated 'the constitutional incapacity of the regional plans to directly force the municipal plans' (Gilli and Offner, 2009). None of the past master plans has significantly influenced the location of warehouses and terminals in the Île-de-France region, and SDRIFs have been ignored in local urban planning.

The region uses another tool in order to regulate logistics activities. The Île-de-France Transportation Plan (PDUIF), approved in 2014, proposes two maps identifying the 'regional logistics framework', which includes the region's 'non-displaceable' multimodal logistics sites. Even if it focuses only on multimodal terminals, this plan provides specific locations on protected sites.

Compared to US metropolitan areas, the Paris region planning policies include logistics issues more clearly. However, the management of logistics land uses and warehouse development remains essentially local, in a region where local municipalities are extremely numerous and small in size, with the exception of the city of Paris. In this context, innovative logistics policies, consisting of developing logistics 'hotels' and other new formats of urban warehouses, arise in specific urban places (section 4). Simultaneously, the regulation is minimal in the outer suburbs, where huge logistics zones are multiplying (section 5).

Public development of logistics sites: freight villages and urban logistics experimentations

In order to limit 'logistics sprawl', and thus to comply with sustainability goals, public authorities facilitate the supply of logistics facilities in inner areas, complementary to the one supplied by large logistics real estate investors in peripheral areas. This new public policy is focused on city centres. The result is a 'dualization' of logistics geography, between urban and peri-urban logistics (Heitz, 2017). In the Île-de-France region, this dualization is illustrated by various planning modes for logistics facilities, with on the one hand the development of 'freight villages' (FVs), mostly in the suburbs, and on the other hand the development of urban logistics, mainly in Paris, in the form of urban real estate experimental projects. One of the most prevalent planning modes for many European local governments when it comes to freight transport and logistics is the development of public, or private/public, logistics zones commonly known as FVs.

Freight villages and suburban logistics development

Freight villages (FVs) are publicly developed business zones dedicated to logistics, managed by a single public or private manager, offering specialized services such as catering, safety or security, repair of vehicles for freight and logistics operators (Savy 2006; Du and Bergqvist 2010; Higgins *et al*, 2012). For Savy (2006), 'In the general development of logistics, FVs occupy (...) a singular place. They (...) link the 'hard' (infrastructure) and the 'soft' (management), the public (municipalities) and private (companies) interests, the long term (spatial planning) and the short term (flexibility of the market)'. Most FVs are located in Europe, particularly in France, in Italy (*interporti*), and in Germany (*Güterverkehrszentren*, or GVZ).

For Boile *et al* (2011), FVs play a positive role at the environmental level, reducing negative externalities. They allow for optimization of urban flows, in particular when they are associated with intermodal terminals. In some cases, they result in a relocation of transport and logistics companies in a single place (resulting in the polarization of logistics facilities), thus reducing nuisances related to the logistics sprawl and fragmentation of warehouse location. The literature on FVs also emphasizes the growing need to protect and secure land availability for warehouses in the future, to which FVs or logistics parks provide a satisfactory response.

In Île-de-France, Bounie (2017) identifies different types of logistics zones, highlighting the existence of four specific stakeholders. In this typology, two formats correspond to a freight village.

The first, and most common, type of logistics zone is the result of a development operation initiated by local (municipal) or national governments with the aim of developing logistics activities. In this case, municipalities or public agencies acquire and develop the land (depollution, connection to networks, infrastructure). Once the development phase is complete, public authorities can sell the land to developers that specialize in logistics real estate. The resale of land in the form of lots can generate a financial margin, offsetting the expenses for the development of the area.

The second type corresponds to publicly developed FVs that remain the property of a public or quasi-public park manager. The Sogaris FV, located in the southern suburbs of Paris, is managed by the semi-public logistics real estate investor (Sogaris), which is directly accountable to the city of Paris.

The third type corresponds to FVs carried out by transport infrastructure managers, such as river ports or airports. Infrastructure managers are public stakeholders, usually under the direct control of the national government (Raimbault, 2014). In the case of a projected FV on the property of an infrastructure manager, the manager will be responsible for the development of the site and will rent lots over a long period, through administrative leases, to actors wishing to develop logistics buildings for their own use or to rent them (Magnan, 2016). Developing FVs brings property incomes to infrastructure managers, which are often higher than the revenues generated by the use of their intermodal terminals. Even if logistics activities are set up near a large rail or river terminal, they are not necessarily users of these facilities. The land can be simply a good opportunity to locate in close proximity to the heart of the city. An example of this opportunity effect is the 2017 opening of an Amazon parcel-sorting centre in Bonneuil-sur-Marne (south-east of Paris). The new facility was developed and is operated internally by Amazon Logistics. It makes it possible to deliver to e-commerce customers six days a week. Amazon does not intend to use the port terminals. The proximity of the port to the city centre remains an attractive factor for the location of warehouses, especially for express parcel transport activities. New trends, such as 'instant deliveries' (Dablanc *et al*, 2017), may increase the need for new buildings close to the city centre to optimize deliveries. Ports' strategy to accept non water-based logistics activities, allows the location of logistics activities to persist in the dense areas (Heitz, 2017).

The last type of logistics zone corresponds to private logistics parks, which are more and more numerous in Île-de-France and in the US metropolitan areas, especially in the outer suburbs. The initiative most often comes from a real estate developer and investor who sees the development of a private logistics zone as an opportunity to enhance the value of his or her real estate assets and to secure land for further development. However, the initiative can also come from public authorities, which have the task of initiating an area dedicated to logistics, but which do not want to develop or manage, because of associated (financial) risks, so they rely on the private sector (Raimbault, 2016). In this case, the real estate developer and investor must take charge of the entire development and, then, of the property management of the zone.

According to the data provided by the Regional Census of Logistics Buildings (Heitz *et al*, 2017) and the Census of Logistics Zones (Bounie, 2017), 48 logistics zones can be identified in the Île-de-France region: 25 per cent are located in the 'petite couronne', the dense part of the Paris region. Overall, 44 per cent of logistics facilities are located in freight villages or other logistics zones (Figure 4.1).

Figure 4.1 Typology of freight villages in Île-de-France

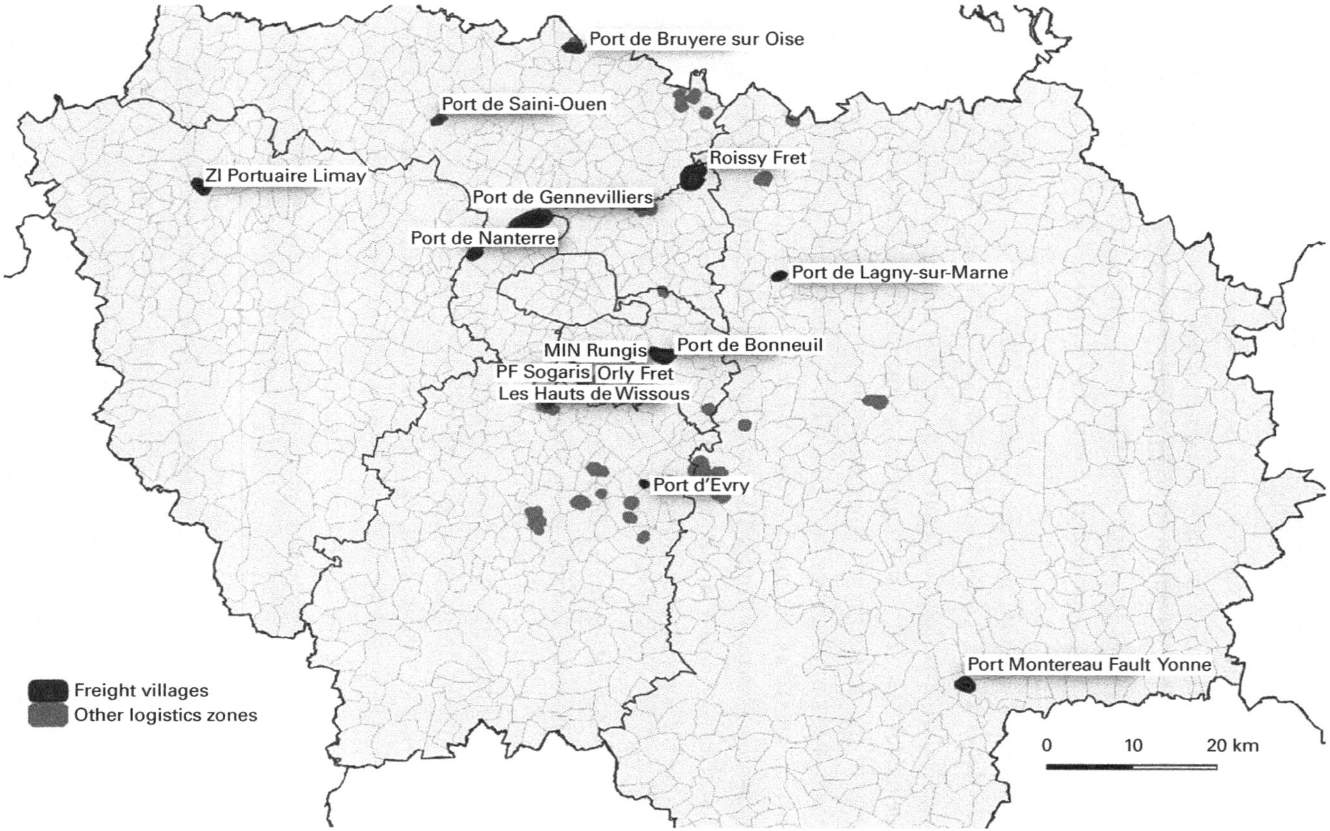

SOURCE author: Heitz, 2018; original source: Bounie, 2017

Developing logistics buildings in Paris: innovative planning and experimentation

Innovative planning of logistics activities in Paris

In Île-de-France, the City of Paris has, for several years, integrated logistics issues into the city planning documents and processes, proposing a new model of logistics facilities dedicated to the dense area. Drawing inspiration from Japanese achievements and interpreting the principles of urban logistics discussed by experts and researchers (Diziain *et al*, 2012), its action is based on two instruments: planning and experimentation.

Initiated in 2006 and developed in 2013 in a partnership framework involving public authorities and private stakeholders (carriers and shippers), the Paris 'logistics charter' promotes best practices for freight and deliveries. The 2013 document is an operational document, including as one of its targets the development of new types of urban warehouses and micro-hubs for logistics. Also, in 2018, Greater Paris (the authority for the Metro area) has proposed a 'pact for logistics activities in Greater Paris'. This new charter includes 131 municipalities and proposes new regulation and harmonization of planning logistics facilities. Moreover, this charter promotes logistics experimentation and makes funds available to finance projects.

In the 2006 Paris zoning code, 'major urban service zones' (UGSU) opened the way to urban logistics innovations or logistics real estate projects. They especially targeted former railyards as well as the banks of the Seine river. The stated objective is to develop logistics facilities, among other activities (waste management, medical facilities, etc). The development of logistics infrastructure is supposed to induce a modal shift to reduce the use of road freight transportation and its negative externalities. The 2016 zoning code, replacing the 2006 one, extends the areas where logistics uses are encouraged (or even made mandatory). The opportunities to locate logistics facilities in the city centre have increased as a result.

The city of Paris has therefore created a policy framework favourable to the development of urban logistics. However, in order for this urban logistics infrastructure development policy to succeed, other actors must support it. The challenge, for the City of Paris, is to convince private investors of the value of urban logistics by providing a favourable policy framework and available land for the development of this type of real estate.

In its 2016 zoning code, the Paris City Council has set up a new category of CINASPIC (Constructions and Installations Required for Public Services or Collective Interests) dedicated to urban logistics, reserving some land for small warehouses from which, for example, electric vans and cargo cycles can be operated, or allowing logistics activities to be integrated into urban projects. These urban logistics areas are defined as spaces dedicated to the reception of activities related to the delivery and removal of goods, which may include short-term storage and withdrawal by the recipient. For the time being, repackaging and permanent storage operations are excluded. Apart from the floor dedicated to logistics, the rest of the building must be intended for other functions. Mixed use real estate projects combining housing or office/recreational and logistics activities are now encouraged.

The legal definition of logistics as a service of interest to the public (CINASPIC) excludes many logistic activities, requiring longer-term storage. Therefore, they clearly revolve around specific logistics activities such as express parcels deliveries, excluding other sectors of logistics.

Logistics real estate and urban experiments

The City of Paris is directly involved in the development of specific urban logistics projects. It funds projects such as the consolidation centre of Beaugrenelle for Chronopost (a major French parcel express operator), the consolidation centre of Les Halles or the Chapelle 'logistics hotel' run by the city-owned logistics real estate investor Sogaris (Dablanc *et al*, 2018). A logistics hotel is a multistorey urban building where several types of activities coexist with logistics activities. These experiments open the way for testing new practices in terms of logistics and freight transport, in collaboration with logistics or freight transport operators. They are supposed to serve as an example to other municipalities by demonstrating the viability and the benefits of these facilities.

The Chronopost facility of Beaugrenelle, opened in 2012, is located in the 15th arrondissement and is composed of 3,000 square metres spread over two levels. This project had to receive a high number of authorizations to be built, in particular from the official Architects of Buildings of France, as the regulatory and architectural constraints were significant.

The Urban Distribution Centre of Montorgueil is another project backed by the City of Paris in the heart of Paris, as part of the diesel reduction municipal objective. Located in one of the densest areas of Paris, it will deliver to stores in the neighbourhood of Montorgueil. Freight operators will be required to pool their flows if they wish to have access to the 600 square metres made available for this project. The municipality wants to create a favourable environment for consolidating deliveries from different carriers. However, in a very competitive freight transport sector, the space proposed by the City of Paris appears too small for carriers who have trouble in finding a viable business plan. The project is currently struggling to succeed.

In 2010, a call was launched for the construction of a logistics facility that could also include offices, sports facilities and housing in the north of the 18th arrondissement. Sogaris proposed a logistics 'hotel' located within a larger zone open for housing redevelopment. The logistics hotel goes hand in hand with an urban project that includes 900 housing units and 80 SOHOs ('Small Office, Home Office'; spaces that combine places of work and housing). The logistics hotel hosts an urban rail terminal, several small storage facilities, a state school, a farm (urban agriculture), tennis courts, sport and leisure facilities and a datacentre. The purpose of this cohabitation is that these activities bear a portion of the cost of building and land, since they are more profitable. This financial equalization strategy allows logistics to return to dense urban areas at an acceptable cost. This logistics hotel, inaugurated in June 2018, is a double experiment for the City of Paris, as it tests the concept of a logistics hotel, and tests the use of rail for the delivery of goods in Paris. The urban rail terminal (TFU) required a lot of work and innovations such as the control of specific and adapted cranes and adapted containers. The inability to use standard techniques increased the cost of the project. The development of the Chapelle logistics hotel has been a complex operation involving multiple authorizations (Dablanc *et al*, 2018). The City of Paris also had to change the local zoning regulations in order to authorize higher buildings, to allow for the financial capacity of the project, and to adjust to the technical constraints of the construction of the rail facility and the use of railways. The results of this experiment tend to show that the support of public authorities is crucial in these projects, which can slow down the diffusion of this type of logistic format because it can make investors risk averse.

The City of Paris and the semi-public company Sogaris are the main stakeholders in the development of these urban logistics facilities. While private actors are involved in the development of suburban logistics zones, they are just emerging in the development of dense urban logistics buildings (UPS, for example, has just opened an urban facility of 7,000 square metres in the eastern part of Paris).

The expansion of suburban logistics facilities are often the result of local governance arrangements in which private stakeholders dominate local governments (Raimbault, 2014), especially through the development of private logistics parks. On the contrary, urban logistics infrastructure has, to this day, relied mostly on public initiative (Debrie and Heitz, 2017). The planning and programming of urban logistics is today largely the prerogative of the City of Paris but tends to spread to other municipalities in the Greater Paris area. Some suburban municipalities are becoming more aware of logistics issues as, for example, in Saint Denis in the north or Vitry in the south-east, with two logistics hotel projects.

Context-based governance of logistics land uses and warehousing development

The way the majority of logistics activities are located remains largely outside the scope of regional planning or real estate and urban experiments. Faced with increased pressure from the development of distribution centres, how do local planners and policymakers take account of logistics activities in their planning processes? Cidell (2011) notes the inherent difficulty of local governments faced with the development of logistics sites: 'in a world of flows and networks, [planners] work within bounded territories'. The irruption of logistics activities in this pattern is met with diverse reactions. Jobs are welcome but the low tax revenues per acre and absence of sales taxes of this type of development are often resented.

In this context, logistics zones are largely developed by the logistics real estate industry, which leads to a strong dynamic of spatial standardization. Nevertheless, an analysis of the Paris region and Atlanta shows that the local and regional historical and institutional contexts are key determinants of the way current logistics sites are regulated. In this way, changes in the modes of production of logistics sites significantly structure the changing geography of logistics terminals, goods flow and workplaces of logistics employees in the two regions. (For a similar comparison between the Paris region and the Frankfurt metropolitan region, see also Barbier *et al*, forthcoming.)

The incremental and silent transformation of industrial zones into logistics zones

The first mode of governance corresponds to the development of logistics activities in industrial zones from the 1970s to the early 1990s. During this period, logistics providers and shippers were looking for land in major urban regions, in order to build the warehouses that they needed.

They first found suitable spaces in the existing industrial zones, replacing former factories or, more often, built on plots that became available when the demand for new manufacturing sites started to decline. This led to a silent conversion of industrial zones into logistics zones. In other words, industrial places have become logistics places *naturally* because of this spatial legacy, which follows a 'path dependence' (Pierson, 2000).

The development of these logistics sites did not rely on complex political arrangements, or specific real estate or land development operations. The land, usually developed by public land developers, was available for any kind of industrial purpose, whether manufacturing or logistics. Municipal authorities were only asked to give their formal agreement by signing the building permits. The shift to logistics on these former industrial sites was therefore almost invisible, without explicit public discussion or negotiation between public and private stakeholders.

In the Paris region, the historical industrial suburbs, known as the 'red belt' because of their strong communist history, became the focus of most of the logistics sites over this period (Raimbault, 2014). The population of these municipalities is poorer than the regional average. The shift to logistics was consistent with development trends in the industrial world. Relying on 'low-skilled' jobs, logistics activities could find the necessary labour force among local jobless workers. At the same time, they paid local taxes that enabled the municipalities to continue implementing social redistribution policies.

The twin municipalities of Mitry-Mory and Compans, located south of Roissy-Charles de Gaulle airport, constitute an example of the logistics development of the 'red belt'. In the 1970s, the State created a large industrial zone spread over the two municipalities. This has gradually attracted a large number of logistics establishments for a total of approximately 600,000 square metres of warehouses (DREIA, 2018), one of the largest areas of logistics concentration in Île-de-France. Logistics development is therefore not the result of local policies but of the evolution of a vast industrial zone developed (and therefore imposed) by the State. Owing to the proximity of the airport and the presence of chemical establishments in the industrial zone, the municipalities are subject to numerous urban planning constraints. In particular, residential development opportunities are limited. In this context, logistics offered and still offers an unexpected local development opportunity, bringing jobs and taxes. The industrial zone represents 7,500 jobs, the majority of which correspond to logistics jobs. The local interest in hosting logistics establishments lies even more in tax gains, which fund approximately one-third of the municipal budgets. They are two 'rich municipalities populated by poor inhabitants' (interview with the mayor of

Compans, 8 April 2011). Local tax gains are much higher than the grant transferred by the State. The two municipalities are therefore dependent on these taxes to make up their budgets and to implement social redistribution policies (transport subsidies for schoolchildren, sports and cultural activities of residents, etc).

In Atlanta, some areas followed the same path from manufacturing to logistics, as early as in the 1970s such as Fulton Industrial Boulevard (FIB). In the 1980s and 1990s, although remaining an important focus for logistics activities, FIB lost some of its attractiveness because of rather small and outdated warehouses, with low ceilings and small and unwired spaces. Today, many warehouses require some degree of retrofitting and upgrading, and FIB faces direct competition as newer logistics facilities are being developed in nearby counties. The assets of Fulton Industrial Boulevard are its central location as well as the low prices of the facilities. It benefits from its proximity to the centre of the metropolitan area as well as immediate access to two major highways. A handful of major real estate companies (Avison Young, Millers Logistics, Ackerman and Co, Grubb and Ellis, Prologis) own a majority of the southern area of FIB and have done an important job in reorganizing land parcels, enlarging them to provide scope for larger buildings.

Local policies targeted towards the development of logistics zones

The increasing demand for logistics spaces led to a second mode of governance. Many local governments or authorities took advantage of this demand to develop new business zones dedicated to logistics activities.

In the Paris region, this strategy of economic development was adopted in particular by several new towns such as Evry, Marne-la-Vallée and, most of all, Sénart. These new towns were entirely designed and planned by public land developers – 'Établissement Public d'Aménagement' (EPA) – directly accountable to the central government and, conversely, independent of municipalities and local politics. Since the 1990s, logistics have been seen by these public corporations as an easy way to attract businesses in a 'post-industrial context' (interview with the head of economic development, EPA Sénart, 2011, quoted in Raimbault, 2017).

The case of Sénart is particularly emblematic. In this new town located 35 kilometres south-east of Paris, EPA Sénart designed a development programme for several logistics zones connected to the area's main motorway nodes. The goal of the agency was to increase the number of jobs according to the population growth they had planned in the new town. The policy was supported by the municipalities[9] insofar as it brought in substantial tax revenues. Slow to start during the 1970s and the 1980s, the development began in earnest in the 1990s: more than 470,000 square metres were built between 1985 and 1997.[10] This development accelerated at the end of the 1990s, with the rate of construction doubling to 900,000 square metres until 2009. This chronology is also closely linked to the development of three motorways in the area during the 1990s. The strategy of EPA Sénart was to develop large logistics zones, thought to be attractive to the logistics companies, and close to the main motorway nodes. In order to attract logistic facilities quickly to these zones, EPA Sénart established strong links with domestic property developers, which built warehouses for rent on the different sites. Its last logistics zone, the 'A5 park' (200 hectares; 550,000 square metres of warehouses), has developed since the early 2010s and is almost totally occupied by five huge distribution centres. In this way, Sénart became one of the region's main logistics poles with more than 2 million square metres of warehouses[11] (12 per cent of the warehouses of the region).

It should be noted that some local governments, which first implemented economic development policies based on logistics zones, shifted from logistics, generally in order to upgrade their socio-economic profile. This strategy was adopted by Gwinnett County in the suburbs of Atlanta. The county experienced the bulk of its logistics developments in the 1980s and 1990s. The government has constantly promoted low-rise buildings. 'This served us well in the past' (interview with local manager, quoted in Dablanc and Ross, 2012), and gave way to a boom in logistics facilities in addition to major retail developments. But the strategy, today, is changing. The county wants to attract mixed-use developments, offices and other high-rise buildings, in the way other northern Atlanta counties have been doing. Urban sprawl is recognized as a major issue, generating traffic congestion and a rapid reduction of available land. Higher densities are now considered a valid option for the county's future economic development. Also, logistics facilities are going further east towards Barrow and Jackson counties on Interstate 85 and current logistics facilities in Gwinnett may face a risk of remaining empty. The county's 2030 comprehensive land use plan emphasizes mixed-use activities, at the expense of logistics zones. The county has therefore chosen to promote a 'transition' away from traditional logistics activities towards upper scale mixed-use activities.

In the absence of strong regional planning policies, local governments implement economic development policies based on logistics zones. These local public strategies are a response to the growing demand for logistics spaces. In both urban regions, this results in logistics zones spreading towards suburban and outer-suburban areas, generally in zones of lower housing density (Dablanc and Ross, 2012).

Private logistics parks

Since the 1990s, logistics firms have tended to opt for flexible real estate solutions and thus to look for warehouses to rent rather than building and managing their own facilities. This has contributed to the emergence of a development and investment market in logistics real estate (Hesse, 2008; Raimbault, 2016), which is connected to the general dynamic of the financialization of real estate (Halbert and Attuyer, 2016). The financialization of logistics real estate is tied to a third mode of governance.

The logistics real estate market is dominated by international firms, which specialize in logistics and manage global investment funds.[12] These companies take direct charge of the development of the warehouses they buy as investment fund managers. In order to reduce their dependence on negotiations with local public authorities, they also tend to be the developers of the logistics zones in which they invest. In other words, instead of building warehouses scattered around different business zones, the industry leaders develop private logistics zones containing several warehouses. These 'logistics parks' are entirely owned and operated by the same investment fund manager responsible for property management. They are fenced and protected by private security.

This business model leads to the privatization of a number of local policies. Logistics real estate firms privatize land development policies, since in the past business zones were directly developed by local governments. To the extent that logistics parks are entirely private, real estate firms become the *de facto* owners and managers of the streets and green spaces that constitute the public spaces in the business parks. Moreover, the model also enables real estate companies to decide on local economic development issues, insofar as they select the firms that settle in the municipality, which considerably affects the latter's economic specialization and prospects.

However, local governments retain control of every legal resource. At present, logistics parks must be authorized and supported by local governments, which are responsible for issuing spatial planning documents and building permits. In other words, the production of logistics parks implies that the local authorities accept this dynamic of privatization. Case studies show two different political mechanisms that explain why local governments accept privatization.

First, some local authorities in the outer suburbs, because of a lack of financial, technical and even political resources, are looking for private investors able to establish private business zones. For example, in Île-de-France between 2002 and 2009, Val Bréon local authority undertook a project for a large, dedicated, 200-hectare logistics park.[13] However, the local authority lacked the administrative, technical or financial resources to develop it. It therefore welcomed the proposal of the real estate firm PRD to develop a private logistics park. The company was responsible for financing the total operation and developing the site and buildings. Moreover, with regard to land development, the main challenge was to resolve a legal conflict with an environmental group, which objected to the impact of the development project on local wetlands. The local authority asked the private land developer to negotiate with the association. The developer proposed selling the wetlands to it for one euro for protection. In this way, the real estate company undertook many of the activities usually carried out by local government (Raimbault, 2017).

Second, some outer suburban municipalities argue that the private logistics park model is superior to traditional publicly developed business zones. This explains how Prologis, the world leader in logistics real estate, chose Sénart as the location for its main logistics park in France, buying a large agricultural plot there in the early 2000s. The firm immediately negotiated with the municipality (Moissy-Cramayel, part of new town Sénart) on the possibility of developing a logistics park. Three arguments regarding the differences between the logistics park and the logistics zones developed by EPA Sénart convinced the mayor. First, the general design of the park and the fact that it was fenced and secure seemed to be an improvement. Second, as both development and management were totally private, it made no demands on the public purse. Third, the property manager Prologis would be solely responsible for the entire park and would negotiate directly with the mayor over any request. This gave the mayor a greater sense of control over his territory compared with the situation with the logistics zones developed by EPA Sénart. Indeed, the latter did not need the mayor's authorization to develop a logistics zone and would not subsequently control the long-term management of the zones (since the plots would be owned by different investors) (Raimbault, 2017).

Logistics real estate investments also explain the contemporary development of logistics zones in the outer suburbs of Atlanta. In Henry County, logistics activities developed in the 1990s and especially in the 2000s. A newcomer in the logistics map of Atlanta, Henry County now sees its focus on distribution centres reinforced. New land parcels were opened up to logistics development (mostly from agricultural or forest use). The zones are organized in major logistics parks, holding very large distribution centres, many serving companies that trade with Florida. These logistics parks resulted from the strategies of the main logistics property investors: a major company buys a large amount of land, plans out and builds the roads and other mandatory amenities, and resells plots to other companies, either direct users or other real estate companies, with a profit. This was encouraged by the county, eager to promote fast economic development. The county, which grew from 59,000 people in 1990 to 200,000 in 2010, remains a 'bedroom community'[14] and logistics is considered an essential part of the strategy to provide more local jobs.

The consequences of this last mode of governance, dominated by the logistics real estate industry, are twofold. At the local scale, local governments negotiate only with property developers and investors. They rarely meet the users of the warehouses, the workers or even the logistics firms themselves. Managing relationships with the firms that rent the warehouses becomes the task of the property manager alone. In consequence, logistics issues are seen as a question of real estate, disconnected from matters relating to logistics activities and employment, such as employee transport or transfer of goods flows from road to rail or river modes. At the regional scale, private logistics parks directly challenge planning policies. As these real estate products are particularly attractive for outer-suburban areas, where local authorities do not have the resources or the desire to develop logistics zones alone, the financialization of logistics real estate largely contributes to logistics sprawl since the 1990s.

Conclusions

Spatial planning dedicated to logistics facilities and activities has emerged in many urban regions. This dynamic is clearer in the case of the Paris region than in the case of US metropolitan areas such as Atlanta. The current Paris regional master plan and transport plan introduce specific orientations concerning the location of major logistics facilities.

The main question remains the implementation of practical regulations on the development of logistics activities. The local decisions in this domain are pre-eminent, leaving the real estate industry taking the strategic decisions and the local communities deciding on the desirability of logistics establishments. This context stimulates logistics sprawl, and its impacts on congestion and pollution, in the outer suburbs.

In parallel, some logistics real estate innovations are implemented in denser areas, and especially in the city of Paris. They lead to new practices in terms of urban logistics services, in relation to stakeholders such as logistics or freight transport operators. However, as regulation remains minimal in the outer suburbs, the result of these policies is a dualization of logistics geography, between urban and peri-urban logistics (Heitz, 2017).

Thus, a greater collaboration and agreement between places within urban regions regarding issues of zoning and the location of logistics sites is still needed. Compared to the present piecemeal approach to logistics planning, greater coordination would support the development of more consistent planning and zoning at the various scales of local and regional policies. Joint decision-making relative to logistics locations and support for critical logistics networks might include revenue sharing with coordinated approval of site locations and shared provision of required infrastructure. A primary benefit would be a region-wide and more comprehensive approach to congestion mitigation resulting in an improvement in goods movements. A regional approach could actually reduce the competitive attitudes of cities leading to an accumulation of tax breaks and subsidies to incoming warehousing facilities that, in the end, can be detrimental to local governments. A regional view could also prevent, on the other hand, very organized communities rejecting freight facilities in the 'backyard' of some less organized ones. Additionally, this perspective could tackle the issue of the local employment base as well as training programmes locally or regionally available for warehousing jobs.

Another important issue in freight planning is the necessary attention given to noise and pollution reduction at facilities' level, through such equipment as low noise asphalt on the access roads and parking areas of facilities, as well as energy saving and environmentally friendly architecture of logistics facilities.

Eventually, whatever the instruments used, what counts is the implementation of effective interventions taking into account logistics issues in planning and urban development policies.

References

Barbier, C, Cuny, C and Raimbault, N (forthcoming) The production of logistics places in France and Germany: A comparison between Paris, Frankfurt-am-Main and Kassel, *Work Organisation, Labour & Globalisation*

Bogart, W (2006) *Don't Call it Sprawl – metropolitan structure in the twenty-first century*, Cambridge University Press, p 218

Boile, M, Theofanis, S and Ozbay, K (2011) Feasibility of Freight Villages in the NYMTC Region, Center for Advance Infrastructure and Transportation, Rutgers, The State University of New Jersey

Bounie, N (2017) La zone d'activité logistique comme levier de développement économique des territoires, PhD Thesis, Université Paris-Est

Cidell, J (2011) Distribution centers among the rooftops: the global logistics network meets the suburban spatial imaginary, *International Journal of Urban and Regional Research*, **35** (4), pp 832–51

Cox, K (2004) The politics of local and regional development: the difference the state makes and the US/British contrast, in *Governing Local and Regional Economies, Institutions, Politics and Economic Development,* ed A Wood and D Valler, Ashgate, Aldershot, pp 248–75

Czerniak, C, Lahsene, J and Chatterjee, A (2000) Urban Freight Movement, What Form Will it Take? *Transportation Research Board*, paper: A1B07: Committee on urban goods movement [Online] http://www.nationalacademies.org/trb/publications/millennium/00139.pdf

Dablanc, L and Andriankaja, D (2010) The impacts of logistic sprawl: How does the location of parcel transport terminals affect the energy efficiency of goods' movements in Paris and what can we do about it? *Procedia, Social and Behavioral Sciences*, **2** (3), pp 6087–96

Dablanc, L and Frémont, A (2015) *La Métropole Logistique, le Transport de Marchandises et le Territoire des Grandes Villes*, Armand Colin, Paris

Dablanc, L, Morganti, E, Arvidsson, N, Woxenius, J, Browne, M and Saidi, N (2017) The rise of on-demand 'instant deliveries' in European cities, *Supply Chain Forum: An International Journal*, **8** (4), pp 203–17

Dablanc, L and Ross, C (2012) Atlanta: A Mega Logistics Center in the Piedmont Atlantic Megaregion (PAM), *Journal of Transport Geography,* **24**, pp 432–42

Dablanc, L, Rouhier, J, Lazarevic, N, Klauenberg, J, Liu, Z, Koning, M, Kelli de Oliveira, L, Combes, F, Coulombel, N, Gardrat, N, Blanquart, C, Heitz, A and Seidel, S (2018) CITYLAB Deliverable 2.1, Observatory of Strategic Developments Impacting Urban Logistics (2018 version), European Commission, p 242

De Lara, J (2013) Goods movement and metropolitan inequality, in *Cities, Regions and Flows,* ed PV Hall and M Hesse, pp 93–110, Routledge, Abingdon

Debrie, J and Heitz, A (2017) La question logistique dans l'aménagement de l'Île-de-France: formulation d'un enjeu métropolitain versus absence de concrétisation dans les projets urbains? *Géographie, économie, société,* **19** (1), pp 55–73

Direction Régionale et Interdépartementale de l'Equipement et de l'Aménagement (DRIEA) (2018) Les dynamiques des constructions d'entrepôts dans les franges, les couronnes et le pourtour de l'Île-de-France (1980–2014), DRIEA, SCEP/DADDT, Paris

Diziain, D, Rippert, C and Dablanc, L (2012) How can we bring logistics back into cities? The case of Paris Metropolitan Area, *Procedia – Social and Behavioral Sciences*, pp 267–81

Du, J and Bergqvist, R (2010) Developing a conceptual framework of international logistics centres, 12th CTR, p 28

Gilli, F and Offner, J-M (2009) *Paris, Métropole Hors les Murs: Aménager et Gouverner un Grand Paris*, Presses de Sciences Po, Paris

Giuliano, G (2007) The Changing Landscape of Transportation Decision Making, Thomas B Deen Distinguished Lecture, Transportation Research Board 2007 Annual Meeting

Gordon, P and Richardson, H (2001) The sprawl debate: let markets plan, *Publius,* **31** (3), pp 131–49

Halbert, L and Attuyer, K (2016) Introduction: The financialisation of urban production: conditions, mediations and transformations, *Urban Studies*, **53** (7), pp 1347–61

Hall, PV and Hesse, M (ed) (2013) *Cities, Regions and Flows*, Routledge, Abingdon

Heitz, A (2017) La Métropole Logistique, structures métropolitaines et enjeux d'aménagement. La dualisation des espaces logistiques métropolitains, PhD Thesis, Université Paris-Est

Heitz, A, Launay, P and Beziat, A (2017) Rethinking data collection on logistics facilities: new approach for measuring the location of warehouses and terminals in metropolitan areas, *Transportation Research Record: Journal of the Transportation Research Board*, **2609**, pp 67–76

Hesse, M (2004) Land for logistics: locational dynamics, real estate markets and political regulation of regional distribution complexes, *Tijdschrift voor Economische en Sociale Geografie*, **95** (2), pp 162–73

Hesse, M (2008) *The City as a Terminal. The urban context of logistics and freight transport*, Ashgate, Aldershot

Hills, R and Schleicher, D (2010) The steep costs of using noncumulative zoning to preserve land for urban manufacturing, *The University of Chicago Law Review*, pp 249–73

Higgins, C, Ferguson, M and Kanaroglou, PS (2012) Varieties of logistics centers. Developing standardized typology and hierarchy, *Transportation Research Record: Journal of the Transportation Research Board*, **2288**, pp 9–18

Lee, B and Gordon, P (2007) Urban spatial structure and economic growth in U.S. metropolitan areas, Western Regional Science Association 46th Annual Meeting, Newport Beach, California, February

Magnan, M (2016) La production et la gestion de l'espace portuaire à vocation industrielle et logistique. Les grands ports maritimes français: gestionnaires d'espaces infrastructurels, PhD Thesis, Université Paris 1

Pierson, P (2000) Increasing returns, path dependence, and the study of politics, *American Political Science Review*, **94** (2), pp 251–67

Raimbault, N (2014) Gouverner le développement logistique de la métropole: périurbanisation, planification et compétition métropolitaines, PhD Thesis, Université Paris-Est

Raimbault, N (2016) Ancrer le capital dans les flux logistiques: la financiarisation de l'immobilier logistique, *Revue d'Economie Régionale et Urbaine*, **1**, pp 131–54

Raimbault, N (2017) Le développement logistique des grandes périphéries métropolitaines: régimes (péri-)urbains et privatisation silencieuse de la production des espaces logistiques, *Métropoles*, **21** [Online] http://journals.openedition.org/metropoles/5564

Savy, M (2006) Logistique et territoire, *La documentation française*, p 63

Notes

1. With permission of Armand Colin publishers, this chapter uses parts of Chapter 11 of *La Métropole Logistique* (Dablanc and Frémont, 2015). We thank Armand Colin for their kind authorization.
2. MPO: Metropolitan Planning Organization.
3. '(...) [No] private property [shall] be taken for public use, without just compensation' (Fifth Amendment to the US Constitution).
4. The authors mention, in their article, that they are both residents of a newly gentrified area of Brooklyn with some remaining industrial activities, which may also explain part of their position.
5. ARC: Atlanta Regional Commission.
6. www.sandag.org/uploads/2050RTP/F2050rtp_all.pdf
7. In France since 2014, metropolitan authorities are authorized to implement land use zoning instead of municipalities. But very few metropolitan authorities have adopted a truly metropolitan land use strategy, preferring to piece together municipal land use plans.
8. These facilities, in the northern (Garonor) and the southern (Sogaris) suburbs, were designed as the two main gateways for goods bound for the capital.

These two freight villages still exist today, and continue to serve the city of Paris as well as the Paris region but with very different functions from what was initially planned (Sogaris, 1997). Geographically, they are now located in inner dense suburbs.

9 Sénart new town is made up of 10 municipalities.

10 Source: Sit@del2 database, French Ministry for the Ecological and Inclusive Transition. This database is a collection of information on the construction of housing and non-domestic premises (information on building permits, demolition permits and preliminary declarations).

11 Source: Synthèse du Contrat de Développement Territorial de Sénart (2013).

12 The market leaders are Prologis (United States), Global Logistic Properties (GLP, Singapore), Goodman (Australia) and Segro (United Kingdom).

13 Val Bréon is an intermunicipal district of 15,000 inhabitants and 10 municipalities about 50 kilometres east of Paris.

14 In 2000, nearly 70 per cent of the working population of Henry County commuted to another county.

The dualism of urban freight distribution 05

City vs suburban logistics

SÖNKE BEHRENDS AND JEAN-PAUL RODRIGUE

Introduction

As the world continues to urbanize, the paradoxes between urban freight efficiency and urban sustainability are getting more significant. Demographic trends underline that from 1990 to 2015, the urban population increased from 2.3 billion people (43 per cent of world's population) to 4 billion, accounting for 54 per cent of the world's population. As urbanization and overall growth of the world's population is projected to continue, this figure is expected to rise to 66 per cent by the middle of this century (UN Habitat, 2016). This demographic trend is clearly linked with growing urban freight flows for production and consumption. Furthermore, there are behavioural shifts in consumption patterns with e-commerce growing significantly accounting in 2015 for 8.4 per cent of all retail sales in Europe and 12.7 per cent in the United States (CRR, 2016). This trend results in a growing number of urban freight flows in the form of home deliveries of parcels.

In response, cities around the world have engaged in extensive experimentation to manage the challenges of city logistics. They include, for instance, the usage of alternative vehicles and modes, off-peak deliveries and the setting of distribution facilities better placed to support urban deliveries (MDS Transmodal, 2012). A substantial body of research has emerged to address the dilemma of environmental impacts and efficiency of urban freight transport (NCFRP, 2013). Yet, most of these approaches focus on one particular dimension of urban freight movements: last mile deliveries to retail stores in central business districts (CBD) or other high-density areas that are the nexus of urban commercial activities. Freight operations in suburban areas, on the other hand, are widely underrepresented in urban freight research as well as in urban transport policy and planning initiatives. This gap is not surprising since it is the high-density central areas, particularly in the CBDs, where the conflicts between efficient logistics and impacts of freight traffic are the most severe and evident.

However, these freight flows represent a declining share of all freight flows in urban areas, as current urbanization patterns across the world are characterized by urban sprawl and lower density-based suburbanization (UN Habitat, 2016). Suburbia in advanced economies, is typically characterized by higher income households in single detached houses with the private automobile use as a dominant mode of commute (Moos and Mendez, 2015). It remains important as an urban development paradigm and is well documented as a prevailing element of the urban spatial structure (eg Mieszkowski and Mills, 1993). What is less considered are the new forms of urban freight distribution that suburbia has created. Urban freight policy actions and research therefore pay little consideration to a substantial share of urban freight activity and only address a small part of urban freight challenges.

In this chapter, it is argued that, given the enduring trend of suburbanization, urban freight distribution may require a new focus that complements the conventional perspective. Does suburban logistics warrant a distinct dimension of urban freight transport policy and research?

Placing city and suburban logistics in their context

Urban freight is a multifaceted and complex activity, particularly since it involves diverse freight flows generated and attracted by a variety of land uses. Thus, there are two key factors affecting city and suburban logistics: first, the various forms of urban freight flows serving different urban supply chains; and second, the urban spatial setting in which they take place. By combining these factors, the fundamental differences between city and suburban logistics can be derived.

Types of urban freight flows

Cities are places of consumption, production and distribution of material goods. Urban freight distribution includes all activities ensuring that the material demands of these activities are satisfied. As a city hosts a large number of different economic sectors, it is provisioned by a multitude of different supply chains, making urban logistics very complex, diverse and not prone to generalization. However, each economic activity taking place in an urban environment can be associated with a specific freight generation profile, which is relatively consistent from one city to another (Dablanc, 2011), even though cities throughout the world differ in terms of size, geographical conditions, history, economy, cultural and political values. The following categories of urban logistics with common transport characteristics can be identified:

- **Delivery to retail stores.** Urban areas host a wide range of retail facilities, which are responsible for the bulk of urban delivery activity. From a logistics perspective, two types of retailers with different goods supply systems can be distinguished. The first one is **chain retailing**, which is served by centralized supply systems. The large retail chain stores are making use of consolidated deliveries in larger vehicles on a scheduled basis, which helps to limit the number of deliveries required. The second group involves small and medium-sized **independent specialist stores**. Their logistics differ significantly from the major retail chains in the organization of deliveries, as they are not served through centralized distribution systems. Supply is usually organized directly by their diverse suppliers, often using their own-account vehicles. As a result, independent specialist stores can receive significantly more deliveries than chain stores and are therefore responsible for considerable freight vehicle activity (Cherrett *et al*, 2012; Dablanc, 2011).
- **Courier, express and parcel services** (CEP) are one of the fastest-growing urban transport businesses owing to e-commerce. Courier and express services deal with the fast transport of documents and lighter parcels with additional value-added services, while parcel services focus on heavier parcels up to 30 kilograms (MDS Transmodal, 2012). CEP operators maintain a global network of logistical facilities where shipments are consolidated for delivery tours in urban areas using large vans or small to medium-sized trucks.
- One segment of the parcel business is **home deliveries.** While conventional retail channels are composed of two trips, that is a delivery from

a distribution centre to a retail outlet and a consumer shopping trip from a retail outlet to a residential home, home deliveries include a single trip from a DC to residential areas. Online shopping has grown significantly and represented, in 2015, 8.4 per cent of all retail sales in Europe and 12.7 per cent in the United States (CRR, 2016). Home deliveries are challenging operations characterized by high delivery failures, empty trip rates and a lack of critical mass in areas with limited demand, resulting in high distribution cost and emissions (Gevaers *et al*, 2011).

- **Consumer shopping trips.** The products sold in retail stores are usually brought home by consumers on their own account, using passenger cars, public transit or walking and cycling. These consumer shopping trips, including the trip to the retail outlet to purchase the product and the trip to transport it home, can be responsible for a significant share of the freight transport energy used in the supply chain from raw material sources to retail outlet, depending on the mode of transport, the quantity of goods transported and the trip distance attributable to shopping (Browne *et al*, 2006). Further, these trips are often chained with other purposes, underlining their complexity (Ye *et al*, 2007).
- **Food deliveries** are a significant generator of urban freight traffic. The food service industry prepares and delivers food and beverages for hotels, bars and restaurants, canteens and catering. The final customers often require specific services presenting different logistics and organizational constraints for these distribution channels, which are often referred to as cold chain logistics (Morganti and González-Feliu, 2015). The sector is generally characterized by unpredictability, and hence orders are generally very small and deliveries are often required on a just-in-time basis, which leads to frequent deliveries (MDS Transmodal, 2012). An emerging market that combines parcel and food deliveries is the home delivery of fresh food.
- **Industrial and terminal haulage.** Cities are not only places of consumption but also places of production and distribution. Production facilities are often elements of global supply chains, sourcing parts from suppliers and distributing intermediate and finished goods. These facilities are commonly found in proximity to ports, airports and rail terminals, which are transit points to regional or global transport networks. Industrial and terminal haulage thus generates freight flows that are not necessarily related to local consumption, but which overlap with city logistics activities.

Figure 5.1 Types of urban freight flows and freight clusters

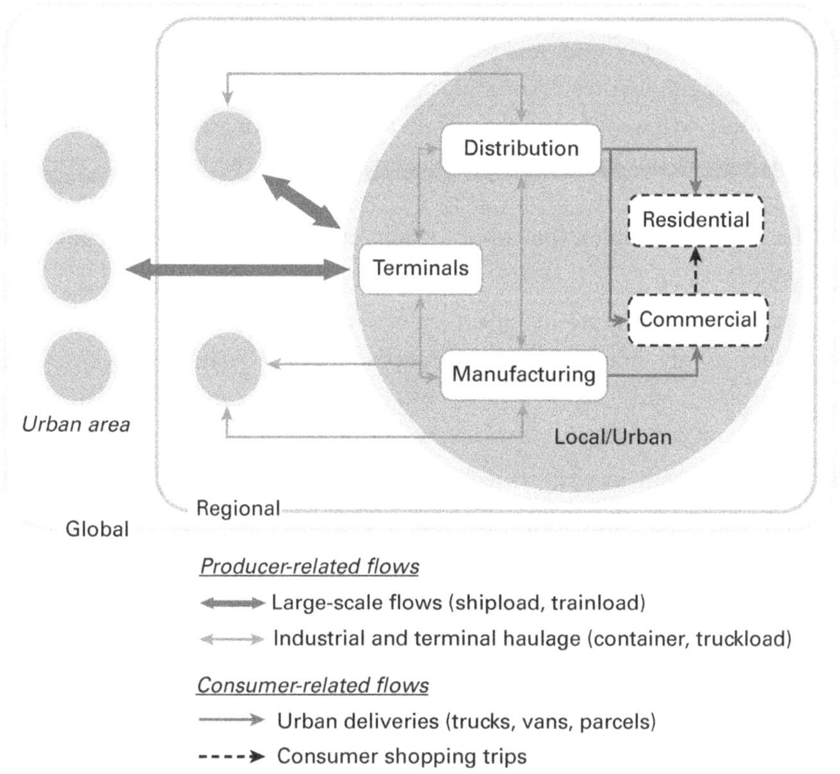

The distribution activities of urban freight flows take many different forms, which can be clustered in two main functional classes of urban freight distribution (Figure 5.1): producer-related distribution and consumer-related distribution (Rodrigue, 2013). **Producer-related distribution** includes two types of flow. The first is large-scale flows, such as interregional and global freight flows in large-scale transport modes such as vessels and trains. The second flow is industrial and terminal haulage, which usually comes in unit loads such as containers and trailers, originating from or destined for terminals, production or distribution facilities within the urban area. **Consumer-related distribution** includes intra-urban freight flows, usually as part loads and parcels originating from distribution facilities and destined for commercial facilities or residential households, as well as private shopping trips from retail outlets to residential areas. These forms of urban logistics are usually clustered in certain areas, resulting in five major types of specialized freight generators (Rodrigue, 2017):

- **Terminals**, such as ports, airports and rail terminals, are transit points of freight flows to local, regional or global transport networks (gateways). Terminals handle a wide variety of freight, that is bulk, containers, full truckloads (TLs) and less-than-truckloads (LTLs). The hinterland of terminals can involve destinations (distribution centres and manufacturing sites) within the city area itself or flows having to transit through urban areas on their way to other destinations. The impact of a transport terminal on the urban area is obviously related to the intensity of the terminal activity, the supply chains it services and the extent of its hinterland.
- **Manufacturing areas** include production facilities often consisting of global supply chains producing intermediate goods and finished goods. They are mainly generators of unit loads, for example containers or truckloads involving all forms of road traffic.
- **Logistics zones** include distribution facilities, such as warehouses and distribution centres, where distribution activities are carried out, which includes consolidation, deconsolidation, cross-docking and storage. These facilities generate unit loads (containers and truck loads) originating from manufacturing districts or terminals.
- **Commercial districts** are zones hosting retail facilities that are the destination of the bulk of urban deliveries through LTLs. Commercial zones also include the clustering of office towers and large institutions (seats of government, universities, museums, etc) that generate a high demand of parcel deliveries.
- **Residential areas** are the place of consumption; hence they are the destination of the bulk of private shopping trips by car and transit as well as home deliveries from e-commerce activities.

Urban freight flows, like most freight flows, are imbalanced in their reciprocity. This is particularly the case for consumer-related flows that are usually unidirectional and have empty backhauls. For instance, retail deliveries (most commonly from distribution centres) are one-way freight flows with the delivery vehicle returning empty or with small loads of returned goods or recyclables (eg empty boxes). Commercial to residential freight flows almost exclusively involve consumers carrying their purchases from stores to their place of residence. Because urban freight flows differ in terms of flow sizes and balance, the flows differ significantly in terms of vehicle operations and externalities that they impose on cities, where space constraints and emission impacts are most severe. The freight flows with high space consumption are shopping trips by car (parking space) and large-scale flows (land use of terminals). Therefore, depending on the setting in which these flows take place their externalities will vary.

The spatial pattern of urban freight flows

The urban spatial structure describes the distribution of population and employment density within an urban area, which can be categorized by its level of centralization. Scholars generally distinguish between monocentric and polycentric structures. The classic monocentric approach (Alonso, 1964; Mills, 1967; Muth, 1969) conceptualizes the city as a circular residential area surrounding one CBD where all the employment is concentrated. The more recent polycentric approach assumes the existence of more than one centre, that is a number of employment and population centres of higher density, clustered some distance away around a CBD (Anas *et al*, 1998). Until the 1970s, the monocentric city model was the dominant paradigm for analysing the internal structure of cities, but against the background of rapid and complex urban change resulting in city structures with multiple employment centres, the model became increasingly deficient for describing modern cities. One empirical consistency, which can be observed between cities worldwide, is that density declines with distance from their established centres (Anas *et al*, 1998). Hence, the urban spatial structure is usually divided into high-density areas and low-density areas with the transition between both commonly evident in the urban landscape.

Population density is also a crucial determinant for the environmental impact of transport operations, for example externalities increase with the number of people being exposed to air pollutants or noise (Bickel and Friedrich, 2004). Hence, the externalities of comparable transport operations are significantly higher in high-density areas than in low-density areas. For example, it was estimated that on average the external costs of particle emissions in urban areas (>1,500 inhabitants/km^2) are approximately 4 times higher than in suburban areas (>300 inhabitants/km^2) and 10 times higher than in ex-urban areas (<300 inhabitants/km^2) (RICARDO AEA, 2014).

These characteristics of the urban spatial structure have implications for urban freight distribution as their preconditions differ between central, suburban and ex-urban areas. **Central areas** (often referred to as CBD or 'City') are the most accessible part of the urban area. There is a high level of competition for a limited amount of urban space, and consequently land values are highest. Central areas are usually characterized by a high level of spatial accumulation of commercial, administrative and cultural activities, and are therefore the destinations of the bulk of urban deliveries. Traffic density is high and congestion widespread, which is particularly reinforced in the context of narrow streets and designated pedestrian zones or streets, which are dedicated to public transport only. Central areas are also very sensitive to traffic noise, accident risks and air pollution due to population density and increasing demands on an attractive urban environment. High-density areas impose a limit to the freight intensity of activities because of high land cost and congestion.

Compared to central areas, **suburban areas** have lower levels of accumulation of urban activities, offering higher availability of land with lower rent values. As suburban areas offer accessibility to markets (the urban core as well as neighbouring suburban areas), they are highly conducive to logistics activities by permitting higher levels of freight intensity. There are generally more residential and fewer commercial activities in suburban areas, which are commonly multi-centric with clusters of production and distribution activities as well as large terminal facilities (ports, airports, rail). Suburbia handles the majority of the interface between the urban area and national as well as global freight networks, but also large flows of urban deliveries originate here. Due to a lower density, suburban areas are less sensitive to traffic externalities. Distribution is highly reliant on road transport, as there are limited opportunities for alternative forms of distribution. Parking difficulties are rarer and streets wider so that heavy trucks are able to circulate on most of the major roads (Rodrigue, 2017).

The areas beyond the suburbs of a city are commonly defined as **ex-urban areas**. In these low-density areas, the predominant land use is residential. Freight demand and sensitivity to traffic externalities are low.

The dualism of urban freight: city vs suburban logistics

A prevalent perspective concerning urban planning is that higher densities are preferable since they generate various economies and are perceived to be a suitable goal towards more sustainable cities, particularly in terms of public transit use. However, from a freight distribution perspective density is associated with several diseconomies, including congestion and higher levels of energy consumption and emissions (Rodrigue *et al*, 2017). Hence, urban freight can be considered as a dualism, which is driven by urban density. To clarify matters, it is argued that urban freight distribution is composed of city logistics and suburban logistics settings:

- **City logistics** involves consumer-related freight flows in high-density urban areas, including both commercial distribution as well as private consumer shopping trips to and from retail stores in these high-density central areas. It captures the 'low hanging fruit' of urban freight distribution, since in these high-density areas parking along the streets is limited and distribution vehicles often double-park. The challenges of urban freight distribution, such as congestion and environmental externalities, are salient in central areas while at the same time opportunities for using load consolidation and alternative modes to road transport are most prevalent.
- **Suburban logistics** involves urban freight distribution taking place in low and medium-density urban areas. It includes the whole range of urban freight flows, both consumer-related and producer-related distribution. There are generally more residential and fewer commercial activities in suburban areas, which are commonly multi-centric with clusters of production, distribution activities, terminal facilities (ports, airports, rail) as well as commercial activities (office space and shopping malls). Constraints from congestion and especially parking are usually less prevalent than in high-density areas. Consumer-related distribution is highly reliant on road transport, as there are limited opportunities for alternative forms of distribution.

Figure 5.2 underlines the expected effect of density on unit delivery costs in the respective realms of city and suburban logistics. In low-density areas delivery costs per unit are higher due to the longer delivery distances and lower density of delivery points. The same number of deliveries requires longer distances compared with the same deliveries taking place in more central areas. Mid-range density suburban areas represent a close to ideal environment for deliveries since delivery costs are lower as shorter delivery distances are experienced while very few constraints, particularly parking, are impacting. As density increases constraints are becoming more acute, particularly parking for deliveries, which is commonly the most prevalent city logistics problem. Delivery costs thus increase rapidly in high-density areas. For retailing, higher density is related to higher sales per floor space (which is highly desirable), but also less space is available for storage. This high sales to inventory ratio requires more frequent deliveries where there is usually limited parking and greater competition for the use of road and

Figure 5.2 Relationship between urban density and commercial freight deliveries

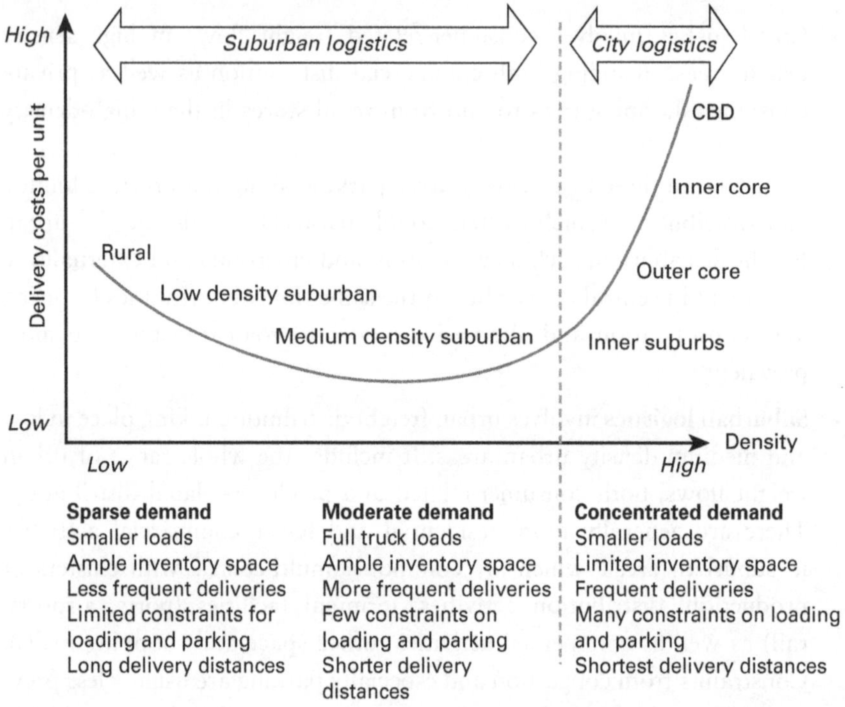

curb space. This requires the usage of smaller delivery vehicles (either by choice or imposed by regulation), which results in more frequent and higher delivery costs. At the highest density, delivery vehicle size may be limited, further increasing trip frequency and cost. This is the main reason why freight distribution in higher density areas commonly requires mitigation strategies and the use of alternative modes.

Factors of divergence between city logistics and suburban logistics

A possible practical implication of the emerging dualism may be a compartmentalization of distribution between central and suburban areas. Traditionally, carriers operate in more or less similar ways and do not develop adapted logistics solutions for specific urban preconditions (Dablanc, 2007). Recently, however, specific logistics distribution strategies emerged to cope with the restrictions of high-density urban areas. Examples of these adapted city logistics distribution concepts include off-hour deliveries (eg in New York City: Holguín-Veras *et al*, 2014), last mile deliveries with small electric vehicles or cargo bikes from urban consolidation centres (eg in the Netherlands: van Rooijen and Quak, 2010; and Copenhagen: Gammelgaard, 2015) or from inner-city mobile depots (eg in Brussels: Verlinde *et al*, 2014). Hence, an implication of emerging dualism may be that carriers develop dual distribution strategies: a city logistics distribution channel with adapted vehicles and operations, and a suburban distribution channel with standard operation procedures. The question remains: which factors are at play inciting the growth of this dualism?

A first factor of divergence between city logistics and suburban logistics can be increasingly constraining policy measures in sensitive high-density urban areas. In order to solve local environmental problems and conflicts with residents, cities frequently use weight/size restrictions, parking regulations and low-emission zones (MDS Transmodal, 2012).

A second factor of divergence can be the current urban planning practices. A dominant perspective in urban planning is that higher densities are preferable as they enable public transit or alternative forms of transportation to more effectively service populations. However, these decisions regarding the newly derived land use designs and patterns associated with smart growth are often disconnected from decisions regarding investment in freight. Smart growth strategies have multiple environmental and social benefits but they also raise demand for goods movement within the urban area (Wygonik *et al*, 2015). Furthermore, trucks may experience slower travel speeds and detours due to the compact land use, dense road network, road-use restrictions resulting from walkable neighbourhood designs, and interference with the increased volumes of pedestrians, bicycles and mixed traffic. Moreover, goods movement patterns will be affected as well in terms of shipment sizes, types of trucks used, pickup and delivery scheduling, or commercial vehicle trip chaining behaviour. There is a strong risk that smart growth strategies could lead to unintended consequences, such as increased congestion, higher logistics costs, parking and safety issues in the short term. In the long run, the freight distribution industry could respond by servicing smart growth neighbourhoods in a less efficient and reliable manner, resulting in higher costs for some goods (eg grocery goods). This could reshape freight distribution and logistics patterns at the local, regional and even global scales, which may not always be in an efficient way.

Figure 5.3 Logistics facilities supporting e-commerce

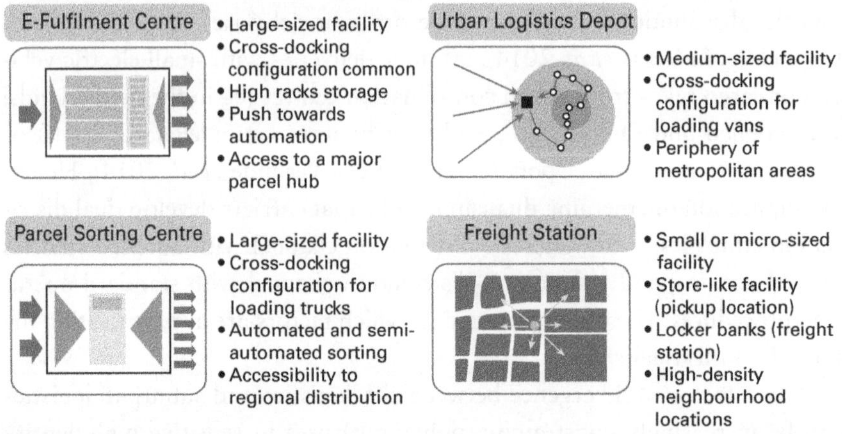

SOURCE adapted from LaSalle, 2013

Finally, another factor contributing to divergence is related to the emergence of e-commerce. Since e-commerce is the fastest growing segment of urban freight, the scaling up of home deliveries taking place in a variety of density and socio-economic settings could lead to a divergence as different strategies in high-density and low-density areas are observed. High-density areas create benefits of consolidation due to higher loads and concentrated demand, while low-density areas that offer higher accessibility and fewer parking constraints are prone to the benefits of lower delivery cost. The introduction of autonomous delivery vehicles such as drones and delivery robots may be more suitable in a suburban setting owing to their smaller capacity. Another factor of divergence is the observed difference in delivery requirements, as urban residents are significantly more inclined to same-day or instant deliveries than rural residents (Joerses *et al*, 2016). These differences may further induce dual distribution strategies as e-commerce provides additional impetus to the divergence between urban and suburban logistics. This is particularly noticeable in the locational behaviour of the logistics facilities supporting e-commerce (see Figure 5.3).

Conclusions

This chapter attempted to conceptualize city logistics and suburban logistics as two distinct forms of urban freight distribution involving two very different functional and operational characteristics. It was therefore argued that urban freight distribution can be considered as a dualism. Several questions arising from the emerging dualism remain, which present further research directions. To begin with, since density is a fundamental discerning factor in the operational characteristics of city logistics, it is important to identify density thresholds for this dualism. Medium-density suburban areas represent a close to ideal environment for deliveries, while delivery costs increase rapidly in high-density areas, inciting the development of divergent distribution strategies. There is a need for empirical research to investigate potential threshold levels for this divergence in a sample of urban settings.

Moreover, is the dualism only relevant in large metropolitan areas like New York (Manhattan), Paris (within the ring road), Tokyo or London (within the congestion pricing zone), or can it be observed also in medium-sized urban areas? An additional issue for further research is the form that the divergent distribution strategies may take. Will the expected dualism involve different operations, vehicles and modes depending on whether city or suburban logistics are involved? Will it have implications on costs and reliability or will it simply be functional? Finally, there is a need to understand the relevance of urban policies, that is regulations and planning decisions, for the emerging dualism. It has been argued that density and regulations are two possible dimensions that drive the divergence between suburban and city logistics distribution strategies. In cases where regulations drive the divergence, it is suggested that future studies should investigate the level of burden that is imposed on carriers and what unintended consequences may result from it.

Acknowledgements

This work was supported by the Volvo Research and Educational Foundations [EP-2014-09, COE-2012-01].

References

Alonso, W (1964) *Location and Land Use: Towards a general theory of land rent*, Harvard University Press, Cambridge, MA

Anas, A, Arnott, R and Small, KA (1998) Urban spatial structure, *Journal of Economic Literature*, **36**, pp 1426–64

Bickel, P and Friedrich, R (2004) *ExternE: Externalities of energy: Methodology 2005 update*, EUR-OP

Browne, M, Allen, J and Rizet, C (2006) Assessing transport energy consumption in two product supply chains, *International Journal of Logistics Research and Applications,* **9**, pp 237–52

Cherrett, T, Allen, J, McLeod, F *et al* (2012) Understanding urban freight activity – key issues for freight planning, *Journal of Transport Geography,* **24**, pp 22–32

CRR (2016) *Online Retailing: Britain, Europe, US and Canada 2015* [Online] http://www.retailresearch.org/onlineretailing.php

Dablanc, L (2007) Goods transport in large European cities: difficult to organize, difficult to modernize, *Transportation Research Part A: Policy and Practice,* **41**, pp 280–85

Dablanc, L (2011) City distribution, a key problem for the urban economy: guidelines for practitioners, in *City Distribution and Urban Freight Transport,* ed C Macharis and S Melo, Edward Elgar, Cheltenham

Gammelgaard, B (2015) The emergence of city logistics: the case of Copenhagen's Citylogistik-kbh, *International Journal of Physical Distribution & Logistics Management,* **45**, pp 333–51

Gevaers, R, van de Voorde, E and Vanelslander, T (2011) Characteristics and typology of last-mile logistics from an innovation perspective in an urban context, in *City Distribution and Urban Freight Transport,* ed C Macharis and S Melo, Edward Elgar, Cheltenham

Holguín-Veras, J, Wang, C, Browne, M *et al* (2014) The New York City off-hour delivery project: lessons for city logistics, *Procedia – Social and Behavioral Sciences,* **125**, pp 36–48

Joerses, M, Schröder, J, Neuhaus, F *et al* (2016) *Parcel Delivery: The future of last mile,* McKinsey & Company

LaSalle, JL (2013) E-commerce boom triggers transformation in retail logistics: Driving a global wave of demand for new logistics facilities, White Paper

MDS Transmodal (2012) DG MOVE European Commission: Study on Urban Freight Transport, Brussels

Mieszkowski, P and Mills, ES (1993) The causes of metropolitan suburbanization, *The Journal of Economic Perspectives,* **7**, pp 135–47

Mills, ES (1967) An aggregative model of resource allocation in a metropolitan area, *The American Economic Review,* **57**, pp 197–210

Moos, M and Mendez, P (2015) Suburban ways of living and the geography of income: how homeownership, single-family dwellings and automobile use define the metropolitan social space, *Urban Studies,* **52**, pp 1864–82

Morganti, E and González-Feliu, J (2015) City logistics for perishable products. The case of the Parma Food Hub, *Case Studies on Transport Policy,* **3**, pp 120–28

Muth, R (1969) Cities and housing: the spatial patterns of urban residential land use, *University of Chicago, Chicago,* **4**, pp 114–23

NCFRP (2013) *Synthesis of Freight Research in Urban Transportation Planning,* Transportation Research Board

RICARDO AEA (2014) Update of the Handbook on External Costs of Transport – Final report for the European Commission: DG-MOVE

Rodrigue, J-P (2013) Urban goods transport, in *Planning and Design for Sustainable Urban Mobility: Global report on human settlements 2013*, ed United Nations Human Settlements Programme (UN-Habitat), pp 57–74, Routledge, New York

Rodrigue, J-P (2017) *The Geography of Transport Systems,* 4th edn, Routledge, New York

Rodrigue, J-P, Dablanc, L and Giuliano, G (2017) The freight landscape: convergence and divergence in urban freight distribution, *Journal of Transport and Land Use,* **10**, pp 557–72

UN Habitat (2016) Urbanization and development: emerging futures; world cities report 2016, UN Habitat, Nairobi

van Rooijen, T and Quak, H (2010) Local impacts of a new urban consolidation centre – the case of Binnenstadservice.nl, *Procedia – Social and Behavioral Sciences,* **2**, pp 5967–79

Verlinde, S, Macharis, C, Milan, L *et al* (2014) Does a mobile depot make urban deliveries faster, more sustainable and more economically viable: results of a pilot test in Brussels, *Transportation Research Procedia,* **4**, pp 361–73

Wygonik, E, Bassok, A, Goodchild, A *et al* (2015) Smart growth and goods movement: emerging research agendas, *Journal of Urbanism: International Research on Placemaking and Urban Sustainability,* **8**, pp 115–32

Ye, X, Pendyala, RM and Gottardi, G (2007) An exploration of the relationship between mode choice and complexity of trip chaining patterns, *Transportation Research Part B: Methodological,* **41**, pp 96–113

Port cities and urban logistics 06

MICHAEL BROWNE AND JOHAN WOXENIUS

Introduction

Cities and metropolitan areas serve a wide variety of functions. Those cities that have a port function may be subject to significant increases in traffic flows (Allen *et al*, 2012; Woxenius, 2016). Thus, in recent years port activities have at times been viewed as a problem by those responsible for traffic planning in the city with which the port is connected (Olsson *et al*, 2016).

This chapter considers the port–city interactions over time and highlights how these have changed. A new phase of these interactions may be at hand with significant implications for urban freight movements. Ports' strategies are constantly evolving and port managers seek to make better use of the port's assets. One of the main assets is land and here there are some emerging trends that have important implications for the port–city interface. In addition, city authorities are increasingly looking for opportunities to use non-road modes for some of the movements of goods to, from and possibly within their cities. Cities that are connected to a port have some interesting opportunities in this area. These developments imply a new period of more intense port–city interaction.

The research is exploratory and considers journal papers that provide insights into the port–city interface and the hinterland transport issues, and reports and other grey literature from a sample of ports that highlight changes in planning and policy with regard to land use that is under the control of (or can be influenced by) the port authority.

The chapter is structured as follows: in section two port–city developments and the port–city interface are discussed; section three considers the implications for traffic and land use; while section four summarizes two important initiatives that are relevant to the port–city interface involving land use planning and the use of non-road transport. Section four contains a short case study of Gothenburg to illustrate the impact and potential for these developments to lead to greater port–city interactions. The final section contains the conclusion.

Port–city development stages and the port–city interface

When ports develop, so do the surrounding cities and, of course, also the port–city interaction. Hoyle (1968) and Hayuth (1982) were among the early researchers to comment on and assess this topic resulting in many citations in more recent work. However, a series of studies by the OECD concerning the competitiveness of global sea-ports (Merk, 2014) and the international port-city organization AIVP's edited book *Port-City Governance* (AIVP, 2014) and its conferences added much momentum to the field. Journals and other publications – see, for example, del Saz-Salazar and García-Menéndez (2016); Tichavska and Tovar (2015); Dooms *et al* (2015); Fenton (2015) – have helped to establish the field as a topic of applied research.

The size of the port in relation to the size of the city is central to port–city interface studies. Ducruet and Lee (2006) illustrate this in a matrix based on 'Centrality', an urban functional measure, and 'Intermediacy', a maritime-based measure (see Figure 6.1).

Hayuth (1982) used the term port–urban interface and Hoyle (1989) described the interface as:

> a geographical line of demarcation between port-owned land and urban zones, or an area of transition between port land uses and urban land uses. Equally, an interface may be conceptualized as an interactive economic system, especially in terms of employment structures; or as an area of integration in transport terms or of conflict in policy formulation and implementation.
>
> Hoyle (1989, p 1)

As both ports and port cities are dynamic phenomena, port-cities' characters often move within the matrix over time. Reasons behind such changes include developments in industry, trade, port competition, port and infrastructure investments as well as policy on national, regional and local levels. Merk (2014) presents a table that goes beyond the matrix in Figure 6.1, considering the question of how the port and the city may grow or shrink. To capture this development over time, Ducruet and Lee (2006) adopt a sine-like curve (see Figure 6.2).

Figure 6.1 A matrix of port–city relations

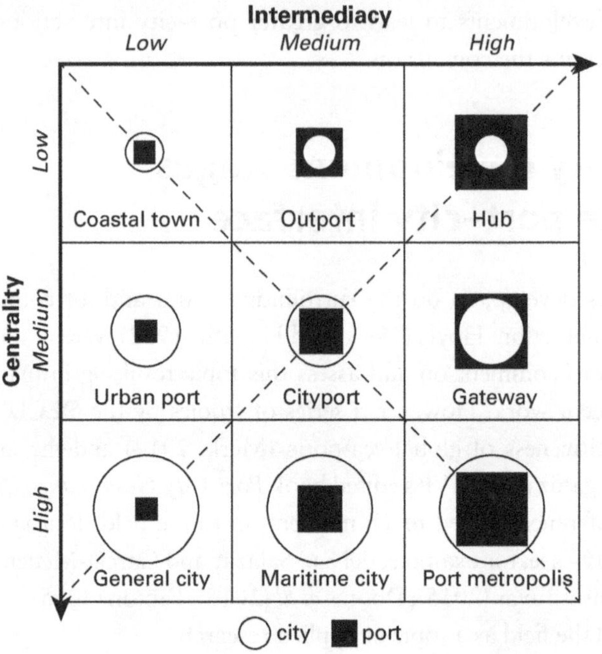

SOURCE Ducruet and Lee, 2006

Figure 6.2 Port–city spatial and functional evolution

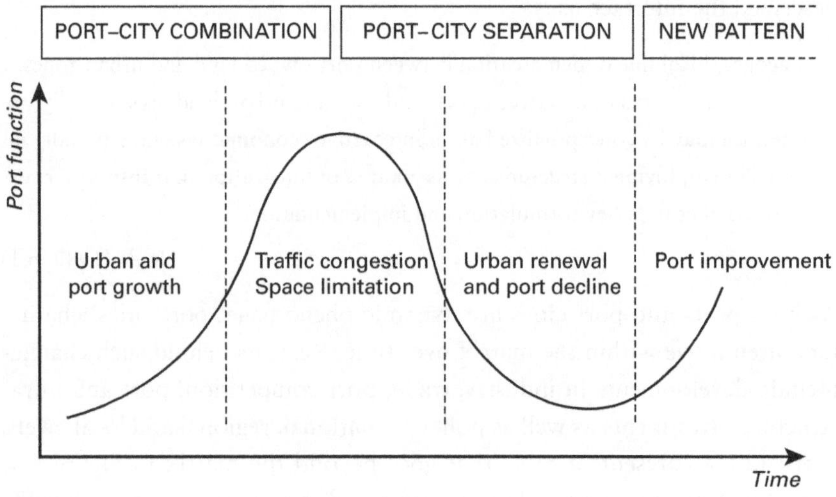

SOURCE Ducruet and Lee, 2006

Dramatic changes in world trade in the post-war years resulted in saturation in city-centre ports. In the **Port–city combination** era, with simultaneous **Urban and port growth**, shipping lines used break-bulk ships and flexible general cargo ships for manual stowage of units such as pallets, slings, nets, piles, sacks and drums. Loading and unloading was very labour intensive and ships could be in port for weeks. Finger pier construction and the use of larger dockside warehouses alleviated but did not solve the problem. Major technological developments were needed and with the coming of larger and more specialized ships (for many different types of cargo) the era of **Port-city separation** began. However, it was the advent of containerization with standardized load units and much improved mechanical handling that finally overcame the problems of the port as the bottleneck for general cargo. Also container handling required new port areas with straight quays, vast container stacking surfaces as well as new highways and railway lines.

With a surrounding city, the new areas were often found closer to the ocean for the many older ports established a bit upstream in rivers, such as London, Bremen and Gothenburg, but many container ports are still located within cities (Hall and Jacobs, 2012) as they have continued to grow around the port. In many cities, shipyards also abandoned vast downtown areas ready for **Urban renewal** – see, for example, Hayuth (1982); McCalla (1983); Hoyle (1989) and (2001); Merk (2014); Wang (2014). Ducruet and Lee (2006) combine the urban development phase with **port decline**, but most large ports actually saw growing volumes at their new sites due to increased trade and productivity gains. This was, however, difficult to comprehend by the citizens and even by many local policymakers. Attempting to generalize upon the development, Hoyle (1989) describes five stages of the port–city interface.

Written much later, Ducruet and Lee (2006) observed that many port cities, entered a **New pattern** era with a **Port improvement** phase. One way was to add services to the port portfolio, including distribution warehousing, advanced logistics and auxiliary services in new stakeholder constellations (Pettit and Beresford, 2009). This development has strengthened over the last 10 years.

Traffic and land use issues arising from the port–city interface

Road transport to and from ports adds severely to congestion affecting the sustainability of port cities in terms of economy by, for example, lost working time, capital cost for goods and higher fuel expenses, environment through unnecessary emissions, as well as social welfare through noise and reduced mobility. Port-related road traffic affects citizens severely causing DePillis (2015) to denote ports 'the new power plants' in terms of a non-wanted neighbour.

In some cases, however, it seems that policymakers overestimate the contribution of port traffic to urban freight flows, as analysed by the World Bank (2017) in the case of Mombasa, as parts of this traffic has an origin or destination at industries located in the proximity of the port but not related to maritime transport. Much port traffic is nevertheless still moved on city streets and roads on its hinterland journey and this causes problems for the city that is connected or near to the port. Many port cities (eg Los Angeles/Long Beach, Rotterdam, Southampton and Gothenburg) have accordingly made major efforts to shift port-related traffic to non-road modes (van den Berg, 2015). Usually this has meant the shift of movements from road to rail but it can also include opportunities for waterborne transport in the capillary parts of the route (Roso *et al*, 2015).

In a study on freight transport and urban form Allen *et al* (2012) demonstrated that major freight generating or transshipment points located within the urban area (such as a large freight-handling sea port in the case of Bristol and Southampton) can result in an urban area attracting truck movements from remote locations. The research considered 14 cities in the United Kingdom, and Southampton and Bristol (both of which have large ports relative to the size of the city) had significantly higher levels of tonnes lifted per square metre of commercial and industrial floorspace than the other cities (which included London where the major port activity is outside the metropolitan boundary). Road freight activity in Southampton measured in tonnes lifted, was 10 tonnes per square metre of commercial and industrial floorspace and Bristol was 8 tonnes compared with an average of less than 4 tonnes for the other 12 cities. Vehicle kilometres performed by heavy goods vehicles on journeys to, from and within these two cities were also considerably higher than for the other 12 cities (160 vehicle kilometres per square metre of commercial and industrial floorspace in Southampton compared with an average of 50).

Alongside the development of strategies to deal with port-related traffic in port cities there has also been an increase in the development of distribution property near ports – in part as a result of increased interests in 'port-centric' logistics but also as port authorities seek new sources of revenue. Being landlord for warehouses is not so different from being landlord for port facilities.

Developments influencing the port–city interface

Ports are changing and the views of city policymakers about ports are also changing. The trend towards port-centric logistics (Monios *et al*, 2018) has influenced thinking among policymakers and highlighted the role the port can play in bringing employment to the city region in which it is located. In addition, cities are searching for ways to increase the non-road options for freight movements to, from and possibly within the city. The role of ports could be important here. Referring to Figure 6.3, it could be argued that a sixth stage is developing in which there will be a reintegration of the interests of the city and the port. This change will, however, also lead to tensions since the size of the port is very significant in terms of land use and the behaviour is a complicated mix between public and private. Two developments are relevant to this discussion:

- land use planning decisions by port authorities and port cities that have led to increased focus on distribution property near ports;
- scope to use waterway links for urban freight which then connects to the role of ports as part of the urban logistics system.

Figure 6.3 Port–city evolution focusing on the waterfront

STAGE	SYMBOL ○ city ● port	PERIOD	CHARACTERISTICS
I Primitive port/city		Ancient/medieval to 19th century	Close spatial and functional association between city and port
II Expanding port/city		19th–early 20th century	Rapid commercial/industrial growth forces port to develop beyond city confines, with linear quays and break-bulk industries
III Modern industrial port/city		mid-20th century	Industrial growth (especially oil refining) and introduction of containers/ro-ro require separation/space
IV Retreat from the waterfront		1960s–1980s	Changes in maritime technology induce growth of separate maritime industrial development areas
V Redevelopment of the waterfront		1970s–1990s	Large-scale modern port consumes large areas of land/water space, urban renewal of original core

SOURCE Hoyle, 1989

Each of these is reviewed in more detail in the following paragraphs and illustrated in the case of Gothenburg in the next section of this chapter.

Land use planning

With growing population, urbanization and densification, there is increasing competition for land within urban areas surrounding a port. Land use is both direct by the maritime cluster in terms of fenced port terminals, access infrastructure and increasingly also by detached container depots for stuffing and stripping, inspections, repair and empty stacking, road hauliers' facilities, intermodal terminals and warehouses, and indirect by port-dependent industry. In addition, keeping an appropriate safety distance around port terminals and industries, and along infrastructure to limit the effects of accidents with hazardous cargo and disturbance by noise, implies high opportunity costs of land use (Olsson *et al*, 2016). Planning agencies also reserve land around ports and other terminals and along roads and railway lines to safeguard coming expansions of infrastructure.

Land use planning decisions can have a major impact on the nature of the development in and around port cities. In many cases ports have significant influence on land use planning, either attributed to national infrastructure interests or by being important revenue generators for cities owning the ports. Over time many port-related activities have been relocated away from ports – a typical pattern in container transport is for import containers to be transported to the port from inland terminals and export containers to move in the other direction. This means that employment is shifted to such inland locations and, in addition, value-adding services may also be created far away from the port. Many of these changes have been argued to be highly efficient from a logistics perspective, but from the port and port city perspectives this may be seen as a loss of revenue.

To counter this trend ports have begun to focus on the use of land near the port for distribution and logistics activities. This has meant that land which traditionally was reserved for port-related activity becomes available for a wider range of uses – often still with a logistics function but not necessarily with a specific link to the port. The past 10 years has seen a major rise in the demand for large distribution properties in strategic locations (ie with access to good transport infrastructure, main consumer markets and an appropriate workforce).

The impact on the port–city interface is complex. Economic development and job creation has positive impacts. In addition, the scope for products to be stored and distributed from nearer to the city may also have an impact on reducing the distance travelled by products – leading to a reduction in transport externalities. However, distribution activity typically leads to increased transport activity and much of this is likely to be road based. As a result, there are additional infrastructure costs that must be borne by the city or region. There is also the impact on congestion that can result from such developments. Despite attempts to shift activities in distribution to non-peak hours it remains the case that much of the transport activity takes place at times that overlap with peak car travel trips.

Waterborne urban freight

Despite the fact that so many cities are located on major rivers or near to the coast, the use of water for urban freight has not reached a high level. Nevertheless there are some examples of waterborne urban freight projects/initiatives especially in the Netherlands and France (Arvidsson *et al*, 2017):

- the Beer Boat (Utrecht) for deliveries to local shops, hotels and restaurants;
- Mokum Maritiem (Amsterdam) for deliveries to local shops and waste transport;
- Vert Chez Vous (Paris) for parcel deliveries;
- DHL floating distribution centre (Amsterdam) for parcel deliveries;
- Franprix (Paris) for supermarket deliveries.

Janjevic and Ndiaye (2014) analysed a range of waterborne freight initiatives arguing that there appeared to be significant potential for such actions and that a wide range of goods could be dealt with in this way. They also noted that road transport would have to be combined with waterborne movement in cities where the waterway network density was low. Lindholm *et al* (2015) also showed that waterway transport could be applicable for the movement of bulk materials. In their research, they noted that the use of large vessels would lead to the most sustainable system (ie compared with the use of road or even rail). Arvidsson *et al* (2017) investigated how waterborne freight transport can relieve the streets of Stockholm and Gothenburg. The main applications were found to be removal of waste, moving excavated material from infrastructure construction to port extensions and distribution vans from parcel terminals to the city centre. A simulation approach was adopted by van Duin *et al* (2017) to consider the opportunity for waterborne transport in Amsterdam. The study concluded that a waterborne city logistics concept with a small number of hub locations can compete with truck deliveries and seems to be a sustainable solution for other cities with large canals as well.

The impact on the port–city interface may be rather modest at present given the scale of the activity related to waterborne urban freight transport. Importantly, if the opportunities and initiatives grow then it does provide a new role for port-related infrastructure. In addition, the skills of those involved in port and maritime management may be a vital asset for cities wishing to develop such initiatives.

The case of Gothenburg

With its 550,000 citizens, Gothenburg is a medium-sized city with a comparatively large port situated at the mouth of the Göta river, draining Lake Vänern, which is the largest lake in the European Union and third largest in geographical Europe. Half of the annual port volume of 40 million tons is petroleum; almost half is unitized as lorries, semi-trailers and maritime containers, and the rest consists of vehicles. There is no dry bulk handling. The port–city separation era (Ducruet and Lee, 2006) in the 1970s resulted in dedicated terminals and transport-intensive industry located further out towards the sea. The oil and vehicle flows are mostly local to the port area, relating to the three oil refineries and two Volvo factories for cars and trucks in the vicinity of the Port of Gothenburg (PoG), but much of the unitized traffic transits the city. Particularly the two ferry ports with city-centre terminals imply pulses of heavy traffic after ship arrivals. Starting in the 1990s, the abandoned port and shipyard areas have been revitalized into high-end residential areas and offices like in many other cities (Hall and Jacobs, 2012). Hence, there are conflicting interests complicating the port–city interface.

Like many ports, PoG is owned by the city, which affects the port–city interface, and PoG operates the energy port itself but the ferry/RoPax, RoRo, container and vehicle terminals have been privately operated on concessions since 2012.

Land use planning

The city is responsible for the city streets and the Swedish Transport Administration for the main roads and railway tracks. The intermediate governance level, Region Västra Götaland with 1.7 million inhabitants, has a planning role for the transport system and recently issued a freight transport strategy and an action plan for West Sweden. The Swedish municipalities have a land use planning monopoly and they are significant land owners, but as PoG is identified as a 'national interest' in the infrastructure planning process, the national level has its say in land use planning affecting port access and the state also has a land use veto on environmental grounds.

Being a small export-dependent country with a public sector contributing half of the GDP, Sweden has a tradition of intense cooperation between industry and the public sector. In Gothenburg it means that Volvo Cars and the Volvo Group (producing trucks, buses, marine engines and construction equipment) influence city politicians affecting land use in the port area, as their factories and logistics facilities are located in proximity to the port. PoG is obviously also influential being owned by the city, feeding back dividends and attracting industry and jobs to the city.

PoG has shifted from being strongly focused on developing railway shuttles for containers and semi-trailers to developing logistics facilities in the port area (Heitz *et al*, 2018), implying that containers are to be stuffed and stripped in the vicinity of the port rather than transited directly to and from the hinterland. In cooperation with real estate developers, PoG has influenced municipality land use planning and it also invests directly in warehouses, widening the concept of being a landlord beyond port terminals (Kårestedt, 2016).

Waterborne urban freight

Gothenburg's location at the mouth of the Göta river enables waterborne urban freight in a range of goods, including construction materials, urban distribution and container hinterland flows.

Construction

Gothenburg grows significantly with ongoing or planned building and infrastructure construction projects amounting to about 100 billion euros. Consequently, road and rail infrastructure has to be improved and several projects involve tunnels and larger construction works, resulting in the need to relocate significant masses. Arvidsson *et al* (2017) find that using barges to move the masses to reclaim land for new port terminals in the river mouth can be feasible as a tool avoiding further congestion of city streets.

Urban distribution

Rivers constitute ancient transport routes and it is common for road and rail infrastructure to follow the river to connect cities along the river. Gothenburg is no exception and the major LSPs have located their consolidation terminals along these roads and, hence, also along the river. River crossings are bottlenecks in Gothenburg's traffic and Arvidsson *et al* (2017) found a potential for using barges to move distribution vans between the consolidation terminals and the city centre on the other river bank. The revitalized port and shipyard areas were planned for less car ownership implying that more goods need to be transported to the area by LSPs, and the river is seen as a high-capacity infrastructure connecting the area with the LSP terminals further upriver. A pilot test using a barge bringing in consumer goods from the LSP terminals and moving waste to a waste-fuelled power plant was performed during two weeks in spring 2016 with good results (Svanberg *et al*, 2017). The results confirmed earlier research in the sense that no major barriers were observed – rather developing solutions that are cost-competitive in comparison to road transport is the main challenge (Janjevic and Ndiaye, 2014).

Hinterland container flows

The Göta river is currently used primarily for bulk and product tanker shipping but new low bridges hamper navigation, and locks upstream of Gothenburg need to be replaced to allow for continued traffic. There are, however, concrete plans to start a twice-weekly container service between Port of Gothenburg and Port of Kristinehamn in Lake Vänern (Swedish Orient Line, 2018) relieving the congested roads and railways (Rogerson *et al*, 2018). Initiatives like this are likely to motivate investment in the new locks.

Conclusions

Major changes have occurred in the port–city interface over the years. Ferry terminals are often still located in city centres, but the heavier freight flows have moved out and are no longer an intrinsic part of city life. This has resulted in changes in traffic patterns on ring-roads and the growing importance of a coordinated and well thought out land use strategy to accommodate the needs of port operations and other logistics operations in the port city. However, this is a complicated topic because ports are in many cases able to act in their own interests or on a national scale and these interests may not always be in the interest of their adjacent city. Also port-city politics need to compromise between manufacturing and logistics industry development with tax revenues on one side and a liveable city attracting service and high-tech firms, education and other institutions on the other side.

To understand the changing nature of the port–city interface it is essential to take a long-term view and relate this to the growing body of research that has taken place since the 1970s. Indeed, the changes go back further than that, starting with the major shifts in international trade in the post-war world with steeply rising flows and technology shifts such as large-scale bulk shipping and containerization.

The chapter argues that despite the tensions between the port and the city there are signs of new opportunities as well as immediate needs for close cooperation and indeed a new era in port–city interfaces. The case of Gothenburg, which is comparatively well researched in various research and pilot projects, can be used as a starting point to explore this development, and future research and field trials will test the validity of this proposition.

References

AIVP (2014), *Port-City Governance,* Sefacil Foundation/AIVP – The worldwide network of port cities, Oceanids Collection, Le Havre

Allen, J, Browne, M and Cherrett, T (2012) Investigating relationships between road freight transport, facility location, logistics management and urban form, *Journal of Transport Geography,* **24**, pp 45–57

Arvidsson, N, Garme, K, Kihl, H, Lantz, S, Ljungberg, AJ, Sundberg, M, Tufvesson, E and Woxenius, J (2017) *Vattenvägen – den intermodala pusselbiten (The water road – the intermodal jigsaw puzzle piece),* Lighthouse Maritime Competence Centre, Gothenburg

del Saz-Salazar, S and García-Menéndez, L (2016) Port expansion and negative externalities: a willingness to accept approach, *Maritime Policy & Management,* **43** (1), pp 59–83

DePillis, L (2015) Ports are the new power plants – at least in terms of pollution. As shipping traffic rises, activists try to keep the air in adjacent neighborhoods from getting worse, *The Washington Post*, 24 November 2015

Dooms, M, Haezendonck, E and Verbeke, A (2015) Towards a meta-analysis and toolkit for port-related socio-economic impacts: a review of socio-economic impact studies conducted for seaports, *Maritime Policy & Management,* **42** (5), pp 459–80

Ducruet, C and Lee, S-W (2006) Frontline soldiers of globalisation: Port–city evolution and regional competition, *GeoJournal,* **67** (2), pp 107–122

Fenton, P (2015) The role of port cities and transnational municipal networks in efforts to reduce greenhouse gas emissions on land and at sea from shipping – an assessment of the World Ports Climate Initiative, *Marine Policy,* **75**, pp 271–77

Hall, PV and Jacobs, W (2012) Why are maritime ports (still) urban, and why should policy-makers care?, *Maritime Policy & Management,* **39** (2), pp 189–206

Hayuth, Y (1982) The port-urban interface: an area in transition, *Area,* **14** (3), pp 219–24

Heitz, A, Dablanc, L, Olsson, J, Sánchez-Díaz, I and Woxenius, J (2018) Spatial patterns of logistics facilities in Gothenburg, Sweden, *Journal of Transport Geography*

Hoyle, B (2001) Urban renewal in East African port cities: Mombasa's Old Town waterfront, *GeoJournal,* **53** (2), pp 183–97

Hoyle, BS (1968) East African seaports: an application of the concept of 'Anyport', *Transactions of the Institute of British Geographers,* **44**, pp 163–83

Hoyle, BS (1989) The port-city interface: trends, problems and examples, *Geoforum,* **20** (4), pp 429–35

Janjevic, M and Ndiaye, AB (2014) Inland waterways transport for city logistics: A review of experiences and the role of local public authorities, in *20th International Conference on Urban Transport and the Environment*, ed CA Brebbia, pp 279–90, WIT Press, Algarve

Kårestedt, M (2016) Trender i logistik – Göteborgs Hamn (Trends in logistics – Port of Gothenburg), *Logistics facilities in West Sweden,* Royal Academy of Engineering Sciences, Gothenburg, 14 September, pp 1–23

Lindholm, M, Olsson, L, Carlén, V and Josefsson, A (2015) The potential role of waterways in sustainable urban freight – a case study of excavated materials transport in Sweden, *Transportation Research Board, The Annual Meeting,* Washington, January, pp 1–16

McCalla, RJ (1983) Separation and specialization of land uses in cityport waterfronts: the cases of Saint John and Halifax (Canada), *Canadian Geographer,* **27** (1), pp 48–61

Merk, O (2014) *The Competitiveness of Global Port-Cities: Synthesis Report,* OECD Publishing

Monios, J, Bergqvist, R and Woxenius, J (2018) Port-centric cities: the role of freight distribution in defining the port-city relationship, *Journal of Transport Geography,* **66**, pp 53–64

Olsson, J, Larsson, A, Woxenius, J and Bergqvist, R (2016) *Transport and logistics facilities expansion and social sustainability: A critical discussion and findings from the City of Gothenburg, Sweden,* University of Gothenburg, Working Paper Series of the Logistics and Transport Research Group, Gothenburg

Pettit, SJ and Beresford, AKC (2009) Port development: from gateways to logistics hubs, *Maritime Policy & Management,* **36** (3), pp 253–67

Rogerson, S, Santén, V, Svanberg, M, Williamsson, J and Woxenius, J (2018) Realizing modal shift to inland waterways, Work-in-progress, 30th NOFOMA Conference, Kolding, 13–15 June, pp 1–3

Roso, V, Styhre, L, Woxenius, J, Bergqvist, R and Lumsden, K (2015) Short sea shuttle concept in north-eastern Europe, *MarIus,* **459**, pp 237–62

Svanberg, M, Santén, V, Halldórsson, A, Finnsgård, C and Daun, V (2017) Logistics demonstrations as a participatory research design, Logistics research network conference, Southampton, 6–8 September

Swedish Orient Line (2018) New container shuttle between Gothenburg and Lake Vänern – Shipping an environmentally friendly transport and logistics solution, Press release, 10 January

Tichavska, M and Tovar, B (2015) Port-city exhaust emission model: an application to cruise and ferry operations in Las Palmas Port, *Transportation Research Part A: Policy and Practice,* **78**, pp 347–60

van den Berg, R (2015) *Strategies and New Business Models in Intermodal Hinterland Transport*, TU Eindhoven

van Duin, JHR, Kortmann, LJ and van de Kamp, M (2017) Distribution using city canals: The case of Amsterdam, 10th International Conference on City Logistics, Phuket, June

Wang, H (2014) Preliminary investigation of waterfront redevelopment in Chinese coastal port cities: the case of the eastern Dalian port areas, *Journal of Transport Geography,* **40**, pp 29–42

World Bank (2017) *Mombasa: options for the port city interface – final report, COWI, Woxkonsult, Syagga & Associates*, Washington DC

Woxenius, J (2016) Review of port-city interactions, *DEVPORT 2016*, Le Havre, France, 19–20 May, pp 1–19

PART TWO
Urban logistics diversity

The logistics of parcel delivery 07

Current operations and challenges facing the UK market

JULIAN ALLEN, TOM CHERRETT, MAJA PIECYK AND MARZENA PIOTROWSKA

Introduction

This chapter discusses the UK parcel market, and the associated delivery and collection operations in London. Insight is provided into the hub-and-spoke next-day/economy and point-to-point same-day sectors. The material presented in this chapter has been largely produced through the authors' work on the 'Freight Traffic Control 2050 (FTC2050): Transforming the energy demands of last mile urban freight through collaborative logistics' research project (www.ftc2050.com) funded by the UK Engineering and Physical Sciences Research Council. However, many of the developments and challenges discussed in this chapter in relation to London and the United Kingdom are relevant to urban areas in developed countries more generally.

Parcel distribution is a fundamental and growing part of urban logistics operations with the majority of parcel deliveries taking place in urban areas. It has been estimated that approximately 300,000 vans are used in the parcel and mail sector in the United Kingdom (which is equivalent to about 10 per cent of the total van fleet) (FTA, 2016). Last mile deliveries of parcels and mail by vans is mostly concentrated in urban areas given the large proportion of final delivery points (both commercial and residential) located in towns and cities. A survey on Regent Street, a major shopping street in central London, found that 21 per cent of all motorized goods vehicles observed were operated by parcel carriers (Transport for London, 2009). Certain types of land use receive especially substantial flows of parcel traffic. For example, a study of a major office block in central London found that more than 40 per cent of all goods vehicle deliveries were associated with parcel and mail flows (Browne *et al*, 2016).

Traditionally, business-to-business (B2B) flows accounted for the greatest proportion of these parcel volumes, followed by business-to-consumer (B2C) flows. These B2B parcel flows are sent and received by all business sectors of the economy, with office, administrative and retail establishments being especially important receivers of these parcel deliveries in urban areas. However, in recent years, the growth in online shopping has resulted in rapid growth in B2C parcel flows as well as the emergence of consumer-to-all-parties (C2X) parcel flows. Customers of parcel carriers are demanding ever-greater service levels, with the time taken for the typical parcel to be transported from point of collection to point of delivery becoming ever shorter. Next-day parcel delivery has become the norm for the majority of parcels transported in the United Kingdom, and now the demand for same-day services, and even fulfilment within one to two hours, is growing. This poses significant operational and financial challenges for parcel carriers, who are having to invest in additional logistics infrastructure to handle the increasing parcel throughput and meet increasing service level requirements but are struggling to pass on these additional costs to their customers. New, startup, 'on-demand' same-day carriers are entering the urban parcel sector, increasing supply of B2C carrier services and thereby exerting further downward pressure on prices. The ever-faster lead times of these parcel movements in urban areas offer reduced scope for parcel consolidation and thereby threaten to increase the transport and environmental intensity of these logistics services. Multiple next-day and same-day parcel carriers compete to provide these services in urban areas and, as a result, busy commercial and retailing streets are visited each day by the vehicles of many competing companies. The very same large buildings, such as office blocks, are visited by many different parcel delivery vehicles each day, which compete for road and kerbside space and time.

The term 'parcel' is used throughout this chapter to refer to the goods moved by parcel carriers. However, it is important to note that this term refers to a range of product sizes, weights and appearances including envelopes, documents, packages and boxed items.

The size of the UK parcel market

In 2014 there were 11,765 parcel delivery companies registered in the United Kingdom (Keynote, 2015). The vast majority were relatively small and specialized in providing bespoke services or focusing on particular geographical locations; 47 per cent and 87 per cent of these companies had turnovers of less than £50,000 and £250,000 respectively with only 3.1 per cent (360 companies) recording turnovers of between £1 million and £4.9 million in 2014 (Keynote, 2015). Approximately 15 parcel carriers have networks that provide services across the entire United Kingdom (Royal Mail, 2015a; Postal and Logistics Consulting Worldwide, 2015) and an even smaller number provide international services.

In 2014, approximately 250,000 people were employed in the UK parcel market across 11,765 companies with 90 per cent employing fewer than 5 people and only 35 companies employing more than 100 (Keynote, 2015). Approximately 11 per cent of the companies in the UK parcel market are based in London, while another 15 per cent are based in the rest of the south-east of the United Kingdom (Keynote, 2015).

It has been estimated that the total UK parcel market handled 2.8 billion items and generated revenues of £10.1 billion in 2016, and that there had been approximately 65 per cent growth in items and revenues over the previous four years (Mintel, 2017). It was reported that 9 out of 10 people had sent or received at least one parcel in the previous 6 months (Mintel, 2017) and forecasts estimate a 33 per cent increase in the volume of parcels handled by 2021 (22 per cent increase in revenues), with much of this growth emanating from e-commerce and online retailing (Mintel, 2017).

Sectors in the UK parcel market

The UK parcel market can be divided into two key sectors: the hub-and-spoke, next-day and economy parcel sector; and the point-to-point, same-day parcel sector.

In the hub-and-spoke, next-day and economy parcel sector, multiple parcels are collected and delivered by vehicles, usually vans, from multiple addresses as part of a single vehicle round. These vehicles operate from local depots (spokes) throughout the working day. Collections are then picked up from each local depot and direct from major customers during the evening using larger, heavier goods vehicles and transported to a centralized hub depot for overnight sorting. Here the goods are unloaded and automatically sorted by destination, and loaded back onto these larger, heavier goods vehicles for transport back to the local depot in the early hours of the morning. By consolidating and sorting flows of parcels destined for the same and adjacent locations together, and by carrying out multi-drop vehicle collection and delivery rounds, it is possible to achieve operational cost savings compared to making direct deliveries and collections.

By contrast, the point-to-point, same-day parcel sector involves the collection of a single parcel or a small number of parcels from a given location followed by the direct transportation to the destination on the same day. This sector provides a faster delivery service compared to the hub-and-spoke next-day sector but has much higher costs per parcel given the lack of consolidation on the vehicle, and the consequent vehicle and labour requirements per parcel handled. Such point-to-point, same-day services are usually limited to parcels that are deemed time-critical by their shippers and receivers.

The hub-and-spoke and next-day parcel sector accounts for approximately 85–90 per cent of the total domestic parcel market by revenue in the United Kingdom, while the same-day point-to-point parcel sector generates turnover that accounts for the remaining 5–10 per cent of the total UK parcel market (Allen *et al*, 2018).

The hub-and-spoke, next-day and economy parcel sector

The hub-and-spoke, next-day and economy sector can be further subdivided into three subsectors: business-to-business (B2B); business-to-consumer (B2C); and consumer-to-all-parties (C2X). B2B refers to products sold by one business to another that are sent via hub-and-spoke parcel carriers, while B2C refers to products sold by businesses to a private individual. Traditionally, B2C involved home shopping via magazines and brochures but has increased rapidly as a result of e-commerce. The main parcel carriers in the United Kingdom B2C subsector are Royal Mail, Yodel and Hermes Parcelnet (Postal and Logistics Consulting Worldwide, 2015). C2X refers to the subsector in which consumers send parcels either to other consumers or to businesses including C2X private sellers on eBay and other internet sites as well as via printed magazines and local newspapers. It also includes small businesses selling via these same media that do not have enough volume to qualify for a business account (Postal and Logistics Consulting Worldwide, 2015). It is estimated that in 2015 B2B accounted for 54 per cent of the UK hub-and-spoke, next-day market by revenue, with B2C, 34 per cent and C2X 12 per cent (Apex Insight, 2015 quoted in Herson, 2015).

Hub-and-spoke, next-day carriers have to handle far more parcels in the B2C and C2X sectors to generate the same revenue compared to B2B operators. Another estimate suggests that B2C and C2X parcel deliveries accounted for almost two-thirds of UK parcel volume in 2016, while B2B accounted for just over one-third (Royal Mail, 2016).

The UK hub-and-spoke, next-day parcel market is predicted to continue to grow due to increasing B2C and C2X e-commerce and online shopping volumes. Royal Mail forecast 4.5 to 5.5 per cent per annum growth in the medium term (Royal Mail, 2016) with the number of parcels delivered on a next-day basis accounting for 57 per cent of total UK domestic volume during 2016/17 (Ofcom, 2017).

The same-day, point-to-point parcel sector

The B2B same-day parcel sector has traditionally been subject to high levels of competition, with many small carriers participating on a local and regional basis. This competition has been due to two key factors: 1) local passenger taxi companies who also provide parcel transport as an additional service with their existing fleets; and 2) the low entry barriers to the market – essentially only a vehicle and a means by which customers could communicate orders (originally telephone) are required with the vehicles used being typically small vans, motorbikes and bicycles. The UK B2B and B2C same-day point-to-point parcel delivery market had a turnover of approximately £1 billion in 2016, which represented an approximate doubling in size since 2012 (Mintel, 2017) with B2B accounting for over 95 per cent of this (Apex Insight, 2017). However, unlike the B2B same-day subsector which is expected to remain static, B2C is expected to see rapid growth over the next couple of years from a value of approximately £50 million in 2016 to an estimated £687 million by 2020 (Apex Insight, quoted in CitySprint, 2017).

Players in the UK parcel delivery market

Hub-and-spoke next-day and economy parcel carriers

The main hub-and-spoke third-party parcel carriers providing next-day and other services in the United Kingdom are (in alphabetical order): APC,

DHL International, DPD, DX, FedEx, Hermes Parcelnet, Royal Mail including Parcelforce Worldwide, TNT, Tuffnells, UK Mail (which was acquired by DHL in 2016), UPS and Yodel. In addition, Amazon, the major online retailer provides its own in-house hub-and-spoke parcel delivery services.

Of these, the formerly publicly owned national postal operator Royal Mail was responsible for approximately 33 per cent of all domestic parcels handled in the United Kingdom by revenue in 2013/14, and Parcelforce, its division for larger, heavier parcels, 6 per cent (a combined market share of approximately 40 per cent of all domestic parcels by revenue) (Postal and Logistics Consulting Worldwide, 2015). DPD, DHL, TNT and UPS each had between 7 and 10 per cent of the domestic parcel market by revenue in 2013/14 (Postal and Logistics Consulting Worldwide, 2015) with APC, DX, FedEx, Hermes, UK Mail and Yodel each having a 1–5 per cent share (Postal and Logistics Consulting Worldwide, 2015).

The average revenue per parcel across the sector was £3.82 in 2016/17 for next-day services, and £2.25 for services longer than next-day (Ofcom, 2017) with APC, DPD and Parcelforce earning an average revenue of £7–8 per domestic parcel handled in 2013/14 and FedEx, Hermes, Royal Mail and UK Mail, £2–5 (Allen *et al*, 2016). The differences in average revenue per parcel are due to three key factors: 1) the size and weight of the items handled; 2) the elapsed time in which the customer wants the parcel to be delivered; 3) the additional services and time guarantees that the customer wishes to purchase. Typically, customers sending B2B parcels want these delivered more quickly than those sending B2C and C2X parcels and, generally, B2B parcels are subject to more time guarantees and additional service requirements compared to B2C and C2X parcels. Hermes, Yodel and Royal Mail predominantly serve the B2C and C2X markets, while APC and DPD handle a majority of B2B parcels, many with time guarantees.

Point-to-point, same-day parcel carriers

A couple of these major hub-and-spoke next-day carriers, including UK Mail and TNT, also provide same-day, point-to-point operations. However, most of the same-day parcel market is handled by specialist same-day carriers. These include CitySprint (the market leader), Royal Mail's Same-Day Courier Service, eCourier (acquired by Royal Mail in 2015), Addison Lee (which offers both passenger and parcel services), Rico Logistics, Absolutely, GLH and many other smaller companies, often operating in specific geographical areas. Even among the named companies, not all of them offer entire national coverage. Some retailers including Amazon and Argos also operate in-house, same-day delivery services for their online shopping customers.

In addition, a few startup companies offering 'on-demand' services have also entered the UK same-day delivery market, aiming to serve the growing online (or 'gig') economy with rapid delivery services. These include Gophr, Quiqup, Shutl, Stuart and the crowdshipper, Nimber (Allen *et al*, 2018). However, at present, the market share of these companies remains small and they typically only offer short-distance urban journeys in one or more UK cities.

Same-day delivery does not offer the opportunity for overnight parcel consolidation as in next-day parcel operations, which improves drop density and facilitates multi-stop local delivery and collection rounds using vans. The price charged per parcel is therefore considerably higher for same-day than for next-day/economy delivery per unit of distance travelled, reflecting the dedicated point-to-point transportation required. An analysis of CitySprint accounts, the market leader in same-day deliveries in the United Kingdom, suggests an average revenue of approximately £16 per parcel despite lower average journey distances and parcel size/weight than next-day parcels (using data in CitySprint, 2017). Many same-day parcels are transported over relatively short distances within a single city, with cycle couriers in London typically earning between £2 and £10 per job (with an average of £3.25–3.50 per job in central London), while motorbike and van drivers earn a higher rate to reflect fuel and vehicle costs (Day, 2015; Employment Tribunal, 2017a; Employment Tribunal, 2017b; Wood, 2016). Therefore, on a per unit weight, size and distance basis there is a major difference in the prices (and costs) of items transported on a same-day basis compared with slower parcel services.

Challenges facing the UK parcel market

Hub-and-spoke, next-day and economy parcel sector

Hub-and-spoke, next-day and economy parcel carriers currently face three key market pressures in the United Kingdom emanating from: 1) the growth in the total number of parcels handled due to the increase in B2C parcels associated with e-commerce and online shopping; 2) competition and overcapacity in the sector; and 3) the static revenues per parcel that customers are paying. As a result, national parcel carriers are trying to better control their operational costs while at the same time making infrastructural investments to remain competitive.

Table 7.1 Changes in total domestic parcels handled by national hub-and-spoke carriers in the United Kingdom, by volume and revenue

Time Period	Volume	Revenue
2013–14 to 2014–15	+5%	+6%
2014–15 to 2015–16	+13%	+11%
2015–16 to 2016–17	+7%	+1%

SOURCE Ofcom, 2015, 2016, 2017

The total number of parcels handled domestically on a next-day or slower basis by UK hub-and-spoke carriers has increased by both volume and revenue in recent years (see Table 7.1). Much of this growth has been driven by increases in e-commerce relative to B2C parcel flows with UK online retail sales exceeding £130 billion in 2016, up 16 per cent compared to 2015 (IMRG, 2017). Table 7.1 also indicates that for the two most recent years for which data is available, growth in parcel volume has outstripped growth in revenue.

This growth in B2C parcel volumes has led to the need for carriers to invest in new hubs and depots to cope with demand and remain competitive. UK Mail, DPD, Parcelforce, Yodel, DHL and Hermes have all invested in such a way that has further increased total parcel handling capacity across the market (Postal and Logistics Consulting Worldwide, 2015; Ofcom, 2017).

The entry of Amazon into the parcel carrier market with the creation of its own logistics and delivery capability (Amazon Logistics) in some locations in the United Kingdom (rather than using existing parcel carriers) has added to this competition. It has been suggested that Amazon Logistics already delivers as many parcels in the United Kingdom as some of the largest national carriers (Royal Mail, 2015b). The degree of competition in the parcel sector (together with the growing importance of B2C and C2X parcel volumes) has resulted in falls in the revenues that carriers receive per delivery (Pooler, 2016). Royal Mail believes that there is already approximately 20 per cent overcapacity in the parcel market and that this is still growing as rivals expand their network infrastructures (Royal Mail, 2015b), which will result in increasing downward pressure on prices for the national carriers (Royal Mail, 2015a).

Retail customers of these parcel carriers and their consumers are demanding ever-faster, more reliable and convenient delivery services, which have led carriers to offer timed delivery windows, parcel traceability and alternative delivery location options, including collection points and locker banks, all of which have cost and investment implications (Copenhagen Economics, 2013; Taylor, 2015). However, these additional services, including a relative shift towards next-day rather than slower services, are being requested from carriers at the same time that their customers are also requesting more attractive rates per parcel.

In addition, B2C deliveries have attributes that typically make them more expensive for carriers to fulfil which include: the substantial first-time failure rates associated with deliveries to residential addresses; the sizeable product return rates in some product categories such as clothing; and the proportion of single-parcel B2C deliveries compared to multiple items per consignee in B2B operations. B2C deliveries also involve more suburban and ex-urban delivery locations, with lower drop densities and higher inter-drop distances compared to B2B.

The intense competition, with increasing importance of lower revenue B2C activity coupled with the investment drive to meet ever-stringent customer demands, has resulted in the average price per parcel among national parcel carriers decreasing by 5 per cent between 2015/16 and 2016/17 (Ofcom, 2017). This pressure on delivery rates is likely to continue as the parcel distribution sector becomes increasingly crowded with the emergence of other non-traditional entrants such as Amazon, and possibly Uber in the future (Jinks, 2016; Lieb and Lieb, 2014; Oliver Wyman, 2015; Sumner-Rivers, 2015).

Several other recent factors have also increased the degree of competition in the next-day parcel market. The growth of e-commerce retail marketplaces is leading to the disintermediation of the relationship between parcel carriers and the shippers (ie their customers). As an example, eBay has developed its own network of collection points where retail consumers can drop off and pick up goods through its partnerships with Argos and Sainsbury's leading to reductions in bulk shipping rates (Royal Mail, 2015b).

Local collection point networks have also emerged, providing pickup and return points in local shops for use by carriers and end consumers. These have been most successful when located in shared-use facilities and not as stand-alone dedicated premises (Price, 2017). Click-and-collect services provided by physical retailers have also seen considerable growth, allowing customers to have their online orders delivered to the retailer's local store for collection in person, depriving parcel carriers of some delivery-to-door demand.

There are other factors outside of the parcel market that have increased the operating costs of parcel carriers. Worsening road traffic conditions and difficulties finding suitable kerbside parking space in urban centres have increased the time taken and hence cost per delivery. Affordable local depots from which to operate next-day parcel deliveries are becoming increasingly difficult to find due to rising land values in UK cities. This is leading to parcel carriers relocating their local delivery depots ever further from the urban centre (Hesse, 2008; Cidell, 2010; Dablanc and Rakotonarivo, 2010). Often referred to as 'logistics sprawl' (Dablanc *et al*, 2014), this has the effect of increasing delivery distance, and the operating costs of central urban parcel collections and deliveries.

Point-to-point, same-day parcel sector

Many of the market challenges facing hub-and-spoke, next-day carriers are also faced by point-to-point, same-day carriers. B2B same-day parcel volumes are expected to decline further as a result of reductions in the quantity of documentation that requires physical transportation in banking, legal and other business sectors. Meanwhile, B2C same-day demand is expected to rise with the growth in e-commerce and online shopping.

The recent emergence of startup 'on-demand' carriers and the offering of same-day delivery services by retailers such as Amazon and Argos have increased capacity in the same-day sector. This is likely to exert a downward pressure on prices. Additionally, Amazon may at some future point offer its same-day delivery services to other customers on a third-party basis, thereby directly challenging the market share of traditional same-day carriers.

As demand from retailers and their customers for same-day B2C services increases, this will require same-day carriers to invest in greater urban depot space than is required for typical same-day B2B operations, which are predominantly made directly from collection point to delivery point. These facilities will be required to consolidate flows from retailers' distribution centres destined for delivery to their customers in urban locations, introducing an additional location and transport leg into the same-day delivery operation. Neither traditional same-day carriers nor disruptor startups have such networks of suitably located local depots within urban centres in the United Kingdom from which to operate same-day services at present. Acquiring such a network of suitably located depots from which to operate same-day B2C deliveries will be extremely expensive given urban land values and property rental costs in the United Kingdom (Piecyk and Allen, 2017).

Many same-day carriers use drivers/riders who are self-employed and this employment status has generated unhelpful media coverage for some same-day carriers. This is now subject to government scrutiny, the longer-term outcome of which could be higher labour costs for same-day carriers (Allen *et al*, 2018).

Parcel carrier operations

The overwhelming majority of deliveries in both the next-day/economy, and same-day parcel sectors take place in urban areas. The following sections provide an overview of these delivery operations in both sectors.

Hub-and-spoke, next-day or slower parcel operations

Hub-and-spoke, next-day parcel deliveries (B2B and B2C) usually take place using vans with a gross weight of up to 3.5 tonnes, but some companies also make use of goods vehicles up to 7.5 tonnes especially when transporting larger, heavier parcels and when delivering bulk loads. Deliveries and collections in urban areas typically take place during the working day (between about 9 am and 5 pm) on weekdays (Monday to Friday), however growth in B2C deliveries is increasing the extent of weekend activity.

Vehicles are based at local depots from where deliveries and collections are made. For deliveries in UK city centres, these depots are often located outside the central urban area owing to the high cost of land. Goods to be delivered from the urban depot are received during the night/early morning and are then sorted onto the delivery vehicles, either by drivers or depot staff. Each vehicle/driver is typically allocated to a given geographical area in order to limit the distance driven between each delivery point. A vehicle/driver may be responsible for the delivery and collection of up to approximately 300 parcels per day or more when demand is high. Each vehicle/driver is responsible for carrying out a multi-drop vehicle round, usually departing from the depot between 8 and 9 am, in order to arrive at business addresses when staff are present to receive the parcels.

Total driving distances on delivery and collection rounds once the vehicle is in the central urban area are typically low, with the distance to and from the depot and the catchment area often exceeding the distance driven between delivery and collection points within the catchment area. In central urban areas, drivers usually spend a large proportion of their day away from their vehicles while collecting and delivering parcels, and walking distances can be substantial. Drivers are usually responsible for determining their vehicle routing and scheduling decisions, and there is a substantial difference between the performance of experienced drivers who have familiarity with the catchment area compared to novice drivers. Carriers attempt to keep their drivers on the same delivery rounds to build up their knowledge of the particular round and the addresses served, help them learn the most

Table 7.2 Driver tasks involved in multi-drop, next-day or slower parcel operations

Sequence	Description of Task
1	Vehicle scheduling decisions – the order in which to carry out the parcel deliveries
2	Loading sequence of the parcels onto the vehicle
3	On-route vehicle navigation decisions
4	Picking the best vehicle stopping location
5	Last mile delivery ability and consignee recall skills – deciding how many addresses to deliver to each time the vehicle is parked and locating the parcels required for delivery on the vehicle
6	On-foot decision-making – deciding how many delivery addresses to deliver to on-foot each time the vehicle is parked and in which order
7	Optimizing walking routes – from the parked vehicle to the delivery points
8	Locating point of entry to the building – which may not correspond with the delivery address on the parcel
9	The journey inside the building to the point of delivery – and gain whatever proof of delivery is required
10	Make decisions about what to do when no one is available to receive the delivery
11	Accepting collections – drivers must be able to decide whether to accept a collection request from the depot while carrying out their delivery round

SOURCE Bates *et al*, 2018

efficient driving and walking strategies, build personal relationships with customers and thereby increase their operational efficiency.

Research in the Freight Traffic Control 2050 project identified 11 tasks that drivers have to carry out during their working day, often without the use of any computer-based support, all of which influence the operational efficiency of the vehicle round (see Table 7.2).

The extent of time-guaranteed deliveries varies between carrier – those working predominantly in the B2B parcel subsector have a greater proportion of time-critical parcels than those focused on the B2C and C2X subsectors.

As part of the FTC2050 project, a detailed survey was carried out of 25 multi-drop vehicle delivery rounds in central London operating from three

Table 7.3 Characteristics of delivery rounds in the central London survey of next-day or slower parcel operations

		Depot A	Depot B	Depot C	Overall Average
Number of Rounds		8	8	9	8
Round duration (hours)	Min	7.7	5.6	5.1	
	Max	10.3	7.2	9.1	
	Average	8.8	6.6	6.7	7.3

urban depots of two different hub-and-spoke parcel carriers. Surveyors accompanied and recorded the driving and walking activity of these parcel delivery operations to business and residential addresses over a three-day period (25–27 October 2016) in the WC1, WC2 and W1 areas of central London. In addition, GPS tracking equipment was used to continually record the vehicle and driver locations. For the purpose of presenting the survey's results, the three London depots studied are referred to as A, B and C; Table 7.3 presents the characteristics of their delivery rounds. All delivery rounds were carried out by vans up to and including 3.5 tonnes gross weight.

The surveys considered all time spent from the point of leaving the depot until returning to the same depot at the end of the round. Additional time spent at the depot (eg for loading the vehicle) was not considered here.

Distance and time statistics

Across the 25 vehicle rounds that were studied, the average round time (ie the time from when the vehicle left the depot until its return) was 7.3 hours, with a range from 5 to 10 hours. Depot A was located further from the central London catchment area compared to the other two depots, indicated by the significantly longer stem distances (the distance from the depot to and from the delivery and collection area) (see Table 7.4).

Table 7.4 Driving distances in the central London survey of next-day or slower parcel operations

	Depot A	Depot B	Depot C	Overall Average
Average stem distance (km)	22.9	3.8	8.3	11.9
Average driven delivery distance (km)	14.2	15.3	7.2	11.9
Total	37.1	19.1	15.5	23.8

The average distance driven within the delivery area, excluding stem mileage, was 11.9 kilometres while the calculated average distance walked was 7.9 kilometres, indicating that walking constitutes a substantial proportion of daily delivery rounds for parcel carriers. Parcel delivery can also involve considerable travel inside buildings, as well as to and from them, especially in multi-tenanted commercial offices and high-rise residential developments. An altimeter and GPS tracker carried by a driver during the survey indicated that approximately 25 per cent of delivery and collection addresses served by the driver involved walking upstairs or taking a lift within multistorey buildings (Figure 7.1 provides an example from one vehicle round).

The proportion of time that was spent driving ranged between 23 per cent and 67 per cent between the 25 rounds studied, with a mean of only 38 per cent. For the remaining 62 per cent of time spent, the vehicle was parked while delivery/collection work or breaks were undertaken. In absolute terms, the average time spent parked during a round was 4.6 hours with 95 per cent of the recorded stopping locations being 'on-street' (ie at the kerbside and typically on double yellow lines), and 'off-street' unloading areas (ie in car parks and loading bays on private space) were used in only 5 per cent of instances. This highlights the pressure that this activity places on kerbside space and demonstrates that in central London courier vans spend considerable amounts of time parked on-street, which may be of interest both to couriers, in negotiating the amount of insurance they have to pay for vehicle use, and to Transport for London, in determining policy for freight provision (eg of kerbside loading bays).

Vehicle stopping strategies, addresses visited and time spent on deliveries and collections

The daily vehicle round structures were identified in advance and were usually permanent, unless the volume of work was too high for a driver to complete, in which case it would be distributed across other drivers. The sequence in which the assigned tasks were performed was decided individually by the drivers unless parcels were subject to specific delivery time guarantees and no route optimization software was used. There were frequent discrepancies observed between the registered business addresses of consignees and the actual point of delivery for the premises. Such issues, coupled with the combination of driving and walking, mean that standard routing and scheduling software is often unable to provide accurate routes and schedules for such operations.

Figure 7.1 Elevation profile from a next-day or slower parcel carrier driver over a one-day vehicle round in central London obtained using a Garmin tracker

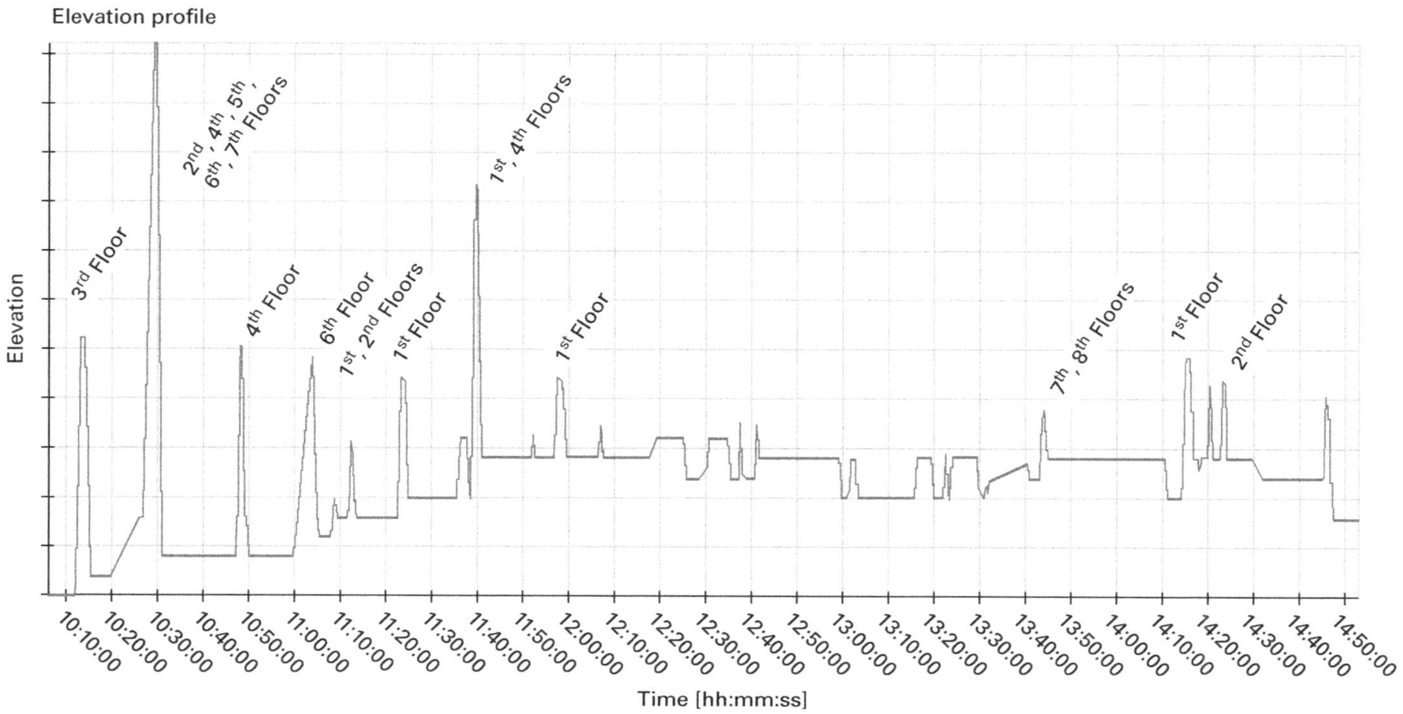

For those parcels subject to delivery time windows (eg delivery before 9 am, 10 am and midday), the preferred driver strategy was to typically 'get them out of the way' to the exclusion of any other deliveries, even if this meant returning to the same areas two or three times during the day. Parking on-street as close as possible to the delivery or collection address was the preferred driver strategy but sometimes parking restrictions or the road network topology (eg one-way streets) led to the driver choosing to park further away (eg on a side street) and then perform a walking tour around a number of different customers that were relatively close to one another. Sometimes this would involve a return to the vehicle to pick up more parcels ('hotelling'), as the driver could not transport them all in one trip. On average across all the rounds, there were 1.9 customers served per vehicle stop; however, individual round averages varied substantially: from 1.1 to 5.2 customers per stop, the former suggesting that some drivers preferred to move the vehicle from customer to customer (minimize walking), and the latter indicating more clustering of customers on walking tours. For the driver intent on minimizing walking, the vehicle would typically be moved only a short distance (eg 50 metres) between stops.

The average number of parcels delivered or collected on each round was 126, to an average of 72 customers, during 37 stops (see Table 7.5). This equates to an average of 1.8 parcels per customer and 3.4 parcels per stop. On average, 3.9 minutes were spent per parcel delivered (or collected), calculated as the total round time divided by the total number of parcels.

Point-to-point, same-day parcel operations

Same-day parcel deliveries (B2B and B2C) take place using a range of vehicle types: bicycles, motorbikes, electrically assisted cargo bikes, cars and vans. These deliveries are typically made during the working day (between about 9 am and 7 pm) on weekdays (Monday to Friday). The rise of B2C same-day deliveries is likely to increase the extent of weekend activity. Bicycles are usually limited to central and inner urban areas, whereas the other vehicle types can cover a larger geographical area given their speed advantages on faster roads. Bicycles and cargo bikes have speed advantages over motorbikes and vans in central and inner urban locations that suffer from traffic congestion. While parcel B2B and B2C deliveries take place between virtually any two locations, medical work usually involves movement between hospitals, surgeries and laboratories.

Table 7.5 Number of stops, addresses served and items delivered/collected in the central London survey of next-day or slower parcel operations

	Depot A			Depot B			Depot C			
	Min	Max	Average	Min	Max	Average	Min	Max	Average	Overall Average
Stops	22	59	40	25	48	34	14	72	38	37
Addresses served	53	102	70	32	86	57	48	120	86	72
Items (delivered/collected)	93	336	164	58	105	83	74	177	132	126

Same-day parcel delivery drivers/riders often work all day (ie 10–12 hours) and most work five days per week. Many have self-employed or dependent worker status, with relatively few employees in the sector. The number of same-day deliveries made by a driver/rider depends on several factors including: 1) the distance between each collection and delivery; 2) the extent to which the driver/rider is allocated overlapping jobs that allow him or her to carry more than a single delivery at a time; 3) the level of demand from customers; 4) the number of drivers/riders being used at any one time by the carrier; and 5) the controller's relationship with, and views on the efficiency of the driver/rider.

A cyclist typically achieves 15–35 urban delivery jobs and covers 50–100 miles per working day in London (Butler and Osborne, 2017; Day, 2015; Employment Tribunal, 2017a; Employment Tribunal, 2017b; Morgan, 2011; Pender, 2007; Sparkes, 2009; Wood, 2016). For drivers/riders using other vehicle types, journey speeds in busy urban areas are likely to be slower and hence involve fewer delivery jobs per day. However, vans and cargo bikes offer larger and heavier carrying capacities so are better suited to transporting multiple items and several deliveries at once, whereas cyclists are limited to carrying multiple items only in the case of documents and very small packages. Vans, motorbikes and cars are also best suited to deliveries that involve long-distance journeys with a collection or delivery location remote from the urban area.

The main differentiation in same-day service levels is whether collection is instantaneous (say within 15 minutes) or at an unspecified time of day, and whether a guaranteed delivery time is attached to the same-day service. Such time requirements place the planning and operation of same-day parcel services under even greater constraints.

The majority of same-day carriers are relatively small organizations that operate on a regional or local/city basis. Employee numbers are usually low (including management, administrative staff and controllers), with the number of drivers/riders, who are often self-employed, usually exceeding the employed office and planning staff (Gruber *et al*, 2014; Maes and Vanelslander, 2012).

Fleet controllers employed by same-day carriers allocate incoming collection and delivery jobs to drivers/riders. The drivers/riders roam the city performing jobs or waiting for their next job to be allocated to them by a controller who may be responsible for as many as 50 drivers/riders. In most same-day carriers, the controller has to retain a mental map of where each driver/rider currently is, the job/s they are working on, and their direction of travel to decide whom best to allocate each job to. The controller also has to allocate these jobs in such a manner that each driver/rider is able to earn a worthwhile income and/or has an equitable workload. In order to earn a sufficient income, drivers/riders are preferably dealing with more than one job at a time, thereby earning income from several customers at the same time as they travel around the city. Ideally, an experienced courier may be carrying approximately 4–6 parcels at any given time, which is often referred to as a 'run' (Fincham, 2006) but, many jobs involve a single point-to-point journey of a single parcel.

The greater the number of drivers/riders overseen by a controller, the more organized and skilful the controller needs to be in visualizing, planning and distributing the jobs between couriers as they arise. The controller will typically seek to allocate drivers/riders to particular locations as much as possible and often undertakes the role without the use of routing and scheduling software (Fincham, 2006).

Jobs are allocated to drivers/riders by controllers on a real-time basis, which can result in some waiting between jobs for drivers/riders. The frequency and duration of waiting times for the next job to be allocated vary and typically range from about 10 to 60 minutes with longer gaps often occurring around the middle of the day when customers are taking lunch breaks. The drivers/riders are expected to remain wherever they are, on standby for their next job from the controller (Employment Tribunal, 2017a).

Once a driver/rider has been allocated a job by a controller, he or she is responsible for: 1) collecting the parcel from the customer; 2) transporting it to its destination as quickly as possible (along with the other parcels for other customers); 3) finding the building the item is destined for, delivering the parcel to the consignee; and 4) obtaining a Proof of Delivery (PoD) (typically a signature) to prove delivery was successful. If the drivers/riders have any queries about jobs they are working on – such as they cannot find the building, or cannot gain access to it – they will contact the controller for advice. Experienced drivers/riders will rarely contact controllers for such assistance, but less experienced drivers/riders will make greater use of a controller's knowledge.

Being a controller or driver/rider is a pressurized job. For controllers this stems from having to retain and compute vast quantities of information and make rapid decisions as new work arises. For drivers/riders, the pressure is based on having to quickly decide on the best routes to take for their jobs and then make rapid journeys across often congested urban environments, taking into account all the hazards and traffic risks that exist. A couple of the larger same-day carriers have replaced their human controllers with computer-based controllers in their efforts to increase efficiency and reduce costs.

Initiatives to reduce the transport and environmental impacts of parcel delivery operations in urban areas

Within the Freight Traffic Control 2050 project a range of logistics management initiatives are being analysed that have the potential to reduce the transport and environmental impacts of next-day and same-day parcel delivery operations in urban areas. These initiatives vary in terms of whether they can be implemented by a carrier alone, or require agreement and implementation by multiple supply chain parties; their ease and likely timescale of implementation; and their potential impact on driving distances and times, parking durations, vehicle fleet requirements, and air quality and carbon emissions.

In the case of the hub-and-spoke next-day/economy parcel sector the following initiatives have been identified as having potential merit and are receiving research attention in terms of desk-based modelling, analysis with carriers and/or actual trials:

- computer-based tools to assist vehicle parking and driver walking strategies;
- other technological aids to improve the efficiency of novice drivers;
- portering delivery systems (the use of on-foot delivery personnel who rendezvous with vehicles to be replenished with further parcels to deliver);
- micro-consolidation centres/mobile depots (to reduce stem mileage/counteract logistics sprawl);
- land use planning policies for logistics facilities (to reduce stem mileage/counteract logistics sprawl);
- relaxing the proportion of timed guaranteed deliveries/collections;
- carrier collaboration in sharing parcel delivery work between themselves;
- the intervention of a 'Freight Traffic Controller' who determines work allocation between carriers across a given geographical area;
- delivery retiming;
- vehicle fleet/type choice;
- pricing delivery services to reflect internal and external costs (challenging the 'free delivery' notion);
- in-house logistics/concierge services for large and multi-tenanted buildings;

- collaborative procurement by receivers (to reduce the number of suppliers/carriers visiting the building or local area;
- increased onsite storage facilities at receivers' businesses to reduce the frequency of deliveries;
- determining the most appropriate location for personal B2C deliveries: workplace, home, collection point, locker bank.

In the case of the point-to-point same-day parcel sector the following initiatives have been identified as having potential merit and are receiving research attention in terms of desk-based modelling, analysis with carriers and/or actual trials:

- consolidating parcel collections by grouping them together and serving them with a single vehicle that then makes all these deliveries, thereby moving several customers' orders at the same time;
- merging together same-day sectors currently operated separately by carriers (eg parcels and medical items);
- green delivery pricing – pricing strategies that promote less transport intensive services that still provide customers with same-day, albeit less rapid, deliveries;
- adopting more environmentally sensitive transport vehicles (eg electric cargo cycles rather than diesel vans and cars).

In investigating each of these potential initiatives, account needs to be taken of the operational and financial implications, as well as their transport-intensity and environmental impacts, as without a sound business case, it will not be viable for same-day and next-day carriers to implement these solutions and remain commercially competitive.

Conclusions

Parcel flows in urban areas are forecast to increase in the coming years as a result of the continued rapid growth in e-commerce and online shopping. This is likely to be accompanied by the demand for ever higher parcel delivery service levels, including time guarantees, same-day deliveries, and even deliveries within one or two hours of orders being placed. The marketplace of carriers offering next-day and same-day parcel delivery services has become increasingly competitive, with falling revenues per parcel, especially in the B2C sector, which is where the growth in demand is occurring.

One major next-day carrier, City Link, ceased trading in the United Kingdom in the last three years, and a startup, 'on-demand' same-day entrant, Jinn, left the UK market in 2017 (Allen *et al*, 2016; Allen *et al*, 2018). It is likely that more carriers will struggle to remain in business in the long run, with others exiting the marketplace. Amazon has been the fastest growing parcel carrier in the B2C sector, and the last mile fulfilment and delivery infrastructure that it has built is a major threat to other carriers if it commences offering third-party services.

The growth in parcel vehicle activity levels has been exacerbated by many retailers offering 'free' or under-priced deliveries in order to generate sales turnover. Coupled with this, the demand for ever-faster same-day services has serious potential implications for the quantity of parcels carried by each vehicle at any one time, and hence the transport and environmental intensity of parcel delivery in urban areas. Policymakers in the United Kingdom and elsewhere have so far failed to develop strategies and initiatives to counter this threat to society and the environment. Some of the environmental challenges posed by growing parcels-related traffic levels will be countered by the adoption of more stringent vehicle emissions standards, Low Emission Zones, and measures to encourage the uptake of alternatively fuelled vehicles. However, these interventions will do nothing to address the growing demand for road and kerbside space and time that these new parcel delivery services are generating.

In order to cope with the additional pressures that these activities are placing on the urban road network, policymakers will need to consider and assist in the development of additional innovative measures. These will need to either require or encourage opportunities for improved vehicle load consolidation, reduced vehicle dwell time at the kerbside, and improved vehicle routing and scheduling that takes account of the walking component of parcel delivery. Examples of initiatives that offer such potential are being investigated in the FTC 2050 project and were summarized in the previous section.

Portering solutions, in which the final leg of urban parcel deliveries is made by on-foot porters rather than delivery drivers, have recently been trialled as part of the FTC 2050 project. These solutions show considerable promise in terms of reducing kerbside stopping duration as well as the vehicle distance travelled, together with potential financial viability from a carrier perspective (Clarke *et al*, 2018). Such portering solutions could also be used in future in conjunction with autonomous vehicles when these become available for general use in urban areas, and would overcome the safety, security and operational challenges associated with the proposed use of aerial drones and pavement droids in urban environments.

There is much scope for collaboration between retailers and parcel carriers to make better use of existing vehicle and logistics infrastructure capacity in urban areas. However, at present, most of these companies are unwilling to work with each other in terms of delivery services, even if it can be demonstrated to lead to lower operational costs. The advent of big data and new analytical tools, together with case studies showing how trust, loyalty, legal and allocation issues can be addressed in shared delivery solutions have the opportunity to play an important role in making urban parcel deliveries more efficient, thereby reducing their undesirable impacts.

If these vehicle technology and logistics management initiatives by carriers and policymakers fail to provide reductions in the transport and environmental intensity of parcel deliveries in urban areas, it may become necessary for policymakers to consider intervening more directly. This could include ensuring that the price charged to consumers for parcel (and other) delivery services reflect the traffic and environmental costs of these activities, in order to reduce demand for the most inefficient and harmful of these urban vehicle operations.

Acknowledgements

The authors would like to acknowledge the work of their academic colleagues on the 'Freight Traffic Control 2050' (FTC2050) project (www.ftc2050.com): Oliver Bates, Tolga Bektas, Kostas Cheliotis, Adrian Friday, Fraser McLeod, ThuBa Nguyen and Sarah Wise.

References

Allen, J, Piecyk, M and Piotrowska, M (2016) Analysis of the parcels market and parcel carriers' operations in the UK, report as part of the Freight Traffic Control 2050 project, University of Westminster

Allen, J, Piecyk, M and Piotrowska, M (2018) Same-day delivery market and operations in the UK, report as part of the Freight Traffic Control 2050 project, University of Westminster

Apex Insight (2015) UK Business to Business Parcels: Market Insight 2015, Apex Insight

Apex Insight (2017) UK Same Day Delivery Market Insight Report 2017, Apex Insight

Bates, O, Friday, A, Allen, J, Cherrett, T, McLeod, F, Bektas, T, Nguyen, T, Piecyk, M, Piotrowska, M, Wise, S and Davies, N (2018) Transforming last-mile logistics: opportunities for more sustainable deliveries, in Computer Human-Interaction (CHI) 2018 Proceedings: ACM, New York, ISBN 9781450356206 (In Press)

Browne, M, Allen, J and Alexander, P (2016) Business improvement districts in urban freight sustainability initiatives: a case study approach, *Transportation Research Procedia*, **12**, pp 450–60

Butler, S and Osborne, H (2017) Courier wins holiday pay in key tribunal ruling on gig economy, *The Guardian*, 6 January [Online] https://www.theguardian.com/business/2017/jan/06/courier-wins-holiday-pay-in-latest-key-tribunal-ruling-for-gig-economy

Cidell, J (2010) Concentration and decentralization: the new geography of freight distribution in US metropolitan areas, *Journal of Transport Geography*, **18**, pp 363–71

CitySprint (2017) Annual Report and Accounts 2016, CitySprint

Clarke, S, Allen, J, Cherrett, T, McLeod, F and Oakey, A (2018) Report on the Portering Trial, Transport for London Consolidation Demonstrator project, Gnewt/Freight Traffic Control 2050 [Online] http://www.ftc2050.com/reports/Final_report_portering.pdf

Copenhagen Economics (2013) E-commerce and delivery: a study of the state of play of EU parcel markets with particular emphasis on e-commerce, European Commission

Dablanc, L and Rakotonarivo, D (2010) The impacts of logistics sprawl: How does the location of parcel transport terminals affect the energy efficiency of goods' movements in Paris and what can we do about it?, The Sixth International Conference on City Logistics, *Procedia Social and Behavioral Sciences*, **2** (3), pp 6087–96

Dablanc, L, Ogilvie, S and Goodchild, A (2014) Logistics sprawl: differential warehousing development patterns in Los Angeles, California, and Seattle, Washington, *Transportation Research Record: Journal of the Transportation Research Board*, **2410**, pp 105–12

Day, J (2015) The secret life of a cycle courier, *The Guardian*, 1 May [Online] https://www.theguardian.com/books/2015/may/01/my-life-cycle-courier-london-cyclogeography

Employment Tribunal (2017a) Ms M Dewhurst v CitySprint UK Ltd: 2202512/2016, Employment Tribunal decision, 5 January, Employment Tribunal

Employment Tribunal (2017b) Mr C Gascoigne v Addison Lee Ltd: 2200436/2016, Employment Tribunal Decision, Published 14 August 2017, Employment Tribunal

Fincham, B (2006) Back to the 'old school': bicycle messengers, employment and ethnography, *Qualitative Research*, **6** (2) pp 187–205

Freight Transport Association (2016) Van Excellence Report, Freight Transport Association

Gruber, J, Kihm, A and Lenz, B (2014) A new vehicle for urban freight? An ex-ante evaluation of electric cargo bikes in courier services, *Research in Transportation and Business Management*, **11**, pp 53–62

Herson, M (2015) Metamorphosis of UK Parcels Market, 22 June, *Post & Parcel* [Online] https://postandparcel.info/65831/news/metamorphosis-of-uk-parcels-market/

Hesse, M (2008) *The City as a Terminal: The urban context of logistics and freight transport*, Ashgate, Aldershot

IMRG (2017) UK online sales exceed £130 billion in 2016, fuelled by sales growth on smartphones, 17 January, *IMRG* [Online] https://www.imrg.org/media-and-comment/press-releases/uk-online-sales-in-2016/

Jinks, D (2016) The Uberfication of Deliveries: Why Uber's move into logistics will transform the delivery market and encourage 'The Sharing Economy Revolution', Parcelhero Industry Report

Keynote (2015) Courier & Express Services: Market Report 2015, Keynote

Lieb, R and Lieb, K (2014) Is Amazon a 3PL?, *Supply Chain Quarterly*, Quarter 3

Maes, J and Vanelslander, T (2012) The use of bicycle messengers in the logistics chain, concepts further revised, The Seventh International Conference on City Logistics, *Procedia – Social and Behavioral Sciences*, **39**, pp 409–23

Mintel (2017) Delivery Market Posts £1 Billion Increase in Sales in 2016, press release, 5 July, Mintel [Online] http://www.mintel.com/press-centre/retail-press-centre/courier-and-express-delivery-market-posts-1-billion-increase-in-sales-in-2016

Morgan, E (2011) Cycle messengers: a really trying way to work, *The Independent*, 18 July [Online] http://www.independent.co.uk/life-style/cycle-messengers-a-really-tyring-way-to-work-2315850.html

Ofcom (2015) Annual monitoring update on the postal market: Financial year 2014–15, Ofcom

Ofcom (2016) Annual monitoring update on the postal market: Financial year 2015–16, Ofcom

Ofcom (2017) Annual monitoring update on the postal market: Financial year 2016–17, Ofcom

Oliver Wyman (2015) Amazon's Move into Delivery Logistics, Oliver Wyman

Pender, K (2007) Bicycle messengers are pedaling uphill against the Internet, *SFGate*, 17 July [Online] http://www.sfgate.com/business/networth/article/Bicycle-messengers-are-pedaling-uphill-against-2581034.php

Piecyk, M and Allen, J (2017) Land availability in London, *Logistics & Transport Focus*, November, pp 38–40

Pooler, M (2016) Online orders boost UK parcel market, *Financial Times*, 5 January

Postal and Logistics Consulting Worldwide (2015) Review of the Impact of Competition in the Postal Market on Consumers, Final Report to Citizens Advice, Postal and Logistics Consulting Worldwide [Online]

https://www.citizensadvice.org.uk/Global/Public/Policy%20research/Documents/Final%20CA%20final%20report%20market%20review%202-07-15.pdf

Price, R (2017) London delivery startup Doddle is closing most of its stores after burning through tens of millions of pounds, *Business Insider*, 24 April [Online] http://uk.businessinsider.com/doddle-closing-stores-laying-off-staff-revenues-click-and-collect-2017-4

Royal Mail (2015a) Annual Report and Financial Statements 2014–15, page 5, Royal Mail

Royal Mail (2015b) Response to Ofcom's July 2015 Discussion paper: Review of the regulation of Royal Mail, 18 September, Royal Mail

Royal Mail (2016) Market Overview, Royal Mail

Sparkes, M (2009) Feared by pedestrians, despised by cabbies: the life and hard times of a London courier, *The Guardian*, 17 September [Online] https://www.theguardian.com/environment/green-living-blog/2009/sep/17/bicycle-courier

Sumner-Rivers, R (2015) Amazon's Prime Ambition, Parcelhero Industry Report

Taylor, I (2015) Royal Mail parcels growth offsets decline in mail revenues, 19 November, *Post & Parcel* [Online] https://postandparcel.info/69477/news/e-commerce/royal-mail-sees-parcels-growth-offset-decline-in-mail-revenues/

Transport for London (2009) Regent Street – Delivery and Servicing Regent Street Site Survey, August 2009, report prepared by Ove Arup and Partners, Transport for London

Wood, Z (2016) 'Love the job, hate the way we're treated': life on the frontline of UK's delivery army, *The Guardian*, 31 July [Online] https://www.theguardian.com/money/2016/jul/30/job-pay-workers-gig-economy

E-commerce trends and implications for urban logistics

08

LAETITIA DABLANC

Introduction

In 2017, e-commerce represented 607 billion euros in Europe (Ecommerce Foundation, 2018), or about 9 per cent of Europe's retail. Despite this still modest share of retail in value, very few activities have changed urban freight as much as e-commerce has since it started developing at a fast rate (about 15 to 20 per cent each year, in value of retail goods sold, in Europe since 2003).

Impacts on urban freight range from increasing the number of urban delivery (and pickup) trips, changing the types of vehicles, operators, time and place of deliveries, increasing technological and economic innovations, disrupting labour organization and conditions, and transforming local traffic and planning policies: in summary, nearly all dimensions of urban freight have been impacted by e-commerce. E-commerce represents a much larger share of the total number of deliveries in cities than its share of retail value (see section 2 on data). The volume of parcels linked to e-commerce and delivered in cities 'will continue to increase by about 7 per cent per year'[1] for a few more years.

Freight transport in urban areas is the result of logistics decisions specific to each of the many sectors of activity that make up a city. Each sector sets up specific logistics chains that meet its own production or distribution requirements. On the freight transport system, two opposing forces are at work. The first is towards more 'mass' freight mobility: consolidated and less frequent deliveries, in larger vehicles, to achieve economies of scale. This, for example, has happened in grocery retail in dense urban areas, with a decrease in independent stores and an increase in chain retail. This is especially true for large cities, where independent retail (outside the city centre) is the fastest disappearing economic activity. While an independent store can see several deliveries per day, a chain supermarket will receive only one or two, with goods consolidated on pallets in a large lorry.

Conversely, other forces are pushing for 'fragmentation' and individualization of deliveries: made on a case-by-case basis, with greater frequency, in smaller vehicles. Behind many of these forces towards fragmentation are e-commerce supply chains. At the extreme of this development are the new individual demands for 'instant' e-commerce delivery (Dablanc *et al*, 2017b). Visser *et al* (2014) argue, from a global review of works on the topic, that options exist to reduce the fragmentation in the retail channel induced by e-commerce.

This chapter describes some of these changes, and when possible quantifies them. One cautionary word, however: data on e-commerce induced urban freight traffic are still in very poor supply. Simple information on the number of urban deliveries and pickups related to e-commerce, for example, is not easy to provide. Because of its crucial importance to understanding trends, the availability of **data** will be the focus of section 2. The remaining sections will look at the main areas of change: in section 3, **consumers'** new behaviours; in section 4 the supply of **delivery services**; in section 5, urban freight **innovations** related to e-commerce; in section 6 a focus on **'instant deliveries;'** and in section 7 the impact of e-commerce on **urban warehousing.**

Data on e-commerce urban freight flows

Data on e-commerce urban freight flows are not sufficient yet. However, some questions can begin to be answered.

Does e-commerce reduce shopping trips?

As Gardrat *et al* (2016, p 5) observe, 'consumer shopping trips are already a relatively well-tackled subject today (...), however these datasets and the subsequent models do not include home deliveries or pickup trips. These data being in fact essentially derived from household mobility surveys and hardly identifying e-commerce related trips.' Several works have actually looked at the impact of e-commerce on personal mobility. In Weltevreden and Rotem-Mindali (2009) or Edwards *et al* (2010), the question was: does e-commerce reduce or increase personal mobility (and the CO_2 attached to it)? For the most part, these articles conclude that it depends. A Swedish survey on consumer buying and travel habits based on the travel diaries of regular and non-regular online shoppers (Hiselius *et al*, 2012) shows that on the whole, those who shop regularly online make the same total number of trips as those who do not. There is no large difference in individual trip length between those who shop regularly online and those who do not, nor is there difference in the mode travelled. Contrary to the Swedish survey, US studies show that ordering online can reduce urban traffic. For Levinson (2014), using 2010 Travel Survey results from Minneapolis and Saint Louis, shopping trips in 2010 were less than 9 per cent of all trips down from 12.5 per cent in 2000 due to the substitution of online shopping (although the economic downturn of 2008–10 may have played a role). Each delivery truck may replace dozens of car-based shopping trips (Cortright, 2015). A study from Wygonik and Goodchild (2012) on US grocery delivery shows that, theoretically, delivery vehicles incur fewer vehicle miles travelled (VMT) when compared with corresponding individual trips to collect these goods. This is partly confirmed by a study from Durand and González-Feliu (2012) in the Lyon region. However, apart from the Swedish study (Hiselius *et al*, 2012), these are simulations only, not empirical studies of what online shoppers actually do in terms of shopping mobility.

How much does e-commerce increase freight trips?

There is another question, closer to the urban freight topic, which is much less discussed in literature: how much urban **freight** mobility does e-commerce generate? In other words, how many delivery/pickup trips are necessary to service e-commerce users? And how do these delivery trips compare within the whole urban freight mobility? This question is important not just for increased knowledge and good data. It is important because it helps predict the upcoming challenges (traffic management, urban planning, pollution and congestion) urban areas will have to face because of e-commerce growth. Some work such as Comi and Nuzzolo (2015) makes simulations, concluding that e-commerce in the future will have an important impact on the increase in urban freight traffic. Very few actual data, however, are reported in the literature.

In this regard, the most accurate figures found to support this chapter come from New York in the United States and Lyon in France, with some interesting elements from London and a few other cases.

In the New York metro area, in 2016, the application of the models developed by Rensselaer Polytechnic Institute to the US zip code Business Pattern Data (J Holguín-Veras[2]) estimates that for **establishments** (business-to-business, or B2B, deliveries), the generation rate of per capita freight operations (deliveries and pickups) is 0.12 per person per day.[3] For deliveries and pickups to **households** (business-to-consumer, or B2C, deliveries) the estimate is that the generation ratio has reached 0.12 operations per person per day (the same as for B2B).

In Lyon (metro area), a detailed data collection on deliveries to households was made by Gardrat *et al* (2016). They looked at what they call 'deferred purchases and receptions' (DPR), including home deliveries, deliveries at pickup points (note: both can be generated by a shopping trip, not only by online orders) and deliveries at grocery click-and-collect points. Their pilot survey shows that, on average, households generate approximately 19.2 DPR per year in the Lyon metro area. The paper identifies several categories of goods:

- groceries and catering (7.2 DPR per household per year);
- clothing (3.8);
- high tech and culture (3.1);
- household appliances, furniture, others (2.6);
- healthcare and cosmetics (2.5).

Considering an average size of household in Lyon of 1.9 (2014), we find a ratio of 10 DPR per person per year, or 0.03 per person per day (four times less than in New York).

In the United Kingdom, the following has been calculated by Allen *et al* (2017) (Table 8.1):

Table 8.1 Annual B2C deliveries in the United Kingdom, 2016

Type of Online Retailing Sector	Annual B2C Deliveries for 2016
Grocery	86 million orders
Non-food small items	890 million parcels
Non-food large items	8.6 million items
Takeaways and other home-delivered meals	270 million orders

SOURCE Allen *et al*, 2017, Table 3.1 p 25

If it is estimated that Londoners exhibit more or less the general UK e-commerce patterns, which may not be the case (especially because people of working age, who tend to order more online than the general population, are overrepresented in large cities), these national figures would represent for London around 121 million parcels, 37 million meals, 1.2 million large items and 12 million grocery orders received by households in 2016.

The number of items ordered, or even delivered, is not strictly equivalent to the number of deliveries and pickup operations, as a parcel can be returned (adding a pickup operation), and a parcel can be delivered together with another parcel (reducing delivery operations). Nevertheless, based on the approximation above, the London figures identified from Allen *et al* (2017) represent around 0.05 operations per person per day, about half the figure provided from New York.

Are 'same day deliveries' a significant new trend?

A new survey (6T-bureau de recherche, 2018)[4] of a representative sample of people living in the City of Paris (population 2.2 million) and in Manhattan[5] (population 1.6 million) provides additional elements. These quintessential 'urbanites' have specific features compared with the rest of the people living in both metro areas: higher revenues and more ethnic diversity. They also enjoy numerous and diverse local physical stores. Here are the main results of the survey.

First, people living in Manhattan and Paris order a lot online, especially in Manhattan: 82 per cent of Manhattanites order online at least 6 to 10 times a month (and 26 per cent at least once a week). For Parisians the figures are 67 per cent and 9 per cent respectively.

Also interesting is the significant share of same-day deliveries in all e-commerce activity: 12.2 per cent of orders in Manhattan and 10.2 per cent in Paris are delivered on the same day. Same-day deliveries include two-hour deliveries, which already make up 4.5 per cent (Manhattan) and 3 per cent (Paris) of total e-commerce deliveries. In this group, the use of 'instant delivery' apps and 'food apps' (see section 5 below) is becoming a major feature of online activity for Parisians and even more so for New Yorkers in Manhattan: 16.2 per cent of respondents in Manhattan are using a food app several times a week (4.5 per cent in Paris), and another 15.6 per cent once a week (7.9 per cent in Paris).

Both populations differ, however, in their mode of delivery: 22 per cent of Parisians mentioned collection points or automated lockers as the place of delivery for their latest purchase, while they represent only 3 per cent of pickup places for Manhattanites. New York building superintendents, or the Parisian *concierge*, currently have a very important role: 27 per cent of Manhattan deliveries and 13 per cent of Paris deliveries are handled by them. This relates well with another survey (Rodrigue, 2017), outside of Manhattan: in an apartment building of 300 apartments (served by one lobby) in northern New Jersey, with mostly upper-middle-income residents, 65 parcels per day were received in 2016. This does not take into account food deliveries.

As a general conclusion about urban freight traffic data involved with e-commerce, let's just say (while hoping that more data will be available in the future) that e-commerce induced freight mobility (B2C) seems already very important in cities in Europe and the United States: it represents 30 to 100 per cent of freight operations serving businesses and administrations (ie B2B, which has always been regarded as representing the totality of urban freight). In other words, urban freight, if defined as freight involving a transport operator (own account or third party) as opposed to freight transport made by a household while shopping, has increased enormously in recent years with (and mostly with) the development of e-commerce.

Growing urban regions, consumers and e-commerce

Today's urban population

Cities, especially large cities, capture an increasing share of population and activities to the detriment of smaller cities or the rural world. They represent interconnected residential and activity nodes (people live in one place and work in another, consume cultural and leisure activities or shop elsewhere in the metropolitan area). City centres increasingly concentrate both wealthy households (with or without children) and young working people or students, rich and poor, including immigrant populations. The mobility of metropolitan residents, in general, is increasingly diversified in its modes (bicycle, car sharing, ride hailing), in its motives and in its schedules. People in metropolitan centres use their private vehicles less often, either because they prefer public transport or alternative modes serving urban work and leisure, or because they no longer own a vehicle. This 'demotorization' of households is particularly marked in the city centre and for the youngest households. These behaviours cumulate with changes in consumption behaviour. Convenience stores, particularly high-end food retail chains, and catering businesses tend to relocate to the city centre, while ethnic businesses increase in urban centres and immigrant neighbourhoods. On the other hand, in the more or less distant peripheries where a growing proportion of the population is located, car ownership remains high, because of a lack of public transport, services and shops, obliging young parents in particular to make complex daily journeys.

E-commerce is now multichannel and extends to groceries

E-commerce adds new dimensions, and some changes, to metropolitan life. E-commerce is now widespread in all segments of the population, no matter where they live – dense urban, suburban or suburban/rural. Metropolitan consumption is now multichannel: households alternately, or at the same time, visit physical shops and order remotely, and receive deliveries in an increasingly diversified way (at home, at a pickup point, at the workplace or at a neighbour's address). This observation must be nuanced for what concerns the online food market. Because until recently it has not been able to offer more attractive prices online than in stores, this segment has developed later and in a more differentiated way than non-food trade. The emergence of click-and-collect services, which imply final mobility of households to collect their shopping, has recently allowed development of remote food orders in suburban areas. In France, the expansion of drive-through outlets for click-and-collect groceries bought online (they are called '*drives*', in English, by the French) has developed very quickly, making the French the European leaders of online grocery shopping (Nielsen, 2018).[6] It is one of the most cost-efficient solutions in metropolitan areas to cope with the growing number of mobile and active shoppers (in particular young active couples with children). Today, all the major grocery retail brands in France have adopted this model (Seidel *et al*, 2016). In 2017, there were 4,036 click-and-collect outlets, more than the total number of large suburban supermarkets. Some (the majority) are attached to the store with no storage (which closely resembles the in-vehicle pickup quite common in the United States), while others are separated from the stores. Click-and-collect services help compensate large retailers for the loss of shoppers and stagnation of sales in large supermarkets. Leclerc's first 'pedestrian *drive*' in Lille offers more products than a city supermarket – 12,000 versus 6,000 stock keeping units (SKUs) at lower prices (on average, 17 per cent reduction), without additional transport costs. Supply to the depot is made through suburban stores continuously. The facility is small (50 square metres), in order to reduce costs and promote rotation. This new organization generates additional freight traffic, with six or seven round trips per day (O Dauvers, quoted in Pierrat, 2017), between the periphery and the centre of Lille.

Table 8.2 Trends for reception point networks in Europe, 2008–2012

Company	Service Type*	Country	Number of Sites 2008	Number of Sites 2012	Growth Rate 2008–12	Parcel Volumes 2012
ByBox	APS	UK	1,000	1,300	+30%	N/A
Collect Plus	PP	UK	Not available	5,000	N/A	N/A
Packstation	APS	Germany	1,000	2,500	+150%	N/A
PaketShop (Hermes)	PP	Germany	13,000	14,000	+7.7%	N/A
ByBox	APS	France	Not implemented	170	N/A	N/A
Cityssimo	APS	France	20	33	+55%	N/A
Kiala	PP	France	3,800 (with MR)	4,500	+18%	15 million
Pickup Services	PP	France	3,100 (à2pas)	5,200	+68%	9 million
Mondial Relay (Point Relais)	PP	France	3,800 (with Kiala)	4,300	+13%	12 million
Relais Colis (Sogep)	PP	France	4,000	4,200	+5%	23 million

*Key: APS = automated pack station; PP = pickup point

SOURCE Morganti *et al*, 2014

Increased expectations from consumers

Overall, e-commerce represents a sort of equalizing force in a metropolitan consumer universe that has known important social differentiation. In parallel, the growing maturity of metropolitan consumers brings with it new desires and expectations. E-commerce's fast development started in 2002/03 when prices of products sold online became more attractive than prices in physical stores. Today, expectations other than price emerge. At the top of the wish list, consumers expect fast delivery and convenience throughout each step of the buying process. People are becoming increasingly aware of the power they have as consumers, and technology continues to move power from producers to consumers. Consumers expect freedom of choice in terms of delivery methods and delivery times. They expect smooth access to a return system. Fast service at all hours becomes more widespread and creates new, higher expectations with respect to accessibility and speed. Customers' expectations routinely go as far as 'instant deliveries'. How does the supply of last mile services cope with these metropolitan behaviours?

Inefficiencies, profitability and logistics solutions for the 'last mile'

In e-commerce, the last mile is the final leg in a business-to-consumer delivery service whereby the consignment is delivered to the recipient either at the recipient's home or at a collection point. Figure 8.1 shows various ways in which e-commerce last mile deliveries combine different elements of the urban supply chain.

Last mile delivery challenges

The last mile is currently regarded as one of the most expensive, least efficient and most polluting segments of the entire urban logistics system. Challenges encountered include:

- The 'not-at-home' problem, leading to high rates of delivery failure. It substantially affects the cost, efficiency and environmental performance, as well as security (risk of theft of a parcel left at the door). Alternative solutions emerge: special locks on the apartment door wirelessly connected to the owner's smartphone, with a camera recording activity (*The Economist*, 23 December 2017).

- Concierges and janitors refusing to accept deliveries. As seen above in section 2, New York residential building lobbies can receive around 60 to 100 parcels a day. A change in the janitors' national collective agreement in France at the end of 2017 acknowledged the issue, allowing janitors not to accept parcel deliveries that require a signature or with a weight above 30 kilograms or dimensions of more than 2 metres.
- Office receptionists facing an increase (difficult to quantify) in employees receiving parcels at work. Some companies are willing to accommodate these deliveries, as a service to employees, while others have banned them. This discussion is ongoing in the United Kingdom.
- Lack of critical mass in some areas or regions, which will also affect the cost. For example, large supermarkets in Dijon tend to concentrate their home delivery service for goods in urban or dense suburban areas in order to optimize delivery costs (Motte-Baumvol *et al*, 2012).
- Increase in returns. Consumers expect smooth, and free, processing of their return for online purchases, as they tend to buy several products in different sizes to choose from.
- Environmental concerns due to the high use of vans, which results in higher emissions per parcel compared with B2B deliveries (Gevaers *et al*, 2011).

Figure 8.1 Supply chain configurations for e-commerce last mile deliveries

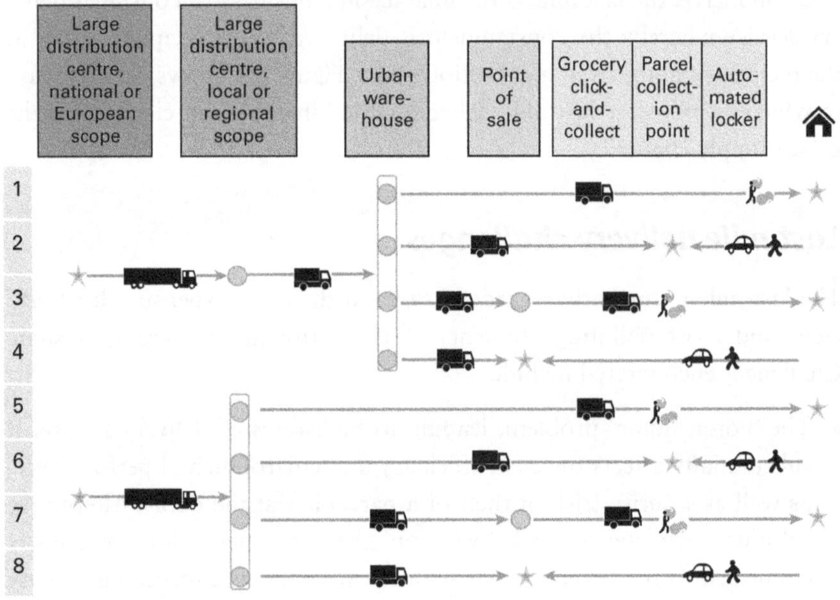

SOURCE JL Perrin, ©institutducommerce

Express parcel operators, specialized operators

Postal and express parcel operators provide the bulk of e-commerce deliveries. They appreciate the new opportunities but feel the cost: 'Economics will require more innovative ways to deliver goods ordered online, instead of only delivering individual items to residences, which is expensive' (FedEx Annual Report, 2017). In an increasingly competitive market, specialized operators have appeared, such as the French Star Service focusing on home delivery of grocery; or pickup point networks, some of them now part of very large groups (Belgian Kiala is part of UPS). While homes remain the main place for current e-commerce deliveries, click-and-collect gains momentum. Back in 2009, Augereau *et al* (2009) had already identified two categories of collection point: **pickup points**, comprising networks of local stores (dry cleaners, florists, etc) and **automated lockers** (referred to as '*packstations*' by DHL in Germany). Both networks have since then developed, especially in Europe (Table 8.2), Asia and, at a more recent stage, in North America, such as Amazon lockers. Automated lockers are implemented routinely in student halls of residence or city centre condominiums. They are an integral part of the design of lobbies in new residential developments in Chinese cities.

A detailed analysis of click-and-collect development in France (Morganti *et al*, 2014) shows that the deployment of networks of collection points is directly linked to population density and frequency. This means that urban areas have larger numbers of pickup points than suburban/rural areas. And in suburban and rural areas, pickup points are more likely to be located in the centre and main commercial streets. Overall, however, coverage is very good. In the Seine-et-Marne department in the Paris region, Morganti *et al* (2014) showed that overall, 80 per cent of the Seine-et-Marne population is less than 8 minutes from a collection point: 8 minutes by car on average for remote suburban homes; and 8 minutes by foot for urban residents.

According to a study in Toulouse, France (Angot, 2018), the implementation of pickup points in central areas seems increasingly difficult because of the reluctance of shop owners to participate. For the author, the pickup-point network model in the future may well be better adapted to suburban and less populated areas, where shop owners see a direct advantage in an additional stream of resources and passers-by.

Retailers are innovating

Brick-and-mortar activities now adopt an 'online-to-offline' (O2O) strategy to use online channels to attract customers to physical stores. Retailers use online virtual shop windows as well as offline physical shops to maximize their exposure to consumers. The physical facility is not just a shop to sell products but a multifunctional space including a showroom/warehouse where customers can experience or pick up products seen online. Walmart is transforming physical stores to multifunction facilities including showroom, mini-fulfilment centre and pickup point. In the United Kingdom, many major store-based online retailers offer click-and-collect services in which customers collect their goods from the store of their choice or other stand-alone collection facility, rather than having them delivered at home. Sports Direct, a London high street and online sports goods retailer, introduced a click-and-collect service that attempts to generate in-store sales as well. Consumers are charged £4.99 for click-and-collect orders, but in return are provided with a £5 voucher that can be spent only in the store.

E-retailers are more involved in logistics services

In the e-commerce logistics service market, lines between supply chain players become increasingly blurred as new business models are challenging incumbent players. Some marketplaces are becoming logistics operators and are developing strong delivery capabilities. This puts logistics service providers in competition with e-retailers or startups that provide innovative solutions to satisfy the requirement of urban consumers in a hurry, such as Shutl in the United Kingdom (bought by eBay). Amazon has entered the parcel carrier market with, in some locations, its own logistics and delivery capability, Amazon Logistics (Allen *et al*, 2017). Amazon Logistics already delivers, in some countries, as many parcels as some of the largest carriers operating in the country.

On the other hand, smaller stores in local areas suffer due to competition from online and large-scale retailers. One response to this has been the creation of last mile delivery brokers within a variety of urban areas, allowing people to buy items from local stores or restaurants and have them delivered by local drivers to the home or office location that is most convenient at the moment. Google launched Google Shopping Express (now Google Express) in San Francisco and the Silicon Valley in 2013. In 2017, all US states were covered (Lermite, 2017). It allows consumers to order goods from a range of brands available locally (eg Target, Walgreens, Staples, L'Occitane) online or through a mobile application (Google Express). A Google truck will pick up and transport all the parcels to its sorting centre, and a small vehicle will redistribute the goods to their destinations according to each order. The cost of each delivery is from zero to US $4.99 and over.

Innovations, e-commerce and urban freight

E-commerce plays a special role in pushing forward technological and other types of innovation that directly impact urban freight.

Urban freight innovations are mostly related to e-commerce

In city logistics in general, there is a strong contrast between the bubbling of innovative ideas from startups and digital entrepreneurs, university research or municipalities,[7] and the relative timidity of concrete achievements. The transition from micro-niche to economically viable deployment is not easy for many logistics innovations (Libeskind, 2015). This is a field where full-scale tests are expensive. This prevents innovation, especially in a context where incentives to innovate are relatively low, as delivery service is perceived by users (consumers) as generally satisfactory (which was not the case for taxis challenged by new ride hailing services). All kinds of recurrent city logistics utopias have not materialized, the only major changes remaining, in the end, those carried out by the e-commerce giants. Indeed, technological and organizational innovations with low implementation costs that have been successful are generally linked to the development of e-commerce. Collection points have become mainstream, providing an alternative to home delivery. Kiala (part of UPS since 2016) had the idea in the early 2000s to streamline the traditional mail-order relay point by extending partnerships to a large number of e-merchants, automating parcel processing and tracking, and professionalizing the management of partner stores. Automated lockers are emerging, in public spaces (train and bus stations, supermarkets) or private ones (a building's lobby). New partnerships emerge for click-and-collect networks, such as between Walgreens and FedEx in the United States. New **conciergeries** should also be mentioned, bringing an additional range of services in office buildings such as dry cleaning, shoemaking and delivery/shipping parcels. Groom Box, for example, has already installed digital lockers in western Paris and suburbs.

The use of digital applications on smartphones to connect freight transport providers and demanders already translates into the operational reality of delivery companies, especially for the B2C market. 'Instant deliveries' have developed very quickly, becoming a mass pattern of urban consumption. These new digitally driven forms of delivery in the city (see section 6 below) have brought about changes in working conditions of delivery workers.

Cross-border e-commerce drives other types of innovation, not so much technological but also organizational, such as Cainiao which has set up in China duty-free bonded warehouses for foreign manufacturers (*The Economist*, 26 October 2017).

Electric delivery vehicles

As far as vehicles are concerned, technological developments in the world of urban delivery, still limited, are much driven by e-commerce. Electric vehicles are not yet ready for the urban delivery mass market. They remain expensive to buy, with few variants per model (volume, height), and their range remains limited despite increasingly efficient batteries. The second-hand market is not yet developed. Even in Norway, where sales of passenger cars are 25 per cent electric, electric vans represent only 2 per cent of the van market. However, the use of electric delivery vehicles raises many hopes. In current operating conditions and taking into account total cost of ownership, Camilleri (2018) estimates a potential market share of 20 per cent by 2032 (in a scenario where diesel prices grow by 20 per cent). Many companies related to e-commerce are testing vehicles. The French La Poste operates the largest fleet of electric commercial vehicles in France. Star Service, a company specializing in grocery home delivery, has installed a car park in Paris with 50 charging stations for its fleet of Kangoo ZE vans. The company operates 200 electric vans. UPS will roll out 35 Arrival electric trucks in Paris and London in the autumn of 2018. Accelerated take-up of electric vans could happen, with some additional push from municipalities (subsidies or regulations).

Electrically assisted cargo cycles have made a notable appearance in the centres of major European cities in recent years. Cargo cycles are tricycles equipped with a fairly large container (between 1 and 1.5 square metres base). They are operated by delivery companies, from small ones such as The Green Link in Paris, who often work for large express parcel operators, or directly by large companies (Amazon owns and operates two cargo cycles in the centre of Strasbourg, France). Star Service bought La Petite Reine, a company that historically was the first in France (and in Europe) to provide deliveries by cargo cycle and even manufactured and distributed one of the main models in circulation today.

Autonomous vehicles, delivery robots

Autonomous vehicles are the subject of considerable technological research and many applications. The rapid technological progress on driving assistance and connectivity (vehicle-to-infrastructure links, vehicle-to-vehicle links, intelligent traffic management) could lead to the routine use of AVs in the not too distant future. Applications in the world of urban deliveries are also the focus of attention of vehicles' manufacturers. They raise the same issues as those for passenger transport, including safety of urban road users, but also specific issues, such as security against theft or the management of the last metres.

For the moment, there is little prospect of an urban future for drone deliveries, especially because of tight regulations concerning urban air traffic. DHL predicted, in a 2014 report, a future for drones but mainly for hard-to-reach geographical areas, more rural than urban. In the spring of 2018, the Chinese e-retailer JD launched a drone delivery service to 100 mountain villages, using 40 drones. Drones have a low capacity (one package at a time), reducing the total productivity of a drone system in an urban environment by '94 per cent' (McKinnon, 2016) compared to delivery rounds by van. However, progress in technology has considerably decreased cost per parcel, provided drones do not cover long distances. This requires that drone departure bases be near end consumers. In cities, this results in real estate costs. Solutions considered include creating departure points from trucks, including autonomous trucks, entering the city for a limited period of time. The delivery point must be suitable for drone landing, which is hardly the case in apartment buildings. In May 2018, a regular drone delivery line opened in Reykjavik, Iceland.

We note the emergence of small robots rolling along the ground, capable of delivering parcels at home (the recipient, notified by text message, meets the robot to open the locker protecting the product). Domino's Robotic Unit was tested in New Zealand for pizza delivery. Starship Technologies is developing in this niche in California and the United Kingdom. JD has university campus delivery rounds made by robots, such as Alibaba's Cainiao logistics company.

The use of big data

At a very different scale, big data will also reshape e-commerce urban logistics. Online retail sites such as Amazon, hold data on individual consumption habits, which can guide and anticipate home deliveries. This brings the mobility of goods into the world of artificial intelligence. Fevad, the French federation of distance selling companies, has created an e-commerce logistics observatory (www.deliver-analytics.com), which uses anonymized data from its members[8] to obtain analytical information presented on a 'dashboard': indicators such as the average time it takes to receive parcels from customers, by type of goods, or the rate of successful deliveries, for different types of e-commerce markets, are monitored.

Focus

When asked[9] 'What is innovation in urban logistics?', a representative from a major player in freight and logistics in Sweden responded with these points:

- flexibility of IT systems (information technology);
- robotization;
- architectural innovation for urban warehouses, mixed uses and new economic models, time-sharing;
- understanding that uses and behaviours are more advanced than logistics professionals or municipal officials think: 60 per cent of our customers would accept packages left on the porch, without signature;
- anticipating the type of consumers that today's teenagers will become, whose online social practices are 'absolutely misunderstood' by adults today;
- quality of service, quality of service, quality of service. Interactivity with the deliverer: chat live, offer alternative delivery solutions (of course via smartphones);
- do not stupidly block incremental innovation (in London, companies are starting to prohibit the delivery of packages to employees at their workplace, when this is a particularly successful way of optimizing urban last mile logistics).

On-demand 'instant deliveries' and food apps

The competition of e-commerce in urban areas is moving into the area of 'instant deliveries', with e-retailers proposing to deliver to customers in less than two hours. This service is typically now part of the 'gig economy', carried out by self-employed individuals who accept assignments through digital platforms (Dablanc *et al*, 2017b).

Increasing types of goods, diversity of companies

The type of products involved ranges from ready meals (restaurants and caterers) to general groceries and, increasingly, consumer products in individual parcels. In Oslo, Zoopit offers instant deliveries in collaboration with several online stores covering products like electronics, pharmaceuticals and clothes. Amazon Prime Now allows members to order more than 25,000 items (as well as food from local restaurants) and get free delivery within two hours (one hour with a fee) in major cities in the world (North America, Europe, China, India, Japan). Some services are dedicated to very specialized markets such as large objects.

Some services are based on crowdsourcing, or collaborative economy, of the 'pure' type: individuals are invited to take advantage of personal trips (by car, bicycle, public transport...) to transport goods. In Europe, the DHL MyWay test in Stockholm is the most advanced to date. Recruited via Facebook, several thousand individuals, called 'mywaysers', compensated up to 1 or 2 euros per delivery, delivered e-commerce packages at home when their itinerary corresponded to a delivery request. The service was abandoned due to the reluctance of e-merchants and recipients to pay for the service. Some services employ private individuals dedicated, when delivering, to the delivery (not driving somewhere for other purposes). In the United States and the United Kingdom, Amazon has successfully developed Amazon Flex, which hires individuals to deliver Amazon packages. Most services use registered self-employed delivery people dedicated to the tasks while delivering them.

Many instant delivery companies have been set up as local startups and are currently growing to regional markets (Europe: Delivery Hero and Deliveroo; the United States: Postmates, Instacart, DoorDash, GrubHub; China: Tencent Meituan, Alibaba Ele.me; Indonesia: Go-SEND).

How many 'instant deliveries' in cities today?

Freight trips generated by instant deliveries are rather significant already. It is estimated that there are about 100,000 instant deliveries every week in Paris (Dablanc *et al*, 2017b). This means that there are 100,000 pickups in the same area, as instant deliveries generally require a physical proximity between pickup and delivery places. Instant deliveries therefore may represent about 12 per cent of B2C related deliveries and pickups, and 3 to 5 per cent of total deliveries and pickups in the Paris region.

In Paris, instant deliveries are mostly made by bicycle. A local survey (Dablanc *et al*, 2017b) showed that bikes make up 88 per cent of deliveries, motorbikes and mopeds (9 per cent), and other means – pedestrian, public transport – 3 per cent). This is very different from urban freight in general, made at 57 per cent by vans, 39 per cent by lorries, 3 per cent by motorbikes, and 1 per cent by bikes and cargo cycles in Paris in 2012 (Serouge *et al*, 2014). The dominant use of bicycles for instant deliveries in Paris is probably an extreme case, due to the French legislation on third-party freight transport: any head of a company, or self-employed individual, providing a freight transport service with use of a motor vehicle (including mopeds, motorbikes and vans) must be registered in the national freight transport register. This can be done after a three-day training course, the guarantee of a fixed sum on a bank account for each vehicle used, and with a clean police record. This rather strict legislation deters independent couriers from using motor vehicles, although many violations of the rule are observed.

Fragile business model, labour issues

An innovative solution in the search for a more profitable model for customized, flexible and cheap delivery services in urban areas, instant deliveries' business model is fragile. In Europe, TakeEatEasy and TokTokTok went bankrupt. Foodora left the French market in summer 2018. In the United States, Shyp recently closed down. Despite a fast increase in volumes, TakeEatEasy did not convince investors to respond to a third call for funds. Highly competitive, the market is perhaps saturated and begins to self-regulate. Postmates, a company operating in the United States, created in 2011 by a German entrepreneur based in San Francisco, is a lasting success story. The company has diversified from a service dedicated to restaurants to become a generalist serving shopkeepers, large and small, positioning itself as an 'anti-Amazon'.

Several companies like Deliveroo or Foodora/Delivery Hero have experienced labour movement and protests (notably in Milan, Berlin, Paris and London). This is part of a mounting wave of criticism in some European countries against the gig economy and 'uberization' of jobs, that is an increase in the share of jobs carried out by independent contractors at the supposed expense of salary-based employment. Though not as publicized as controversies with ride hailing services, instant deliveries are a key part of the discussion. Gig jobs are considered precarious and devoid of benefits such as the right to unionize, good insurance or retirement benefits. In the delivery business, they are also accused of favouring dangerous behaviour on the road, as the revenue made is usually correlated to the number of delivery tasks accomplished.

Promoting better work protection for independent contractors is one way forward. A California bill proposal pushed for independent contractors to be able to form their own negotiating organizations. The bill would have required technology companies to meet and negotiate with organized groups of independent contractors. It passed the California Assembly Labour and Employment Committee in 2015 but was abandoned because of anti-trust concerns.[10] The French law 2016-1088 on Labour, Social Dialogue and Career Protection introduced the following changes to the Labour Code applying to independent contractors using digital platforms:

- If they decide on the 'characteristics' of the service and its price, digital platforms have a social responsibility towards the workers using them.
- Digital platforms must organize or pay for insurance for work-related accidents (for workers earning a minimum annual revenue).
- Workers using these platforms have a right to professional training and the digital platform must pay for it (for workers earning a minimum annual revenue).
- Workers can unionize and their bargaining actions – if reasonable – cannot be used as a motive for dismissal.

In addition to allowing independent contractors to form their own bargaining organizations, unions also promote the reclassification of independent workers as employees. In the United States, several lawsuits in the instant delivery sector have resulted in such reclassifications. Instacart reclassified some or all of its contractors into employees. One lawsuit came from four former drivers working for Amazon Prime Now in Los Angeles and specifically for its subcontractor Scoobeez, a courier company based in Orange County. 'Amazon goes much further than Uber in controlling drivers' schedules and work activities. Amazon Prime Now drivers work regular shifts for an hourly rate and do not have the option to decline deliveries. They also wear Amazon Prime Now uniforms and are not allowed to work for other firms' (quote from a plaintiff, from *LA Weekly*, 29 October 2015). It was reported that Amazon pressured its subcontractor Scoobeez in settling the case, because of the bad publicity and potentially large penalties.

Cooperative-type organizations are timidly setting up to federate independent workers in the delivery sector. In Belgium, a mutual society of artists and self-employed people (SMart) invoices self-employed couriers for their services, making them 'semi-salaried'.

Two surveys made in Paris among couriers (Dablanc and Saidi, 2018) showed the transition of a population of 'dilettante' workers (students and employees delivering in their leisure time for extra resources, often passionate about cycling) to a less-educated population for whom deliveries constitute the main job. These couriers come from the working-class suburbs and have a difficult commute by bicycle – or using public transport with their bicycle. All couriers agree on the challenges of the job: bicycle theft, long waiting times in restaurants, low premiums when traffic conditions are more difficult.

A new challenge to urban policy and planning

City managers now have to deal with these new services. First, in terms of traffic management: the addition of tens of thousands of deliveries by bicycle or moped, or even on in-line skates and scooters, in the streets of large cities increases the heterogeneity of road use, always feared by traffic engineers. Cities must also deal with consequences in terms of urban construction and urban planning: guaranteeing delivery in less than two hours means that the point of departure (picking) of the goods must be close to the consumer's point of arrival. To serve the majority of Los Angeles residents, Amazon operates five Prime Now warehouses, of 5,000 to 6,000 square metres each in the city, at strategic locations, all very urban ones. Existing zoning ordinances are not always welcoming to such buildings (see section 7).

It is still early to imagine the future development of instant delivery, an emerging activity whose economic and social model is fluctuating. Uber succeeded (with lows and highs) in passenger transport because customers were facing a quality issue (insufficient taxis, high prices). In the freight transportation sector, the service is provided and generally of good quality. Profitability is also difficult to achieve, because of a well-known phenomenon for urban delivery: high costs (delivering in the city is complex) but low prices (the delivery market is very competitive, and consumers are increasingly reluctant to pay the real cost of a delivery). It is not certain that the main innovation of instant delivery – the use of a pool of couriers available on demand – will be enough to meet the challenges of this market, at least under acceptable social conditions. However, the growth in consumer demand for instant deliveries, especially in very large cities, seems inexorable. Urban teenagers, in particular, are already eager users, which will guide the behaviour of the adult consumers that they will become.

E-commerce and urban warehousing

Types of warehouse

Warehouses for e-commerce are growing in number. E-commerce requires two types of logistics facilities: fulfilment centres, where products are stored and picked for order preparation; and cross-docking terminals, or sorting centres, where parcels are quickly sorted for last mile delivery tours. While a lot of e-commerce parcel traffic is going through cross-dock facilities operated by regular parcel post and express transport companies (DHL, UPS, La Poste, USPS ...), dedicated facilities operated by e-retailers are also emerging.

The evolution of Amazon facilities in France (Figure 8.2) exemplifies the changes in e-commerce warehousing:

- Amazon opened its first fulfilment centres away from the Paris region: Orleans in 2007, Montélimar in 2010, Sevrey (North of Lyon) in 2012, Lille in 2013, Amiens in 2017.
- The last mega centre will open much closer to Paris: at the end of 2018, Amazon will operate a 142,000 square metre warehouse (representing 500 to 1,000 jobs) in Brétigny-sur-Orge, 30 kilometres south of Paris.
- In 2016 Amazon opened its first urban warehouse to facilitate its new instant delivery service (Prime Now). It is located on Boulevard Ney in the 18th arrondissement, within the city of Paris. The terminal, converted from a former warehouse, serves Paris and 20 nearby cities. It is much smaller (4,000 square metres) than the fulfilment centres.
- Since 2017, Amazon has been operating a third category of warehouse: two cross-dock facilities (urban sorting centres) of around 10,000 square metres each (and about 80 jobs) were built close to Paris, one 15 kilometres to the north-east, close to highways, industrial zones and Charles de Gaulle airport; the other 13 kilometres to the south-east close to residential suburbs as well as major industrial zones. Local contractors operate final deliveries from these two centres. 'These terminals are here because Amazon is committed to deliver parcels when and where customers want them' (Head of Amazon Logistics France, 2017).

An emerging niche of urban warehouses

As shown by the Amazon example, the development of same-day delivery requires logistics facilities to be closer to customers in order to reduce time to delivery. Online retailers and their transport providers (such as UPS) are

Figure 8.2 Amazon warehouses in France

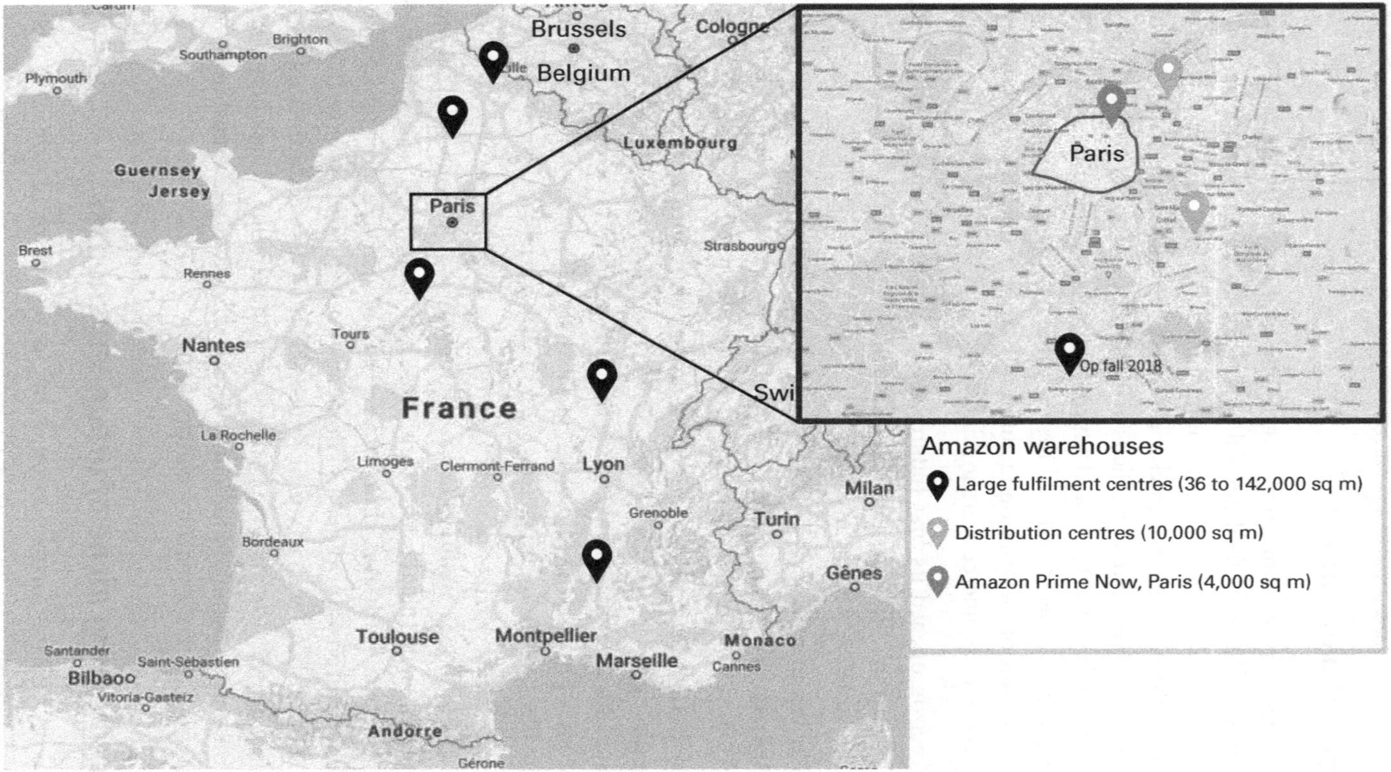

SOURCE Dablanc *et al*, 2018; map: J Rouhier

increasingly willing to pay a premium for relatively small, well-located and well-equipped sites that allow them to gain an advantage over their competitors. E-commerce companies and other retailers are looking for 'infill' locations within urban areas that are repurposed for logistics. An infill area has usually already been developed, but is now vacant and can be repurposed for new users (Spencer *et al*, 2016). The best-known example of urban warehouses is the expansion of Amazon Prime Now facilities in major cities around the world, including one in Manhattan. If the facilities are not in city centres, they will be located in suburban areas near major highways accessible in 30 minutes during non-rush-hour periods (Phillips, 2016). Figure 8.3 shows the Amazon Prime Now warehouse in the centre of Barcelona, Spain. A local publishing company's headquarters was transformed into a warehouse.

Express parcel delivery companies also open small-sized facilities in dense urban centres in order to be closer to their destinations (Heitz and Beziat, 2016). Chronopost, a major express transport operator in France (group La Poste), operates from Beaugrenelle terminal, a former elevated parking structure in the 15th arrondissement converted into an urban warehouse. UPS opened a 7,000 square metres terminal in the eastern part of Paris in 2017. The City of Paris now requests bids for tenders to transform abandoned or underused sites into urban logistics hubs, most often within mixed-use development projects, to reduce impacts from growing urban freight traffic.

In London, most e-commerce warehouses are located outside, often very far outside, the city limits, as far as the Midlands (Birmingham–Leicester–Northampton). A growing warehousing area for e-commerce last

Figure 8.3 Amazon Prime Now's urban warehouse in Barcelona, Spain

SOURCE Google Street View and Google Maps

mile deliveries is around the M25 ring road, between Heathrow, Gatwick, Luton and Stansted. This is due to the lack of sufficient availability in urban areas for urban logistics warehouses needed for last mile fulfilment (Addleshaw Goddard, 2017). The demand for land in London and the land values are so high that warehousing demand often loses out to land uses with higher values such as residential and office development. However, in recent years, warehousing facilities emerged in inner and outer London as a result of the requirements of the online shopping market. From these centres last mile deliveries depart heading to consumers in both residential and commercial buildings. Sainsbury's recently opened its first purpose-built urban fulfilment centre, which can handle 25,000 orders per week, from which it has been testing same-day deliveries. It proposes home delivery to customers, in the time slot following the order (in less than 1 hour), every day of the week. In order to allow fast service, the order is prepared from the nearest store or warehouse, depending on the location of the customer. A click-and-collect service is also available.

Innovative concepts and architecture

With the emerging niche of urban warehouses, which need to better integrate into the city and share expensive land charges, new architectural forms are appearing that try to bring together, in the same building, logistics and other activities. Logistics activity itself can be divided into several floor levels, as in Japan or Korea where some warehouses have eight to ten storeys, all accessible to trucks. These multistorey multi-use facilities are called 'logistics hotels', under the general concept of 'vertical logistics'.

A concept of 'time sharing' has been proposed by the French Post's real estate division, which allows several companies to use a building at different times. A first building opened in Bordeaux in June 2018 serving several subsidiaries dedicated to parcel deliveries.

In general, attention to environmental, energy and aesthetic quality of urban warehouses is increasing, although much progress is needed by municipalities in freight planning processes, as well as in architectural training and education (Behrends and Dablanc, 2017).

Conclusions

E-commerce is both a factor of growth and a major disruptor of urban freight. It represents the main area of increase in urban freight traffic. It accelerates changes in business models. E-commerce has given rise to many successful technological and organizational innovations, in a 'low cost–low price' urban freight market previously prone to short-term city logistics concepts and pilots. Leading e-commerce companies, with Amazon, JD, Alibaba, eBay and Rakuten in the lead, view themselves as logistics service companies in nature. They decide on full logistics services and in some cases they operate them directly, investing in warehouses, vehicles and IT systems to make deliveries to consumers more efficient. They cooperate with traditional freight operators (Amazon is the most important client of many postal operators in Europe and the United States), but also now compete with them. This brings many changes in the last mile logistics industry.

Consumers are the key variable in understanding the trends associated with e-commerce. Consumers living in large urban areas around the world have never had so many options for acquiring goods and services, while their patterns of mobility are also changing quickly. Consumers' demands for home deliveries are, as a result, increasingly sophisticated. High quality of service in terms of reliability of delivery, ease of returns and faster delivery times, all this at low delivery fees, are expected. A proportion of consumers are aware that these requirements can translate into fragmented deliveries and increased freight trips in cities, generating negative impacts on pollution and congestion. New services such as 'instant' deliveries are associated with poor working conditions for self-contracted couriers earning a living by maximizing the number of deliveries at the expense of their safety. However, so far, few people are willing to acknowledge the impact of buying habits on the urban freight system, and even fewer to change it. Consumers' requirements may need to be taken as a given as behaviour is unlikely to change with awareness alone. There are other mechanisms that can be put in place to guide the e-commerce urban delivery system in a more sustainable direction. Urban freight policy is indeed challenged by e-commerce and needs to innovate. Traffic management, urban planning and enforcement policies must promote cleaner delivery vehicles, consolidation of goods flows as well as architectural innovation for new urban warehouses. Land use planning of logistics facilities must be integrated into the master planning of large urban regions.

References

6T-bureau de recherche (2018) E-commerce et pratiques de mobilité: regards croisés entre Paris et New York (E-commerce and mobility practices: comparison between Paris and New York), to be published

Addleshaw Goddard (2016) How soon is now? The disruption and evolution of logistics and industrial property, Company report [Online] www.addleshawgoddard.com/logisticsreport

Allen, J, Piecyk, M and Piotrowska, M (2017) An analysis of online shopping and home delivery in the UK, Report as part of the Freight Traffic Control (FTC) 2050 project

Angot, L (2018) Les points-relais, outils logistiques au coeur de la fabrique urbaine: constats, évolutions et perspectives Le cas de la métropole toulousaine (Pick-up points, logistics instruments for urban development, the case of Toulouse metropolitan area), Presentation at *Commerce of the Future, Future of Commerce,* University of Le Havre conference, Le Havre, France, 1 June

Augereau, V and Dablanc, L (2009) An evaluation of recent pick-up point experiments in European cities: the rise of two competing models? in *Innovations in City Logistics*, ed E Taniguchi and RG Thompson, pp 303–20, Nova Science Publisher, Inc, New York

Berhends, S and Dablanc, L (2017) Planning processes in high-density development projects: how does freight fit in? Case studies from Gothenburg and Paris, INUF International Urban Freight Conference, 14–17 October, Long Beach, California

Camilleri, P (2018) Market potential for electric delivery vans, PhD dissertation, University of Paris-Est, Marne-la-Vallée, France

Comi, A and Nuzzolo, A (2015) Exploring the relationships between e-shopping attitudes and urban freight transport, The 9th International Conference on City Logistics, 17–19 June, Tenerife, Spain

Cortright, J (2015) [accessed 21 June 2018] Growing e-commerce means less urban traffic, *City Observatory* [Online] http://cityobservatory.org/growing-e-commerce-means-less-urban-traffic/

Dablanc, L, Savy, M, Veltz, P, Culoz, A and Vincent, M (2017a) Des marchandises dans la ville, Report for Terra Nova think tank, June, 113p

Dablanc, L, Morganti, E, Arvidsson, N, Woxenius, J, Browne, M and Saidi, N (2017b) The rise of on-demand 'instant deliveries' in European cities, *Supply Chain Forum – an International Journal*, **18** (4), pp 203–17

Dablanc, L, Rouhier, J, Lazarevic, N, Liu, Z, Kelli de Oliveira, L, Koning, M, Blanquart, C, Combes, F, Coulombel, N, Gardrat, M, Heitz, A, Klausberg, J and Seidel, S (2018) Observatory of Strategic Developments Impacting Urban Logistics, CITYLAB Deliverable 2.1, European Commission, 198p

Dablanc, L and Saidi, N (2018) On-Demand Instant Deliveries: New Questions for Cities, American Association of Geographers Annual Meeting, New Orleans, 10–14 April

Durand, B and González-Feliu, J (2012) Urban logistics and e-grocery: Have proximity delivery services a positive impact on shopping trips? *Procedia – Social and Behavioral Sciences*, The 7th International Conference on City Logistics, **39**, pp 510–20

Ecommerce Foundation (2018) [accessed 10 June 2018] Ecommerce Europe-European B2C Ecommerce Country Report 2017 [Online] www.ecommercefoundation.org/download-free-reports

Edwards, J, McKinnon, A and Cullinane, S (2010) Comparative analysis of the carbon footprints of conventional and online retailing. A 'last mile' perspective, *International Journal of Physical Distribution & Logistics Management*, **40** (1/2), pp 103–23

Gardrat, M, Toilier, F, Patier, D and Routhier, JL (2016) The impact of new practices for supplying households in urban goods movements: method and first results. An application for Lyon, France, VREF Urban Freight Conference, Gothenburg, Sweden

Gevaers, R, Van de Voorde, E and Vanelslander, T (2011) Characteristics and typology of last-mile logistics from an innovation perspective in an urban context, in *City Distribution and Urban Freight Transport: Multiple perspectives*, ed C Macharis and S Melo, pp 56–71, Edward Elgar, Cheltenham, UK; Northampton, USA

Heitz, A and Beziat, A (2016) The parcel industry in the spatial organization of logistics activities in the Paris Region: inherited spatial patterns and innovations in urban logistics systems, *Transportation Research Procedia*, **12**, pp 812–24

Hiselius, L, Rosqvist, L and Clark, A (2012) E-shopping and changed transport behaviour, European Transport Conference, Glasgow, United Kingdom

Lermite, C (2017) Google-Walmart: Google Express, une arme vraiment efficace contre Amazon? LSA Commerce connecté, 28 August

Levinson, D (2014) [accessed 16 July 2018] Peak shopping and the decline of traditional retail, *OUPblog*, 12 February [online] https://blog.oup.com/2014/02/transportation-peak-shopping-traditional-retail-decline/

Libeskind, J (2015) *La logistique urbaine, les nouveaux modes de consommation et de livraison (urban logistics, new modes of consumption and delivery)*, Editions FYP, Limoges

McKinnon, A (2016) The possible impact of 3D printing and drones on last-mile logistics: an exploratory study, *Built Environment*, **42** (4), pp 576–88

Morganti, E, Dablanc, L and Fortin, F (2014) Final deliveries for online shopping: the deployment of pickup point networks in urban and suburban areas, *Research in Transportation Business & Management*, **11**, pp 23–31

Motte-Baumvol, B, Belton-Chevallier, L, Schoelzel, M and Carrouet, G (2012) Les effets de la livraison à domicile sur l'accès aux produits alimentaires: le cas des grandes surfaces alimentaires et des cybermarchés de l'aire dijonnaise (Impacts of home deliveries on access to food: the case of large grocery retailers and online grocery retailers in the Dijon metropolitan area – In French), *Flux*, **88**, pp 34–46

Nielsen (2018) [accessed 16 July 2018] Grande consommation & e-commerce: la France championne d'Europe avec 6,6 per cent des achats réalisés online (Mass retail and e-commerce: France is European champion with 6.6 per cent of grocery sales online) [Online] http://www.nielsen.com/fr/fr/insights/news/2018/grande-consommation-e-commerce-la-france-championne-europe.html

Phillips, R (2016) [accessed 16 July 2018] Tackling E-commerce's 'Last Mile' Warehouse Networks, *NAIOP Newsletter*, Winter 2016–17 [Online] http://www.naiop.org/en/Magazine/2016/Winter-2016-2017/Business-Trends/Tackling-Ecommerces-Last-Mile-Warehouse-Networks.aspx

Pierrat, F (2017) Drive piéton, le concept qui pourrait révolutionner les centres villes (pedestrian click-and-collect depots, the concept that could revolutionize city centres), *Le Figaro*, 11 April

Rodrigue, JP (2017) [accessed 16 July 2018] Residential Parcel Deliveries: Evidence from a Large Apartment Complex, Metrofreight Project Report Number: 17-5.1d [Online] https://www.metrans.org/sites/default/files/research-project/MF%205.1d_Residential%20Parcel%20Deliveries_Final%20Report_030717.pdf

Seidel, S, Marei, N and Blanquart, C (2016) Innovations in e-grocery and logistics solutions for cities, *Transportation Research Procedia,* **12**, pp 825–35

Serouge, M, Patier, D, Routhier, JL and Toilier, F (2014) [accessed 5 September 2018] Enquête Marchandises en Ville réalisée en Île-de-France entre 2010 et 2013 (Urban goods movement survey in the Paris region, made between 2010 and 2013 – In French), LAET internal report [Online] https://halshs.archives-ouvertes.fr/halshs-01727717/document

Spencer, C, Caton, C and Conwell, B (2016) [accessed 16 July 2018] Final Delivery: The Last Mile, Urban Land Institute Fall Meeting, E-commerce Session [Online] http://uli.org/wp-content/uploads/ULI-Documents/Caton_FinalDelivery.pdf

Visser, J, Nemoto, T and Browne, M (2014) Home delivery and the impacts on urban freight transport: a review, 8th International Conference on City Logistics, *Procedia – Social and Behavioral Sciences*, **125**, pp 15–27

Weltevreden, J and Rotem-Mindali, O (2009) Mobility effects of B2C and C2C e-commerce in the Netherlands: a quantitative assessment, *Journal of Transport Geography*, **17**, pp 83–92

Wygonik E and Goodchild, A (2012) Evaluating the efficacy of shared-use vehicles for reducing greenhouse gas emissions: a U.S. case study of grocery delivery, *Journal of the Transportation Research Forum*, **51** (2), pp 111–26

Notes

1. La Poste manager, interview in spring 2017, referenced in Dablanc *et al* (2017a).
2. Graciously provided by José Holguín-Veras from his ongoing work at Rensselaer Polytechnic Institute, e-mail exchanges, May 2018.

3 It is also interesting to note that because New York is one of the few US metro areas where freight surveys were made in the 1960s, RPI could calculate that today's deliveries to establishments are about 20 per cent lower in number (in total) than deliveries made in the 1960s.

4 Measuring the impacts of online shopping on mobility practices: the case of Paris and New York City. Data collection made in December 2017 by 6T consultancy and the Rudin Center of Transportation Policy & Management at New York University. Data analysis is ongoing. These figures were graciously provided by N Louvet, who agreed they be mentioned as such in this chapter.

5 More exactly, Manhattan without Harlem and with a few neighbourhoods of Brooklyn.

6 With 6.6 per cent in value of all grocery shopping in France in 2017. 80 per cent of online grocery shopping in France is picked up at click-and-collect ('*drives*'). Increasing competition and increasing quality of service can be noted in this market. Amazon Prime Now in Paris announced in May 2018 a partnership with Monoprix, a high-end grocery retail chain, to include food offerings on its instant delivery platform.

7 In terms of public policies, 'innovative city logistics' is now part of the mobility strategy of large municipalities. Paris&Co, the innovation agency of the City of Paris, has opened an incubator for logistics startups in 2018.

8 Amazon, the first e-retailer in France, and the first client of the main express parcel transport operators in the country, is not a Fevad member, however, which makes the data not representative enough of the actual situation.

9 Interview in March 2017 by the author.

10 https://techcrunch.com/2016/04/21/california-bill-to-give-gig-workers-organizing-rights-stalls-over-antitrust-concerns/

Food and urban logistics 09

A fast-changing sector with significant policy and business implications

ELEONORA MORGANTI

Introduction

A high and increasing proportion of food consumption takes place in urban areas, supported by ever-changing food distribution and transport systems. The number and variety of distribution channels by which food is supplied to urban consumers has changed and risen dramatically in recent years. Food is available not only in supermarkets, minimarkets, corner shops, cafés, restaurants and food trucks, but also at different shops whose main business is non-food items, such as pharmacies and book shops, at a growing number of vending machines and at a wide range of facilities (eg gyms, recreational centres). In the distribution networks, there are many changes – the shift to out of town retail supermarkets from the 1960s and then in more recent years the move back to city centres is just one example. Destinations change as more food is ordered by consumers for delivery to home.

Transport and the associated logistics activities of handling and storage have made possible these changes in food distribution channels, raising new issues for the operators (Dani, 2015). The need for speed, the small consignment sizes, the fragmentation of the deliveries, the questions around food safety standards and the need to ensure traceability of products are the demanding tasks which have increased with the constant transformation of the retail sector and generated new challenges for the transport industry.

Rapid technological development, in particular in information technology and artificial intelligence, has contributed to the development of transport services and logistics tools to partially solve these issues. Digital products and services, the internet and mobile technology, and new business models resulting from these advances have led to the redesign of delivery operations in order to offer higher performance and to cope with fast-changing consumer habits.

There are many challenges in urban food logistics including: 1) the challenge of complexity; 2) the challenge of distribution nodes and markets; 3) the challenge of achieving higher levels of sustainability. There are many others but these three profoundly influence the need for more focus on how urban food logistics can be managed more effectively.

This chapter discusses several important themes starting with the complex links between food distribution and urban logistics in section two. Sections three and four explore two significant trends occurring in cities around the world. The first trend focuses on wholesale produce markets and food hubs as crucial nodes of food distribution at local and regional level. The second trend is the importance of food deliveries on urban traffic combined with initiatives from the private sector for improving environmental impact. Section five looks at the transformation generated by online shopping for food. The final part contains the conclusion and recommendations for relevant strategies in urban food planning and city logistics.

The complex links between food distribution and urban logistics

Understanding food distribution channels

Food and urban logistics in modern cities and metropolitan areas are systems inextricably linked between themselves and with other urban systems such as land use and waste management. The urban food distribution system is extremely diverse and complex and it includes many organizations, for example farmers, food processors, wholesalers, markets, retailers, third-party logistics, transport operators, local and regional governments. In many cases there is a complex interaction between the public and private sectors as well – for example, the public sector can be seen as a major customer (school meal provision, hospitals, military bases). At the same time public authorities have the responsibility to set and enforce regulations related to food safety standards – many of these are connected with the logistics of transport, handling and storage. It is also typical for greater complexity to lead to higher logistics costs. Of course, organizations within food logistics seek to manage this complexity and prevent extra cost burdens.

Some of these organizations are very powerful, exerting considerable control over the food supply chain. In recent years many have observed the growing power of major food retailers within market-based economies (Lang, 2003; Hingley, 2005; Morgan *et al*, 2008). This power has direct implications for the decisions made on questions of transport and logistics all along the supply chain, including the last mile (Fernie *et al*, 2010). As a result, some popular trends are visible and common in various cities around the world; nevertheless, food logistics operations are multiple and diverse, reflecting the existing vast landscape of food outlets and services, from the ethnic food shop to fine dining, from the organic vegetable shop to the event caterer. Shaped on the needs of the distribution channel they serve, delivery operations are characterized by load unit, type of vehicle and type of carrier (Morganti and González-Feliu, 2014; DG Move, 2012), with different degrees of consolidation and efficiency.

In Table 9.1 the urban food distribution channels are presented in a simplified classification, divided between food retailing and hotel, restaurant and catering (HORECA). Within these two macro-sectors, various supply chains are defined based on the business model of the distribution channels, such as 'corporate' (major retail chains) vs 'independent' for food retailing and 'organized' vs 'non-organized' for HORECA. Additional supply chains are identified for e-grocery, online orders for prepared meals and alternative schemes for food shopping (eg farmers' markets). Depending on the national context and on the specific features of each city, it is possible to observe a more dominant role of corporate retailers and large hotels, fast-food chains and franchises (eg London), or a large majority of food outlets run by small, independent retailers and family-owned 'non-organized' HORECA (eg Lisbon). The success of online shopping and the progress of alternative channels for food are also aspects highly impacted by the specific urban culture, technology penetration and consumers' attitudes at local level. As a result, it is clear that urban food logistics exhibit many variations according to context.

Food logistics operations for the main distribution channels

Scenarios describing fragmented, frequent and small deliveries to urban food outlets have been presented in different studies, for European cities of various sizes, for example Paris, France (PIPAME, 2009), Winchester, United Kingdom (Cherrett *et al*, 2012); Parma, Italy (Morganti and González-Feliu, 2014).

Table 9.1 Urban food distribution channels and degree of consolidation of deliveries

Urban Food Logistics Efficiency	Food Retail		HORECA (hotel, restaurant, catering)	
High degree of consolidation of deliveries	Corporate retailers (major retail chains)	– Supermarkets and hypermarkets, eg Carrefour, Walmart – Convenience retailing, eg Carrefour Express, Tesco Express – Specialized retailers, eg Iceland (frozen food), Whole's Food (healthy food)	'Organized'	– Hotel chains, eg Accor Group, Best Western – Restaurant chains eg Nando's, Burger King – Café chains, eg Le Pain Quotidien, Starbucks – Catering industry for the hospital market, schools, work canteens, eg Sodexo, Aramark
Low degree of consolidation	Independent retailers	– Mom-And-Pop shops – Specialized shops	'Non organized'	– Non-affiliated restaurants, cafés, bars, hotels
Various degrees of consolidation	E-grocery	– Click and mortar, eg Asda – Online retailers, eg Ocado, Amazon	Online order	– Fast-food and restaurant chains, eg Domino's – Non-affiliated restaurants
N/A	Alternative	– Box schemes – Farmers' markets		

SOURCE author's own elaboration based on Morganti and González-Feliu, 2014; DG Move, 2012

Corporate retailers and major hotel and restaurant chains have invested heavily in distribution networks to take control of deliveries and increase overall supply chain efficiency, consolidating supplies upstream of stores at centralized distribution centres. By doing this they have been more strongly positioned to achieve economies of scale through centralized, more consolidated and less frequent deliveries. The increased proportion delivered in consolidated loads from retailer-controlled distribution centres and a corresponding decline in the multiple drop deliveries of manufacturers and wholesalers promoted the consolidation of loads in larger vehicles, making better use of each vehicle's carrying capacity (DG Move, 2012).

Independent retail and the HORECA are sectors characterized by small and medium-sized Mom-and-Pop shops, family-owned restaurants, bars, non-affiliated hotels, etc. These businesses differ significantly from the major retail chains in terms of delivery operations. They often do not control deliveries, with wholesalers or suppliers being responsible for goods transport (using transport on their own account or through third-party carriers); they usually do not pay for the transport directly and have no contact with the carrier except for the receipt of the delivery. Freight deliveries to these local stores contribute significantly to urban road congestion as they are supplied between three and ten times a week, they have diverse suppliers, with a predominant use of own vehicles and low vehicle fill rates (DG Move, 2012; Morganti and González-Feliu, 2014).

The retail sector demonstrates how fragmentation of demand for deliveries (eg numerous independent retail outlets and HORECA located in a city centre) combined with fragmentation of supply of food products (eg numerous wholesalers and other suppliers using their own vehicles to make just-in-time deliveries) results in a greater number of movements with only part loads than would be the case if both demand and supply were more concentrated (DG Move, 2012).

Distribution nodes and food hubs

Challenges for the transport industry and impact of the food distribution landscape

Among the variety of urban freight systems, food logistics presents specific constraints related to food safety and traceability, such as short lead time and distinct handling procedures. In the case of fresh, frozen and prepared food, temperature-controlled technology is required together with just-in-time deliveries and dedicated facilities and vehicles. The receivers set increasingly high performance standards that must be met, including shorter time windows and higher frequency of deliveries. Empty runs and long dwell times at loading and unloading points are frequent and they can represent a significant waste of resources.

Compared with other non-highly perishable food and non-food supply chains, these constrains often result in higher consumption of energy, lower levels of consolidation and lower efficiency, leading to additional costs for transport operations. Profit margins for companies engaged in food logistics can be low. For the transport operator it may be difficult to pass on to powerful customers all the extra costs associated with urban food logistics operations. The last mile of food logistics is therefore seen as a highly competitive industry, with low margins and high risks.

Nevertheless, this industry plays a vital part in the way cities function, providing uninterrupted and constant flows of food products to urban dwellers. Urban food transport and logistics support the variety of distribution channels (corporate, independent, organized and non-organized), which compose the urban food provisioning landscape, resulting in wider food accessibility.

In this context, cities appear as key actors leading a transition process addressing problems related to urban food provisioning and interconnected with transport, health, land use and local economic development (Morgan, 2009). In a growing number of cities including San Francisco, New York and London, policymakers are thus setting a variety of measures to better integrate food issues in the urban policy agenda, and, together with the community and supply chain actors, they are implementing innovative projects dealing with sourcing and distributing food.

Initiatives on distribution nodes, consolidation and food hubs

Most of these urban food strategies include significant connections with urban logistics, even if these connections are not always clearly labelled this way. Noticeable projects, relevant for both food sustainability and city logistics, set four main objectives: 1) to contribute to the enhancement of food access and quality; 2) to support regional economy and reinforce the urban–rural connection; 3) to improve cost effectiveness of the transport of goods; 4) to reduce air pollution.

Policies related to the redesign of wholesale produce markets and the creation of food hubs are good examples of initiatives with similar targets. The idea of focusing on traditional produce markets started with the renovation efforts planned by the markets' authorities around Europe and in various countries to overcome the commercial decline that originated with the growing power of the major retail chains (WUWM, 2011). The renovation was also supported by some small and independent shops and 'non-organized' HORECA services, which traditionally relied on wholesale produce markets to source their products, where local farmers used to sell.

New organizational concepts have been discussed by operators, practitioners and researchers under the model known as regional and/or alternative food hubs, defined as 'partnership based arrangements that coordinate the distribution of a range of food products from producers of a uniform provenance to conventional or hybrid markets' (Morley *et al*, 2008). Although most of the wholesale produce markets present numerous sources of products at both global and local levels and only few markets are dedicated to 'producers of a uniform provenance', organizational elements of the food hub concept can be adopted by market authorities. Enhancing the role of the existing wholesale produce markets by improving the transport and logistics services offered in situ and by renewing the consolidation functions that have historically been part of it, has a potential positive impact on the degree of efficiency of deliveries. According to Barham (2013), it is possible to relate and enlarge the role of the wholesale market to food hubs, intended as (existing) supply chain intermediaries playing a new or renewed role in the urban food provisioning and distribution system, driven by environmental social and economic criteria.

From an urban logistics perspective, a food hub is an important distribution node that can offer:

1. Consolidation, distribution and wholesale.
2. Active coordination of marketing, communication and logistics services.
3. A permanent facility.

Food hubs and markets that foster consolidation and aggregation of food deliveries to food outlets (mainly to independent shops and 'non-organized' services) reduce inefficiencies in transport operations and contribute to reducing the costs of deliveries. Both the transport industry and the receivers benefit from a better use of resources and larger economies of scale. Moreover, it is possible to identify a reduction of environmental impact, air pollution and road traffic.

Among the few documented cases that received high levels of support from local authorities are Parma and Padua in Italy. The first project was a wholesale produce market, which started consolidation operations for local producers and wholesalers, delivering fruit and vegetables with natural gas vans to outlets in the historic city centre of Parma (Morganti and González-Feliu, 2014). The second case offered food deliveries as a service of a generic urban distribution centre. In France similar consolidation projects have been applied to food deliveries to school cafeterias in Paris (Newton.Vaureal Consulting, 2013) and also for transport operations generated at the wholesale produce markets in Lyon (Gardrat *et al*, 2013).

Examples of food hubs are not restricted to Europe and North America. There is growing interest in enhancing urban food distribution in Latin America (Palacios-Argüello *et al*, 2017). The city of Bogotá and its policy on promoting a new food supply system (called SAAB) offer a good example of this new trend. Direct exchange between producers and retailers is fostered through different initiatives: a virtual marketplace, a network of regional consolidation centres and new logistics platforms in Bogotá. The final goal is to reduce intermediary and transport costs and then increase the supply of fresh food at a fair price for consumers.

Raising sustainability levels for urban food logistics

The importance of food deliveries in urban freight movements

Food deliveries to urban outlets account for a significant part of urban freight movements. Although data on food deliveries are limited and often outdated, surveys at city level are able to provide some more detailed information on the relevance of last mile for food. In London, results from TfL studies (2015) estimate around 15–17 per cent of vans and trucks entering central London are involved in making food deliveries. At a more local level the importance of food deliveries in the total mix of freight movements is clear from a survey of Regent Street, where the HORECA sector covers some 39 per cent of deliveries including items such as food and beverages, linen and other catering requirements for organizations such as restaurants, cafés and fast-food outlets within Regent Street (Figures 9.1 and 9.2). From studies like this one, organizations working within the HORECA sector could be

Figure 9.1 and Figure 9.2 Freight and food movements in Regent Street, London

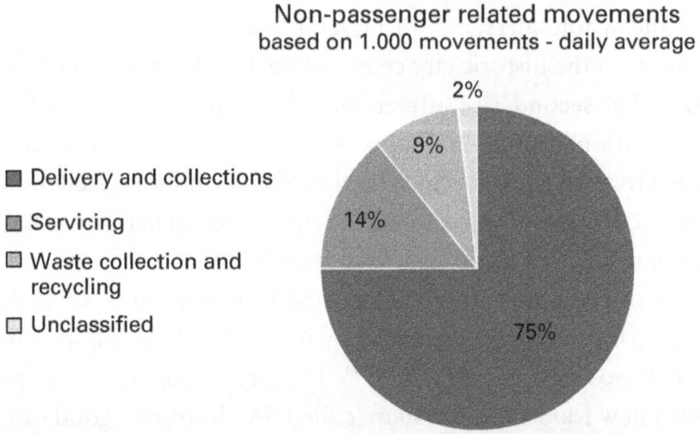

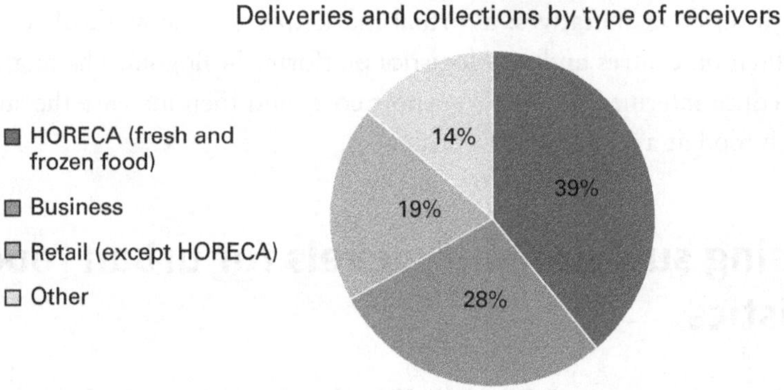

SOURCE adapted from TfL, 2015

prime candidates for consolidation and these deliveries could be managed through a logistics supplier specializing in chilled and frozen goods. Another example is provided by Leeds, where the field observation conducted in the city centre recorded that vehicles delivering food and drink account for 55 per cent of all observed vehicles (Aecom 2014, limited access report).

There are many examples of good practices and innovation in the freight transport and logistics involved in urban food logistics (see below). Innovation in the use of clean vehicles has been important in showing what is possible and providing insight into the scope for reducing environmental impacts. However, it remains the case that many urban food deliveries are made by old diesel vehicles, such as small trucks and vans of more than

10 years, which consume large quantities of fossil fuel and also generate high quantities of pollutant emissions such as nitrogen dioxide (NO_2) and particulate matter (PM) (Morganti and Dablanc, 2014).

Initiatives reducing environmental impacts of urban food deliveries

There are projects other than food hubs that focus on increasing the environmental sustainability of food logistics without being necessarily embedded in the broader political agenda for food provisioning and distribution. These are initiatives led by private companies, for both transport and retail industries, aiming at testing new solutions and adopting new delivery methods. FoodLogica, for example, is a logistics project in Amsterdam bundling deliveries from multiple suppliers within a maximum range of 100 kilometres to small shop and café owners located in the city centre, which usually ask for small and frequent shipments and do not have an optimized delivery scheme. The delivery services are provided by solar-powered electric cargo bikes instead of trucks, reducing air pollution and congestion in the streets of the capital. In 2014 the pilot project started with recycled containers as micro-logistics platforms and two e-trikes delivering to five receivers. Four years later the fleet is composed of 18 e-trikes, providing options of multiple drops-offs and pickups for various food products including bread, fruit and vegetables to an increasing number of cafés, shops and restaurants.

Another project, developed in Paris, focuses on waterways for last mile deliveries. The French food retail company Franprix, together with the logistics service provider Norbert Dentressangle and with support from local administrations, developed and implemented a multi-modal transport solution for supplying Franprix stores located in Paris. Previously, the stores were supplied by trucks directly from the company's distribution centre 20 kilometres outside Paris. Now, a barge shipping 26 containers enters the city every day at 5 am (the trip lasts 3 hours) and drops off containers at the quai de la Bourdonnais, not far from the Eiffel Tower. Trucks pick up the containers and deliver the products to about 80 supermarkets. According to an ex ante assessment, the use of the barge avoids the equivalent of about 450,000 vehicle-kilometres by trucks per year, when fully operational. This is equivalent to a 37 per cent reduction in CO_2 emissions for the trip between the regional warehouse and the stores (as cited in Morganti and Dablanc, 2014).

Online food ordering and new delivery practices

In the short-term future, cities will have to address the issues related to food distribution arising from forthcoming digital innovation and from the growth of online shopping for food. Among the new distribution channels there are, for example, 'ghost restaurants', food services without a physical location but with a delivery-only menu. Robots and automated vehicles for delivery services and 3D food printers as domestic equipment are some of the ongoing changes that will further transform food logistics in urban areas.

Currently, the most debated event is the rapid growth of online food ordering and related home delivery for groceries and prepared meals offered within two hours and known as 'instant delivery'. Historically, home deliveries were limited to certain local grocery stores, some pizzerias and some Chinese restaurants. In recent years, online food delivery services received large amounts of investment and the sector is expected to show an annual growth rate of 11 per cent until 2022 (Statista, 2018).

The growing popularity of food deliveries is partly explained by the proliferation of applications for smartphones and by multiple platforms offering online ordering services, including Facebook with its 'Food Order' feature in restaurant profiles and Google, which signed an agreement with US restaurant chains to allow users to order meals directly from search results.

Some instant delivery providers began as startups operating in big cities (Deliveroo in the United Kingdom, Foodora in Germany, Tok Tok Tok in France, for example). The early start gave them an advantage over major international players that are now responding with aggressive strategies to acquire more dominant positions. These include Uber and its delivery services (UberRush and UberEats) and Amazon (Prime, Prime Now and Fresh).

At present, consumers have access to a broader range of products, including high-end restaurants and high-quality ingredients. As described by Dablanc *et al* (2017) the ordering options can be divided into three categories:

- delivery of prepared meals (such as Deliveroo and JustEat);
- delivery of meals with recipes and kits of ingredients (such as HelloFresh or Gousto);
- grocery and alcohol delivery, including farm subscriptions (this category includes Ocado, a pioneer in e-marketplaces, and Farmdrop) and the various options offered by the major traditional retailers.

Most instant delivery companies defined themselves as technology platforms that connect users (either private or commercial) with transport service providers, who are independent third parties under contract to perform collection and delivery operations. The focus is on their role as intermediaries, instead of logistics providers or as carriers. Deliveroo, for example, 'acts as an agent on behalf of the Partner Restaurant when it presents Meals, taking orders on their behalf and delivers food to consumers' (extract from Deliveroo, Terms and Conditions of Service, July 2018).

The business model also includes specific strategies on how to promote the service to the public. The price of the delivery advertised to the consumer does not reflect the actual cost of the service: depending on the case, the real cost of the last mile is split in varying proportions among the restaurant and the consumer, without providing transparent information. The free or discounted delivery service is therefore an effective marketing tool for attaining consumer loyalty and gaining market share. In the medium term, this translates into a business model that does not appear viable in the already strongly competitive industry of food logistics, unless very high and consistent volumes of deliveries are secured.

From the point of view of urban logistics, the impact of online food orders raises questions about the volumes of deliveries, which are not obvious to measure and monitor. The flows of instant deliveries – not always optimized – are believed to contribute to an increase in transport operations and therefore in traffic, although some of these online orders were previously made over the phone. It remains to evaluate the impact on air quality, most deliveries being made by bicycle, or even the reduction in the number of journeys for grocery shopping purposes, driven by these new habits.

Conclusions

The complex links between the food distribution channels and the transport and logistics industries raise challenging tasks for city logistics policies aimed at reducing the impact of traffic directly generated by food deliveries. Food logistics in urban environments present inefficiencies and a lack of coordination, in particular among independent retailers and non-organized HORECA businesses. The delivery operations for these distribution channels offer high potential for optimization with the support of policymakers, promoting food hubs and other consolidation platforms with both commercial and logistics functions. At the private level, both transport operators and retail companies have shown small but promising initiatives to increase the environmental sustainability of food transport operations, including modal shift and redesign of the last mile of the supply chain. Moreover short-term challenges for city planners and practitioners are represented by technological innovation and the rapid growth of digital food distribution channels, such as e-grocery and online ordering for prepared meals, which are influencing trends in food consumption and purchasing habits of urban dwellers.

The unprecedented pace of urbanization and its effects on cities make it urgent for local administrations to develop urban policies oriented towards redesigning food distribution and logistics operations on the basis of new types of social, economic and environmental relationships among food producers, suppliers, retailers and consumers. The new strategies have higher chances of success if they are able to combine city logistics and urban food provisioning aspects in integrated policies.

References

Barham, J (2013) Clarifying the food hub concept, *Rural Connections*, **6** (10), pp 7–10

Cherrett, TT, Allen, J, McLeod, F, Maynard, S, Hickford, A and Browne, M (2012) Understanding urban freight activity – key issues for freight planning, *Journal of Transport Geography*, **24**, pp 22–32

Dablanc, L, Morganti, E, Arvidsson, N, Woxenius, J, Browne, M and Saidi, N (2017) The rise of on-demand 'Instant Deliveries' in European cities, *Supply Chain Forum*, **18**, pp 203–17

Dani, S (2015) *Food Supply Chain Management and Logistics: From farm to fork*, Kogan Page, London

Deliveroo [accessed 2 July 2018] Terms and Conditions of Service [Online] https://deliveroo.co.uk/legal

DG Move (2012) [accessed 28 June 2018] Study on Urban Freight Transport – 210041R4_final report [Online] https://ec.europa.eu/transport/sites/transport/files/themes/urban/studies/doc/2012-04-urban-freight-transport.pdf

Fernie, J, Sparks, L and McKinnon, A (2010) Retail logistics in the UK: past, present and future, *International Journal of Retail & Distribution Management*, **38** (11/12), pp 894–914

Gardrat, M, González-Feliu, J and Routhier, J-L (2013) Urban goods movement analysis as a tool for urban planning, in 5th ECTRI-FERSI YRS, 5–7 June, Lyon, France

Hingley, KM (2005) Power imbalance in UK agri-food supply channels: learning to live with the supermarkets, *Journal of Marketing Management*, **21**, pp 63–88
Lang, T (2003) Food industrialization and food power: implications for food governance, *Development Policy Review*, **21** (5–6), p 555
Morgan, K (2009) Feeding the city: the challenge of urban food planning, *International Planning Studies*, **14** (4), pp 341–48
Morgan, K, Marsden, K and Murdoch, J (2008) *Worlds of Food: Place, power and provenance in the food chain,* Oxford University Press, Oxford
Morganti E and Dablanc, L (2014) Recent innovation in last mile deliveries, *SpringerBriefs in Applied Sciences and Technology*, pp 27–45
Morganti, E and González-Feliu, J (2014) City logistics for perishable products. The case of Parma's Food Hub, *Case Studies in Transport Policy*, Elsevier
Morley, A, Morgan, S and Morgan, K (2008) Food Hubs: The Missing Middle of the Local Food Infrastructure? BRASS Research Report for Welsh Government
Newton.Vaureal Consulting (2013) *Etude de diagnostic du fonctionnement, bilan et préconisations pour améliorer la logistique d'approvisionnement des restaurants administratifs de la Ville de Paris*, Rapport Final, Municipalite de Paris
Palacios-Argüello, L, Morganti, E and González-Feliu, J (2017) Food hub: Una alternativa para alimentar las ciudades de manera sostenible, *Revista Transporte y Territorio*, **17**, pp 10–33
PIPAME (Pôle interministériel de prospective et d'anticipation des mutations économiques) (2009) *Logistique mutualisée: la filière fruits et légumes du MIN de Rungis*, Report
TfL – Transport for London (2015) [accessed 28 June 2018] Sustainable delivery and servicing – Lessons from London, presentation by Ian Wainwright [Online] http://www.ukroadsliaisongroup.org/download.cfm/docid/31DA53DC-664B-4164-87603AFECDFAE6C7
Statista (2018) [accessed 2 July 2018] Online Food Delivery [Online] https://www.statista.com/outlook/374/100/online-food-delivery/worldwide
WUWM (2011) [accessed 28 June 2018] The Role and Importance of the Wholesale and Retail Market Sectors for the European Union [Online] https://cms.webbeat.net/contentsuite/tools/fileManagement/getfile.aspx?sit=129&guid=638ac0b4-e1e4-4fc1-9fc0-602912a38216

Consolidation centres in construction logistics

10

GREGER LUNDESJÖ

(Note: This chapter first appeared in *Supply Chain Management and Logistics in Construction* (2015) edited by Greger Lundesjö.)

Introduction

There are many different ways to organize consolidation of materials in construction and we discuss a number of approaches below. To understand what is meant by a construction consolidation centre (CCC) and how it changes the flow of materials to (and in some cases from) a construction site it is useful to consider what typically characterizes the delivery of materials to construction sites.

There are a great number of deliveries:

- Different materials arrive on separate vehicles from individual suppliers.
- There is little or no coordination between deliveries and timekeeping by suppliers is often poor, leading to congestion and waiting time at gates, or vehicles circulating in the local area waiting for a slot.
- Many vehicles arrive much less than fully loaded.
- Often vehicles depart empty or nearly empty yet return logistics opportunities are not exploited.
- Often large quantities are delivered, requiring storage on site over long periods.

- There is a wide range of vehicle types requiring different equipment and often making unloading time-consuming.
- The different trades on site each have their own suppliers and the main contractor has little control over the coordination of deliveries.

All these factors make the gates and receiving areas much busier than warranted by the actual volume of materials. Queuing and waiting frequently cause delay and trade contractors lose productive time waiting for or looking for materials. Construction traffic has a negative impact on the local area causing congestion, noise and pollution.

Using a CCC addresses all these issues. Instead of delivering to site, suppliers deliver to a small warehouse (or distribution centre) where materials are stored in dry and secure conditions. From the CCC consolidated loads, possibly for a number of trades and in some cases even for more than one site, are made up and delivered to site on a just-in-time (JIT) basis. Large items and materials for which a full vehicle load is required at one time bypass the CCC and go directly to site; there is no point in offloading at the CCC just to reload the complete delivery again. Naturally, consolidation is less important in the early stages of the construction of a building, but it comes into its own during the fit-out stages. Excessive packaging can be removed at the CCC and return journeys can be used to remove surplus materials, packaging and waste from the site. Site traffic is drastically reduced and deliveries run on time. Site productivity improves and waste is reduced.

Consolidation is not a new concept in construction and there are many case studies and reports analysing the operation and benefits of using a CCC (see Figure 10.1). Many date from the first decade of the 21st century. Based on the generally excellent feedback from these early examples one would have expected widespread use of CCCs to follow. But while they are in regular use they are by no means the norm in the industry, and it is relevant to ask why, in fact, they are not more widely used.

A few well-documented early CCC projects:

- In 2001 the Heathrow Consolidation Centre (HCC) was set up to serve the ongoing construction work at Heathrow Terminals 1–4. The HCC was set up by Mace and was run by construction logistics specialists Wilson James for BAA. The HCC has been thoroughly studied and covered in articles and books, such as *Managing Construction Logistics* (Sullivan, Barthorpe and Robbins, 2010).
- Between 2001 and 2003 a logistics centre supported a large residential project called Hammarby Sjöstad in Stockholm, Sweden. This centre,

Figure 10.1 Illustration of the principles of consolidation

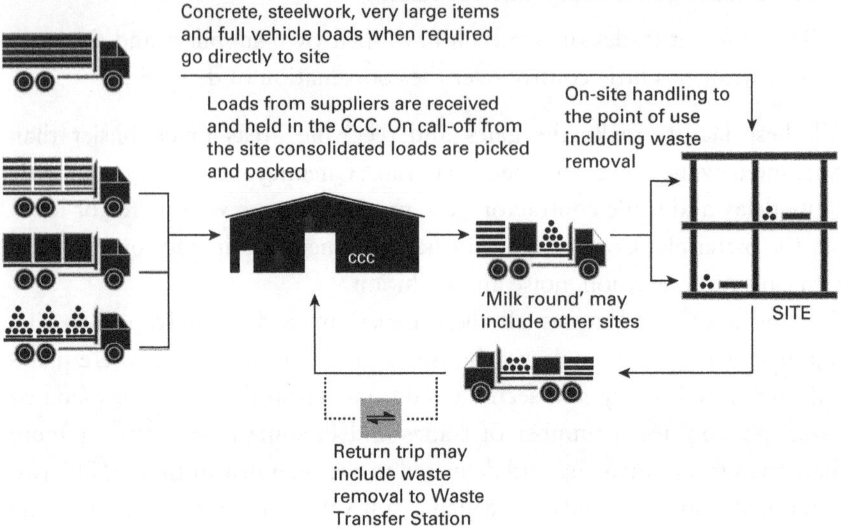

introduced on the initiative of Stockholm City Authorities, achieved its objectives in reducing traffic and related issues such as noise and emissions. The operation was subject to academic studies, which also found other substantial benefits; in particular significant reductions in waste through better storage, reduced product damage and reduced shrinkage (Ottoson, 2005).

- In London, likewise the authorities encouraged the use of construction consolidation. A partnership between Transport for London, developers Stanhope PLC, the construction firm Bovis Lend Lease and logistics company Wilson James (who also operated the facility) set up the London Construction Consolidation Centre (LCCC), which began operation in Bermondsey, south London in 2005. The LCCC was initially created for a pilot study. After the pilot study Wilson James carried on the activity on a commercial basis; it has relocated to Silvertown just south of City of London Airport. The experiences from this operation have been covered in several articles and books, such as *Managing Construction Logistics* (Sullivan, Barthorpe and Robbins, 2010).

All these early examples of CCCs were studied in some depth, and generally regarded as successful. The benefits of using a CCC based on these experiences and some other more recent examples will be set out in this chapter. Transport for London commissioned further studies indicating that London on an ongoing basis could/should support at least six CCCs strategically located around the city (Anderson, 2007). Following these early, much publicized experiences of CCCs, and both academic and business-case support of the concept, one would have expected strong growth in this approach to construction logistics. This has not happened, and at the end of this chapter some of the reasons for this will be discussed.

The resources, functionality and operation of a CCC

Compared to many modern distribution and warehousing operations the processes of a CCC are very straightforward. In simple terms its purpose is to receive materials in bulk from suppliers, store them securely and, on order from the site, make up loads for daily deliveries. The nature of the typical construction project where different subcontractors have control and ownership of their different materials has an impact on how CCCs are run; and there are various approaches, some of which will be discussed later.

The resources and facilities

When discussing CCCs the process of consolidation is more important than the physical facilities; nothing complicated is required. The resources of an ideal CCC operation include:

- A small or medium-sized warehouse. At a minimum an open floor is all that is needed for storage; larger operations will include some pallet racking and shelving areas.
- Preferably a covered area where vehicles can be offloaded/loaded in the dry.
- Outside hard standing for large items and materials not vulnerable to the weather.
- A waste/recycling area for packaging materials and other waste.
- Forklift truck(s) for vehicle loading and handling in the warehouse.
- Vehicle(s) for delivery to site.
- Personnel such as warehouse operative(s), administrator and driver(s).
- Some kind of warehouse management system.

In the guidance note for using CCCs to reduce construction waste and carbon emissions (Lundesjö, 2011) examples are given of the differing sizes and types of CCCs that provide useful service depending on the projects served.

Table 10.1 Large and small resources

	Large Multi-project, Multi-client CCC	Small Single-project CCC
Size of warehouse	10,000 m^2 warehouse space plus large yard area	650 m^2 warehouse space; the operation housed within a 3PL shared user distribution facility
Throughput in PEU (pallet equivalent unit)	50,000 per year	6,000 per year
Vehicles	1 × 26 tonne flatbed with crane 2 × 18 tonne flatbed 1 × 18 tonne curtain-sided with tail lift 1 × LWB Transit 4 × forklift trucks The fleet is regularly adjusted to demand	1 × rigid flatbed lorry 1 × 18 tonne curtain-sided lorry with tail lift 1 × large Transit van 1 × forklift truck
Operatives	Manager, administrator, warehouse operatives and drivers – in total eight employees	A manager, an administrator, one warehouse operative and two drivers
Construction projects supported	Up to six large inner-city projects simultaneously including a major hospital and large commercial and residential developments	Supporting a single development of luxury apartments

For illustration, resources of the largest and smallest are summarized in Table 10.1, which illustrates the rather obvious fact that the resource requirements have to be adapted to the project volume served; they are, however, in warehousing terms neither large nor complex. The focus in consolidation is on the process.

Ordering materials

Trade contractors are usually responsible for ordering and supplying their own materials as part of their subcontract. In a project using a CCC they are asked to request delivery to the CCC rather than to site. The focus of the CCC is to consolidate deliveries to site and not to become a large bulk warehouse. Therefore it is not unusual for CCC operators to require contractors to limit the amount of stock they hold at any one time in the CCC to no more than, say, two weeks' usage. However there is an argument that, given sufficient space, the guiding principles for supplier deliveries ought to be economic and environmental, ie full vehicle loads, and preferably coordinated in time to allow for return logistics opportunities.

It is important to note that this approach will reduce the cost of material supply thanks to faster vehicle turnaround time (see section on the benefits of CCCs) and economical order quantities. It is important for the main contractor (who normally pays for the CCC operation) to ensure that these savings are identified and passed on. This might not be as simple as it seems, with delivery costs not always transparent but hidden within fixed price offers, including delivery.

Receiving materials at the CCC

Ideally, a CCC should include a covered vehicle offloading area to ensure that materials can always be handled in dry and safe conditions. When vehicles arrive, which should be as per agreed schedule to avoid both conflict with other suppliers and unnecessary waiting time, the CCC operative will offload and inspect the delivery against the delivery note. This inspection is limited to product ID, quantity and damage. The CCC operatives handling goods owned by trade contractors do not have the ability or authority to break open packs for detailed inspections. The warehouse management system is updated so that the materials are shown as in stock in the CCC and available for delivery to site. Often a label is produced identifying the materials, the contractor using the materials and any other information deemed necessary. If not required instantly the materials are put away into storage.

Storage of materials

There are a couple of fundamentally different approaches to the organization of a CCC. The most basic arrangement is to have just an open warehouse floor, with areas painted on the floor allocated to different contractors. All materials for contractor 'A' go in area 'A', for contractor 'B' in area 'B' and so on. While this is the easiest method to administrate, particularly if there is no reasonable warehouse management system in place, it does not utilize space efficiently and will require a large area or will be suitable only when there are relatively few contractors.

A typical construction project has a wide range of materials and the ideal CCC would have floor space for large items and items that can be block stacked, an area with pallet racking for palletized goods handled by forklift truck and some shelving areas for small items. In addition there may be a requirement for a fenced-in lockable area providing extra security for high-value items. This arrangement, where one contractor's items may be in all three areas, requires a warehouse management system (WMS). Compared to the WMS running a modern retail operation this can be a very basic system, sometimes as simple as a large spreadsheet. What is required is basically a database where all materials are registered with details of which contractor they belong to, type of materials, article number, order reference, quantities, dates delivered and location in the warehouse. If, as would often be the case, the CCC is operated by a third-party logistics company (3PL) then the WMS requirement can very easily be fulfilled by standard systems that those companies regularly use. What this means for the CCC is that there is no need to separate zones for all contractors. Instead space can be used efficiently and any individual material can still be retrieved based on the WMS information. The inventory records enable contractors to keep check on their stockholding and plan new orders and deliveries, thus improving forward planning.

Output of materials

The fundamental principle of a CCC-based project is that material supply should be according to a JIT pull system. This means that materials are not pushed onto site to be available 'just in case' but are ordered for when they are needed. This is the responsibility of the trade contractors. Typically this is done on a 24- or 48-hour cycle: eg order today for delivery tomorrow or the day after. The contractor must specify materials required, quantity and (in some cases) delivery location on site. One of the benefits of using a CCC is to drastically reduce the amount of materials on site, therefore the quantities delivered should be just for one or two days' consumption. The methods for ordering can vary from simply phoning in orders to the CCC administrator to using text messaging or e-mail. In some instances connection is provided on site with contractors specifying their orders online. Delivery management systems can also be used for this purpose.

Delivery of materials

The CCC will operate a small fleet of delivery vehicles. Based on the site orders received, the administrator makes up consolidated vehicle loads for the day's requirements.

The delivery operation can benefit from a GPS-based traffic management system. With this, very accurate estimated time of arrival (ETA) can be provided, which is extremely useful to traffic marshals and gate operatives, particularly in restricted inner-city areas. It is a common experience that with a CCC operation deliveries are often within plus or minus 15 minutes of target time, whereas in 'normal' projects it is not unusual for delivery accuracy to be no better than 'morning' or 'afternoon' – if that. The CCC approach means that there will be no queuing at gates and no circulating traffic waiting to get access.

When it comes to the delivery of materials on site there are two main options. Either the CCC operation ends at the offloading area with the individual contractors taking responsibility for their materials once they are offloaded, or there is an on-site logistics team responsible for handling to the point of use or to each individual contractor's material lay-down area. The use of CCCs can lead to substantial productivity gains because there is less time wasted waiting for materials; clearly these productivity gains are maximized with the use of an on-site handling team.

Warehouse management systems

The use of WMS technology brings many advantages to the construction project. It gives a level of control over material usage that is not there when individual contractors manage their own supply flow directly to site. The inventory control means that low stock levels can be flagged up so that reordering happens in a timely fashion, reducing the number of emergency orders and late deliveries. The system automatically provides a record of suppliers' delivery accuracy in terms of on-time performance, quantity and specification. The system also gives the main contractor improved visibility of trade contractor performance. Poor planning leading to shortages and delays, and emergency orders will show up, as will over-ordering – a common issue in construction.

Value-added processes

The most common approach is for CCCs to consolidate only at full pallet level; ie they receive truckloads of pallets from different suppliers, then make up consolidated vehicle loads comprising a mixture of pallets for delivery to site. It is unusual for pallets to be broken down or for secondary (outer) packaging to be opened and individual packs/items selected. Compare this approach to modern retailing where roll cages are made up with a mixture of products to match the sequence and location of the product in the supermarket aisle, making replenishment as efficient as possible. The full pallet load on the building site might hold more product than is needed in one location, necessitating repeated handling of the materials on a crowded site; while more than one product might be needed in the location leading to several pallets competing for restricted space. Anyone who has visited or worked on a building site will recognize these problems. Following the examples set by other industries, instead of trade contractors having to move materials from location to location, mixed pallet loads can be prepared at the CCC, supplying materials needed at specific on-site locations. An example of where this can work is the making up of a material kit for each ward in a hospital project. The difficulty in achieving this lies in the fact that it could involve more than one trade contractor, so the mixed kit order will only come about through detailed planning and site management, forcing collaboration between different trades and logistics contractors.

Another area where the CCC can provide useful added value is in relation to packaging. In crowded city-centre sites the volume of packaging presents a handling problem on site and leads to additional traffic for waste removal. For some items it is possible to remove secondary (outer) packaging, and in some cases even primary packaging, at the CCC before delivering to site; it is a short journey and materials are handled by logistics professionals. Special handling units (compare the supermarket roll cage) can be used to protect the product on the final leg and on site, and the emptied units are taken back to the CCC on the return leg of the delivery run.

If a workspace can be provided at the CCC not only can packaging be removed but in some cases subassemblies or other preparatory work can be undertaken, which otherwise would have to take place on site. An example of this strategy was highlighted in the case study Material Logistics Planning, Central St Giles (Lundesjö, 2009b). The contractor responsible for assembling and lagging the air-conditioning system found that it was far more efficient to carry out this work at the CCC; the work environment was good, and the completed units were loaded on pallets for each location on site. The operator explained that on site, this work would have involved cramped conditions, being up ladders and getting in everybody's way! Furthermore, CCCs are sometimes used to manufacture prototype and demonstration interiors for client approval prior to final completion on site.

These examples show that when a CCC is available, creative thinking by project managers and trade contractors can result in new ways of doing things, thereby easing congestion and making the construction process on site more efficient.

The benefits of using a CCC

There are many well-documented benefits of using a CCC. The most obvious benefits stem from the main reason that CCCs were first introduced: to reduce traffic and congestion around sites in urban and inner-city areas, thus reducing noise and emissions of nitrogen oxides, particulate matter and CO_2. In this primary objective CCCs have been very successful and this is why the use of CCCs has been promoted by, for example, Transport for London and the City of Stockholm.

Studying the impact of using CCCs in some of the early applications of the methodology, several further benefits were discovered and in later applications taken into account as part of the rationale for using CCCs.

The construction industry is a major contributor to the overall volume of waste in society. Product damage from poor site storage conditions and frequent moving of materials as work progresses is a common problem in construction. So-called shrinkage (product being stolen or simply lost) is also not insignificant. As a result, over-ordering, often by 15–25 per cent, takes place with the acceptance that material wastage will be high. The CCC, simply by providing a secure, covered, not overcrowded warehouse facility has a direct beneficial effect on reducing waste. Handling materials on site just once and for more or less immediate use drastically reduces site damage-induced waste.

The use of a CCC facilitates an increase in return logistics. Studies have shown (WRAP, 2012) that some 80 per cent of vehicles delivering to a construction site depart empty. The planned consolidated delivery pattern that follows from using a CCC makes it easy to use the delivery vehicles for taking unused and packaging materials back to the CCC. Packaging is a major waste stream in construction and attempts to introduce reusable packaging often fail as the return logistics cannot be achieved economically. The CCC is the natural hub for collecting reusable packaging coming back from site. From the CCC, supplier delivery vehicles can collect the reusable packaging; whereas directly on site there normally is not space to marshal return materials, and time pressures for vehicle turnaround prevent methodical return handling.

The use of a CCC has been found to significantly enhance productivity on site. There are a number of ways in which the working practices that follow from using a CCC drive productivity improvements. On traditional sites a significant part of trade contractors' time is occupied in waiting for materials and handling materials rather than completing their primary construction tasks. The problems often start at the gate. Waiting time at gates and offloading areas, queuing for critical resources such as space, fork-lift trucks, hoists etc steal productive time. The CCC delivers consolidated loads and therefore fewer vehicles on a planned timetable often within plus or minus 15 minutes of schedule, which means that operatives and offloading equipment can be ready and prepared for arrival. This factor alone can have a measurable effect on productivity in an industry where a delivery accuracy no better than within a half-day or day has traditionally not been unusual.

Productivity is also enhanced by the fact that only appropriate quantities of materials are brought to site on a JIT basis. (Note that in construction JIT may refer to, say, daily deliveries; whereas in other industries such as manufacturing it may well be a matter of hours or minutes.) The effect is less material on site. Materials traditionally stored on sites can be in the way, obstruct movement and frequently have to be moved as work progresses into new areas. A working environment clear of clutter promotes productivity. These site-related productivity gains will be enhanced if the use of the CCC is combined with the use of a specialist logistics contractor for the on-site handling to the point of use – utilization of trade contractor time can then be maximized.

The use of a CCC forces the trade contractors to plan ahead at a detailed level. They need to be able to place accurate orders for material delivery on the CCC for their requirements two to four days ahead. The discipline imposed by the main contractor and the CCC operator will not allow them to order excessive quantities 'just to be on the safe side'. Main contractors have expressed the view that this requirement for planning and discipline placed on trade contractors in itself sharpens contractor performance, with fewer conflicts with others on site and a smoother performance.

Using a CCC is also helpful in the promotion of health and safety on site. On-site storage areas are cramped, often out-of-doors and on uneven surfaces ill-suited for storage and handling. Within the CCC materials are handled and stored using appropriate equipment in a safe warehouse environment. Materials are brought to site JIT leaving the site uncluttered; this improvement in the working environment can have a direct impact on site safety. Again the benefit is enhanced if the CCC is combined with the provision of an on-site handling specialist so that handling professionals service the trade contractors to the point of use rather than just to the gate/offloading area.

There are numerous studies that have attempted to quantify these various benefits (some cases are summarized in the text below).

CASE STUDY Hammarby Sjöstad, Stockholm

At Hammarby Sjöstad, Stockholm (Ottoson 2005) the logistics centre (LC) was introduced specifically to ease the effects of construction – traffic, noise, pollution – for local residents. This was to be achieved mainly by reducing the number of small deliveries, defined as those with fewer than four pallets, through consolidation. Some of the results quoted were:

- number of small deliveries reduced by 80 per cent;
- reduced energy consumption and emissions of CO_2, nitrogen oxides and particulate matter;
- improved living conditions at site for new inhabitants (those moving into properties built in the first phases of the project);
- less traffic congestion at the site;
- improved working environment.

On all these counts the project was deemed a success following evaluation by the City of Stockholm. Subsequent studies by academics also pointed to significant reductions in material waste and shrinkage.

CASE STUDY The London CCC

The London Construction Consolidation Centre (LCCC) was set up in 2006 by construction logistics experts Wilson James to serve four projects in central London. The operation was modelled on an original concept established in 2001 at Heathrow Airport (HCC). In *Managing Construction Logistics* (Sullivan, Barthorpe and Robbins, 2010) it is highlighted that many in the industry felt that the CCC concept would be useful only in airport construction projects because of the very particular circumstances that apply:

- the high level of security required;
- the need to deliver the construction project during continuous passenger operations of the airport;
- the stringent commercial needs and absolute requirements to meet handover dates.

In operation, however, the HCC was found to bring further benefits, namely:

- improved productivity on site;
- faster turnaround and better utilization of the suppliers' delivery vehicles, leading to cost reductions;
- reduced damage and waste through better handling methods;
- improved health and safety standards;
- delays due to materials not being available reduced from 6 per cent to 0.4 per cent – a factor of 15, which enhances overall programme certainty and productivity.

These factors contributed to the decision that the consolidation centre concept would be viable also for the central London projects where the main drivers were limited in space on site for offloading and storage, coupled with congested access to sites and the costs of the London congestion charge. Subsequently the LCCC was evaluated in some depth and the following benefits are quoted in the interim and final reports on the LCCC (Transport for London, 2007; Transport for London, 2008):

- a 68 per cent reduction in the number of construction vehicles entering the City of London delivering to the LCCC-served sites;
- an average of two hours reduction in suppliers' journey time by going to the LCCC rather than accessing the central London sites;
- delivery performance of 97 per cent of the right goods delivered correctly first time;
- an approximate reduction in associated CO_2 emissions of 75 per cent (relating to the final stages of the journey);
- significantly reduced product damage and shrinkage leading to an estimated 15 per cent reduction in waste;
- productivity of the LCCC-served site labour force increased by up to 30 minutes per day.

On a site employing 500, this is up to 250 hours per day saved, equating to 30 workers if working an eight-hour shift.

The report Freight Best Practice (Department for Transport, 2007) studied the LCCC from a freight perspective and listed beneficial impact on a number of key performance indicators (KPIs): reduction of freight journeys, reductions in supplier journey times and delivery reliability – with results as stated above.

Table 10.2 Number of vehicles and cost of congestion charges

	No of Vehicles	Cost of Congestion Charges (at £8 per vehicle per day)
Without LCCC	4,099	£32,792
With LCCC	1,461	£11,688
Minimum saving		£21,104

Other KPIs included reduction in vehicle mileage, reduction in number of vehicles used, backloading of pallets and stillages and reduction in waste. The report also looked at the congestion charge savings per annum, as shown in Table 10.2.

The report endorses CCCs as an effective way to reduce both vehicle mileage (and associated fuel consumption and emissions) and traffic congestion in urban areas.

CASE STUDY WRAP

WRAP, the Waste and Resources Action Programme, is a not-for-profit company funded by government and public sector organizations in the United Kingdom that promotes the sustainable use of resources in virtually all sectors of society: consumer, retail, construction etc. As the construction industry is a major contributor to overall waste volumes, WRAP has focused on this industry and one of the strategies has been to promote good logistics practice as a way to reduce waste and carbon emissions. (All WRAP studies are available through the website at **www.wrap.org.uk** under Construction.) Below are a number of relevant studies for using CCCs to reduce construction waste and carbon emissions (Lundesjö, 2011):

- In the study of Unilever House (WRAP, 2007), a central London refurbishment project using the LCCC, the following was reported:
  - In all, some 13,200 pallets (or pallet equivalent) were handled by the LCCC over a two-year period.
  - 90 per cent of all delivered pallets were returned to the LCCC for collection by suppliers.
- The project also provided an excellent illustration of over-ordering in the industry, and of the waste-reducing effect of using a CCC. At the end of the

project 38 full 26-tonne lorry loads of unused materials worth approximately £200,000 remained at the CCC rather than ending up in waste skips.

- WRAP reports on Barts Hospital (Lundesjö, 2009a) and Central St Giles (Lundesjö, 2009b) show a reduction of vehicle journeys into central London of 74 per cent and 75 per cent respectively, with corresponding reductions in energy usage and emissions.

Types of CCC

There are many different types of CCC. In *Managing Construction Logistics* (Sullivan, Barthorpe and Robbins, 2010) three different solutions are suggested:

- concealed consolidation centre;
- communal consolidation centre;
- collaborative consolidation centre.

The concealed consolidation centre is so called because it is not in a separate location but is contained within the boundary of the construction site. This is a useful approach for large, typically multi-building sites, where a warehouse facility can be accommodated and the CCC operation can be carried out, receiving all goods and servicing all the different parts of the site. So while it is not in a separate location the site will enjoy all the CCC functionality and derive the benefits thereof. The Stockholm example of Hammarby Sjöstad referred to earlier can be said to be of this type.

The communal consolidation centre is a facility serving a number of projects for a single contractor/client. This is a good approach for large urban and city areas where there are several projects running concurrently. The facility would typically be run by the main contractor or a specialist logistics company. Dedicated storage zones can be set up for the different projects or the warehouse space can be shared fully depending on how sophisticated are the warehouse managements systems used. The facility is financed by the client via the main contractor, who in turn will try to recoup the costs from the savings made by the various subcontractors: reduced transport, handling, damage etc.

The collaborative consolidation centre would typically be the largest operation of the three alternatives. This is where one CCC is used collaboratively by a number of different clients and main contractors. Operated by a logistics specialist company it is financed by handling charges levied at the clients, depending on volumes handled.

On the construction logistics area of WRAP's website a slightly different categorization of CCC is outlined. Four types of consolidation centres are described:

- **Hidden consolidation.** This is the same approach as with the concealed CCC described above – a consolidation operation within the boundaries of a large site.
- **Single-user consolidation.** This is where a consolidation centre is set up to support a single project. It is typically set up by the main contractor, hiring a logistics company to operate the centre.
- **Shared consolidation centre.** This is a multi-project consolidation centre and encompasses both the communal and collaborative centres described above. This can support several sites for one or several clients/main contractors.
- **Virtual consolidation.** This is the final suggestion described, and it differs from the earlier approaches. This is where a dedicated CCC is not set up. Instead, by collaborating with a 3PL the construction client/main contractor makes use of the 3PL's existing resources in terms of shared user warehouses or depots.

In using CCCs (Lundesjö, 2011), examples are given of three radically different approaches to construction consolidation:

- A shared facility serving multiple clients and multiple sites. The London CCC in Silvertown, London, is operated by construction logistics specialists Wilson James supporting several projects (at the time the report was written six projects used the facility) for different clients/main contractors across central London.
- A single-user single-project CCC. At Nine Elms, London MLogic operated a CCC on a site owned by the large distribution company DHL, supporting one client, Laing O'Rourke, for a single project: One Hyde Park.
- A single-client, multi-project and multifunctional CCC. This is an operation in Park Royal, London run as a partnership between Sainsbury's and construction logistics specialists Fit Out (UK) Ltd. So while there is a single client (Sainsbury's), there are many sites, with new stores being built and existing stores being refurbished. The CCC is multifunctional in that it not only serves as a CCC but is also a refurbishment centre. During refurbishment projects materials are removed from site and taken back to

the CCC, where they are inspected and if possible refurbished for reuse on the current project or stored for future use.

The above list illustrates that there are many ways to approach construction consolidation and while they are very different they can all be successful:

- They reduce traffic to sites and in the urban areas served.
- They facilitate JIT delivery of materials to sites.
- They provide dry, safe and secure storage conditions and professional materials handling methods that result in reduced product damage and shrinkage.
- By providing controlled material flow to site they contribute to programme certainty and financial performance.

There are many arguments in favour of shared and/or multi-project CCCs. Set-up and fixed costs can be shared over a larger volume and there are more opportunities to maximize utilization of resources thereby reducing unit costs. Only large projects tend to justify the initial cost of starting a CCC operation, but once in place smaller projects can successfully benefit from sharing the resource. The arguments in favour of a single-user CCC are often based on the need for security and the ability to tailor the operation entirely around one client/main contractor's operation. With increased engagement by 3PLs in the construction industry, however, one can expect the shared user model to increase, with the 3PL drawing on its existing resource base as in setting up CCCs.

Locating a CCC

To fulfil its function a CCC must be in the right location. This means:

- Good access for inbound supplier deliveries. The CCC should be on a major road close to motorway/trunk road network. There are two reasons for this:
  - to minimize the impact on local roads and communities of incoming deliveries;
  - to provide fast turnaround for suppliers' vehicles in order to minimize cost.
- A location reasonably close to the site(s) served. As a rule of thumb this means that the drive time to site should be ideally no more than 30–45 minutes. Allowing for loading and offloading times each vehicle can then

do two or three rounds per shift. Fewer than two rounds per shift leads to a high likelihood of poor vehicle and manpower utilization.

In *Using CCCs* (Lundesjö, 2011) these criteria are used to model suitable locations around a number of cities in the United Kingdom, illustrating how easily the benefits of a CCC operation could be provided. In reality, however, there are very few examples, and in the United Kingdom they are centred on London. The case for CCCs in London was analysed in detail by Peter Brett Associates for TfL (Anderson, 2007) and at that time they forecast that London volumes could support six shared-user CCCs on an ongoing basis, for which they modelled suitable locations. However, six shared facilities did not spring up. The LCCC continued in operation and has been joined mainly by single-project CCCs and also some 3PL operations.

Case study summary: Bart's Hospital Phase 2

This summary of experience is based on a report (not in the public domain) made available by Wilson James and prepared by the Department of Engineering and the Built Environment of the Anglia Ruskin University, analysing the effect of logistics and site services on the construction performance of Bart's Hospital Phase 2.

For this central London project Wilson James provided a more integrated level of logistics services than has been seen before. Named the Integrated Logistics and Site Services Support Package (ILSSSP), it was tailored to the requirements at Bart's and included the delivery of construction materials from supplier order to point of use, combined with the provision of a range of site services and support. This was managed and delivered as a single discrete work package to main contractor Skanska.

The report identifies the London Construction Consolidation Centre (LCCC) and the on-site team as vital components of a completely integrated supply chain. Specialist logistics management was provided by Wilson James and was itself fully integrated into the Skanska project management team; the effectiveness of the ILSSSP was based upon the central role that logistics played in the planning and management of the project. The report highlights savings and improvements in many areas; here we will mention two. There was an estimated 2–3 per cent saving in materials used by trade contractors and the productivity improvements were estimated to be 6–10 per cent. Further to this the report identifies many environmental benefits in terms of reduced waste, reduced vehicle journeys/mileage, reduced noise and improved safety. The report states that the ILSSSP enabled the project to achieve its programme and cost targets which otherwise would have been significantly increased by the constricted site and restricted access. Improved logistics efficiency through the use of specialist logistics management, specialist equipment and trained, experienced logistics operatives ensured that timely material availability was achieved and waste minimized. It also reduced the management and resource inputs required from Skanska. Furthermore, it ensured that the operation of the hospital was unaffected throughout the duration of the project.

It is clear from the report that this approach not only pays for itself but also offers significant benefits financially, environmentally and socially.

However, some of the difficulties alluded to in this Chapter were also experienced. The report notes scepticism and inertia among trade contractors not keen on adopting new practices. There is an unwillingness among trade contractors to be open about costs – sometimes a lack of awareness of true costs – which means they are unable to appreciate savings; this in turn makes it difficult for the main contractor to fully exploit the potential extra competitiveness in the tendering situation, and later in the project to realize the savings and benefit fully from the strategy. While the integrated approach adopted by Skanska on St Bart's made significant progress in this area, it seems that the report confirms that to move forward the whole industry needs better insight and understanding of all processes and costs in the supply chain, and a more collaborative attitude. But it is clear that for contractors who can master this approach there is strong potential for improved competitiveness on price, construction time and overall performance.

Conclusions

Both when studying the literature and when talking to managers in the industry one comes to the conclusion that consolidation centres work; projects using CCCs run well and benefit from them. In spite of this, while CCCs are used, they have not penetrated the industry at anything like the level expected, say, 10 years ago in 2005.

In most cases a CCC is used when the main contractor is forced down that route by specific constraints. Those constraints are normally space restrictions on site (limiting storage and/or access via gates) or restrictions limiting vehicle access such as narrow time windows and on-street queuing disallowed by local councils. While these are good and valid reasons for using a CCC, the advantages identified above – environmental benefits, productivity gains, programme certainty and cost savings that can outweigh the cost of using a CCC – mean that CCCs could be considered much more widely as a construction logistics strategy. So why is it that, if not forced down the CCC route by local regulations or severe constraints, CCCs are so seldom considered? One logistics manager at a major UK main contractor stated that to run a CCC near London of about 3,000 square metres supporting a £400 million project in central London costs about £1 million per year to run. In the extremely competitive bidding environment you just cannot win acceptance for that cost, for something that at the end of the project the client does not have! The main contractor has to cover the cost, but many of the savings benefit the trade contractors and their subcontractors, such as hauliers. And while case studies point to many savings, few are willing to trust upfront during the bidding situation that those savings will be fulfilled. And even if the savings are fulfilled, the main contractor paying for the CCC might not be able to claw those back from all the subcontractors and suppliers. We have a known cost against hoped-for savings.

Construction, particularly in cities and densely populated urban areas, is an activity circumscribed by planning regulations, traffic regulations and environmental controls. Perhaps this is an area where local authorities should interfere and insist on the use of CCCs, by regulating site access, and perhaps even promoting shared CCC facilities in suitable locations. That way, everyone in the bidding for projects would have to cover the cost and at the end everyone is likely to be the winner.

References

Anderson, S (2007) Construction Consolidation Centres: An assessment of the potential for London wide use, Peter Brett Associates for Transport for London

Department for Transport (2007) [accessed August 2010] London Construction Consolidation Centre [Online] http://www.freightbestpractice.org.uk

Lundesjö, G (2009a) [accessed 15 February 2015] Case Study: Material logistics planning, Barts Hospital, London, Skanska, *The Logistics Business for WRAP* [Online] http://wrap.org.uk/construction

Lundesjö, G (2009b) [accessed 15 February 2015] Case Study: Material logistics planning, Central St Giles Stanhope, Bovis Lend Lease and Wilson James, *The Logistics Business for WRAP* [Online] http://wrap.org.uk/construction

Lundesjö, G (2011) [accessed 15 February 2015] Using Construction Consolidation Centres to Reduce Construction Waste and Carbon Emissions, *The Logistics Business for WRAP* [Online] http://wrap.org.uk/construction

Ottoson, M (2005) [accessed 15 February 2015] Evaluation Report: New concepts for the distribution of goods, trendsetter report no 2005:7, *Civitas* [Online] http://www.trendsetter-europe.org/

Sullivan, G, Barthorpe, S and Robbins, S (2010) *Managing Construction Logistics*, Wiley-Blackwell, Oxford

Transport for London (2007) London Construction Consolidation Centre Interim Report – May 2007 [Online] http://www.tfl.gov.uk

Transport for London (2008) London Construction Consolidation Centre Final Report – October 2008 [Online] http://www.tfl.gov.uk

WRAP (2007) [accessed 23 February 2015] Material Logistics Plan, Good Practice Guidance: Project code WAS041-001, ISBN 1-84405-370-9 [Online] http://www.wrap.org.uk/sites/files/wrap/MLP%20Guidance%20Document.pdf

WRAP (2012) [accessed 15 February 2015] Case Study: Reverse logistics on construction sites [Online] http://wrap.org.uk/construction

The socio-economic benefits of off-peak hour distribution 11

The case of Stockholm

SÖNKE BEHRENDS, IVÁN SÁNCHEZ-DÍAZ AND ANNA PERNESTÅL BRENDEN

Introduction

Increasing urbanization and the ensuing difficulties to deal with passenger and freight transportation needs have led the public sector and the transportation community to seek alternatives that alleviate traffic impacts while coping with budget and space constraints. In particular, it is evident that densely populated cities suffer from an oversaturated infrastructure during daytime hours, but the same space is then underutilized during the evening, at night or in the early morning, in the so-called off-peak hours. This has motivated initiatives to shift urban freight distribution to off-peak hours to improve utilization of existing infrastructure and enhance the efficiency of goods distribution.

Although shifting freight distribution to off-peak hours has been tried via congestion pricing and traffic restrictions, the most successful scheme is via off-peak hours deliveries (OPHD) programmes. OPHD programmes, often led by the public sector, aim at retiming deliveries from regular hours to off-peak hours. Experiments and regulation to foster OPHD have been implemented in numerous cities, with the most recent and representative being in New York City, implemented in the early 1970s as a traffic control measure (Noel, 1983), *DeliverEASE* implemented in 2006 as an incentive-based programme (Holguín-Veras *et al*, 2013b), *Operation 'Moondrop'* in London in 1968 (Churchill, 1970), the experiment during the 2012 Olympic Games (Olympic Delivery Authority, 2010), the *Night Deliveries* programme in Paris that has operated since 2009 (Devin *et al*, 2014), and the *Night Deliveries* programme in Barcelona that started in 2003 (NICHES, 2008).

Literature generally agrees about the socio-economic effects of OPHD, which includes significant benefits in terms of reduced congestion and emission impacts, but also leads to an increase of noise impacts for residents. However, there is limited research providing any quantitative evaluation of these effects (Holguín-Veras *et al*, 2011; Holguín-Veras *et al*, 2016). Furthermore, conditions such as city size, congestion levels and transport characteristics are rarely taken into consideration. It is therefore difficult to make estimates about the usefulness of OPHD in different cities, which limits the transferability of existing best practice, especially to cities that are smaller than large metropolitan areas like New York, London, Paris or Barcelona. The aim of this chapter is to evaluate the socio-economic benefits of OPHD and to identify the relevance of contextual conditions by comparing the external costs of business-as-usual daytime distribution trips with the distribution trips at off-peak hours based on a pilot project in Stockholm, Sweden.

The chapter starts by introducing the background to OPHD and reviewing previous experiences. Then the case study for assessing the socio-economic effects of the OPHD pilot in Stockholm is described, including an introduction to the pilot project, a description of the assessment method and a definition of the scenarios. Finally, the results are presented followed by a discussion of their implications for policy and research.

Off-peak hour distribution projects: background and experiences

OPHD projects aim at shifting urban freight distribution from regular hours – usually matching overall traffic peak-hours – to the hours of the day when transportation infrastructure is less utilized, ie off-peak hours. Off-peak hours are often divided between night hours (right after business hours), late night or early morning. This distinction is important because it can affect receivers' personnel costs, travel time savings, and noise and environmental impacts (Sánchez-Díaz *et al*, 2016).

Off-peak hour distribution has been tried using different policy approaches, including: 1) a laissez-faire approach, where the market is let alone so that companies that find it more efficient to distribute at night do so; 2) road pricing approaches extended from passenger transportation to freight vehicles for which a fee is charged during peak hours to manage demand and shift traffic to off-peak hours; 3) a public sector-led programme where incentives are provided to voluntary participants; and 4) access restrictions either to only allow freight vehicles during off-peak hours, or to ban vehicles from off-peak hours – this restriction can go together with selective relaxations given the vehicles meet some standards (Sánchez-Díaz *et al*, 2016).

Although in a laissez-faire scenario firms in some sectors such as dairy distribution, newspaper distribution, grocery stores and beverages distribution, receive a share of their deliveries during off-peak hours (*Noel et al*, 1980), the overall amount of OPHD under a laissez-faire approach is too small to generate a benefit in terms of congestion or environmental savings. In essence, different authors have estimated the share of off-peak hour freight traffic under a laissez-faire approach to range from 5 to 11 per cent for cities such as New York City, Amsterdam and London (Vilain and Wolfrom, 2000; Schoemaker *et al*, 2006; Allen *et al*, 2008).

Implementing road pricing initiatives has shown some degree of success for passenger transportation. However, this is not the case for freight transportation, for which the fee to deliver during the day is paid by carriers that prefer to assume this cost or distribute it among their multiple customers rather than convince them to shift their delivery time to off-peak hours (Holguín-Veras *et al*, 2005; Holguín-Veras *et al*, 2006). This has been corroborated with empirical evidence in New York City and London where despite having significant increases in the tolls/congestion fees, freight traffic time patterns did not change significantly (Vilain and Wolfrom, 2000). There are, nevertheless, some reasons to implement such road pricing initiatives, such as funding new freight projects or other OPHD programmes (Holguín-Veras and Aros-Vera, 2014).

The number of public sector-led programmes where incentives (eg public recognition) are often provided have been increasing in the last years, some examples include New York City, São Paulo and Bogotá among others (Holguín-Veras *et al*, 2013b; Holguín-Veras *et al*, 2016). These types of programme are often supported by academia, carriers, large companies interested in OPHD and Business Improvement Districts. Holguín-Veras *et al* (2017) estimate that depending on the types and levels of incentive (eg monetary incentive, public recognition, carriers' discount) offered to the receivers, the share of OPHD can range between 5 and 40 per cent.

Access restrictions to ban vehicles from delivering during peak hours have been tried in China as a way to cope with the imminent impacts of disruptive events (eg Beijing Olympic Games), or in cases of extreme environmental conditions (eg Beijing, Shenzhen and Changsha) (Changsha Bureau of Public Security, 2013; Beijing Traffic Management Bureau, 2014; Shenzhen Bureau of Public Security, 2013; Gang, 2009; Campbell, 1995). However, these measures have been largely ineffective, because carriers find either smaller vehicles or violate the ban and deliver at the time their customers need the goods. In European cities, where it is common to have freight vehicle restrictions to deliver during off-peak hours, the most common

Table 11.1 Summary of pilot test results

Pilot Test	New York City	London	Denmark	Paris	Stockholm (preliminary results)
Travel time savings	1.25 h in a 10 miles tour	38–55% 1 h per trip	8–10% less vehicle miles	50–56%	50–60%
Service time savings	Up to 1 hour	N/A	9–17% overall time savings	27–61% overall time savings	N/A
Environmental impacts	CO_2 reduction: 20–75%	CO_2 reduction: 48–62%	CO_2 reduction: 7% for beverages distribution	CO_2 reduction 36–40%	CO_2 reduction 20–40% based on fuel reduction
Noise assessment/ complaints	No complaints	No complaints Curtains reduce noise 8–10 dB	Some safety issues No noise complaints for most pilots	One complaint over unloading area OPHD done under 60 dB	No complaints Noise logged for evaluation

SOURCE Sánchez-Díaz *et al*, 2016

approach has been to implement technology and practices that allow low noise deliveries during off-peak hours and assess the impacts through pilot tests (Goevaers, 2011; Transport for London, 2015; The City of Paris, 2013; Sánchez-Díaz *et al*, 2016).

Pilot tests of OPHD have been crucial in getting the different stakeholders engaged, in testing low noise technology and guidelines, and assessing the potential benefits of this initiative. These pilots have often derived from larger programmes and, in some cases, in the inclusion of OPHD as a strategy for the mobility plan of cities. Table 11.1 shows a summary of the results from OPHD pilot tests implemented in New York City, London, Denmark, Paris and Stockholm.

Case study: evaluating an OPHD pilot project in Stockholm

The OPHD pilot project in Stockholm

Stockholm is the capital of Sweden with a current population of about 1.5 million people. Demand for goods distribution increases constantly. In Stockholm, there are regulations prohibiting deliveries with heavy vehicles in the city centre between 10 pm and 6 am, to avoid night-time noise. In 2014 the city released the Stockholm Freight Plan 2014–2017 (City of Stockholm, 2014), which included goals to improve accessibility and improve efficiency for urban freight transport. One of the activities outlined in the plan was to conduct an OPHD pilot giving permission for night-time deliveries to two vehicles during 2015 and 2016. In parallel with the pilot, a research project was started to assess the potential efficiency gains from OPHD for the private sector, evaluate the socio-economic benefits for society and to develop low-noise freight distribution solutions.

The OPHD pilot in Stockholm involved two different delivery schemes. The first scheme is a dedicated delivery to a single customer (full truckload, FTL), ie one truck delivers big volumes from a warehouse located 30 kilometres outside the city to three different grocery stores in the city centre, resulting in three routes back and forth between the city and the warehouse each night. The second scheme is a consolidated delivery to various customers (less-than-truckload transport, LTL), ie one truck delivers small volumes from a warehouse to several hotels and restaurants, resulting in one or two routes per night in a multiple-stop delivering scheme. Both trucks were equipped with low-noise technology and certified according to PIEK (Goevaers, 2011) and the handling equipment used in the pilot was specially designed to reduce noise and pollution. GPS data, fleet management data and noise measurements has been continuously collected from the trucks. The pilot project showed that shifting deliveries from daytime peak hours to night increased driving efficiency, delivery reliability and energy efficiency (Fu and Jenelius, 2018).

The assessment method

The negative side effects of transportation are generally defined as externalities, because they are not borne by the transport operators or customers and hence not taken into account when they make a transport decision. The externalities can be expressed in monetary terms and are then referred to as external costs. This case study calculates the external costs of business-as-usual daytime distribution trips and compares them with distribution trips at night-time. To calculate the external costs the CUTS-Assessment model is used (see Behrends (2016) for a model description). The model calculates for a given transport demand a series of key parameters describing the logistics efficiency (the receiver's perspective), transport resource efficiency (the carrier's perspective) and impact intensity (the authorities' perspective). These key parameters are determined by factors characterizing supply chain design, transport solutions and land-use system. This case study is limited to the impact intensity, which represents the socio-economic effects, ie it does not include logistics and transport resource efficiency.

The calculation of external costs in the CUTS model are based on RICARDO AEA (2014) which provides best practice methodology for estimating the external costs of transport. The negative side effects of transport imposed on society are commonly grouped into:

1 congestion;
2 accidents;
3 noise;
4 air pollution;
5 climate change;
6 costs of up- and downstream processes;
7 infrastructure wear and tear for road and rail.

Table 11.2 Congestion, accidents and noise costs in euro cents per vehicle-kilometre of a rigid truck (1.9 passenger car units) in a metropolitan area

Impact Type	Road Category/ Urban Form	External Costs		
		Free Flow	*Saturated*	*Congested*
Congestion	local street	4.8	303.1	460.9
	main road	1.7	268.5	344.5
	motorway	0.0	50.9	116.9
Accidents	local street		0.9	
	main road		1.0	
	motorway		1.2	
Noise (day)	suburban		0.9	
	urban		13.9	
Noise (night)	suburban		2.3	
	urban		35.8	

SOURCE RICARDO AEA, 2014

This case study is limited to 'wheel-to-tank', ie only the external costs of the vehicle operation are included. Neither externalities from fuel production and distribution ('well-to-tank') nor from vehicle and infrastructure production etc are included in the analysis. The reason for this limitation is that these parts are not affected by shifting transport times, ie their impact is the same in both scenarios. Hence, this study includes the impact categories 1–5 and excludes the categories 6 (costs of up- and downstream processes) and 7 (road infrastructure wear and tear).

The following data are needed in order to calculate the external costs of freight transport for categories 1–5 (RICARDO AEA, 2014):

- Congestion costs depend on the *vehicle size* (rigid truck or articulated truck), type of *urban area* (metropolitan areas with a population > 250,000 people; urban areas with a population > 10,000; rural areas), the *road type* (motorway, main roads, other roads); and *traffic conditions*, ie the ratio of actual traffic flow to theoretical maximum traffic flow. Three categories of traffic conditions are defined: free flow (up to 75 per cent of the theoretical maximum traffic flow); saturated (75–100 per cent); and congested (more than 100 per cent).
- Accident costs depend on the *vehicle size* (only one type defined for freight, eg heavy goods vehicle) and *road type* (motorways, other non-urban roads, urban road).

- Noise costs depend on *vehicle size* (light commercial vehicle or heavy goods vehicle); *time of day* (day, night); traffic conditions (dense, thin) and type of *urban area* (urban with 3,000 inhabitants per kilometre road length, suburban with 700 inhabitants and rural with 500 inhabitants). Table 11.2 shows the congestion, accident and noise cost of a rigid truck used in this case study.
- Air pollution costs are measured in cost per unit of emission. Emission parameters included are particles ($PM_{2.5}$), nitrogen oxides (NO_X), hydrocarbons (HC) and sulphur oxides (SO_2). The external costs of $PM_{2.5}$ depend on type of *urban area* (urban area with a population density of more than 1,500 inhabitants/square kilometre, suburban with a density of 300, and rural areas with a density below 150).
- Climate change costs are measured in cost per emission of CO_2 equivalent. Since estimating the costs of climate change is highly uncertain, a wide range of values is presented. Table 11.3 shows the air pollution and climate costs used in this case study.

For all impact categories country-specific cost values are presented, except for climate change. As climate change is a global impact, the unit costs do not depend on any local conditions. Congestion, accident and noise costs are measured in cost per unit of traffic (eg euros per vehicle-kilometre). Air pollution and climate change costs are measured in cost per unit of emission (euros per tonne CO_2). The CUTS model therefore requires input data on emission factors for each vehicle type on the different road categories and in different traffic conditions. In the CUTS model these emissions are calculated based on the approach presented in NTM (2007). As the NTM data do not present emission values for specific traffic conditions, we use

Table 11.3 External costs of emissions in euro cents per gram

Emission	Costs
CO_2	0.01
HC	0.10
SO_x	0.54
CH_4	0.23
PM-urban	19.74
PM-suburban	5.02
PM-rural	1.46

SOURCE RICARDO AEA, 2014

emission data from the Handbook of Emission Factors for Road Transport (INFRAS, 2014). The handbook presents detailed emission data based on a variety of parameters, including vehicle type, vehicle size, technology (gasoline or diesel) emission concept (EURO classes), road type, traffic conditions and road gradient. Accordingly, the following data are needed in order to calculate the external costs of the distribution trips:

- vehicle type (size, engine technology, fuel);
- number of goods transported (load factor of the vehicle);
- the route of the distribution trip including time of day; distance; road type (local street, main road, motorway); urban form (rural, suburban, urban); and traffic conditions (free flow, saturated, congested).

The distribution tours

Two theoretical distribution tours are analysed, which are based on data from the pilot project in Stockholm. The first tour is a *dedicated delivery to a single customer* (full truckload, FTL). The second tour is a *consolidated delivery to various customers* (less-than-truckload transport, LTL). In order to calculate the external costs of these tours, the following data are used:

- Vehicle type: in the Stockholm trial a hybrid truck (FTL) and biogas truck (LTL) are used. In this case study, we use trucks of the same size as in the trial, but we assume conventional diesel trucks without any special low-noise equipment for the sake of generalizability of the results. Hence, we assume the following vehicles: for FTL, a rigid truck, 26t, Diesel, Euro 6; and for LTL a rigid truck, 17t, Diesel, Euro 6. The emission values of these vehicles are displayed in Table 11.4 and Table 11.5 respectively.
- We assume an average load factor of 50 per cent (full truckload at the beginning and empty at the end of the tour).
- Distribution tour: we use GPS data from the Stockholm trial to construct the route, the time and the urban form of the trip. The traffic conditions are based on the data on typical traffic levels from GoogleMaps.

For each tour, two scenarios are constructed: first, deliveries taking place in the daytime (Scenario BAU); and second, a delivery trip taking place in off-peak hours. To estimate the relevance of congestion levels, we conduct a sensitivity analysis by constructing two more scenarios of daytime distribution: one scenario (Table 11.6) with significantly lower (approximately half) congestion levels (BAU low congestion); and one scenario (Table 11.7) with significantly higher (approximately double) congestion levels (BAU high congestion).

Table 11.4 Energy consumption and emissions to air of a rigid truck (Euro 6, 26 ton) by road category and traffic situation

ROAD CATEGORY (DESIGN SPEED)	SPEED	ENERGY CONSUMPTION			EMISSIONS TO AIR (50% CAPACITY UTILIZATION)					
Traffic condition	[km/h]	empty [g/km]	full [g/km]	average [g/km]	CO_2 [g/km]	HC [g/km]	NO_x [g/km]	PM [g/km]	SO_x [g/km]	CH_4 [g/km]
Motorway (80 km/h) free flow	76	159	222	191	603	0.0232	0.1247	0.0031	0.0008	0.0006
Motorway (80 km/h) saturated	59	160	237	198	625	0.0259	0.2153	0.0034	0.0008	0.0006
Motorway (80 km/h) congested	17	357	496	426	1342	0.0752	0.8695	0.0096	0.0017	0.0018
Main road (50 km/h) free flow	47	184	268	225	710	0.0321	0.3081	0.0042	0.0009	0.0008
Main road (50 km/h) saturated	29	229	329	279	879	0.0442	0.4815	0.0058	0.0011	0.0011
Main road (50 km/h) congested	12	441	562	500	1574	0.1073	2.1211	0.0130	0.0020	0.0026
Local street (50 km/h) free flow	41	175	264	219	689	0.0340	0.3544	0.0044	0.0009	0.0008
Local street (50 km/h) saturated	26	229	322	275	867	0.0500	0.7330	0.0065	0.0011	0.0012
Local street (50 km/h) congested	12	441	562	500	1574	0.1073	2.1211	0.0130	0.0020	0.0026

SOURCE INFRAS, 2014

Table 11.5 Energy consumption and emissions to air of a rigid truck (Euro 6, 17 ton) by road category and traffic situation

ROAD CATEGORY (DESIGN SPEED)	SPEED	ENERGY CONSUMPTION			EMISSIONS TO AIR (50% CAPACITY UTILIZATION)					
Traffic condition		**empty**	**full**	**average**	**CO_2**	**HC**	**NO_X**	**PM**	**SO_X**	**CH_4**
	[km/h]	**[g/km]**	**[g/km]**	**[g/km]**	**[g/km]**	**[g/km]**	**[g/km]**	**[g/km]**	**[g/km]**	**[g/km]**
Motorway (80 km/h) free flow	76	142	177	160	503	0.0202	0.1108	0.0026	0.0006	0.0005
Motorway (80 km/h) saturated	59	136	180	158	497	0.0221	0.2045	0.0028	0.0006	0.0005
Motorway (80 km/h) congested	16	276	355	314	988	0.0609	1.0865	0.0079	0.0013	0.0015
Main road (50 km/h) free flow	46	155	204	179	564	0.0277	0.2766	0.0035	0.0007	0.0007
Main road (50 km/h) saturated	29	185	245	215	676	0.0373	0.5029	0.0048	0.0009	0.0009
Main road (50 km/h) congested	12	334	404	369	1162	0.0862	2.5301	0.0109	0.0015	0.0021
Local street (50 km/h) free flow	41	148	199	173	545	0.0297	0.3491	0.0037	0.0007	0.0007
Local street (50 km/h) saturated	26	190	244	217	684	0.0433	0.7714	0.0055	0.0009	0.0010
Local street (50 km/h) congested	12	334	404	369	1162	0.0862	2.5301	0.0109	0.0015	0.0021

SOURCE INFRAS, 2014

Table 11.6 FTL trip composition and traffic conditions (Free: free flow; Sat: saturated; Cong: congested)

		OFF-PEAK HOURS			DAYTIME			DAYTIME (LOW CONG)			DAYTIME (HIGH CONG)		
	Distance [km]	Free [%]	Sat [%]	Cong [%]	Free [%]	Sat [%]	Cong [%]	Free [%]	Sat [%]	Cong [%]	Free [%]	Sat [%]	Cong [%]
Total	*203.8*												
Urban	*28.7*												
local street	11.2	100%	0%	0%	0%	100%	0%	50%	50%	0%	0%	50%	50%
main road	17.5	100%	0%	0%	0%	100%	0%	50%	50%	0%	0%	50%	50%
Suburban	*128.0*												
motorway	128.0	100%	0%	0%	50%	50%	0%	75%	25%	0%	25%	50%	25%
Rural	*47.1*												
local street	14.1	100%	0%	0%	100%	0%	0%	100%	0%	0%	100%	0%	0%
motorway	33.0	100%	0%	0%	100%	0%	0%	100%	0%	0%	100%	0%	0%

Table 11.7 LTL trip composition and traffic conditions (Free: free flow; Sat: saturated; Cong: congested)

		OFF-PEAK HOURS			DAYTIME			DAYTIME (LOW CONG)			DAYTIME (HIGH CONG)		
	Distance [km]	Free [%]	Sat [%]	Cong [%]	Free [%]	Sat [%]	Cong [%]	Free [%]	Sat [%]	Cong [%]	Free [%]	Sat [%]	Cong [%]
Total	*40.9*												
Urban	*24.2*												
local street	12.9	100%	0%	0%	0%	100%	0%	50%	50%	0%	0%	50%	50%
main road	4.5	100%	0%	0%	0%	100%	0%	50%	50%	0%	0%	50%	50%
motorway	6.8	100%	0%	0%	0%	56%	44%	50%	28%	22%	0%	25%	75%
Suburban	*16.7*												
local street	6.0	100%	0%	0%	0%	11%	89%	50%	6%	44%	0%	0%	100%
main road	4.7	100%	0%	0%	31%	69%	0%	15%	70%	15%	0%	70%	30%
motorway	6.1	100%	0%	0%	100%	0%	0%	100%	0%	0%	30%	40%	30%

Figure 11.1 Distribution tours of a) FTL and b) LTL

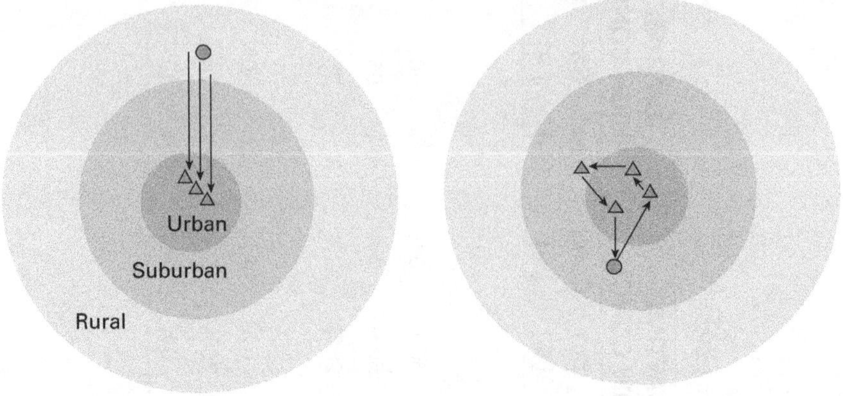

Figure 11.1a shows the distribution tours of the FTL tour. It is based on GPS data from an off-peak tour on 26 January 2016, which took place from approximately 8 pm to 5 am. It included three full-truckload tours from a warehouse approximately 30 kilometres north of Stockholm to three grocery stores in the city centre of Stockholm. Before off-peak hour distribution was introduced, deliveries to the three shops were done by three trucks during morning peak hours, in order to meet the delivery time requirements of the shops. Hence, for the daytime delivery scenario three trips taking place between 6.30 am and 7.30 am are assumed. Table 11.6 shows the distances and congestion levels in both off-peak and daytime distribution. In total, the three tours are approximately 204 kilometres long: 29 kilometres in urban, 128 kilometres in suburban and 47 kilometres in rural areas. Off-peak traffic levels are free flow. During daytime traffic is completely saturated in the urban core, partly saturated on the suburban motorway, and free flow in the rural areas close to the warehouse.

Figure 11.1b shows the distribution tours of the LTL trip. It is based on GPS data from the off-peak hour tour on 26 January 2016, which took place from approximately 2 am to 7 am. During this time, deliveries were made from a warehouse in a suburban area south-west of the city centre of Stockholm to seven destinations in central Stockholm. For the daytime scenario, it is assumed that this trip took place in the morning peak-hour period from 7 am to 12 pm. Table 11.7 shows the trip composition and traffic conditions in both off-peak hour and daytime distribution. In total, the tour is approximately 41 kilometres long: 24 kilometres in urban and 16 kilometres in suburban areas. At off-peak hours, traffic levels are free flow.

During daytime, in the urban core traffic is saturated on the local streets and main roads, while it is partly congested on urban motorways. In suburban areas, it is partly congested on local streets, partly saturated on main roads, while it is free flow on suburban motorways.

Results

Comparing the external costs of daytime and off-peak hour distribution

This section presents the results of the calculations of the external costs of daytime distribution trips (baseline scenario) and compares them with distribution trips at off-peak hours (off-hour scenario). In the baseline scenario, ie daytime deliveries with current congestion levels, the LTL delivery trip causes externalities of about 100 euros and the FTL delivery trip causes externalities of about 134 euros. More interesting than the absolute number of external costs is the relative contribution of the different impact types to the total external costs (Figure 11.2). Though the trips differ in type of delivery pattern (LTL vs FTL), transport distances (approximately 40 kilometres vs 280 kilometres), dominating road types (urban roads vs motorways), there are strong similarities in terms of the relative contribution of different impact types to total externalities of daytime delivery trips. In the daytime, the dominant external cost is related to congestion, which in both cases account for roughly 90 per cent of total externalities. The noise impacts are also in the same order of magnitude for both FTL and LTL (2 and 4 per cent). A difference can be observed for the relative contribution of climate change, which is significantly higher for FTL (9 per cent) than for LTL (3 per cent). This can be explained by the longer transport distances of the FTL case, which mainly take place on motorways in less sensitive rural areas, where congestion, air pollution and noise impacts are negligible. Accident risks and local air pollution are negligible compared with the other categories.

In the off-hour scenario, the total externalities of both transport chains are significantly reduced. The LTL trip's externalities account for 13 euros (–87 per cent in comparison to daytime deliveries) and the FTL trip's externalities are 29 euros (–78 per cent). When analysing the relative contribution of the different impact types to the total externalities, some differences can be observed (Figure 11.2). Noise is the biggest impact type in both cases; however, it is more dominant in the LTL case (72 per cent) than in the FTL

Figure 11.2 Distribution of external costs of daytime delivery trips and off-hour delivery trips

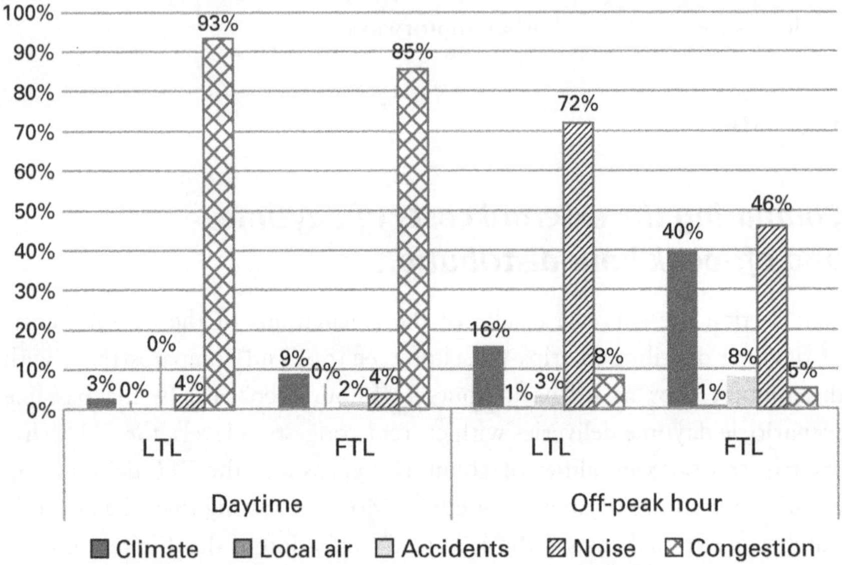

(46 per cent). The second significant impact type is climate, which accounts for 16 per cent in the LTL case; for the FTL case climate is in the same order of magnitude as the dominating noise costs (40 per cent). In the off-peak hours, congestion and accidents are minor impacts (between 3 and 8 per cent in both cases), while contribution to local air pollution remains insignificant (1 per cent).

Although off-peak hour deliveries significantly reduce the total externalities in both cases, there are some differences when analysing the relative changes of the different impact types (Figure 11.3). Naturally, when shifting delivery times to off-peak hours, congestion costs are almost completely eliminated. Driving in non-congested traffic also reduces fuel consumption and emissions; consequently, there are also significant reductions of air pollution and climate impacts. These benefits, however, are achieved at the cost of significantly higher noise impacts if no low-noise technology and standards are introduced. Finally, shifting to off-hours does not affect the impacts on safety.

These patterns are consistent between FTL and LTL despite major differences in composition of the distribution tours. There are, however, differences in the scale of the changes in some impact categories. While congestion benefits (–99 per cent in both cases), the noise burdens (+160 per cent for FTL and 158 per cent for LTL) as well as safety impacts (no change for both cases) are on the same level in both cases, the reductions of air pollution and climate impacts, on the other hand, differ significantly. Since in the FTL case a large share of the trip takes place on rural motorways, which are relatively insensitive to changes in delivery time, climate and air pollution impacts are only slightly reduced (–3 per cent in climate impact and –17 per cent in air pollution impact). In the LTL case, which is dominated by urban and suburban driving, the emission benefits of shifting delivery time are bigger and hence, the reduction of climate and air pollution impacts are much higher (–25 per cent and –63 per cent).

Sensitivity analysis

To test the robustness of the results to congestion levels a sensitivity analysis is conducted. Figure 11.4 shows the relative changes of off-peak deliveries in comparison with daytime deliveries at different congestion levels during daytime, ie with significantly higher levels compared to the BAU scenario ('daytime high congestion') and significantly lower congestion levels ('daytime low congestion'). Despite these significant different congestion levels, there is only a little effect on total externalities, ie there is only a slightly larger reduction in the high congestion scenario (–85 per cent instead of –79 per cent for FTL;

Figure 11.3 Relative changes of externalities between daytime and off-peak hour distribution by impact type

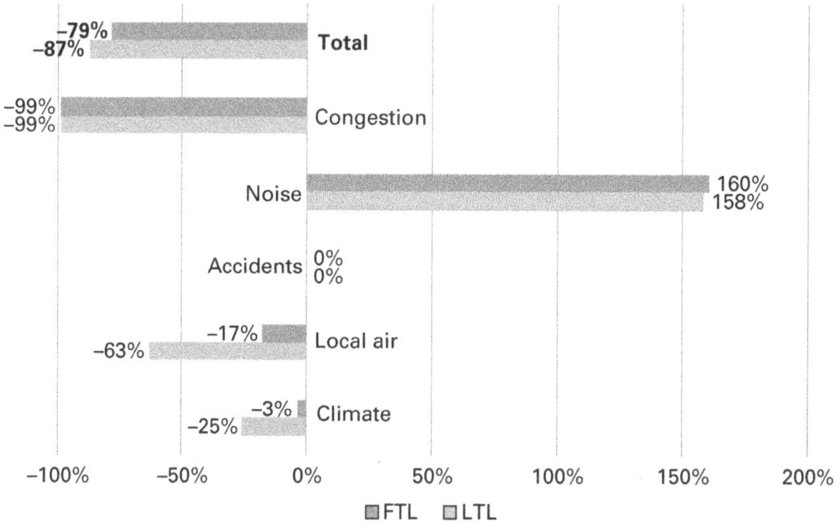

Figure 11.4 Relative changes by impact type at different congestion levels in a) FTL and b) LTL

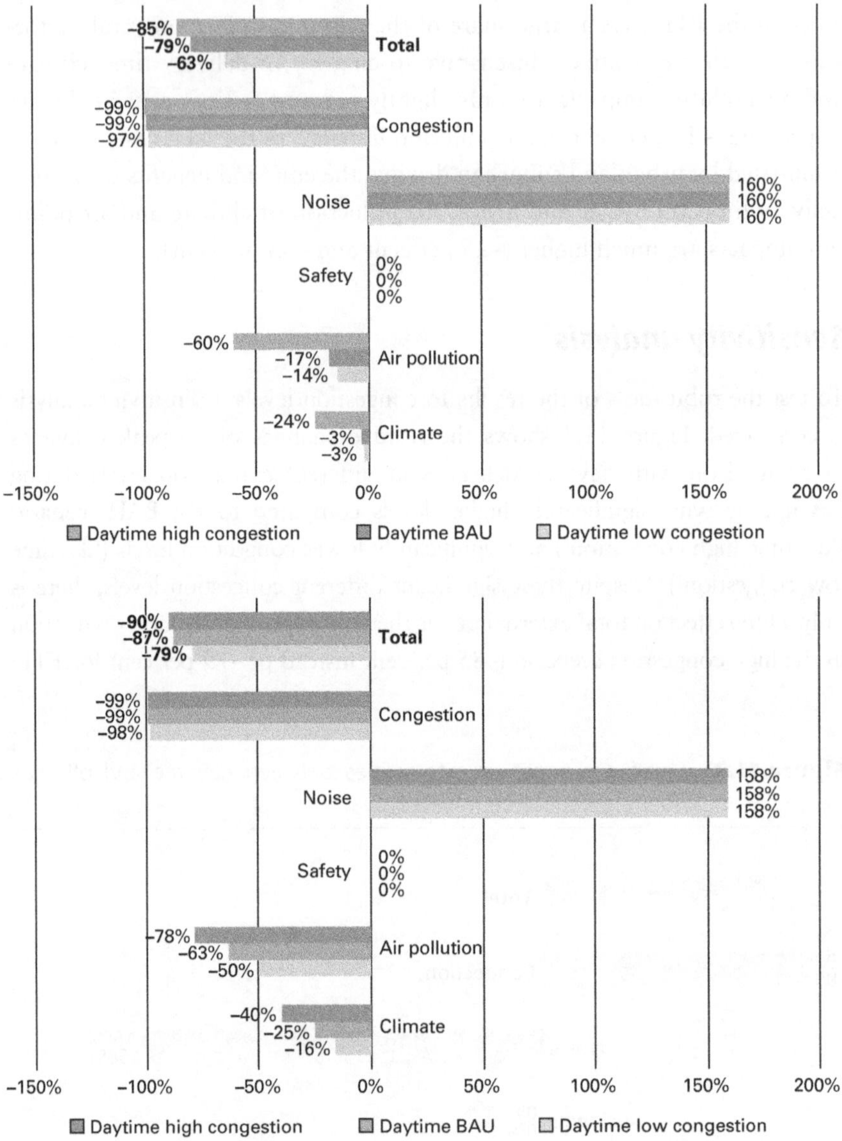

–90 per cent instead of –87 per cent for LTL), and only a relatively small reduction in the low congestion scenario (–63 per cent instead of –79 per cent for FTL; –79 per cent instead of –87 per cent for LTL). The relatively strong robustness of the total reduction potential to changing congestion levels is mainly due to the fact that there is practically no effect of congestion levels on congestion, noise and safety impacts. Air pollution and climate impacts, on the other hand, show a strong sensitivity to congestion levels. The relative improvement of air pollution impacts increases significantly with growing congestion levels (43 percentage points for FTL; and 15 percentage points for LTL) and decreases with smaller congestion levels (3 percentage points for FTL; and 13 percentage points for LTL). The same pattern can be observed for climate impacts on a somewhat smaller scale, ie they increase significantly in the high congestion scenario (21 percentage points for FTL; and 15 percentage points for LTL). In the low congestion scenario, they remain on the same low level for FTL and decrease by 9 percentage points for LTL.

Implications for policy and research

The case study shows some general patterns of socio-economic effects of OPHD. First, congestion is by far the biggest unsustainable impact of daytime distribution trips, as it accounts for a large majority of total externalities. Noise and climate change are minor impacts, while safety and air pollution impacts are almost insignificant. Second, shifting distribution to off-peak hours significantly reduces the socio-economic effects of urban distribution, as they no longer contribute to congestion. Third, there are also moderate climate and air pollution benefits as the better driving conditions reduce fuel consumption and emission levels. These benefits are, however, achieved at the cost of significantly higher noise impacts, which account for the large majority of externalities of off-peak hour distribution. Fourth, the effects of shifting distribution from daytime to off-peak hours on congestion benefits and noise burdens are robust to changing congestion levels, eg the effects are in the same order of magnitude for very low as well as for very high congestion levels. Air pollution and climate benefits, on the other hand, are more sensitive to changing congestion levels, as they decrease with lower congestion levels and increase with higher congestion levels. Fifth, off-peak hour distribution does not have any effect on safety impacts; they are the same in both daytime and off-hour distribution as well as for different congestion levels.

From a transport policy perspective, the results indicate that OPHD are not only a promising measure for megacities like New York City or other large metropolitan areas with urgent congestion problems. Even for smaller cities with moderate congestion levels OPHD provide considerable benefits. In addition, the results are also relevant for large metropolitan areas, where OPHD are mainly applied to reduce congestion and to make distribution more efficient. In these cities, OPHD also lead to substantial benefits in terms of reduced air pollution and climate impacts. Finally, in all cases of OPHD cities have to combine the schemes with measures reducing the noise of urban distribution.

From a theoretical perspective, this case study identifies some limitations of existing assessment models for the valuation of the socio-economic cost of urban distribution. First, the case results indicate that safety impacts do not depend on time of day or congestion levels, which, however is in conflict with several previous research outputs. For example, as Sánchez-Díaz *et al* (2016) note, OPHD can increase safety by reducing the conflicts between trucks, passenger cars, cyclists and pedestrians. On the other hand, a higher average speed can lead to a higher number of accidents as well as increased severity of accidents (Eliasson *et al*, 2009). Second, models for the evaluation of external costs do not provide any indicators for loading and unloading activities, which are much more significant for the noise impact of urban distribution compared to actual driving. Assessments are therefore likely to underestimate the impacts of noise. Furthermore, it is difficult to assess the benefits of low-noise equipment and operational noise reduction measures (Goevaers, 2011; Holguín-Veras *et al*, 2013a; Pernestål Brenden *et al*, 2017) that have been developed as a response to the noise challenge of OPHD. While the existing assessment approach provides many insights, a more detailed understanding of the full range of socio-economic effects will be possible as more sophisticated assessment methodologies are developed.

Conclusions

As the world continues to urbanize, traffic volumes in urban areas are rapidly increasing, resulting in traffic congestion threatening urban air quality and the mobility of citizens and goods. In order to cope with traffic congestion, many cities have initiated programmes to shift urban freight distribution from peak hours to off-peak hours. Obviously, the benefits are highest in large metropolitan areas coping with high levels of congestion, but OPHD provide significant congestion benefits even in smaller cities with moderate congestion levels. In addition, OPHD are also a promising measure to reduce the impacts of local air pollution as well as to reduce the emissions of greenhouse gases. These benefits, however, are achieved at the cost of significantly higher noise impacts, if no low-noise equipment and operational noise reduction measures are applied. Finally, there is need for a more sophisticated methodology for the evaluation of safety and noise impacts of urban distribution measures.

Acknowledgements

This work was supported by the FFI – Strategic Vehicle Research and Innovation [2014–05598]; the Volvo Research and Educational Foundations [EP-2014–09]; the Integrated Transport Research Lab (ITRL) at KTH Royal Institute of Technology in Stockholm and the Urban Freight Platform at Chalmers University of Technology and University of Gothenburg.

References

Allen, J, Browne, M, Cherrett, T *et al* (2008) Review of UK urban freight studies, *Green Logistics project, Universities of Westminster and Southampton*, Universities of Westminster and Southampton, London, 88

Behrends, S (2016) Factors influencing the performance of urban consolidation schemes, in *Commercial Transport*, ed U Clausen, H Friedrich, C Thaller *et al*, pp 351–67, Springer International Publishing

Beijing Traffic Management Bureau (2014) Delivery Time Restrictions [Online] http://zhengwu.beijing.gov.cn/gzdt/gggs/t1348811.htm

Campbell, JF (1995) Peak period large truck restrictions and a shift to off-peak operations: impact on truck emission and performance, *Journal of Business Logistics*, **16**, pp 227–47

Changsha Bureau of Public Security (2013) Announcement about Freight Vehicles Ban in Certain Areas and Routes [Online] http://www.changsha.gov.cn/xxgk/gfxwj/sqzz/sgajjzd/201303/t20130313_437903.html

Churchill, JDC (1970) Operation 'MoonDrop': an experiment in out of hours goods delivery, *Proceedings of the 3rd Technology Assessment Review*, Organization for Economic Cooperation and Development, Paris, pp 135–40

City of Stockholm (2014) The Stockholm Freight Plan 2014–2017

Devin, E, El Moussati, H, Moizan, V *et al* (2014) Livre blanc: les livraisons de nuit en logistique urbaine, in SAS CF (ed), Paris, 78

Eliasson, J, Hultkrantz, L, Nerhagen, L *et al* (2009) The Stockholm congestion – charging trial 2006: overview of effects, *Transportation Research Part A: Policy and Practice,* **43**, pp 240–50

Fu, J and Jenelius, E (2018) Transport efficiency of off-peak urban goods deliveries: A Stockholm pilot study, *Case Studies on Transport Policy*, **6** (1), pp 156–66

Gang, C (2009) *Politics of China's Environmental Protection: Problems and progress*, World Scientific

Goevaers, R (2011) PIEK low noise equipment, off peak hours transport, Presentation at the Transportation Research Board Annual Meeting, January, Washington DC

Holguín-Veras, J, Özbay, K and Cerreño, A (2005) Evaluation Study of Port Authority of New York and New Jersey's Time of Day Pricing Initiative: Final Report, New Jersey Department of Transportation, Trenton NJ, **xiv**, p 476

Holguín-Veras, J, Wang, Q, Xu, N *et al* (2006) Impacts of time of day pricing on the behavior of freight carriers in a congested urban area: implications to road pricing, *Transportation Research Part A: Policy and Practice,* **40**, pp 744–66

Holguín-Veras, J, Ozbay, K, Kornhauser, AL *et al* (2011) Overall impacts of off-hour delivery programs in the New York City metropolitan area, *Transportation Research Record,* **2238**, pp 68–76

Holguín-Veras, J, Marquis, R, Campbell, S *et al* (2013a) Fostering the use of unassisted off-hour deliveries: operational and low-noise truck technologies, *Transportation Research Record: Journal of the Transportation Research Board*, pp 57–63

Holguín-Veras, J, Wojtowicz, JM, Wang, C *et al* (2013b) *Integrative Freight Demand Management in the New York City Metropolitan Area: Implementation phase*, p 459, Rensselaer Polytechnic Institute, New York City Department of Transportation, Rutgers University

Holguín-Veras, J and Aros-Vera, F (2014) Self-supported freight demand management: pricing and incentives, *EURO Journal on Transportation and Logistics,* **3**, pp 1–24

Holguín-Veras, J, Encarnación, T, González-Calderón, CA *et al* (2016) Direct impacts of off-hour deliveries on urban freight emissions, *Transportation Research Part D: Transport and Environment,* **61**, pp 84–103

Holguín-Veras, J, Wang, X, Sánchez-Díaz, I *et al* (2017) Fostering unassisted off-hour deliveries: the role of incentives, *Transportation Research Part A: Policy and Practice,* **102**, pp 172–87

INFRAS (2014), Handbook Emission Factors for Road Transport. July 2014 ed.: INFRAS.

NICHES (2008) Innovative Approaches in City Logistics: Inner-city night delivery [Online] http://www.niches-transport.org/fileadmin/archive/Deliverables/D4.3b_5.8_b_PolicyNotes/14683_pn7_night_delivery_ok_low.pdf

Noel, EC (1983) Night delivery: institutional restraints, *Journal of Urban Planning and Development,* **109**, pp 44–49

Noel, EC, Crimmins, SH, Myers, NK *et al* (1980) A survey of off-hours delivery, *ITE Journal*, pp 18–23

NTM (2007) Calculation methods and default data – mode-specific issues – road transport Europe, Network for Transport and the Environment, Gothenburg

Olympic Delivery Authority (2010) On Time: London 2012 – Olympic Route Network and Paralympic Route Network, *London: Olympic Delivery Authority* [Online] http://www.london2012.com/publications/olympic-route-network-and-paralympic-routenetwork.php

Pernestål Brenden, A, Koutoulas, A, Fu, J *et al* (2017) Off-peak City Logistics – A Case Study in Stockholm, Stockholm

RICARDO AEA (2014) Update of the Handbook on External Costs of Transport, Final Report for the European Commission – DG Mobility and Transport, London

Sánchez-Díaz, I, Georén, P and Brolinson, M (2016) Shifting urban freight deliveries to the off-peak hours: a review of theory and practice, *Transport Reviews*, pp 1–23

Schoemaker, J, Allen, J, Huschebek, M *et al* (2006) Quantification of urban freight transport effects I, *BESTUFS Consortium,* NEA, University of Westminster, PTV, Transman, **76**

Shenzhen Bureau of Public Security (2013) Announcement about Truck Routes and Banned Areas [Online] http://www.szga.gov.cn/NEWWEB/ZWGK/QT/GSGG/201307/t20130718_54558.htm

The City of Paris (2013) Charte en faveur d'une logistique urbaine durable, *Mairie de Paris*, Paris, **54**

Transport for London (2015) Retiming and Out-of-Hours Deliveries [Online] https://www.tfl.gov.uk/info-for/freight/moving-freight-efficiently/retiming-and-out-of-hours-deliveries

Vilain, P and Wolfrom, P (2000) Value pricing and freight traffic: issues and industry constraints in shifting from peak to off-peak movements, *Transportation Research Record,* **1707**, pp 64–72

PART THREE
Making change happen

Stakeholder engagement and partnerships for improved urban logistics 12

MICHAEL BROWNE, ALENA BRETTMO AND MARIA LINDHOLM

Introduction

Until recently urban transport authorities often overlooked freight, concentrating their attention on the movement of people. Even when motivated to tackle urban freight, many city authorities find it difficult to address the complex set of differing views of a large variety of stakeholders. Historically, the role of city authorities, or local authorities within cities, has been confined largely to one of regulation. Correspondingly, until recently there has been limited engagement of private companies in the local authority transport-planning process (Lindholm and Browne, 2015).

Engaging stakeholders is very important as without their involvement it is difficult to motivate changes in the urban freight and logistics system. Successful implementation of effective urban logistics initiatives demands a solid understanding of both freight activity and the supply chains serving the urban area. This makes it essential to find ways to engage with businesses carrying out their activities in the city. It has become clear that to effect change it is necessary to engage the private sector and at the same time to work with public sector decision-makers in order to demonstrate the importance of supply chains to local economies and quality of life.

Holguín-Veras *et al* (2015) have noted these factors and point out the need for disseminating best practices and defining implementation paths that consider the concerns of all stakeholders involved.

This sounds rather straightforward but in practice there are many conflicts among public and private interest groups and these often result in obstacles to success. To foster change that will be accepted by the private sector, public policy must account for businesses' needs and goals, and the constraints under which they operate. The need to find effective ways to engage with stakeholders has received increasing attention (Lindholm and Browne, 2013; European Commission, 2018). Complex policy environments call for high efforts to engage stakeholders and it is evident that urban logistics is often complex because the impacts of changes to policy and planning can have a diverse range of impacts on stakeholders. Structuring a participatory process that accounts for stakeholder opinions and helps in finding suitable solutions can be advantageous in such cases (Le Pira *et al*, 2017).

Urban logistics is at the heart of some major challenges in technological and social trends and the impact on cities. Technological and social trends are affecting how we manage and plan in cities. For example, there is a growing interest in autonomous vehicles. This is also linked to innovation in the use of urban space, which has become a priority for policymakers and city planners. Increasing attention is being paid to the need for more dense patterns of residential and commercial building in order to improve accessibility. These developments have implications for urban freight. If city living patterns become denser and more people decide not to own a car then there is likely to be an increase in last mile delivery trips. This in turn means that goods movement and personal mobility are becoming more and more closely linked. In response to these rapid changes it is more important than ever to widen participation in the discussion about urban logistics. It is essential to find new ways to engage with business and with other areas where there is limited connection – for example architecture, urban design and urban planning.

The aim of this chapter is to discuss a range of stakeholder engagement approaches with the main focus being on freight partnerships or freight networks. The next section will briefly discuss what is meant by stakeholder engagement and the range of stakeholders that need to be considered in urban logistics. This is followed by the insights from several partnerships that responded to a survey to explore the features of their operations that work and the initiatives that are less successful. After this there is a discussion of other types of engagement and particularly ways to improve urban logistics by developing stronger links with existing business and town-centre communities. The chapter concludes with some reflections on the way ahead.

Stakeholder engagement

Freight transport in cities has always been subject to regulation. In many cases this is aimed at the vehicles and the activities they perform. Regulations may be designed to limit vehicles in certain parts of the city according to size or perhaps according to the time of day. Other factors such as the desire of city authorities to reduce emissions mean that regulators also consider the type of fuel used for urban logistics movements. Such restrictions, when imposed without an understanding of the upstream supply chains, risk leading to sub-optimization and to creating a climate of disagreement and confrontations between the public and private sectors. For example, bans on larger vehicles may simply lead to transport operators using an increased number of small vehicles, while time of day bans may also lead to an increase in vehicle activity and miles travelled as companies seek to meet the needs of all their customers who may have placed high demands in the time of day of the delivery.

For many years the role of the public sector (city authorities or the local authorities within cities, eg boroughs, districts and arrondissements) has been confined largely to regulation. Much of this regulation has focused on time of day of operation and limits on vehicle sizes. Therefore, in general, private companies perform freight transport operations in urban areas and the public sector regulates those operations and is responsible for the local infrastructure network. Until recently there has been limited engagement designed to involve private companies in the city authority transport planning process (Lindholm and Browne, 2013).

Creating greater engagement and forming freight partnerships can contribute to more successful freight policymaking. Successful implementation of initiatives to improve urban logistics requires:

- understanding freight activity and commerce;
- engaging the private sector;
- educating decision-makers on urban logistics;
- disseminating best practices.

Range and complexity of urban logistics stakeholders

It is important to distinguish between the three different groups who are capable of implementing changes to the urban freight system, namely:

- **Public policymakers** (especially urban authorities) who make changes to urban freight transport operations through the introduction of policy measures that force or encourage companies to alter their behaviour.
- **Freight transport companies** that implement initiatives that reduce the impact of their freight operations because they derive some internal benefit from this change in behaviour. These benefits can be internal economic advantages from operating in a more environmentally or socially efficient manner, either through improved economic efficiency or through being able to enhance market share as a result of their environmental stance. Instances of company-led initiatives include increasing the vehicle load factor through the consolidation of urban freight, making deliveries before or after normal freight delivery hours, the implementation of IT for communications or planning purposes, improvements in the fuel efficiency of vehicles, and improvements in collection and delivery systems. Some of these initiatives are technology related, some are concerned with freight transport companies reorganizing their operations, and some involve change in the supply chain organization.
- **Receivers** of the supplies delivered have a great deal of power in influencing urban supply chains, though only recently their role has been identified and exploited to foster urban freight sustainability. Inducing receivers to accept deliveries at night is at the core of the off-hour delivery project conducted in New York City (Holguín-Veras *et al*, 2011). Moreover, receivers could be encouraged to consolidate deliveries, as done as part of the Delivery Servicing Plans initiative made by Transport for London (Brettmo and Browne, 2016). These demand modification examples – part of what may be called freight demand management – could lead to dramatic improvements in sustainability. More research is needed to identify the best ways to modify demand.

There are several definitions and classifications of urban freight stakeholders. PIARC (2012) identified four major stakeholders: shippers, freight carriers, residents and administrators, and pointed out that they would often have different goals and implement various initiatives. Thus 'shippers' were said to 'hope to receive and send their goods in a reliable manner which does not violate the designated time window for delivery to lower delivery costs.' For freight carriers the main focus was on the goal of meeting shippers' needs using their 'resources, public infrastructure and information to maximize their profits'. The focus for residents in urban areas was argued to be around minimizing nuisance caused by urban freight transport and to the wish to create a safer and more comfortable community. Finally, administrators play a balancing role in trying to enhance the quality of human life as well as decrease congestion levels within the urban road network and at the same time 'decrease the negative environmental impacts and increase the security of urban freight transport'.

In reality, there are more than four groups of stakeholders. A report from the Regional Plan Association (RPA) in 2016 noted that the success of urban freight strategies requires the involvement of a range of key actors and stakeholders, identifying the following stakeholder groups:

- government;
- communities and residents;
- shippers and truckers;
- distribution and warehouse facilities;
- property owners and managers;
- commercial establishments.

RPA pointed out that exactly who must be involved in what role may vary based on the strategy or political geography.

Interactions between the public sector and private sector urban freight stakeholders (transport operators, retailers and so on) are often focused mainly on complaints (eg noise complaints by residents, problems over kerb space available for unloading and loading etc). However, the establishment of a freight partnership can lead to a better understanding of freight problems and also a change in the nature and usefulness of these interactions between the public and private sectors. Sharing knowledge and the transferability of knowledge between partners can be highlighted as among the most important effects of a greater level of engagement.

Freight partnerships

One possibility to involve stakeholders in urban freight transport planning is to initiate a freight partnership. Freight partnerships have been shown to be an important part of addressing urban logistics and freight transport problems. A freight partnership is a long-term partnership between freight stakeholders concerned with urban freight, that on a formal or informal basis meet regularly to seek solutions to problems and discuss concerns that occur in the urban area (Lindholm and Browne, 2013).

Establishing a freight partnership

To establish a freight partnership, it is important to consider configuration, management and outcomes (Lindholm and Browne, 2015):

- **Configuration:** identifying relevant stakeholders is important. Different cities have different prerequisites, but it is almost always a good idea to involve many different stakeholders, such as transport operators, retailers, trade associations, property owners, authorities etc. Each city should first consider their specific situation and area of focus, and then identify relevant actors that have a specific interest in that area. This helps to ensure that the objectives of the partnership are relevant to the stakeholders.
- **Management:** when a partnership is established, evidence has shown that effective project management is needed in order to sustain the partnership. An action plan or similar document should be created, in order to structure discussions and maintain a long-term perspective. The participants need to be kept to a manageable number (10 to 25) to keep discussions among stakeholders lively. It is equally important that stakeholder representatives have a mandate to impose change within their respective organizations.
- **Outcomes:** outcomes of partnerships are valuable to all stakeholders involved, and it is likely that concrete achievements will be essential to maintaining the momentum of freight partnerships in the longer term. Measures should be considered as business propositions, and it is necessary to accept that urban freight transport issues are complex, ie to avoid seeking single solutions.

Specific action points can be summarized (Table 12.1).

Insights from a survey

A survey of 16 freight partnerships from 11 countries provides some insights into how such an initiative can be successful (Lindholm and Browne, 2014). The survey compared the partnerships, looking at what was similar and what was different and also trying to reach an understanding of the types of initiatives that worked well and those that were less successful. The focus of questions in the survey is illustrated in Figure 12.1.

Table 12.1 Suggested action points for setting up a freight partnership

Action points in setting up a freight partnership
1. Set initial objectives that are specific, measurable, achievable, realistic and timed. 2. Identify and recruit partners that help achieve your objectives. 3. Establish the partnership's management structure. 4. Decide when, where and how often you should meet. 5. Identify funding sources and seek the necessary endorsement. 6. Try to pre-empt potential problems.
Action points in developing a freight partnership plan
1. Identify problems and collect relevant information to clarify their precise nature. 2. Assess the various solutions and reach consensus on what should be done. 3. Draw up a timed action plan for delivering the solutions, identifying who is responsible for each task by when.
Action points for maintaining momentum in a freight partnership
1. Consider how you can maintain interest and keep the momentum going. 2. Use publicity to promote the partnership and its activities. 3. Monitor progress of the process, outputs and outcomes.

SOURCE adapted and summarized from Department for Transport, 2003

Figure 12.1 Survey approach

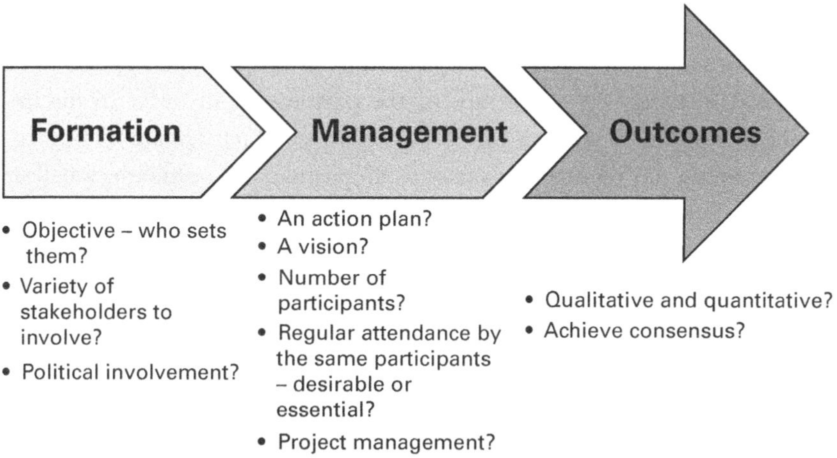

SOURCE based on Lindholm and Browne, 2014

Participating partnerships (see Table 12.2) were from cities of varying sizes. In addition, the structure and organization of the partnerships varied with some having been initiated by city authorities with a broad remit while others were more narrowly focused having been created to address specific problems.

Table 12.2 List of freight partnerships/networks providing information

Tyne and Wear Freight Partnership (UK)
Greater Lyon (France/GLA)
Belo Horizonte (Brazil/BHTRANS)
New York (USA/NYCDOT)
Metrolinx (Canada/Toronto)
Rome (Italy)
Oslo (Norway)
Paris Charter (France)
East Osaka (Japan)
Toulouse Delivery Charter (France)
West Australia regional partnership (Australia)
Gothenburg local freight network (Sweden)
Central London Freight Quality Partnership (UK)
Utrecht (The Netherlands)
Montpellier (France)
Nantes (France)
G93 La Seine-Saint-Denis: regional partnership (France)
City of Leiden (The Netherlands)
Lidköping (Sweden)

SOURCE Freight Quality Partnerships around the world (Lindholm and Browne, 2014)

Meetings and attendants

The number of meeting per year varies, but it seems to be common to have between two and four meetings per year. Some of the partnerships also have additional meetings for subgroups of the partnership in order to discuss specific issues. This is also relevant for the number of participants. The largest partnership has reported as many as 80 participants, while the smallest have only 5 to 10 participants with many reporting numbers of 15 to 25. For the larger partnerships it is evident that some meetings will be in a plenary format but for discussions about specific topics subgroups may be formed.

Funding and governmental status

In general funding for the partnerships is limited. Most partnerships do not receive any funding, while in other cases some partnerships have received funding through a project. In a few cases funding has been obtained by tackling small-scale projects that have received joint public and private funding.

The governmental status of the partnerships is mainly non-formal, without any formal agreements or responsibilities. However, there are some partnerships where the members have signed a charter or terms of reference of the partnership. Three of the partnerships have formal status.

Outcomes and achievements

Outcomes and achievements of the partnerships are of course valuable to all stakeholders involved. The outcomes and achievements are grouped into four main areas: collaboration/cooperation; information; regulations etc; and projects. Collaboration between stakeholders is an important output and also one of the reported strengths of the partnerships (see below). The partnership approach offers a neutral platform for engagement of freight stakeholders in projects, but also creates positive discussion of freight in the city. The platform provides a possibility for the stakeholders and the authority to share views on freight in the urban area during meetings, but as the partnership participants get to know each other, it also creates an indirect possibility to meet and discuss issues between partnership meetings.

Outputs that focus on information are important and this is seen from almost all partnerships. The outputs are typically guidance for freight operators in the form of maps and routing information, dissemination of information through pamphlets, parking guides etc. Input to issues of regulation represents a further output arising from partnerships. The main regulations mentioned are connected to loading and unloading zones in the urban area, but also to providing a simpler regulation for distribution activities, to address problems with parking fines and to deploy different certification schemes. There are also many projects reported as outcomes of the various partnerships. These include: case studies of specific topics in order to study implications of tackling freight issues in different ways, research studies, initiatives on urban consolidation centres and electric vehicles.

Strengths

The respondents identified several strengths relating to the freight partnership reported. Overall there is lot of emphasis on cooperation and information sharing. An important note is that information is not just shared as a one-way communication from the stakeholders to give input to the authorities, but also for the authorities to share information among themselves (ie for different local administrative areas to share details of good practices or changes they are implementing). All partnerships highlight that the network and the cooperation between the participating stakeholders that the partnership encourages are important strengths. On the one hand, the local public authorities receive input to policymaking, through dialogue and information from freight stakeholders regarding problems as well as possibilities. On the other hand, the freight stakeholders receive information from the authorities and have the possibility to ask questions regarding ongoing and upcoming plans and in that way are better informed and prepared (eg forthcoming changes in legislation). The final group of strengths that is reported in the survey are the physical outcomes of the partnership (the maps, signs, guides and so on referred to above). The outputs in general bring real benefits to all stakeholders involved in the discussion.

Weaknesses

There are several weaknesses reported by partnerships in the survey. Weaknesses could be grouped into five main areas: outputs (eg a slow implementation of initiatives, politicians are not included in the process, suboptimal solutions); meeting structure (eg many stakeholders come to meetings without sharing information, no active discussions including all partners); the partnership group/members (eg lack of participation of stakeholders from certain industry sectors, it is hard to reach consensus within the group, the group is either too large or too small); authority activities (eg there is a general lack of understanding of freight activities among authorities); and resources (eg there is a lack of funding to hold meetings, lack of resources in time to attend meetings).

Respondents noted that participation can sometimes be unbalanced with some participants being much more active than others. A specific concern raised by respondents was that when some participants are not fully involved and engaged in a decision or plan then there can be difficulties later. It seems that the need to find ways to engage the full membership of a partnership remains a challenge. Table 12.3 summarizes some of the features that work well and others that do not work as well.

Freight partnership outputs

Many of the partnerships responding to the survey showed a clear focus on operational issues such as loading and unloading arrangements. One reason given was the desire to reduce fines being paid by the private sector for breaking regulations on unloading time allowed. Other motives for this focus included the goal of improving the accessibility to the shops and restaurants in the urban area that are dependent on deliveries made in larger vehicles.

Table 12.3 What works well for freight partnerships and what could be better

The partnership is working well because of:	Drawbacks/things that could be better:
A genuine interest from participants to improve the situation	Same people every time tend to give less variation to the discussions
Continuity and engagement among participants	Members who do not attend on a regular basis
Focusing on long-term possibilities	Members from police and citizen groups are sometimes missing
Good organization/management (a driving spirit is almost always essential)	Politicians and senior management from industry are needed
An interesting and common agenda for the participants	Tends to become a talking shop
	Lack of dissemination

SOURCE based on Freight Quality Partnerships around the world (Lindholm and Browne, 2014)

Table 12.4 A range of outputs from partnership meetings

Physical Outputs	Soft Outputs
• New pilot projects in urban freight • Multilingual delivery and information points for truck drivers • Interactive roadmaps for drivers • Plan of priority sectors for redesign of loading bays/spaces • Regulation for deliveries	• Project collaboration in urban freight research • Analyse impact of CNG vehicle in urban distribution • Technical studies to implement urban consolidation centre • Input on marketing strategies • Exchange of information and guidance of urban goods movement projects • A better dialogue for freight and logistics • Informal networking between meetings

SOURCE based on response to a survey (Lindholm and Browne, 2014)

It is important to note that the focus of the outputs in the survey is more or less equally distributed between physical outputs and soft outputs (see Table 12.4).

A review of the responses provided evidence that almost all the partnerships are achieving valuable results often with relatively limited budgets.

The results from the partnerships highlight the importance of a much better engagement between the public and private sectors. Partnerships are not the only way to achieve this interaction but the survey from various countries does show that freight partnerships are a key approach to working together to improve urban freight and logistics practices.

Stakeholder engagement through business improvement districts

Existing urban business networks also offer opportunities for increasing stakeholder engagement to work on urban logistics matters. For example, many cities have a chamber of commerce that links together businesses located in the city. Town-centre management initiatives can also be found in many smaller urban areas and indeed in the central areas of larger cities. Specific initiatives in shopping malls and shopping centres can also be observed (CITYLAB, 2018), For many of these networks freight and logistics questions have traditionally not featured in their activities or have been at best very low in the interests of their members. However, there are signs of change and one of the partnership approaches that may be well suited to increased stakeholder engagement is Business Improvement Districts (BIDs).

A BID is a business-led body formed to improve a defined commercial area, in which the local businesses have voted to invest collectively to improve their environment. The improvements made by a BID are selected by their business members and can include activities such as street cleaning and security services, recycling, business support, improved infrastructure, area branding and promotion. During the past 10 years, a number of researchers have noted the growing importance of public–private partnerships in relation to urban freight transport (Allen *et al*, 2010; Lindholm and Browne, 2013). In most cases the partnerships being discussed have been established specifically to deal with freight transport matters. However, in the United Kingdom the emergence of a growing number of BIDs provides another organizational structure within which freight issues can be addressed. The BIDs in central London are typically not-for-profit companies, funded by businesses that work closely with local public sector partners (including local councils, Transport for London (TfL), and the Metropolitan Police) to achieve the desired improvements for the area. Several of the BIDs in Central London have now started to work on projects concerned with urban freight transport. Similar initiatives have been identified elsewhere (Browne *et al*, 2016; Brettmo *et al*, 2017).

Forging links with BID-type organizations could be very valuable in encouraging the uptake of sustainable urban logistics initiatives. BIDs have a formal decision-making function and are also composed of public and private sector organizations. This means they are able to act collectively to adopt improvements within a given geographical area. Although only a few BIDs have started to adopt specific urban logistics actions many of them offer a joint procurement service to members (often concerned with waste management and recycling). This approach can be adapted and extended to address purchasing of products that are common across many BID members – for example, office supplies. This in turn can be used to promote a more consolidated delivery pattern.

The range and variety of BID members is also potentially important in widening the net of stakeholder engagement. Previous urban freight research has illustrated the importance of addressing receivers as well as gaining the involvement of carriers (transport operators). Focusing on receivers has been essential in persuading firms to adopt strategies such as retiming deliveries to move the delivery operations out of the peak traffic periods. Combining business interest with sustainable urban logistics initiatives could be a powerful way to approach urban logistics challenges.

Other engagement initiatives that can be considered

Freight capacity building at key agencies

Given the much greater focus among city transport planning authorities on personal mobility it is not surprising that there are relatively few freight planners in many city administrations. Overcoming this lack of resource and expertise takes time but there can be significant benefits from designating a freight person at key agencies (Holguín-Veras *et al*, 2015). Examples of this strategy can be found in many cities including London, Paris, Lyon, Gothenburg and New York. A person (or better still a team) will rapidly become a focal point for communication about urban logistics between the public and private sectors. The increased outreach efforts can also contribute to other goals such as providing relevant information and background details to elected officials.

Elected officials will often be involved in longer-term strategies that influence urban freight and logistics and also in short-term measures such as restrictions and possibly regulations. Having access to freight and logistics expertise can help to create an overall understanding of the economic importance of supply chains in metropolitan areas. Currently, there is a strong focus on making cities more sustainable and liveable and it is important that elected officials receive the necessary information about the way that freight and logistics management contributes to this (Holguín-Veras *et al*, 2018).

Living labs

Private sector organizations can also play a vital role in sharing good practices. Private sector companies need to consider efficiency in their urban logistics operations but at the same time they should also ensure they reduce negative external impacts. This can be difficult when companies cannot access good practice initiatives. One way to support this has been through what is called the 'living lab' approach (CITYLAB, 2018). As the CITYLAB project noted:

> A living lab may be set up to develop a specific product or service and run over a relatively short time period or may be more far reaching and run over a longer period to take advantage of latest technologies and to adapt to changing environments.

The term 'living lab' refers to a local experimental project of a participatory nature. The aim of such an approach is to actively involve all relevant stakeholder and user groups to encourage participation, hear all views, promote innovation, set project goals and agree actions. The focus is on practical implementation, learning, feedback and improvement. A living lab is usually organized around four key principles (CITYLAB, 2018):

1. Practical, 'real life' setting, with on the ground implementation.
2. Multiple stakeholders.
3. Co-creation of innovative solutions and end-user involvement.
4. Iterative learning and development (based on a structured feedback concept).

Goals can be varied given the composition of the stakeholders but will often include environmental concerns (eg improving air quality) as well as a focus on operating more efficiently. There will usually be multiple stakeholders including many of those mentioned earlier in the chapter: public authorities, logistics service providers, research institutes and the public.

Conclusions

Participation in networks and partnerships among stakeholders can be seen as a very important development for urban logistics. Although many of these initiatives start in a modest way there is clear evidence of the growing success of the engagement approach. It is also apparent that there are many ways in which engagement can be taken forwards. Indeed, starting a freight partnership does not in any way preclude also developing interactions with organizations such as Business Improvement Districts.

There is much to be gained through improved dialogue and understanding and increasing the knowledge of what can be done in the context of urban logistics. Structure is important and there needs to be a balance between the public and private sector since it is not possible for one side alone to create major change. In the same way, it is essential that there is top down interest and leadership concerning urban logistics (from both public and private sector organizations). However, this must be supported by increasing the number of people who have skills and knowledge in urban logistics and are able to implement the strategic ideas on the ground.

It is very important that urban logistics is considered in a strategic way and is linked to longer-term initiatives in cities such as the focus on strategic land use planning and infrastructure developments. Freight partnerships are not intended to replace existing networks; rather they can be seen as an essential complement to the structures that are currently in place. While much of the progress has been very encouraging it is important to continue the efforts. There has in the past been a heavy reliance on engagement with transport operators and carriers. It is essential to widen this network to include the customers of the transport operators as well as those responsible for questions of urban design. In many instances urban logistics and freight are still not embedded into the planning strategy within cities and it is essential that urban logistics strategies become features of many more urban and metropolitan areas.

Cities are complex environments where many structures are not used in the way they were originally intended. Therefore, systems including urban logistics have to adapt to these demands. It can be argued that many initiatives are context specific and that the way they are applied will vary considerably between one city and another (as will the impacts). However, improving stakeholder engagement and building partnerships can be seen to be very widely relevant and applicable to the take-up of new ideas that are important for urban logistics.

References

Allen, J, Browne, M, Piotrowska, M and Woodburn, A (2010) Freight quality partnerships in the UK – an analysis of their work and achievements, in *Green Logistics project,* ed Transport Studies Group, University of Westminster, London

Brettmo, A and Browne, M (2016) An exploratory study of the scope for receivers to influence urban freight consolidation through changes in their procurement practices, Paper presented at the Logistics Research Network Conference (LRN) 2016, University of Hull, UK

Brettmo, A, Browne, M, Holguín-Veras, J, Wojtowicz, J and Allen, J (2017) The role of intermediary organisations in influencing urban deliveries to receivers/establishments, Paper presented at the International City Logistics Conference 2017, Thailand

Browne, M, Allen, J and Alexander, P (2016) Business improvement districts in urban freight sustainability initiatives: a case study approach, *Procedia*, **12**, pp 450–60

CITYLAB (2018) [accessed 10 July 2018] City Logistics Living Labs: A way forward with city logistics innovation [Online] http://www.citylab-project.eu/brochure/LL.pdf

Department for Transport (2003) A guide on how to set up and run Freight Quality Partnerships, *Good Practice Guide 335,* DfT

European Commission (2018) Engagement of stakeholders when implementing urban freight logistics policies, Non-binding guidance documents on urban logistics No 3/6

Holguín-Veras, J, Ozbay, K, Kornhauser, A, Brom, M, Iyer, S, Yushimito, W, Ukkusuri, S, Allen, B and Silas, M (2011) Overall impacts of off-hour delivery programs in New York City metropolitan area, *Transportation Research Record*, **2238**, pp 68–76

Holguín-Veras, J, Amaya-Leal, J, Wojtowicz, J, Jaller, M, González-Calderón, C, Sánchez-Díaz, I, Wang, X, Haake, D, Rhodes, S, Hodge, SD, Frazier, RJ, Nick, MK, Dack, J, Casinelli, L and Browne, M (2015) NCFRP Report 33: Improving Freight System Performance in Metropolitan Areas, National Cooperative Freight Research Program, Washington DC, Transportation Research Board: 1–212

Holguín-Veras, J, Amaya Leal, J, Sánchez-Díaz, I, Browne, M and Wojtowicz, J (2018) State of the Art and Practice of Urban Freight Management Part II: Financial Approaches, Logistics, and Demand Management, Under review Transportation Research A

Le Pira, M, Marcucci, E, Gatta, V, Ignaccolo, M, Inturri, G and Pluchiono, A (2017) Towards a decision-support procedure to foster stakeholder involvement and acceptability of urban freight transport policies, *European Transport Research Review*, **9**, pp 54–68

Lindholm, M and Browne, M (2013) Local authority cooperation with urban freight stakeholders: a comparison of partnership approaches, *European Journal of Transport and Infrastructure Research*, **13** (1), pp 20–38
Lindholm, M and Browne, M (2014) Freight Quality Partnerships around the world, Report on a survey published with the support of the Volvo Research and Education Foundations (VREF)
Lindholm, M and Browne, M (2015) Organizing and managing urban freight partnerships, Volvo Research and Education Foundations Research Brief, No 4
PIARC (2012) Public Sector Governance of Urban Freight Transport
Regional Plan Association (2016) Why Goods Movement Matters: Strategies for Moving Goods in Metropolitan Areas

Multi-actor multi-criteria analysis as a tool to involve urban logistics stakeholders

13

CATHY MACHARIS, BRAM KIN AND PHILIPPE LEBEAU

Introduction

European cities are facing a major challenge if they want to fulfil the objective of CO_2-free city logistics in major urban centres by 2030 (European Commission, 2011). Freight vehicles are recognized to be disproportionally polluting (MDS Transmodal, 2012): they are responsible for approximately 25 per cent of transport-related CO_2 emissions, 30 per cent of NO_x emissions and 50 per cent of particulate matter while they represent about 15 per cent of the vehicle kilometres driven in cities (Dablanc, 2011; Schoemaker *et al*, 2006). To address that challenge, a number of best practices have already been implemented across Europe (Bestfact, 2013). At the same time, authorities aim to mitigate the negative impact of urban freight transport (UFT) by implementing measures like low emissions zones, and vehicle weight and size restrictions (Anderson *et al*, 2005; Muñuzuri *et al*, 2005).

In any case, one of the main lessons learned is the importance of stakeholder involvement prior to implementation as a lot of projects and measures do not reach their intended effect and sometimes even have an adverse impact (Ballantyne *et al*, 2013; Bjerkan *et al*, 2014; Lindholm, 2013; Quak, 2008; Stathopoulos *et al*, 2012). Different stakeholders affect and/or are being affected by the challenges caused by UFT (Banville *et al*, 1998; Macharis, 2005). Stakeholders have different, possibly conflicting, interests; therefore, one solution for one stakeholder might lead to a worse situation for another stakeholder (Browne and Allen, 1999; Macharis and Kin, 2017). Conflicting interests are put forward as one of the main constraints of efforts to mitigate the negative impact of UFT. More generally, studies in UFT as well as in other fields show that the difficulty and the lack of stakeholder involvement in the decision-making process is the main shortcoming in reaching intended goals (Beierle, 2002; Lindholm, 2013; Luyet *et al*, 2012; Reed, 2008).

It is therefore argued that consideration of the different interests of the stakeholders is essential to guarantee the success of best practices and policy measures (Behrends *et al*, 2008). In this context, the multi-actor multi-criteria analysis (MAMCA) offers a method to improve the success of measures and projects by assessing to what extent (policy) initiatives contribute to the objectives of the different stakeholders. This method explicitly takes the different stakeholder interests into account in the decision-making process (Macharis, 2005). It has been applied in different cases and mentioned as a suitable methodology in the field of UFT (Balm *et al*, 2014; Bjerkan *et al*, 2014; Buldeo Rai *et al*, 2017; Gatta and Marcucci, 2016; Kin *et al*, 2017; Lebeau, 2016; Macharis *et al*, 2014; Muñuzuri *et al*, 2016; STRAIGHTSOL, 2014; Suescún and Daraviña, 2016; van Lier *et al*, 2016; Zenezini and De Marco, 2016). The MAMCA methodology has been applied several times in workshops, where representatives from the different stakeholder groups are present and provide their input. In addition to input for the evaluation of a set of measures, workshops provide other advantages that will be elaborated in this chapter. Workshops facilitate gathering the diverging interests from a bottom-up perspective. The aim of this chapter is to give an overview of the different settings in which workshops were used regarding the MAMCA methodology as well as the lessons learned. The chapter highlights the contribution that the methodology makes to enhance participatory decision-making in the field of UFT. This is illustrated with real cases (section three). The following section describes the methodology.

Methodology

Compared to a traditional multi-criteria analysis (MCA), the multi-actor multi-criteria analysis (MAMCA) has the specificity of including the stakeholder's interest at the core of the methodology. It uses stakeholder objectives as evaluation criteria of the different solutions that are considered (Macharis, 2005). This way, each solution is evaluated based on the stakeholder's perspectives. The results therefore allow us to identify to what extent the solutions are meeting the objectives of each stakeholder. In this section, the seven steps of the MAMCA that are depicted in Figure 13.1 are discussed.

Step 1: Define alternatives

The first step of the methodology is identifying the alternatives that are considered for implementation. They can take various forms and be more or less narrowly defined. They can be described in terms of infrastructure investments, technological solutions, policy measures, and so on. A base scenario should also be included in the alternatives. This way, the modifications brought by the alternatives to the base scenario can be assessed.

Figure 13.1 MAMCA methodology

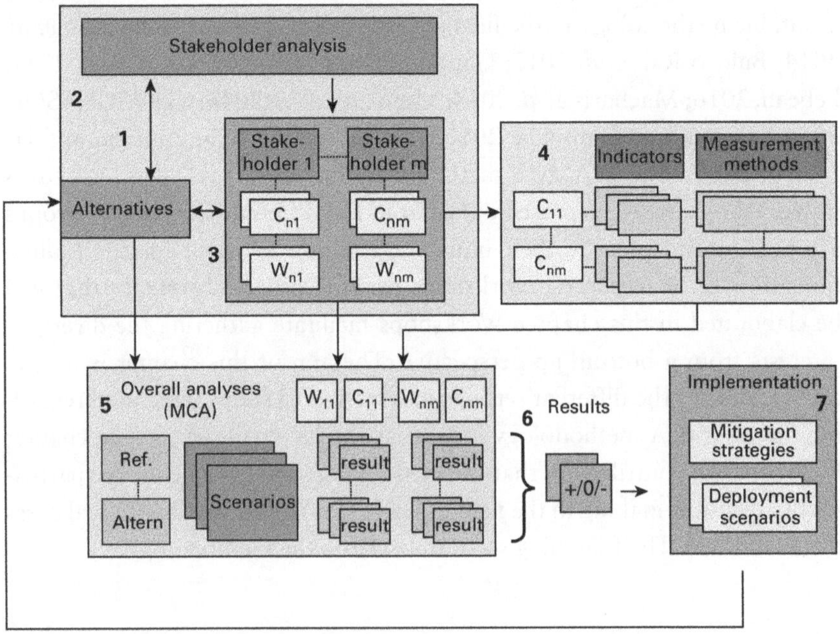

SOURCE Macharis *et al*, 2014

Step 2: Stakeholder analysis

The aim of the second step of the MAMCA is to identify the stakeholders that should be consulted for the evaluation of the alternatives. A stakeholder is, according to Freeman (1984), an individual or group of individuals who can influence the objectives of an organization or can be influenced by these objectives themselves. Stakeholders are thus not only those who are affecting a problem, but also those who are being affected by it (Macharis, 2005). Within the urban freight context these are usually the receivers, shippers, logistics service providers (LSPs), authorities and citizens (Behrends, 2011; Macharis *et al*, 2014). This list is, however, not predetermined and the groups might change depending on the context. Stakeholder analysis should be viewed as an aid to properly identify the range of stakeholders that need to be consulted and whose views should be taken into account in the evaluation process. Additionally, this step might give the opportunity to adapt the alternatives that were defined in step 1.

Step 3: Define criteria and weights

The stakeholder analysis has revealed the different stakeholder groups to consider in the MAMCA. In step 3, the analysis focuses on each of these groups. The aim is to identify their objectives on the one hand and assess the importance they associate to these objectives on the other hand. These objectives will then be used in the MAMCA as evaluation criteria of the alternatives. In the MAMCA methodology, the criteria for the evaluation are the goals and objectives of the stakeholders, and not the effects or impacts of the actions as are usually used in an MCA. In a natural way, these impacts will be reflected in the goals of the stakeholders (if all relevant stakeholders are included). The weight of each criterion is then assessed by the stakeholders themselves according to the importance they attach to their objectives. For the determination of the weights, existing methods can be used such as the allocation of 100 points, direct allocation, pairwise comparison method, and so on (for an overview see Eckenrode, 1965, and Nijkamp *et al*, 1990). Input from the stakeholders can be acquired online, through surveys and in workshops (or seminars). In the latter, stakeholders are actually present (Lindholm, 2013; Macharis *et al*, 2012).

Step 4: Criteria, indicators and measurement methods

The criteria identified in the previous step are used to evaluate the performance of each alternative. In this step, the criteria are 'operationalized' by constructing indicators (also called metrics or variables). This way, the impact of the different alternatives on the criteria can be measured. Indicators are usually quantitative but can also be qualitative. More than one indicator may be required to measure a project's contribution to a criterion and indicators themselves may measure contributions to multiple criteria.

Step 5: Overall analysis and ranking

In this step the different alternatives are being evaluated against the criteria of each stakeholder group. Sometimes it is necessary to further specify in which context these alternatives will be used, in order to be clear on what has to be evaluated. For example, it might be necessary to clarify the assumptions in the socio-economic context, market share and so on, in clear scenarios so that it is possible to evaluate the impact on criteria. The evaluation can be done on an ordinal scale or a continuous scale.

The analysis will then be further executed for each stakeholder group by a multi-criteria analysis method (we often use the PROMETHEE or the AHP method). It will show the overall preference of that stakeholder group for the scenarios. In the multi-actor view, the preferences of the different actors are brought together. Here, no overall aggregation is given as the aim is to give an idea of the different points of view.

Step 6: Results

The multi-criteria analysis developed in the previous step results in a ranking of the proposed alternatives per stakeholder as shown in Figure 13.2. The multi-actor view allows clear identification of the scenario that receives most support from stakeholders (in this case, scenario 3: S3). It can help in finding the Pareto optimal alternative compared with the business-as-usual (BAU) scenario. A single-actor perspective can also depict the MCA results per stakeholder in order to identify critical criteria, explaining their position in the multi-actor view. The MAMCA therefore provides a comparison of different strategic alternatives, and supports the decision-maker in making the final decision by pointing out for each stakeholder which elements have a clearly positive or a clearly negative impact on the objectives of each stakeholder.

Step 7: Implementation

The results of the MAMCA can then be discussed in this final step. They give a good starting point by showing to what extent the different alternatives contribute to their individual objectives. This way, we can avoid

Figure 13.2 Multi-actor results of a MAMCA

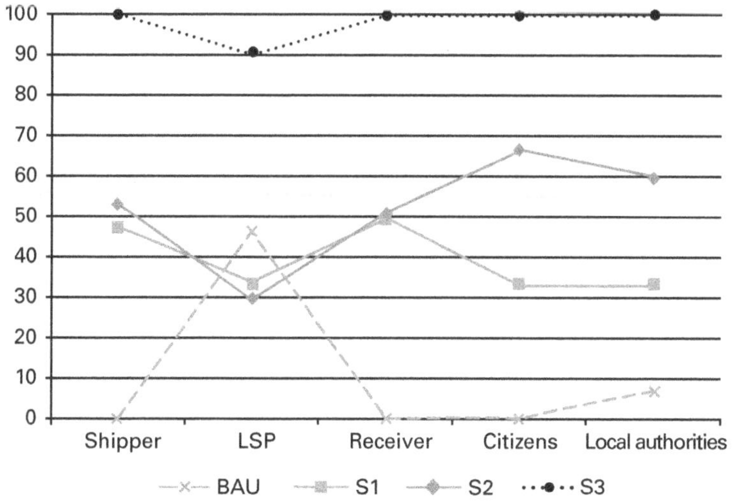

SOURCE adapted from Macharis et al, 2014

discussions where actors remain defensive and protect their own preferred scenario. Instead of having a conflicting situation where actors prefer to choose 'their alternative', this decision support tool allows the discussion to be structured around their underlying objectives. It helps to get insight in where the benefits and disadvantages are situated and how compensatory actions can be taken to overcome some negative drawbacks. Possible new alternatives or modified ones may be proposed for further analysis as more insight into the advantages and disadvantages of a certain alternative for each stakeholder is generated. This would then create a feedback loop towards the beginning of the procedure.

Applications

As elaborated above, the MAMCA methodology allows the incorporation of different stakeholders in the analysis of different alternatives and as a result helps to structure complex decision-making processes. The MAMCA can be used for different purposes. Depending on the time and budget, the methodology can be used as an ex ante or ex post evaluation tool. With participation, preferably in a real-life workshop, it is a way to get many immediate insights into the decision-making problem and it enables all stakeholder groups to achieve a common understanding of the problem as well as of potential solutions. In a workshop, stakeholders can also be informed more clearly about the purpose of the study and the alternatives (Lebeau, 2016). It also contributes to awareness of the problem (Kin *et al*, 2017). Furthermore, it adds to more democratic representation and social learning (Vermote, 2014).

The use of workshops in different contexts will be detailed below. These applications demonstrate the versatility of the methodology and its potential contribution to different discussions. First, the MAMCA has been used to support decisions. Second, a MAMCA workshop can serve as a tool to demonstrate the difficulty and importance of collaboration to actual stakeholders. Lastly, at different institutions an interactive workshop with the MAMCA has been used to teach about cooperation and decision-making issues.

In order to support an efficient discussion, a software has been developed (MAMCA, 2018). It allows the set up of a specific project with different scenarios, the creation of multiple groups with multiple criteria, evaluation of them and visualization of the results thanks to direct computations of the inputs. Practically, participants are divided between different stakeholder groups. Each group is directly connected to the software with a computer or tablet (eg iPad). After discussion within the respective stakeholder group, weights can be attributed to criteria. Depending on the design of the workshop, evaluation of the alternatives can also be done by the participants and can be inserted in the software. All results can directly be visualized centrally, which allows discussion of the results with all stakeholders. All demonstrations discussed below concern decisions in the UFT field. The MAMCA can, however, also be applied to decisions in other fields (Sun *et al*, 2015; Turcksin *et al*, 2011; Vermote *et al*, 2013).

A tool to evaluate demonstrations and future rollout scenarios

In essence, the MAMCA is used as a tool to support decisions and inform the decision-making process and can be applied to different kinds of projects. The initiative can, for instance, be taken by authorities in order to evaluate the support for a specific policy measure by the stakeholders before implementation. The initiative can also come from project developers that aim at estimating the success of an innovative solution among stakeholders. The methodology has been used for European project STRAIGHTSOL where a mobile depot demonstration from TNT Express in Brussels was evaluated (Verlinde *et al*, 2014) as well as demonstrations in six other European cities (STRAIGHTSOL, 2014). The Municipality of Mechelen, in Belgium, used the MAMCA to assess support for different alternative delivery options in the city centre (van Lier *et al*, 2016). Buldeo Rai *et al* (2017) conducted a MAMCA in a workshop to assess different future rollout scenarios for crowdsourced deliveries. Following this workshop, another workshop was organized to evaluate an already existing initiative. In this section, the application of the MAMCA from Lebeau *et al* (2015) is used as an example.

The scenarios consider different implementations of urban consolidation centres in Brussels. Besides the number of urban consolidation centres servicing the city, a number of supporting policies are also included in these scenarios as well as different vehicle technologies used for the last mile. These scenarios were developed by Janjevic *et al* (2016) following the scenario planning methodology of Schoemaker (1995). Their design took into account the current context of UFT in Brussels. Steps 2 and 3 of the MAMCA were based on a workshop organized in the 'Regional Mobility Commission – freight division', which is hosted by the Transport Ministry of the Brussels-Capital Region. This platform gathers together the stakeholders interested in freight transport in Brussels. The identification of the stakeholder groups and their objectives were first achieved based on a literature review (step 2 of the methodology). The results of the review were then submitted to the stakeholders for validation through a survey accompanied by an invitation to the workshop. In that survey, each respondent first had to pick the stakeholder group he or she belongs to, or create an extra one. Then, depending on that choice, the respondent was asked to confirm or adapt the objectives that were identified by the literature review (definition of the criteria from step 3). Thanks to that preliminary work, the workshop could focus on discussion of the final results (step 7). Indeed, the evaluation of the scenario was achieved before the workshop, based on the criteria mentioned by stakeholders in the survey (step 4). We limited, therefore, the contribution from stakeholders during the workshop to the weight assessment of their objectives (last requirement from step 3) and the final results have been directly computed by the MAMCA software, which manages steps 5 and 6.

The workshop attracted 32 participants, which were seated at round tables according to the stakeholder groups they chose during the survey. That attendance figure was sufficient to ensure an efficient discussion within each stakeholder group. Indeed, each group was asked to debate the importance they associate with their objectives and assess them through a pairwise comparison method managed by the MAMCA software. The results were then displayed as shown in Lebeau *et al* (2015). The discussion of these results was unfortunately limited since the assessment took more time than expected. It was therefore difficult to come up with one preferred scenario from all stakeholders, although the results identified two scenarios where all stakeholders were better off than in the BAU scenario. Instead, every actor remained defensive and tried to promote the situation he or she preferred the most. That workshop illustrates well the cooperation problem at stake in UFT. Lebeau *et al* (2015) concluded that the preferences of stakeholders could be used in a second iteration of the MAMCA in order to design a new set of scenarios that would better satisfy stakeholders.

A tool to demonstrate collaboration

Stakeholders in the UFT context are assumed to behave according to their own interests. They are often not aware that in a city context there is ample room for improvement. This might be because 'economic' stakeholders such as shippers underestimate the impact of UFT, especially because it concerns only a minor part of total transportation. As a result, stakeholders are often not aware that the last mile is the most expensive and difficult part, and there is great potential for improvement (Macharis and Kin, 2017; MDS Transmodal, 2012). Also, a city environment might be too complex. Additionally, all stakeholders are constrained by bounded rationality (Macharis *et al*, 2004; Marsden *et al*, 2012). For instance, authorities often cooperate poorly with private stakeholders as they primarily focus on restricting freight flows in urban areas with the aim of limiting congestion and air pollution. At the same time the provision of goods is also important for the liveability of a city (Macharis and Kin, 2017). In other words, authorities often pay attention to environmental and social sustainability, but largely ignore economic sustainability. For companies this might be the other way around.

In this context MAMCA workshops with representatives from actual stakeholder groups have been organized. In this way they get to understand more about what is the impact of UFT on their objectives, what it means for other stakeholders with whom they have to deal, whether they want it or not, and finally, what potential there is to make it more sustainable and cost efficient. In this regard, several workshops have been organized. During a workshop at the Logistics Innovation and Training Centre of Nike, representatives from different stakeholder groups participated in a case study on UFT. Most participants represented large shippers. Others represented transport companies, retailers and governmental organizations. Additionally, there were some supply chain experts from different institutions. All participants were divided between the five stakeholder groups with five or six persons per group. Criteria of the stakeholder groups were based on those identified in the STRAIGHTSOL project (STRAIGHTSOL, 2012). The five groups were divided within a room so their discussions could not disturb those of other stakeholders. Each group had a laptop available to insert the weights and evaluation of the alternatives. Afterwards they were able to see their own results. In the final discussion the separate uni-actor views as well as the multi-actor view were shown centrally to allow each stakeholder group to elaborate on and discuss the results. The case study of this workshop concerned freight distribution in the city of Brussels, which is characterized by one of the highest congestion levels in Europe (TomTom, 2016). The alternatives to the current way of delivery with conventional vehicles (BAU) were: the use of an urban consolidation centre, night deliveries, and the third alternative was left open for discussion by the participants. Eventually, the participants proposed 'shared capacity' as a third alternative. Each group then attributed weights to their criteria. They also evaluated the alternatives. The multi-actor results showed that BAU contributes the least to the criteria of all stakeholders and that out of the three alternatives the alternative with shared capacity has the lowest score. This is in line with what is known in the literature: the problems of shared capacity and thus (horizontal) collaboration are the sharing of costs, benefits and (competitive/sensitive) data (Cruijssen *et al*, 2007; van Lier *et al*, 2014). Overall, both consolidation centres and night deliveries contribute well to the scores of all stakeholders combined.

By using the MAMCA in this context, and as indicated by the participants during the discussion afterwards, it became clear that UFT, especially for the company representatives (ie shippers, LSPs and receivers), is a part of the supply chain that is relatively unknown. Its impact is therefore underestimated. To summarize, the four main lessons for participants during this workshop were:

1. UFT has a large societal, environmental and economic impact, and severely affects the viability of the business models of some stakeholders.
2. There are viable alternatives available which can potentially lead to win-win situations for multiple stakeholders.
3. Stakeholders gained insight into what other stakeholders – customers, for example – have as objectives.
4. Cooperation in this context is inevitable and the MAMCA is a good tool to support it.

A tool to teach cooperation

The application of the MAMCA in a workshop has also been used in an educational setting. By involving students in this way it helps them to take up different points of view, and more importantly, to make clear how difficult are decisions in a context such as UFT when diverging interests are involved. Interactive MAMCA sessions to teach cooperation have, among others, been used at the VUB, Amsterdam University of Applied Sciences and the University of Gothenburg. Although each workshop is linked to cooperation, different topics have been addressed. Whereas the topic during several classes in Brussels and Gothenburg was UFT in general, in Amsterdam it concerned an actual case on construction logistics of a new building for the university (Macharis *et al*, 2016).

During an interactive workshop at the VUB, the MAMCA was applied following a class on UFT within the Supply Chain Management course. The proposed alternatives for UFT in Brussels included: BAU, off-hour deliveries, UCC with urban toll and UCC with electric vehicles. The students were divided between the five stakeholder groups as mentioned earlier. However, owing to the size of the class sub-stakeholder groups were created, meaning that there were three separate groups of LSPs, three separate groups of local authorities and so on. Not only is this relevant for a workshop with a large number of participants, it is also of importance for evaluation purposes. For instance, a stakeholder group like the citizens can consist of those from two different neighbourhoods, whereby each is impacted by UFT in a different way. Alternatively, citizens are often a heterogeneous group as they can, for example, be considered as car drivers, a family who wants to enjoy a pleasant living environment, a shopper and so on. The same goes for other stakeholders. The MAMCA software allows the creation of subgroups within one stakeholder group. It also enables visualizing the results of each subgroup separately. The scores of the separate subgroups can be aggregated per stakeholder group in order to compare in the multi-actor view the preferences for each alternative across stakeholder groups. A boxplot can also be developed in order to visualize the heterogeneity of the preferences within stakeholder groups in the multi-actor view. The exact interpretation of the alternatives was, to a large extent, left open to the students. The same applied to what kind of stakeholder group they considered themselves to be (eg conservative or progressive authority). In total 80 students were divided into 15 stakeholder groups. Each group was connected to the software through a laptop or a tablet. During the discussion after the workshop, they were able to elaborate on how they interpreted their stakeholder group and how this influenced their results. As an example, Figure 13.3 shows how differently the three local authority groups evaluated the criteria.

Figure 13.3 Weight attribution of local authorities

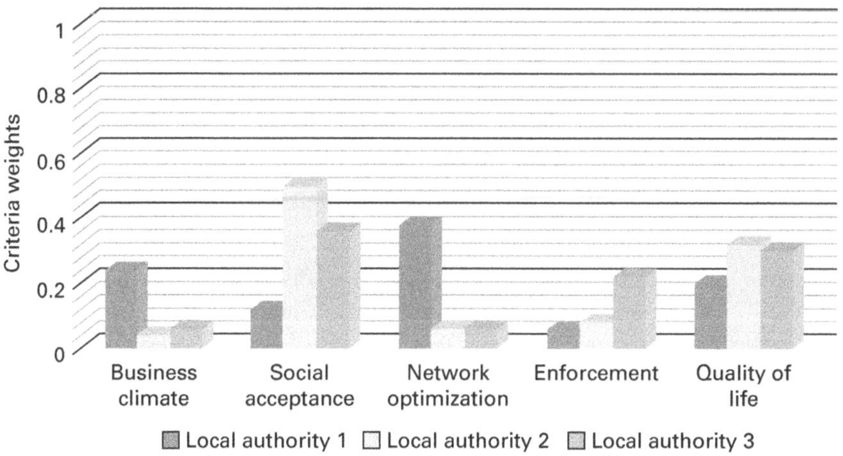

Results for the three local authority groups show that the highest weights are attributed to the criteria social acceptance and quality of life. With regard to the alternative, BAU contributes the least to the criteria of the three groups combined. The use of a UCC with subsequent deliveries by electric vehicles contributes the most to the criteria. This is followed by the alternative whereby a toll has to be paid to enter the city, or alternatively outsourcing deliveries to a UCC.

Using a workshop with the MAMCA in an educational setting obliges students to think about the content of the course. As indicated by students afterwards, it makes difficulties with decision-making in a context setting more concrete. In this specific case, the workshop followed the last class on UFT, or the last mile, within a course of supply chain management. Compared with other parts (eg long haul), within the city different stakeholders have to deal with each other to a larger extent. This workshop also demonstrates that stakeholder groups can be subdivided. This is inevitable with heterogeneous groups that have similar criteria but might evaluate them in a totally different way.

Workshops and their characteristics

Table 13.1 gives an overview of the characteristics of workshops discussed in this paper.

Table 13.1 Different types of workshop and their characteristics

	Workshop Type 1: Demonstrations	Workshop Type 2: Collaboration	Workshop Type 3: Educational	Workshop Type 4: Future Participation
Purpose	Evaluate demonstrations	Demonstrate collaboration	Teach collaboration	Participation
Stage of the MAMCA	Ex ante/ex post	Ex ante	Ex ante	Ex ante/ex post
Design of the alternatives (Step 1)	Predefined by experts	Predefined/ Participatory	Predefined/ Participatory	Participatory
Stakeholder analysis and Weights (Steps 2 and 3)	Survey/ Workshop	During workshop	During workshop	Crowdsourcing
Evaluation (Step 5)	By experts	Participatory/ by experts	By students	Participatory/ by experts

Further work on this topic will enable improved visualizations to help in guiding discussions after the results phase. Adding the perspectives of more stakeholders could also be valuable. In that case the workshop might no longer be a physical gathering, but an online tool that will be used to gather data from many more citizens (ie crowdsourcing). This is illustrated for 'Workshop 4'.

Conclusions

Within the UFT context, five stakeholder groups generally have to be taken into account, namely: shippers; logistics service providers; receivers; citizens; and authorities. In a specific case it might be that some are less relevant or that others should be added, such as shopping mall owners or the regional/national authority. Also subgroups might be created depending on the context of the problem. Each of these stakeholder groups have specific objectives that they would like to be taken into account in decision-making. With the use of the MAMCA methodology this is made possible. In this chapter we described how interactive workshops contribute to evaluation and can further enhance mutual understanding between stakeholders. Three types of workshop were discussed. First, the more traditional workshop, in which BAU is compared with scenarios based on an actual demonstration that is tested in real life, or a potential pilot test prior to the demonstration. Possible rollout scenarios are defined by experts and discussed with stakeholders. Evaluation of scenarios is executed by researchers and the main interaction appears when scenarios and results are tested. In these applications much time is devoted to the definition of good indicators and the collection of good evaluation data. Second, workshops in which potential future measures are being assessed against the objectives of stakeholders. In these interactive workshops, the focus is on discussion about the weights of criteria and evaluation. This leads directly to a common understanding of the problem and better insight is gained about the objectives and concerns of other stakeholders. A third type of workshop is quite similar to the second, but is specifically for educational purposes and so here the exercise is carried out with students.

Policymaking for UFT is very challenging. Not only because of a lack of data or the fact that until now UFT has been mostly neglected in cities, but also because there are many stakeholders that are involved or are influenced by new initiatives. Stakeholder involvement in the UFT context is becoming a mantra due to the complex setting with different, possibly conflicting, interests. With the MAMCA methodology, the different stakeholders are all taken into account by explicitly taking their objectives as the basis by which to evaluate several policy options. The use of such an approach can lead to far better decision-making.

References

Anderson, S, Allen, J and Browne, M (2005) Urban logistics – how can it meet policy makers' sustainability objectives? *Journal of Transport Geography*, **13** (1), pp 71–81 [Online] http://doi.org/10.1016/j.jtrangeo.2004.11.002

Ballantyne, EEF, Lindholm, M and Whiteing, A (2013) A comparative study of urban freight transport planning: addressing stakeholder needs, *Journal of Transport Geography*, **32**, pp 93–101 [Online] http://doi.org/10.1016/j.jtrangeo.2013.08.013

Balm, S, Browne, M, Leonardi, J and Quak, H (2014) Developing an evaluation framework for innovative urban and interurban freight transport solutions, *Procedia – Social and Behavioral Sciences*, **125**, pp 386–97 [Online] http://doi.org/10.1016/j.sbspro.2014.01.1482

Banville, C, Landry, M, Martel, J and Boulaire, C (1998) A stakeholder approach to MCDA, *Systems Research*, **15**, pp 15–32

Behrends, S (2011) *Urban Freight Transport Sustainability. The interaction of urban freight and intermodal transport*, Chalmers University of Technology

Behrends, S, Lindholm, M and Woxenius, J (2008) The impact of urban freight transport: a definition of sustainability from an actor's perspective, *Transportation Planning and Technology*, **31**(6), pp 693–713 [Online] http://doi.org/10.1080/03081060802493247

Beierle, TC (2002) The quality of stakeholder-based decisions, *Risk Analysis*, **22** (4), pp 739–49 [Online] http://www.ncbi.nlm.nih.gov/pubmed/12224747

Bestfact (2013) Best Practice Handbook 1, Deliverable 2.2 [Online] http://www.bestfact.net/wp-content/uploads/2014/01/BESTFACT_BPH.pdf

Bjerkan, KY, Sund, AB and Nordtømme, ME (2014) Stakeholder responses to measures green and efficient urban freight, *Research in Transportation Business and Management*, **11**, pp 32–42 [Online] http://doi.org/10.1016/j.rtbm.2014.05.001

Browne, M and Allen, J (1999) The impact of sustainability policies on urban freight transport and logistics systems, in *Selected Proceedings of the 8th World Conference on Transport Research,* ed H Meermans, E Van de Voorde and W Winkelmans, World Transport Research

Buldeo Rai, H, Verlinde, S, Merckx, J and Macharis, C (2017) Can the crowd deliver? Analysis of crowd logistics' types and stakeholder support, Presented at the 10th International Conference on City Logistics, Phuket (Thailand), 14–16 June 2017

Cruijssen, F, Cools, M and Dullaert, W (2007) Horizontal cooperation in logistics: opportunities and impediments, *Transportation Research Part E: Logistics and Transportation Review*, **43** (2), pp 129–42 [Online] http://doi.org/10.1016/j.tre.2005.09.007

Dablanc, L (2011) City distribution, a key element of the urban economy: guidelines for practitioners, in *City Distribution and Urban Freight Transport: Multiple perspectives*, ed C Macharis and S Melo, pp 13–36, Edward Elgar, Cheltenham

Eckenrode, R (1965) Weighting multiple criteria, *Management Science*, **12** (3), pp 180–92

European Commission (2011) *White Paper Roadmap to a Single European Transport Area – Towards a competitive and resource efficient transport system*, COM(2011) 144 final, Brussels

Freeman, RE (1984) *Strategic Management: A stakeholder approach*, Pitman, Boston

Gatta, V and Marcucci, E (2016) Stakeholder-specific data acquisition and urban freight policy evaluation: evidence, implications and new suggestions, *Transport Reviews*, **36** (5), pp 585–609 [Online] http://doi.org/10.1080/01441647.2015.1126385

Janjevic, M, Lebeau, P, Ndiaye, AB, Macharis, C, Van Mierlo, J and Nsamzinshuti, A (2016) Strategic scenarios for sustainable urban distribution in the Brussels-capital region using urban consolidation centres, *Transportation Research Procedia*, **12**, pp 598–612 [Online] http://doi.org/10.1016/j.trpro.2016.02.014

Kin, B, Verlinde, S, Mommens, K and Macharis, C (2017) A stakeholder-based methodology to enhance the success of urban freight transport measures in a multi-level governance context, *Research in Transportation Economics*, **65**, pp 10–23 [Online] https://doi.org/10.1016/j.retrec.2017.08.003

Lebeau, P (2016) *Towards the Electrification of City Logistics?* Vrije Universiteit Brussel

Lebeau, P, Macharis, C, van Mierlo, J and Janjevic, M (2015) Implementing an Urban Consolidation Centre: Involving stakeholders in a bottom-up approach, URban freight and BEhaviour change, Conference 2015, Rome

Lindholm, M (2013) Urban freight transport from a local authority perspective – a literature review, *European Transport/Trasporti Europei*, **3** (54), pp 1–37

Luyet, V, Schlaepfer, R, Parlange, MB and Buttler, A (2012) A framework to implement stakeholder participation in environmental projects, *Journal of Environmental Management*, **111**, pp 213–19 [Online] http://doi.org/10.1016/j.jenvman.2012.06.026

Macharis, C (2005) The importance of stakeholder analysis in freight transport, *European Transport/Trasporti Europei*, **25–26**, pp 114–26

Macharis, C and Kin, B (2017) The 4 A's of sustainable city distribution: innovative solutions and challenges ahead, *International Journal of Sustainable Transportation*, **11** (2), pp 59–71 [Online] http://doi.org/10.1080/15568318.2016.1196404

Macharis, C, Kin, B, Balm, S and Ploos van Amstel, W (2016) Multiactor participatory decision-making in urban construction logistics, *Transportation Research Record: Journal of the Transportation Research Board*, **2547**, pp 83–90

Macharis, C, Milan, L and Verlinde, S (2014) A stakeholder-based multicriteria evaluation framework for city distribution, *Research in Transportation Business and Management*, **11**, pp 75–84 [Online] http://doi.org/10.1016/j.rtbm.2014.06.004

Macharis, C, Springael, J, De Brucker, K and Verbeke, A (2004) PROMETHEE and AHP: The design of operational synergies in multicriteria analysis. Strengthening PROMETHEE with ideas of AHP, *European Journal of Operational Research*, **153** (2), pp 307–17 [Online] http://doi.org/10.1016/S0377-2217(03)00153-X

Macharis, C, Turcksin, L and Lebeau, K (2012) Multi actor multi criteria analysis (MAMCA) as a tool to support sustainable decisions: state of use, *Decision Support Systems*, **54** (1), pp 610–20 [Online] http://doi.org/10.1016/j.dss.2012.08.008

MAMCA (2018) [Online] https://www.mamca.be

Marsden, G, Frick, KT, May, AD and Deakin, E (2012) Bounded rationality in policy learning amongst cities: lessons from the transport sector, *Environment and Planning A*, **44** (4), pp 905–20 [Online] http://doi.org/10.1068/a44210

MDS Transmodal (2012) DG MOVE European Commission: Study on Urban Freight Transport

Muñuzuri, J, Larrañeta, J, Onieva, L and Cortés, P (2005) Solutions applicable by local administrations for urban logistics improvement, *Cities*, **22** (1), pp 15–28 [Online] http://doi.org/10.1016/j.cities.2004.10.003

Muñuzuri, J, Onieva, L, Cortés, P and Guadix, J (2016) Stakeholder segmentation: different views inside the carriers group, *Transportation Research Procedia*, **12** (June 2015), pp 93–104 [Online] http://doi.org/10.1016/j.trpro.2016.02.050

Nijkamp, P, Rietveld, P and Voogd, H (1990) *Multicriteria Evaluation in Physical Planning*, Elsevier Science Publishers, Amsterdam

Quak, H (2008) *Sustainability of Urban Freight Transport: Retail distribution and local regulations in cities*, Erasmus University Rotterdam

Reed, MS (2008) Stakeholder participation for environmental management: a literature review, *Biological Conservation*, **141** (10), pp 2417–31 [Online] http://doi.org/10.1016/j.biocon.2008.07.014

Schoemaker, J, Allen, J, Huschebeck, M and Monigl, J (2006) *Quantification of Urban Freight Transport Effects I*, BESTUFS consortium

Schoemaker, PJ (1995) Scenario planning: a tool for strategic thinking, *Sloan Management Review*, **36**, pp 25–40

Stathopoulos, A, Valeri, E and Marcucci, E (2012) Stakeholder reactions to urban freight policy innovation, *Journal of Transport Geography*, **22**, pp 34–45 [Online] http://doi.org/10.1016/j.jtrangeo.2011.11.017

STRAIGHTSOL (2012) *Deliverable 3.2. Report on stakeholders, criteria and weights*

STRAIGHTSOL (2014) *Deliverable 5.4. Final evaluation of all STRAIGHTSOL city distribution concepts by use of the MAMCA*, Brussels

Suescún, JPB and Daraviña, PAC (2016) A paradox of sustainable development and urban freight transport – Public space renewal vs deliveries and pick-ups: The case of Cali – Colombia, *World Conference on Transport Research (WCTR)*, 2016, Shanghai, China

Sun, H, Zhang, Y, Wang, Y, Li, L and Sheng, Y (2015) A social stakeholder support assessment of low-carbon transport policy based on multi-actor multi-criteria analysis: the case of Tianjin, *Transport Policy*, **41**, pp 103–16 [Online] http://doi.org/10.1016/j.tranpol.2015.01.006

TomTom (2016) Tomtom Traffic Index. Measuring Congestion Worldwide, [Online] https://www.tomtom.com/nl_be/trafficindex/list

Turcksin, L, Macharis, C, Lebeau, K, Boureima, F, Van Mierlo, J, Bram, S and Pelkmans, L (2011) A multi-actor multi-criteria framework to assess the stakeholder support for different biofuel options: the case of Belgium, *Energy Policy*, **39** (1), pp 200–14 [Online] http://doi.org/10.1016/j.enpol.2010.09.033

van Lier, T, Caris, A and Macharis, C (2014) Sustainability SI: Bundling of Outbound Freight Flows: Analyzing the Potential of Internal Horizontal Collaboration to Improve Sustainability, *Networks and Spatial Economics* [Online] http://doi.org/10.1007/s11067-014-9226-x

van Lier, T, Meers, D, Buldeo Rai, H and Macharis, C (2016) Making urban freight transport more sustainable in a medium sized city: the case of Mechelen, *European Transport Conference 2016: AET Papers Repository*, 5–7 October 2016, Barcelona, Spain

Verlinde, S, Macharis, C, Milan, L and Kin, B (2014) Does a mobile depot make urban deliveries faster, more sustainable and more economically viable: results of a pilot test in Brussels, *Transportation Research Procedia*, **4**, pp 361–73 [Online] http://doi.org/10.1016/j.trpro.2014.11.027

Vermote, L (2014) *Sustainable Mobility and Decision-making: Participatory assessment of mobility policies in Belgium and Palestine*, Vrije Universiteit Brussel

Vermote, L, Macharis, C and Putman, K (2013) A road network for freight transport in Flanders: multi-actor multi-criteria assessment of alternative ring ways, *Sustainability*, 5 (10), pp 4222–46 [Online] http://doi.org/10.3390/su5104222

Zenezini, G and De Marco, A (2016) A review of methodologies to assess urban freight initiatives, *IFAC-PapersOnLine*, **49** (12), pp 1359–64 [Online] http://doi.org/10.1016/j.ifacol.2016.07.752

Off-hour deliveries 14

The importance of outreach and proper planning

JEFFREY WOJTOWICZ, SHAMA CAMPBELL
AND JOSÉ HOLGUÍN-VERAS

Introduction

In many urban areas, traffic and transportation activity has become overcrowded and inefficient, especially during the peak periods of the day. Often it is not feasible to build or expand infrastructure to accommodate increased demand. Dealing with congestion and its environmental impacts necessitates the use of a wide spectrum of public sector initiatives. This provides the rationale for transportation demand management (TDM). TDM encompasses strategies aimed at increasing the efficiency of the overall system by means of inducing changes in demand patterns, such as promoting the use of modes that have higher occupancy over single occupancy vehicle trips (SOV), or switching trips from peak hours to off-peak hours (Seattle Department of Transportation, 2008). Passenger TDM aims to decrease the number of car trips, which will in turn reduce vehicle miles travelled, to achieve key policy objectives such as energy conservation, environmental protection and congestion reduction (City of New York, 2011).

In contrast, only relatively recently, have systematic efforts to improve the performance of urban freight systems been undertaken. Through the creation of a comprehensive planning guide, extensive research was done to identify and catalogue initiatives that could improve freight system performance in metropolitan areas (Holguín-Veras *et al,* 2014a; Holguín-Veras *et al,* 2014b). Within this planning guide a spectrum of supply and demand related strategies are discussed for practitioners to consider. An important group of initiatives, freight demand management or FDM, seeks to induce beneficial changes in freight demand to reduce the negative impacts of freight activity, while fostering beneficial ones. In doing so, FDM strives to reduce the number or change the timing, mode and/or destination of deliveries made to commercial establishments.

Off-hour deliveries (OHD) is a paradigmatic example of FDM, an emerging field that increases the sustainability of freight activity by modifying the nature of demand that generates freight vehicle traffic. The OHD programme exploits the fact that freight carriers travel during congested hours (despite slower trips, higher costs, etc) only because their customers (the receivers of the supplies) demand it. By inducing receivers to accept deliveries in the off-hours (7 pm to 6 am), most carriers will gladly alter their operations, producing dramatic effects in otherwise congested cities. OHD leads to: reduced urban congestion and air pollution; increased economic productivity and lower costs; and enhanced sustainability and quality of life, with reduced conflicts between freight traffic and passenger vehicles, pedestrians and cyclists. It has been found that these benefits can be achieved through incentives offered to receivers in exchange for their commitment to accept OHD. Since incentives remove receivers' opposition, and the carriers are generally in favour, entire supply chains have switched to OHD. Moreover, the commitment of carriers to the use of low-noise delivery practices will minimize the impact of noise on local communities.

As a whole, urban areas of various sizes with significant daytime congestion are ideal candidates. The companies that deliver goods and supplies within cities will benefit, as will the receivers and communities. While the ideal geographic scope is congested urban areas, the benefits extend far beyond those areas. OHD will reduce freight traffic from distribution centres outside the city to the urban core.

Implementing OHD is not straightforward; a great deal of planning and effort is required to make it successful. Without proper considerations, the strategy may fail to be effective. This chapter presents experiences and lessons learned from the implementation of OHD in New York City, including key findings from the outreach efforts, with the intention of offering guidance on how to inform decision-makers of critical points to consider when implementing OHD.

Background to off-hour deliveries and the role of outreach

The research that led to the launch phase of the OHD project was a partnership between Rensselaer Polytechnic Institute (RPI) and the New York City Department of Transportation (NYCDOT). The NYC OHD project was implemented in stages. After a successful pilot phase that concluded in 2010, the United States Department of Transportation (USDOT) Office of the Assistant Secretary for Research and Technology (OST-R) sponsored an implementation phase (Integrative Freight Demand Management in the New York City Metropolitan Area: Implementation Phase), which was launched in June 2011(Holguín-Veras *et al*, 2010; Holguín-Veras *et al*, 2013).

The NYC OHD project has been widely acknowledged as an impactful and business-friendly public sector freight initiative. Among its impacts are changes seen in the economy, the environment and the quality of life in local communities:

- The project has the potential to influence large numbers of deliveries (up to 20 to 40 per cent of key industry sectors like food and retail), with tremendous economic impacts.
- The OHD programme increases economic competitiveness, reduces congestion and environmental pollution, and increases sustainability, quality of life and liveability.
- At a global scale, the environmental impacts of OHD could be tremendous (Holguín-Veras *et al*, 2016). If OHD is implemented in all the metropolitan areas in the world with populations of more than 2 million people, these cities could eliminate the emission of: 297.8 million tons of CO_2, 57.8 thousand tons of reactive organic gases (ROG), 65.8 thousand tons of total organic gases (TOG), 843.1 thousand tons of CO, 120.6 thousand tons of NO_X, 19.7 thousand tons of PM_{10}, and 18.9 thousand tons of $PM_{2.5}$.
- By removing the interferences produced by deliveries, OHD programmes facilitate the implementation of other sustainability initiatives, such as bus rapid transit systems, cycle lanes and enhanced pedestrian walkways that also need kerb space.
- The OHD project has dramatically confirmed the potential of public–private sector and academic cooperation in solving urban congestion. The programme's business-friendly nature has won the enthusiastic support of the private sector (*Journal of Commerce*, 2009, 2010; *Wall Street Journal*, 2010).

- This project has changed freight policy at regional, national and international levels. NYC adopted OHD as part of its sustainability plan (City of New York, 2011), and the Federal Highway Administration (FHWA) and the Environmental Protection Agency (EPA) created a programme to replicate the OHD programme in cities throughout the United States (Federal Highway Administration, 2012). The first grants from this federal programme were awarded to Orlando, Florida and Washington, DC.
- Supported by thorough research, as well as the NYC project's pilot and implementation experience and data, the OHD concept is transferable and adaptable, and its implementation can serve as an example for cities around the world.
- The use of financial incentives in exchange for OHD removes opposition from receivers; while the use of low-noise delivery technologies ensures that communities are not negatively impacted.

An OHD programme can affect entire supply chains, as well as the stakeholders involved, from shippers to receivers to community members. As such, outreach is a key part of the implementation process, both to inform stakeholders, and to gather feedback on issues and concerns that need to be addressed to improve its implementation. Since receivers generally have the most concerns, from added labour costs to security issues, the incentives provided need to outweigh these issues.

Approach to outreach and appropriate outreach strategies

One key element of a successful OHD programme is proper outreach. Without sufficient outreach to both the public and private sectors and the community, there is a high likelihood of failure. The entire outreach effort needs to include various elements of education, recruitment and mediation between stakeholders. The strategies used in NYC address these elements, and should be adaptable to other OHD programmes in other locations. Throughout the NYC OHD programme there were dedicated staff members from both RPI and NYCDOT who were responsible for outreach to potential participants; these points of contact are essential. With meetings, field visits, phone calls and other coordination efforts, the level of effort for outreach is significant and can easily consume at least 30 to 40 per cent of time for someone conducting outreach.

An outreach strategy should be defined at the outset of a project, as without a proper scope it can be difficult to manage all of the stakeholders effectively. It was decided early in the NYC OHD project that RPI and NYCDOT would work jointly on the outreach campaign, talking in parallel to potential participants. In addition, at some venues, such as meetings or trade shows, both teams worked together. Once companies began to show an interest in the programme most of the follow-up communication was carried out by RPI. This was strategic, as RPI was able to sign non-disclosure agreements (NDAs) with the interested parties, to keep their company data secure and to schedule all necessary field visits for data collection. NYCDOT, given their resources, was responsible for the majority of the creation of the branding and marketing campaigns.

Based on lessons learned, the team identified a series of steps that should be followed to successfully implement OHD:

1. Determination of the incentive.
2. Selection of the target industry sectors.
3. Stakeholder engagement.
4. Advertising, marketing and branding.
5. Recruitment.
6. Implementation.
7. Evaluation and enhancement of the programme.

The steps begin prior to actual outreach, and conclude with evaluation and enhancement of the programme, Figure 14.1 shows this process.

Figure 14.1 Flowchart showing steps for implementing off-hour deliveries (OHD)

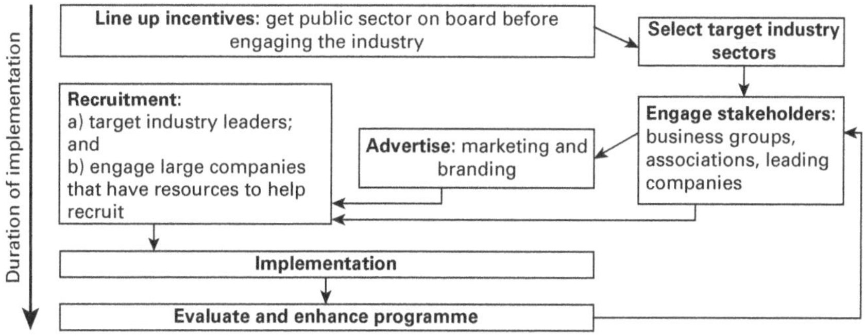

Line up the incentive

The success of OHD largely depends on the incentives in place, so it is critical to determine what incentive programme will motivate participation. Since OHD by nature appeals to carriers, the incentives are directed towards receivers. Receivers hold the power in the relationship between the agents in most urban freight markets, so they determine when deliveries occur. For receivers, the concerns in doing OHD are related to costs, whether increased staff hours for those doing staffed OHD, or suitable security strategies and equipment for those doing unassisted OHD (UOHD). A well-designed public sector intervention is needed to avoid the primary obstacle to OHD: receiver resistance. All necessary public sector agencies must be on board early in the process, and made aware of the suite of incentives that could be provided to participating businesses. Such incentives could include one-time payments, tax breaks, shipping discounts, public recognition or business support services. The pilot conducted in NYC employed both modalities of OHD: staffed OHD and UOHD, where UOHD does not require staff to receive the deliveries. At the end of the pilot those who did UOHD continued to accept OHDs, while those who did staffed OHD could not afford to continue without the incentive. The more sustainable modality for implementation is UOHD, given the cost of maintaining overnight staff. This finding is important in terms of incentive packages for permanent implementation.

In the UOHD implementation phase a stated preference survey was developed to assess respondents' willingness to do UOHD based on various incentives offered. The incentives included: 1) a one-time incentive ranging from US $1,000–$9,000 (in $1,000 increments); 2) a carrier discount ranging from 0 per cent to 50 per cent (in 10 per cent increments); 3) public recognition that would indicate to the public that the business is a participant of a sustainable, community and environmentally friendly programme; and 4) business support services (ie services to help them in running their business). Analysis of the data collected showed the NAICS[1] sectors that were more willing to participate in OHD as well as willingness based on the various incentive packages. The data collected from the sample regarding the incentives offered showed that offering a one-time incentive ranging from US $1,000–$4,000 will be the most efficient use of funds depending on the percentage shift that is desired. Regarding carrier discounts, the data indicated that although there was incremental increase with each additional 10 per cent increase in discount, the largest increase in willingness was from no discount to 10 per cent, which showed a 9.53 per cent increase in willingness. Offering public recognition and business support increased willingness by 3.22 per cent and 4.53 per cent, respectively (Holguín-Veras *et al*, 2017). Further behavioural modelling was done using the stated preference portion of the survey to get a better understanding of the effects of the incentives; for more details on the sample and modelling results see Holguín-Veras *et al*, 2017. The actual incentives used for the NYC OHD launch phase were a one-time US $2,000 payment and public recognition. The participating carriers said in the future they may consider offering a shipping discount to those receivers willing to accept OHD.

The information gained from data collection and subsequent analysis provides useful knowledge in developing an effective incentive package. Also, the public sector should finalize the incentive package prior to engaging the industry. This will ensure that the public sector is on board with the incentives they plan to offer, and the outreach steps can be completed without any confusion to the business community.

Selection of the target industry sectors

Prior to engaging actual businesses in an OHD programme, the industry sectors targeted for participation should be determined. Although it is advantageous for businesses from many industry sectors to switch to the off-hours, it is more manageable to focus on only a few for implementation, as each industry sector will have a different set of requirements that they must consider before shifting. If too many sectors are identified, it will be more difficult to tailor solutions for each of the participants. Within targeted industries, many of the carriers and receivers can help spread the word about the programme, and concentrate their efforts to common receivers. Also, when implementing OHD in other urban areas, it is important to understand the freight trips attracted and produced by the various industry sectors so the most effective sectors can be targeted. For recruitment purposes in the NYC project, the team primarily focused on businesses within the food and retail sectors. These sectors produce a large portion of the deliveries destined to Manhattan (15 per cent and 42 per cent respectively).

It is also important to conduct behavioural research to determine which sectors are among the most inclined to participate in OHD. Essentially, focusing on these sectors offered the highest potential payoff in terms of freight traffic reductions. To this effect, the team conducted a large amount of behaviour research to determine how receivers and carriers would respond to policy measures intended to foster OHD, and integrated the research's chief findings in the Behavioural Micro-Simulation (BMS). The BMS enabled the team to identify the most appropriate policy design, and estimate the OHD market share that could be achieved.

The BMS assesses the effects of alternative policy designs by modelling the decision of the receivers in response to incentives, and the decision of the carriers in response to the choices made by the receivers. The BMS is 'behavioural' because it operationalizes the behaviour research conducted on the response of receivers to incentives, and the response of carriers to the receivers' decisions concerning whether or not to accept OHD. The BMS ensures the realism of the results by: grounding the simulations in the estimated number of deliveries at each analysis zone; and using realistic values of travel times and costs in the local transportation network. Holguín-Veras *et al* (2018) discuss in more detail how the BMS was used to support the selection of industry sectors.

Engage key stakeholders

As with many other projects, implementing OHD requires key stakeholder engagement. All key players, including people from a wide spectrum of groups, must be involved. Most stakeholders are willing to provide feedback to improve the system, but if too much is asked of them they may back out, or provide less thoughtful information. It is also important to consider the geographic scope of the project and to ensure representation from this entire area.

The following groups of stakeholders were engaged in the NYC implementation:

- **Carriers, shippers and large chain businesses.** As the most noticeable actors in freight delivery, these have the largest number of trucks involved in urban traffic, and their daytime activity or lack thereof will be an indication of programme success.
- **Trade groups, business improvement districts, chambers of commerce and receivers.** These groups are able to reach clearly defined groups of businesses and already have established working relationships with the business community.
- **Community.** The residents of the city where the OHD programme is to be implemented are obviously key stakeholders as they are concerned with how the programme will affect them, specifically noise during the night.

It is important to realize that stakeholders can be engaged at various levels. Some stakeholders need to be engaged only at key milestones, while others should be engaged more frequently. The next section provides some details on the advisory groups that were created for the NYC OHD project.

Advisory groups

One of the first tasks related to outreach is the creation of advisory groups. For the NYC OHD programme two advisory groups were created: the industry advisory group and the public agency advisory group (Holguín-Veras *et al*, 2010). These groups are able to provide input from a broad range of stakeholders.

The industry advisory group (IAG) is a group of businesses representing carriers, shippers, receivers, economic development groups and trade groups from various economic sectors and different business sizes. The objective in creating the IAG was to assemble a group that is knowledgeable of urban goods movement from a variety of perspectives, and represents economic sectors and different business sizes from the geographic area.

At the start of the OHD project, the team moved quickly to create the IAG, as the IAG became a vital tool in recruiting OHD participation. The members of the IAG shared their views on freight movement in NYC, their businesses'/groups' perspective and concerns, as well as feedback on various OHD-related ideas. This information was valuable in revising strategies to address additional issues, and in recruitment, as the team became aware of important issues specific to stakeholders. The members also helped spread the word to increase recruitment. The business improvement districts (BIDs) were especially vital in this role, as they were able to facilitate introductions to other groups or companies that could benefit from OHD. Throughout the project there were periodic IAG meetings, as well as individual interactions with members. In summary, the main contributions of the IAG were providing feedback on the programme and outreach and branding strategies, and assisting in participant recruitment.

For the pilot phase, the IAG had six private sector representatives. For the implementation phase, the group grew to include: four BIDs; seven trade groups representing various sectors in Manhattan, including carriers and receivers; and ten businesses, including carriers and receivers, and a mix of chains and non-chains (Holguín-Veras *et al*, 2010; Holguín-Veras *et al*, 2013). Improvements that have come about as a result of the IAG meetings include the development of: press and branding plans; mechanisms that could be used by IAG members for recruitment, such as follow-up surveys for businesses, and a standardized letter for receivers to explain the programme; standardized text for participant websites to publicize the project; and a recognition scheme to reward programme participants.

The public agency advisory group comprised various NYC agencies that are relevant to implementing and sustaining OHD. This included representatives from NYC Economic Development Corporation (NYC EDC), NYC

Small Business Services (NYC SBS), NYC Department of City Planning (NYC DCP), NYC Department of Health (NYC DoH), NYC Department of Environmental Protection (NYC DEP), NYC Department of Buildings, Port Authority of New York and New Jersey (PANYNJ) and NYC Department of Housing and Urban Development (NYC HUD). All applicable agencies associated with the implementation area should be involved.

Advertising, marketing and branding

Branding and marketing are key, as they enable the programme to catch on and grow. Large cities such as NYC, with an approximate population of 8 million, have many marketing ads competing for people's attention. Therefore, a smart professional marketing campaign is necessary to ensure that messages reach their intended audience, relay a programme's benefits, and gain public support. It is desirable for a marketing team to identify a name, logo and tagline for the programme. For example for the NYC OHD project the marketing team identified 'NYC DeliverEASE' as a possible name, which is a play on the word 'deliveries', while conveying that OHD is an easy solution.

The goal of the programme's branding and marketing strategies is similar to those of any other product: to develop a slogan that is catchy and memorable, and a logo that is easily understood and recognizable. These two elements should work hand-in-hand to detail the benefits, and sell the programme to various stakeholders.

Recruitment

Following stakeholder outreach and advertising of the programme, rigorous recruitment of the participants can begin. The recruitment process is long and tedious, but it can yield hefty results, especially if done properly. For the NYC programme there were two main components. The first is recruiting industry leaders or icon businesses that are well respected either locally or nationally. Once the programme has several of these leaders on board it is easier to pitch the idea to other businesses. Other businesses realize that if those icon businesses tried and were successful, they might be as well. The second approach was reaching out to shippers, carriers, receivers of all business sizes as well as trade groups. Many of the small companies were contacted through the trade groups, or the large companies that they conduct trade with. The larger companies were utilized to leverage their position to influence their customers or other smaller companies to switch to OHD.

This resulted in a chain effect, as in some cases if a receiver decides to switch to OHD for a specific carrier they begin to explore the possibility of switching other deliveries they receive to the off-hours as well. In these cases, the outreach team can act as a liaison between the two to assist with the switch, and in other cases the receiver communicates directly with the carrier to make arrangements to receive deliveries during the off-hours.

Without interactions with trade and business groups it would have been difficult for the team to reach their several thousand members. The groups engaged in NYC included: The Real Estate Board of New York (REBNY); Manhattan Chamber of Commerce (MCC); the Food Industry Alliance of New York (FIANY); the New York State Restaurant Association (NYSRA); the NYC Hospitality Alliance (NYCHA); the NYC Hotel Association; and several business improvement districts (BIDs) such as Grand Central Partnership.

Outreach was also done to the individual prospective participants – carriers, shippers and receivers. There were companies that expressed interest in being involved between the pilot and implementation phase, mainly as a result of hearing about the successful pilot. Logically, the outreach team approached these companies first. The team used a scripted interview process, inquiring about characteristics of their business operations, and their willingness to participate in both staffed OHD and UOHD.

As previously mentioned, carriers and shippers favour OHDs, and were naturally enthusiastic to create OHD delivery routes, or add customers to their existing routes. Receivers were more resistant, with issues that were beyond their purview such as lease agreements, community board concerns and union contracts. A major hurdle that was experienced in outreach to the receivers is that they were often busy with the operations of the business. The receivers were typically small establishments with limited resources to pursue further investigation into this, or other programmes, which resulted in short, unsuccessful calls. With the aim of enlisting higher numbers, these receivers were also contacted by their shippers about the programme, when possible. To assist in recruiting receivers to the project through large shipping companies, the team drafted a letter that the shipper could disseminate to its customers. The letter shown in Figure 14.2 outlined the programme benefits.

With the large carriers and shippers, a two-pronged approach was developed: first, the receiver was contacted by a representative of the shipping organization; then if the receiver expressed interest, the outreach team would follow up with more detailed information. This worked well in recruiting small businesses that were serviced by large carriers and shippers. This was

Figure 14.2 Sample outreach letter

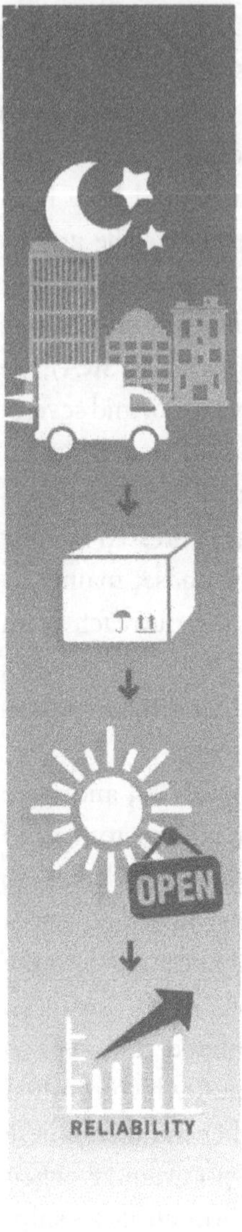

Grand Central PARTNERSHIP

NEW YORK CITY DOT

Request for Participation in the NYC deliverEASE Program

Dear Member of the Grand Central Partnership:

We invite you to participate in NYC deliverEASE, a program to increase off-hour deliveries (typically between 7PM and 6AM) with the goal of reducing congestion, improving quality of life, and increasing the efficiency of urban deliveries. A pilot test conducted in 2009–2010 revealed several benefits to receivers, vendors and the city at-large.

By switching your deliveries to the off-hours your business will:

- Have **more time available to spend with customers**, instead of waiting for a delivery to arrive.
- Receive **on-time deliveries all the time**. After all, your supplies will be there waiting when you open your business in the morning.
- **Reduce the need for extra inventory**, therefore, saving money on inventory costs.

As encouragement to participate in NYC deliverEASE, you will receive a $2,000 financial incentive.

60% of the incentive will be provided for one successful quarter of participation and the remaining 40% for the second quarter. In addition, you will earn **public recognition** as one of the participants in this pioneering program.

In addition, you may also be able to negotiate reduced shipping costs from your vendors.

If you are interested in learning more about this exciting project please complete the form on the following page.

"Whole Foods has enjoyed the ability to take deliveries in overnight. It has allowed us to serve our customers better through better in-stock position. enhanced our commitment to our Green Mission through more efficient trucking operations and improved our collaboration with our vendors."

ROB TWYMAN, Regional VP Whole Foods Market Northeast Region

To learn more, contact Jeff Wojtowicz at RPI at **518-276-2759** or **wojtoj@rpi.edu.** Please email or fax (518-276-4833) the form on the following page. Additional project information and testimonials from participants can be found at cite.rpi.edu/off-hour-deliveries and www.nyc.gov/html/dot/html/motorist/offhoursdelivery.shtml

also a cost effective way to inform potential participants; the companies with ample resources who already had a presence with the receivers were informing them of the programme. Also, using the existing relationship helped with trust, as an unfamiliar third party was not asking them to start changing their delivery patterns.

Site visits to some of the interested receiving establishments were also helpful, as the team was able to identify problems and recommend specific solutions to facilitate OHD. Suggestions could include physical changes like additions, renovations or remodelling parts of the building or adding specific technology such as refrigeration units or access technologies to increase security. In addition, face-to-face discussions were more persuasive than phone or email communication, as they make for easier explanation and understanding of the subject matter. One of the success stories of site visits includes a major high-end hotel that made physical changes such as adding a refrigeration unit, as well as internally promoting the programme to 18 other hotels under the same brand in the NYC metro area.

Implementation

It is critical to work closely with businesses adopting OHD to ensure that all of their questions are answered and that they feel comfortable in the shift. Although the project team may have one schedule in mind, the business community may have other ideas about timing. It is important to be flexible and to work with the constraints of the businesses to ensure successful implementation.

Evaluation and enhancement of the programme

As an OHD programme is being implemented, the progress needs to be monitored regularly to ensure that goals and objectives are being met. As this evaluation is taking place, enhancements will need to be developed to ensure the programme's longevity.

Public agency perspective on outreach and incentives

It is believed that incentives for OHD participation can take many other forms in addition to financial incentives. For many public sector agencies financial incentives and business support programmes are not usually within their toolbox of options. Yet, those types of incentives were identified by the IAG as very important in helping businesses make the shift to OHD. Industry stakeholders stated that the OHD programme is not yet a core focus for any business. Participation will often require supporters to fight internal battles to secure permission from their organizations to participate. Getting involved in OHD must be easy to justify to corporate decision-makers, and even easier to do. Providing incentives to motivate companies to change their behaviour is not a new idea. For example, business incentives are provided by agencies to encourage grocery stores to be opened in underserved neighbourhoods without access to fresh produce. Incentives are also provided to help companies purchase alternative fuel trucks. In order to create the proper incentive packages it may be necessary to build multi-agency collaborations to solve these challenges.

Lessons learned

Implementing OHD in any urban area will require care and attention to detail, especially with outreach efforts. Players at many different levels need to tout the programme's benefits and successes. The NYC OHD team and members of the IAG were instrumental in recruitment and outreach. Representing a diverse group of businesses from across the Manhattan target area, the IAG was also instrumental in promoting the project and generating interest for businesses to participate. Industry champions, such as the IAG members are key in influencing others to participate.

Once a clear and comprehensive outreach plan has been developed, stakeholders can be engaged. Only after the overall programme structure has been defined should community stakeholders be engaged. While early stakeholder engagement is of utmost importance, if stakeholders are brought into the process before there is clear direction, their assistance and involvement could be jeopardized. The remainder of this section presents the key lessons learned.

Developing the incentive structure at the onset of the project is critical. Since receivers generally have the most concerns about added labour costs to security issues, the incentives being provided need to outweigh these concerns. Even before recruiting participants, it is essential to completely understand, and be confident in how the incentives are structured. Having the public sector offer financial incentives for receivers to switch to the off-hours is not a model that can be sustained over a long period of time. Other forms of incentive can be offered, whether tax breaks, business support services and/or public recognition.

Carriers and shippers often benefit from these programmes because of reduced operating costs and improved efficiency in their delivery routes. As the number of OHDs increases it is possible that in the future, some shippers will consider offering shipping discounts to businesses that receive goods in the off-hours. However, in order to make these discounts feasible, the shippers would have to significantly increase the number of off-hour delivery routes. It is likely that in the future, once a certain level of OHDs has been achieved, this shipper discount model could replace the need for a public sector incentive. Additionally, in the future, it may also be possible for shippers to offer an incentive to their sales team to promote OHDs. Since the shipper would have lower operating costs when operating in the off-hours, they may also be able to provide a higher commission to the sales people for all deliveries or accounts switched to the off-hours. This would have to be investigated on a case-by-case basis by each company, but it is a potential mechanism for shippers to increase the amount of OHDs.

'Icon' businesses serve as great role models. Businesses are more likely to trust other businesses before they rely on what public agencies or academia might tell them. If they see that other businesses are successfully implementing OHD without major complications they are more likely to try it. Finding well-recognized or 'icon' businesses to be the participant leaders adds significant value. These icon businesses might be a well-recognized national chain or a prominent local business. Small companies might resist participating unless and until they see an industry leader involved.

Focusing outreach resources on the receivers is most beneficial; in most cases, carriers are more likely to be in favour of switching. This reflects the fact that the receivers, as the carriers' customers, have great power to influence how and when deliveries are made. Changing receivers' behaviour leads directly to changes in carriers' operations, while policies that target carriers do not necessarily lead to broader changes in the behaviour of the receivers. However, it is important to note that working closely with the carriers can help to identify potential receivers that can be switched to off-hour routes.

Define an effective marketing strategy. The business community must be aware of a programme and understand its benefits before it will interact with the project team or participate. A brand name that is easy to remember increases the likelihood that people will recognize and remember the programme. A marketing strategy helps facilitate the work of implementation; name recognition, or any prior awareness of the programme opens doors, eases doubts and makes initial contacts easier. Having a participating signature chain or icon business further enhances people's identification with the programme.

Finding 'champions' within a business was a key lesson learned from the NYC programme. A champion is the primary person at a company with whom the implementation team could interact. In many cases, the champions were the most effective persons to carry the concept of implementing OHD forward within the company. When there was no internal champion, a switch to the off-hours was often difficult to achieve; not because the idea wasn't liked, but because of internal logistics. The dynamic employment market in metropolitan areas further complicates matters. Often, especially in the restaurant and retail industries, the team would find a champion, but that person would either be promoted within the company or change employers. This typically meant that the idea would have to be 'resold' from scratch. Therefore, once a business expresses interest in the programme, it is important to move expeditiously.

Garner high-level support. A powerful message from high-level civic leaders is often required to enact large-scale change. High-level support can yield powerful campaigns and multi-stakeholder support, including trade groups and associations, and leading private companies. Capturing the attention of many businesses of various sizes at once is much more effective than reaching out to one receiver at a time.

Determine the optimal time for them to start switching their operations to the off-hours. Businesses may want to switch to the off-hours when their business is typically slower so switching does not create problems during their peak times. For instance, many businesses are against changing their operations in the fourth quarter of the year (October through December) as this is typically the busiest period, when businesses gear up for the holiday season.

Do not mandate OHD, keep it voluntary. In some cities throughout the world, in particular China, the use of OHD has become mandatory. Yet a voluntary programme is more effective and business friendly. Only the establishments that benefit from OHD participate in it, which guarantees satisfaction, sustainability and an increase in economic welfare.

Allow flexibility into the schedule. Adhering to a schedule is important, but it is important to allow for flexibility in the case of extreme events such as weather disasters or financial impacts. If there are major events, businesses will be focused on getting back to normal, and won't be interested in diverging from their standard practices. Both the pilot and implementation phases in NYC had extreme events impact their schedules. In the pilot the Wall Street collapse impacted outreach efforts greatly, and during the implementation phase Super Storm Sandy slowed progress. Some receivers had to refurbish buildings because of the storm, and some of the participating trucking companies had significant damage to their fleets due to flooding. After the storm, the team proceeded cautiously with outreach efforts; many of the affected carriers, shippers and receivers did not fully recover for nearly five to six months after the storm.

Conclusions

The implementation of off-hour deliveries in major cities has been found to have profound benefits to all stakeholders. The NYC OHD project is widely recognized as one of the most impactful, and business-friendly, sustainability programmes. It is beneficial to the private sector and the economy as it reduces last mile delivery costs by 30 per cent to 52 per cent (COE-SUFS 2016a, COE-SUFS 2016b); it is beneficial to communities as it increases safety by reducing conflicts between pedestrian and freight vehicles, while the use of low-noise-delivery technologies and practices reduces the risk of negative noise impacts; and it is beneficial to the environment because it reduces traffic congestion and vehicle emissions by 55 per cent to 67 per cent (Holguín-Veras *et al*, 2016).

Although implementing OHD can have significant benefits it is important to carefully plan the programme, particularly the stakeholder outreach portion, which is significant and will determine the success of the programme. For best results it is suggested to build private–public–academic partnerships (PPAP). Building a diverse PPAP will help with the overall outreach as many of the leaders within the PPAP can influence other groups that they may work with. The public sector can define the vision to be accomplished and use its coordinating power to bring other public sector agencies together. It can also provide various types of funding and support to conduct the necessary research and implementation of the OHD programme. The private sector can provide critical input to define the scope of the OHD programme and identify constraints faced by participating companies. The involvement of the private sector can include individual businesses but also trade groups and business improvement districts. The private sector can help validate research findings and help recruit participants. Lastly, the private sector can engage local leaders to ensure the long-term success of the OHD programme. Academic partners can conduct research to determine the most effective ways to foster OHD. Academic partners are often looked at as an honest broker and can serve as intermediaries between the public and private sectors. The private sector is typically reluctant to share detailed data about its operations; however, the academic sector can also serve as the custodian of confidential data and analyse the impacts of OHD. The involvement of academia also provides a safe space, free of political and other economic outside pressures, for collaborative innovation to take place.

As mentioned in this chapter and based on the lessons learned from the NYC OHD programme, the following steps are recommended for successful implementation of OHD:

1. Determination of the incentive.
2. Selection of the target industry sectors.
3. Stakeholder engagement.
4. Advertising, marketing and branding.

5 Recruitment.
6 Implementation.
7 Evaluation and enhancement of the programme.

Additionally, the amount of human resources required to implement OHD should not be underestimated. A dedicated staff is necessary, one prepared to make countless phone calls and emails to potential participants, and to not be discouraged when people are too busy with day-to-day business to respond immediately. If the lessons learned and steps presented in this chapter are followed, and with ample private, public and academic support, a successful implementation of OHD can be achieved.

References

City of New York (2011) [accessed 1 May 2011] PlanNYC: A Greener, Greater New York: Update 2011 [Online] http://www.nyc.gov/html/planyc/downloads/pdf/publications/planyc_2011_planyc_full_report.pdf

COE-SUFS (2016a) [accessed 14 April 2016] Webinar #13: Updates on Off-Hour Delivery Pilots Part I: The Experiences of Sao Paulo, Brazil and Copenhagen, Denmark, Peer-to-Peer Exchange Program [Online] https://coe-sufs.org/wordpress/peer-to-peer-exchange-program/webinar13/

COE-SUFS (2016b) [accessed 15 June 2016] Webinar #14: Updates on Off-Hour Delivery Pilots Part II: The Experience of Bogota, Colombia, Peer-to-Peer Exchange Program [Online] https://coe-sufs.org/wordpress/peer-to-peer-exchange-program/webinar14/

Federal Highway Administration (2012) [accessed 1 July 2012] Federal Grant Opportunity Request for Applications (RFA): Off Hours Freight Delivery Pilot Project [Online] http://apply07.grants.gov/apply/opportunities/instructions/oppDTFH61-12-RA-00016-cfda20.200-cidDTFH61-12-RA-00016-instructions.pdf

Holguín-Veras, J, Amaya, J, Jaller, M, Wang, C, Wojtowicz, J, González-Calderón, C, Sánchez-Díaz, I, Hodge, S, Browne, M, Rhodes, E and Haake, D (2014a) *Public Sector Freight Strategies in Metropolitan Areas II: Pricing, Logistics, and Demand Management*, Transportation Research Board 93rd Annual Meeting, Washington DC, Transportation Research Board

Holguín-Veras, J, Encarnación, T, González-Calderón, CA, Winebrake, J, Kyle, S, Herazo-Padilla, N, Kalahasthi, L, Adarme, W, Cantillo, V, Yoshizaki, H and Garrido, RA (2016) Direct impacts of off-hour deliveries on urban freight emissions, *Transportation Research Part D: Transport and Environment,* **61** (A), pp 1–20 [Online] DOI: http://dx.doi.org/10.1016/j.trd.2016.10.013

Holguín-Veras, J, Hodge, S, Wojtowicz, J, Singh, C, Wang, C, Jaller, M, Aros-Vera, F, Ozbay, K, Marsico, M, Weeks, A, Replogle, M, Ukegbu, C, Ban, J, Brom, M, Campbell,

S, Sánchez-Díaz, I, González, C, Kornhauser, A, Simon, M, McSherry, S, Rahman, A, Encarnación, T, Yang, X, Ramirez-Rios, D, Kalahashti, L, Amaya-Leal, J, Silas, M, Allen, B and Cruz, B (2018) The New York City Off-Hour Deliveries Program: A business and community-friendly sustainability program, *Interfaces,* **48** (1), pp 70–86

Holguín-Veras, J, Jaller, M, Amaya, J, Wang, C, González-Calderón, C, Sánchez-Díaz, I, Browne, M, Wojtowicz, J, Hodge, S, Rhodes, E and Haake, D (2014b) *Public Sector Freight Strategies in Metropolitan Areas I: Governance, Supply Side, and Traffic Operations*, Transportation Research Board 93rd Annual Meeting, Washington DC, Transportation Research Board

Holguín-Veras, J, Ozbay, K, Kornhauser, AL, Shorris, A and Ukkusuri, S (2010) *Integrative Freight Demand Management in the New York City Metropolitan Area – Final Report*, United States Department of Transportation [Online] http://transp.rpi.edu/~usdotp/OHD_FINAL_REPORT.pdf

Holguín-Veras, J, Wang, C, Sánchez-Díaz, I, Campbell, S, Hodge, SD, Jaller, M and Wojtowicz, J (2017) Fostering unassisted off-hour deliveries: the role of incentives, *Transportation Research Part A: Policy and Practice,* **102** (August), pp 172–87 [Online] DOI: http://doi.org/10.1016/j.tra.2017.04.005

Holguín-Veras, J, Wojtowicz, JM, Wang, C, Jaller, M, Ban, XJ, Aros-Vera, F, Campbell, S, Yang, X, Sanchez-Diaz, I, Amaya, J, González-Calderón, C, Marquis, R, Hodge, SD, Maguire, T, Marsico, M, Zhang, S, Rothbard, S, Ozbay, K, Morgul, EF, Iyer, S, Xie, K and Ozguven, EE (2013) *Integrative Freight Demand Management in the New York City Metropolitan Area: Implementation Phase*, Rensselaer Polytechnic Institute, New York City Department of Transportation, Rutgers University, RITARS-11-H-RPI, United States Department of Transportation [Online] http://cite.rpi.edu/news/16-off-hour-delivery

Journal of Commerce (2009) New York delivers at night, *Journal of Commerce*, **10** (35): 4A

Journal of Commerce (2010) New York to Expand Off-peak Truck Program, *Journal of Commerce* [Online] https://www.joc.com/trucking-logistics/new-york-expand-peak-truck-program_20100702.html

Seattle Department of Transportation (2008) Best Practices in Transportation Demand Management, in *Seattle Urban Mobility Plan Briefing Book*, City of Seattle

Wall Street Journal (2010) [accessed 2 July 2010] Congestion Fight Runs Into Night [Online] http://online.wsj.com/article/SB10001424052748704334604575339292960610492.html

Note

1 The North American Industry Classification System (**NAICS**) is the standard used by Federal statistical agencies in classifying business establishments for the purpose of collecting, analysing and publishing statistical data related to the US business economy.

The procurement process 15

A key to improved urban logistics efficiency

OLOF MOEN

Introduction

In its most rudimentary form, a transport service is carried out between origin 'A' and destination 'B', and a procurement process precedes this service. It may be a basic pickup and delivery service based on a standard agreement, wherein goods are registered, retrieved and delivered in line with a specified tariff; on the other hand, it may involve a more complex distribution network where the transport service, contract period and price are determined through a procurement process that, in its simplest 'textbook' form, takes place in three steps: define the specifications, select the supplier and conclude the contract agreement (van Weele, 2010). For transport buyers in general, the strategy for competitive bidding (while working in arm's-length supplier relationships) has resulted in ongoing negotiations both before and after concluding the contract agreement (cf Rogerson *et al*, 2014). The conventional (and established) procurement process in Sweden has focused mainly on oral rounds of negotiations between parties, followed frequently by a melodramatic dissolution that determines price per delivery or price per hour or day; from there, the transport service provider is delegated logistic, operational and follow-up responsibilities (Moen, 2016a).

Regardless of the complexity of the transport service, if the parties agree on the stipulations set out in the contract, the deal is in equilibrium, from a market perspective; however, the procured service may not be transport efficient from an environmental or societal (ie sustainability) perspective. It is only at the time of procurement – in fact, at the time of signing the contract – that transport buyers can regulate and be assured of the quality of key economic ratios, as well as the responsibilities and the level of transport efficiency in agreements with transport service providers, and they directly affect both economic outcomes and environmental impact (Sandberg, 2007). Furthermore, although a great deal of the transport activity resulting from these decisions takes place outside cities and over long-distance routes, many have start and/or end points in urban areas. Therefore, procurement and purchasing decisions have a direct impact on urban freight flows.

Changes that increase transport efficiency – while also offering cost savings to transport buyers – can be achieved by embracing new procurement processes. The status quo in Sweden's transport sector, however, suggests that such change is slow to come. The results of the 'Freight Purchasing Panel' survey of 175 Swedish companies in trade and manufacturing showed that contract agreements tended to last over extended periods (Lammgård *et al*, 2013). It was found that the transport buyers had, on average, long-term transport agreements with eight transport service providers (ie more than one year each); however, the largest contract (in terms of value) accounted for 48 per cent of the total volume of freight transported. The length of the largest contract was on average two years, but in practice, contracts were renegotiated and a business deal had lasted an average of 10.3 years. This is a remarkable time frame for any business relationship, given that in one decade major changes have occurred in technological developments in particular and in the world in general. Studies have shown that within supply chains, a lack of competitive tendering is the single greatest hindrance to transport efficiency enhancements (Engström, 2004).

Trends in urban freight

Business and industry have fundamentally restructured themselves, with a geographic concentration of production nodes and supply chains; this has taken place at the cost of low fill rates and thus low transport efficiency (Transport Analysis, 2011). This has occurred, despite the fact that the transport environment has evolved to offer substantially better road standards and more transport-efficient vehicles. Transport buyers have noted these circumstances, and have started demanding changes to the planning, operations and monitoring of the transport services procured. Certain trends relevant to how the procurement process in freight transport will evolve – such as shifts in power with regard to transport services, the impacts of digitalization and the consolidation of goods – can be identified, and in terms of restructuring, changes will need to occur within these areas of the transport sector.

It is obvious that there has been a shift in power within transport supply chains, from transport service providers (intermediaries and transport companies) to transport buyers. Individual companies cannot, for obvious reasons, oversee the entire transport system; rather, those involved in transport services – such as suppliers, transport companies, intermediaries, and recipients – act in line with their own business models and strategies (cf Teece, 2010). Furthermore, there has been a notable lack of innovation and investment that would otherwise serve as a basis for new business models; from a societal perspective, there has also been a lack of development in regulations conducive to sustainable solutions in the freight transport sector (Quak, 2008; Russo and Comi, 2010). Given that freight transport is considered a mission-critical part of a company's supply chain, the attitude of transport buyers in the 21st century has changed rapidly, in line with cost increases in the transport sector; of equal importance has been society's increased focus on climate and the environment (Swahn, 2013).

The transport sector can be characterized as a loosely coupled system bearing high complexity, where stakeholders are concurrently interrelated, but autonomous, and many decisions are managed operatively (Weick, 1976; Dubois and Hulthén, 2014). A more tightly coupled system or connected system would involve changes towards the digital processing of orders, waybills and other analogous documents, and the integration of scanning and various business systems to streamline administrative procedures and provide better monitoring and control. The lack of information technology (IT) in the transport sector is notable compared to other vertical industries like financial services, where all transactions occur digitally, or retail, where barcodes follow products throughout the supply chain. The transport sector lacks the tools, procedures and business models needed to integrate digital information into operational activities (Marchet *et al*, 2009). In the aftermath of big data, one can anticipate that the transport sector will become as digitalized as these other vertical industries that have already developed automated business processes (Waller and Fawcett, 2013). In the near future, not being digital may imply exclusion from procurements and, hence, transport contracts.

There is a distinct trend towards fragmentation in the freight sector; it can be seen as stemming from sub-optimization within existing transport networks, and it generates inefficiency in the transport system. Sub-optimization is brought about through the use of just-in-time delivery and specific time windows, to increase the service level to end customers; this will, in turn, lead to lower fill rates (Taniguchi, 2003). Attentiveness to consumer demands and adaptation to specific delivery conditions in freight transport have resulted in more downtime and 'slack' in transport planning, in terms of both capacity utilization and driving routes (van Duin *et al*, 2007). Slack in planning leads inevitably to an increase in vehicle kilometres of travel (VKT) and lower fill rates, but it especially has negative environmental (and therefore societal) impacts, as it leads to increased carbon dioxide emissions (Santén, 2016). In counteracting the trend towards lower fill rates, the consolidation of goods constitutes a key concept in increasing efficiency within manufacturing or retail supply chains (Lumsden, 2007; Coyle *et al*, 2008). There is coherence between authorities and the research community such that, with more efficient planning and consolidation – both of which can increase the fill rate – a large proportion of heavy trucks could be removed from the streets (Piecyk and McKinnon, 2010; Transport Analysis, 2012; Vierth *et al*, 2012).

Business model innovation in urban freight

Business model innovation and technological development are two closely related processes that influence each other; as such, they create a highly complex context for the change process, since they involve all stakeholders within a transport supply chain. These circumstances can collectively erect a barrier to innovation processes (Williamsson and Moen, 2017). Nevertheless, the application of modern IT tools has created new possibilities to make planning more efficient, and to control networks of transported goods (eg Weigel and Cao, 1999). One prime obstacle is that the transport sector generally lacks measurability, standardization and incentives to register distance and time in transport services. An unconditional requirement for streamlining the transport sector (or any other vertical industry for that matter) is the use in all parts of the supply chain of digital information (Mason *et al*, 2003). This implies that digital planning is absolutely essential, but it nonetheless requires parallel backing from a customized procurement process. Consequently, conventional business models lack digitalization with control and transparency with respect to the transport services provided – or from the transport buyer's perspective, in procurement of transport services (Marchet *et al*, 2009; Moen, 2016a).

While both of the case studies presented in this chapter involve the integration of IT tools into the procurement process of new business models, no development has taken place from a technical viewpoint. The tool used is the off-the-shelf software package WinRoute, which leverages vehicle routing problem (VRP) algorithms (WinRoute, 2012). In this chapter, commercial software packages are discussed in terms of 'route optimization', where the aim is to optimize driving routes and thereby increase transport efficiency by minimizing VKT (ie 'deadhead driving', in route optimization terminology). Thus, technology is not the primary threshold, since the new business models presented are based on the functionality of standardized route optimization software – something that is already well developed – and there are many performance-wise equivalent products on the market (Hall, 2006). There is a bias in development circles, where mathematical modelling and algorithm development have tended to dominate the operational research (OR) agenda and deal with vehicle routing; this focus has resulted in the publication of thousands of scientific papers (Laporte, 2009). With few exceptions, applied studies and implementation methods based on best practices in transport modelling (OR) remain conspicuously absent (cf Hesse and Rodrigue, 2004).

Laporte (2009: 408) points out that the 'VRP can be simply defined as the problem of designing least-cost delivery routes from a depot to a set of geographically scattered customers, subject to side constraints'. VRP algorithms can be described in terms of the complexity of the scheduling process, and they are available in a multitude of variations; generally speaking, they are designed as extensions of the core VRP (Golden *et al*, 2010). They involve many constraints and parameters, from rudimentary solutions with regard to vehicle capacity and time windows, to more advanced VRPs with multiple depots, multiple vehicle uses, fleet composition, pickups and deliveries in the same route, dynamic planning, customer constraints and road network regulations, inter alia (Nanda Kumar and Panneerselvam, 2012). Nevertheless, algorithms alone cannot determine the outcome of operational work. On the contrary, it is the dispatcher interacting with the computer's geographical interface and using attribute data from register files who, in practice, executes transport modelling (Kant *et al*, 2008).

However, in Sweden, the power of route optimization software has been underestimated; in particular, the transport industry there has had doubts, as evidenced in a negative attitude towards applicability and potential gains (Arvidsson *et al*, 2013). As a point of reference, there are significantly lower rates of route optimization application in Sweden than in, for example, the United States or the BeNeLux countries, where usage is more widespread among logistics and transport service providers. The main obstacle is that route optimization depends directly on organizational development and changes in business models, along with demands for behavioural changes among stakeholders, to achieve the information transparency that digital planning demands (cf Brynjolfsson and McAffe, 2012). In general, software tools used in urban freight tend to lack R&D that examines the adaptation and behavioural changes required by organizations (cf Laporte, 2009; Browne and Goodchild, 2013). The following two case studies clearly show that it was not technology that constituted the major obstacle: the obstacle was the initial hesitation to create a centralized planning function with insight and transparency in information exchange, with both internal and external partners (cf Kohn and Huge-Brodin, 2008; Jonsson *et al*, 2013).

Methodology: action research as agent of change

Building on the discussion above, the rest of this chapter concentrates on two case studies, both of which hinge on practice and were developed through action research. In action research, the researcher–innovator participates actively in interpreting, analysing and changing the procurement process, in tandem with the stakeholders (cf Somekh, 2006). Action research is a powerful method that is particularly conducive to organizational change, based as it is on an inductive approach that bears methodological similarities to practical philosophy (Carr, 2006). The researcher–innovator's prior knowledge governs both preparation and execution through consecutive steps of plan, action, observation and reflection, in what is frequently portrayed as an intellective loop; this is followed by a new loop with a new plan that is based on the previous loop's action, observation and reflection.

The first case study represents a modification of the urban consolidation centres (UCC) business model used in city logistics (Browne *et al*, 2005). The (so-called) municipal 'co-distribution of goods', in line with the *Swedish Public Procurement Act* is based on route optimization, which works as a tool in both the procurement and operational phases.

In the second case study, the same principle is developed for commercial freight transport. In the five-step model, cost is determined by a contract agreement based on route optimization and open book accounting (OBA). Transport buyers have used new business models (the case studies) in the procurement process, and all are based on the above-mentioned trends of digitalization, consolidation and a shift in power within the transport supply chain. Although these examples come from Sweden, both business models are generic and can be adapted to EU regulations, or by private companies in Western economies.

Case study 1: municipal co-distribution of goods

In the case of Swedish UCC, the initial focus is on overcoming traffic congestion and accessibility problems in the central areas of larger cities (Swedish Road Administration, 2009). These problems relate to city logistics, which in turn relate to optimizing the logistics and transport activities of private companies in urban areas (Taniguchi et al, 2001). However, in Sweden – where there is a long tradition of social welfare programmes – the concept has assumed an extra dimension and been used by local authorities to distribute publicly owned goods, as part of a business model involving the co-distribution of goods. Sweden's conventional business model offers free delivery, with transport starting with the supplier (sender) and ending at a municipal unit (recipient); in this model, transport is included as a hidden surcharge in the price of the goods. To create change, the transport service and the goods will need to be procured separately, with goods from external suppliers being delivered to a UCC for co-distribution to schools, kindergartens, nursing homes and hospitals. The largest share of transport costs relates to food supplies, which accounts for approximately 1 billion euros per year – a value equivalent to roughly 5.5 per cent of all food sales in Sweden (Swedish Competition Authority, 2011: 63).

The major change will be the transfer of legal responsibility (and hence power within the transport supply chain) from suppliers to the municipality. In general, freight transport within municipal administration has been a subordinated area with a low level of knowledge, in terms of both managing its own (internal) practices of public authority and traffic planning (Lindholm, 2012) and specific knowledge in (external) procurement issues (Braic *et al*, 2012). The main driver for change has been reducing fossil-fuel emissions by reducing the number of deliveries by 70–80 per cent, depending on the number of suppliers. On average, municipalities have five food suppliers and five suppliers of other goods, which can be reduced to two weekly deliveries (Levin *et al*, 2016). Additionally, there have been strong incentives to allow for purchases of locally produced food; this has been next to impossible under the *Swedish Public Procurement Act,* where transport is the major barrier to local suppliers' participation in the municipal procurement process (Moen, 2017).

The initial innovation of the co-distribution of goods dates back to 1999, with a cluster collaboration among three municipalities in the province of Dalarna; out of this came what is called the Borlänge model (Backman *et al*, 2001). The Borlänge cluster applied the transport industry's conventional business model, meaning that the contracted transport service provider is responsible for shipments from suppliers to its own distribution centre, for marshalling and loading goods, and for transport planning with distribution to municipal units. The business model developed administratively in 2010, when the municipality of Växjö integrated co-distribution and e-commerce (Braic *et al*, 2012). This led to co-distribution being conceptually integrated into the official 'single face to industry' (SFTI) standard for e-commerce, as commissioned by government agencies and coordinated by the Swedish Association of Local Authorities and Regions (SFTI, 2011). The business model has evolved further, into the Ystad–Österlen model of 2013, where the municipality as transport buyer takes over from the transport service provider both planning and follow-up, thus making for a thoroughly disruptive innovation (Moen, 2013).

The Ystad-Österlen procurement model

The *Swedish Public Procurement Act* wholly controls the municipal tendering process, and in the case of the Ystad–Österlen model, it fundamentally changed how transport service providers quote their price in a tender: unlike the conventional business model of quoting price per delivery or per hour or day, the new model quoted price based on VKT and working hours. Figure 15.1 shows the digital pricing model used to submit a tender as part

Figure 15.1 The Ystad–Österlen model; the municipality digital pricing model for the tender of the municipal co-distribution of goods, based on the framework of the *Swedish Public Procurement Act*

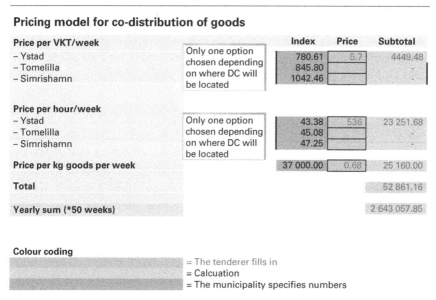

Pricing model for co-distribution of goods

		Index	Price	Subtotal
Price per VKT/week	Only one option chosen depending on where DC will be located			
- Ystad		780.61	5.7	4449.48
- Tomelilla		845.80		-
- Simrishamn		1042.46		-
Price per hour/week	Only one option chosen depending on where DC will be located			
- Ystad		43.38	536	23 251.68
- Tomelilla		45.08		-
- Simrishamn		47.25		-
Price per kg goods per week		37 000.00	0.68	25 160.00
Total				52 861.16
Yearly sum (*50 weeks)				2 643 057.85

Colour coding

= The tenderer fills in
= Calcuation
= The municipality specifies numbers

SOURCE Moen, 2014, p 492

of the procurement process in the new business model. This model contains a number of steps that are discussed below.

Define the specifications

Simulations with route optimization define the transport requirements for the consolidation of goods. Preparation for simulations is of utmost importance, and is based on surveys of the delivery addresses, stop times and transport volumes of existing transport services. The simulated results are put into what is called a resource-optimized tender document, where tenderers have access to measurable figures that represent the resource requirements (ie the number of vehicles, VKT, driving time and sequenced driving routes).

Select the supplier

In the digital pricing model in Figure 15.1, one enters the tenderer's price per kilometre, cost per hour worked and price per kilogram of transported goods. The lowest bid to meet the specified quality requirements wins the contract, in accordance with the *Swedish Public Procurement Act.* Since the municipality's priority is reducing environmental impact, the pricing model gives three simulated alternatives for a UCC localization in each municipality's central city. Offered prices are multiplied by simulated entry values for each UCC location and then scaled up to an annual cost, so that the tenders are directly comparable. Ystad received the lowest values (in terms of environmental rebate) by virtue of the population's 'centre of gravity', as it contains approximately one-half of the three municipalities' inhabitants, and thus also one-half of all goods delivered to the municipal units. On the other hand, Simrishamn was penalized in environmental terms, since the UCC is 40 kilometres from the 'centre of gravity' and hence has a significantly longer feeder distance to delivery addresses.

First, let us examine the monetary terms used to calculate the environmental rebate. The tender of a UCC located in Ystad is based on the per-kilometre price of 5.70 Swedish crowns (SEK), an hourly rate of 536.00 SEK and a per-kilogram price of 0.68 SEK for goods handled in the UCC. This derives the quoted tender price of approximately 2.6 million SEK per year. In comparison, the environmental rebate for Ystad is calculated based on 780.61 kilometres × 5.70 SEK per kilometre = 4,449 SEK, implies that a tenderer in Tomelilla would have to put in an offer of 5:26 SEK per kilometre (4,449 SEK / 845.80 kilometres) or 8 per cent in environmental rebate; alternatively, to beat the Ystad bid, a per-kilometre price of 4:27 SEK

(4,449 SEK / 1,042.46 kilometres) or 25 per cent in environmental rebate, would be required of a UCC in Simrishamn, assuming that the time cost and the per-kilogram price were kept constant.

Contract agreement

Payment will be made by way of 'reverse billing', where the transport service provider gets paid for time and distance (registered in real time) for each performed driving route. Follow-up takes place as part of the contract, and it requires the transport company (as the subcontractor) to install a mobile vehicle-monitoring device that provides full information exchange transparency. Reports compare the results to the sequenced planning, thus determining whether deviations occurred along the route. In this way, the reports serve as a basis for reverse billing, in that vehicle monitoring specifies to the transport buyer what should be invoiced, and deviations are checked before payment is made.

It should be noted that the environmental rebate is based on route optimization, which compares three transport plans as tender specifications; there, the municipalities' environmental goals override to some extent the supranational EU legal principles of equal treatment, non-discrimination and transparency. In this way, the municipality's environmental policy reflects goals and measurable requirements, through the resource-optimized procurement procedure. The co-distribution of goods implemented by the municipalities of Ystad, Simrishamn and Tomelilla reduced deliveries to recipients, from 26,245 to 6,300, ie a 76 per cent reduction (Moen, 2013). These figures are noteworthy in relation to the results achieved in the field of city logistics, given that the implementation efforts were self-funded and have been sustainable over time (Quak and DeKoster, 2009).

Implementation in Sweden

What is noteworthy is that 41 of Sweden's 290 municipalities (14 per cent) had implemented the co-distribution of goods business model by 2017, with 22 of these implementations taking place between 2015 and 2017. It is expected that the number of municipalities will increase and exceed 100 in the early 2020s, and this implies that innovation is close to reaching a breakthrough and achieving a paradigm shift within Swedish municipal administration. Furthermore, another five municipalities in 2018 will implement the radical innovation of the Ystad–Österlen model, in which logistics will be taken over by the municipality; additionally, four municipalities will implement 'from scratch' and one will upgrade its existing co-distribution to a new procurement process. This means that there will be eight implementations, and this gives implicit legitimacy to the Ystad–Österlen model as a disruptive innovation that challenges the conventional transport industry's business model.

The Ystad–Österlen model received numerous awards for innovation and creativity in the transport sector. The municipalities involved won the 'Logistics Municipality of the Year' in 2014, were nominated in 2014 for the Swedish Post's (PostNord) 'Great Logistics Prize', and together with the transport service provider won in 2015 the Swedish Transport Administration's prestigious 'This Year's Best Lift' prize; as well as international attention, the EU project Intereg South Baltic awarded Ystad municipality the 'Low carbon logistics award 2018', with the statement that the municipal institution was a pioneer in city logistics. This was done in competition with the private sector, with the same ambitious innovations in freight transport. Furthermore, the Swedish government through the Swedish Energy Agency funds a national centre for the development and deployment of the business model of municipal co-distribution of goods. For municipalities, the co-distribution of goods is mainly a procurement issue, but the result will ultimately benefit the environment and increase transport efficiency. However, the new business model is not a win–win solution; it is a radical innovation that changes the current game plan and significantly increases transport efficiency.

Case study 2: the five-step model

Starting with the co-distribution of goods as the conceptual framework, the same methodology is used in the five-step model to accommodate transport buyers in the private sector (Moen, 2016b). The five-step model was developed through action research and tested empirically in the case study of a transport service using static driving routes.

The five-step procurement model

What primarily differentiates the five-step model from the transport industry's conventional business model is its unconditional demand for transparency in the procurement process. The difference is most noticeably seen in the transparent resource-optimized tender document, where both parties have access to measurable figures that represent the resource requirement of the procurement (ie the number of vehicles, VKT, driving time and sequenced driving routes), and where both parties have facts and a proposed solution (transport planning) as a basis for negotiations. Another prominent change is the outcome, where the five-step model increases transport

Figure 15.2 Development of price for transport services over time in the conventional transport procurement process. Payment is per delivery or per hour or day; the five-step model, in comparison, features payment per kilometre driven and hours worked

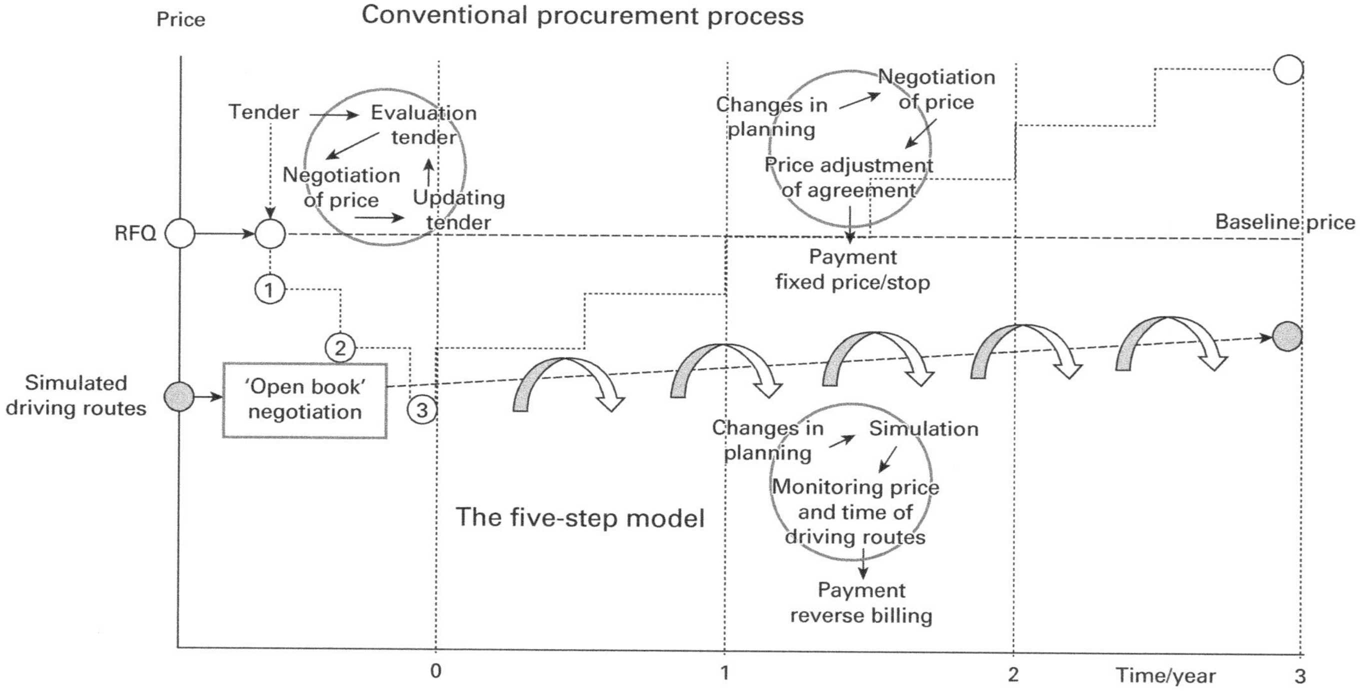

SOURCE Moen, 2016a, p 177

efficiency and concurrently lowers costs. Figure 15.2 summarizes the two business models and differences are discussed below.

In the conventional procurement process (upper-left circle), the starting point is a request for quotation (RFQ) with statistical information, including delivery addresses and customer data. The transport service provider is expected to establish transport planning with driving routes, and this becomes the basis for a bid with a fixed price per delivery address or a fixed price per hour or day. In the second step, the transport buyer starts the selection process that takes place in rounds, where received bids are evaluated and the number of potential suppliers reduced. It is noteworthy that the process is based on tenderers planning the driving routes, and the transport buyer pushes the price in negotiations until one company has been selected. Thereafter, the transport buyer and the selected supplier negotiate the details of the contract agreement – such as driving routes and responsibilities – but ultimately it is a matter of price per delivery or fixed price per hour or day. During the operational phase, unforeseen changes occur in driving routes not included in the procurement documentation (ie the RFQ); these increase the price in a stepwise fashion along the curve (upper graph) and with ongoing negotiations (upper-right circle) throughout the whole contract period.

The five-step model also starts with specifications, a selection process and a contract agreement, but differs in the preparation phase, by virtue of the transparent resource-optimized tender document; this document is based on simulated driving routes, with considerably higher demands for expertise on the transport buyer's side. That a procurement model features route optimization and the ambitious use of digital information at all stages of the transport supply chain implies that at least some of the dispatching and operational tasks will be automated (cf Hassall *et al*, 2012). The procurement process determines price per kilometre and hours worked, in the same way the Ystad–Österlen model does; in comparison, the driving routes change only slightly, since the algorithms in a new simulation will minimize VKT and make the optimal selection based on new conditions. This process is represented by arrows in the lower graph, in which the price moves around an average value during transparent and digital replanning.

The digital format constitutes the single largest divergence in operations, compared with the manual replanning in the transport industry's conventional business model. Replanning leads to a renegotiation with adjusted price levels for the transport service (the climbing steps in the upper graph), in which the transport service provider is in possession of the whole of the

Figure 15.3 Flowchart of the conceptual framework of the five-step model

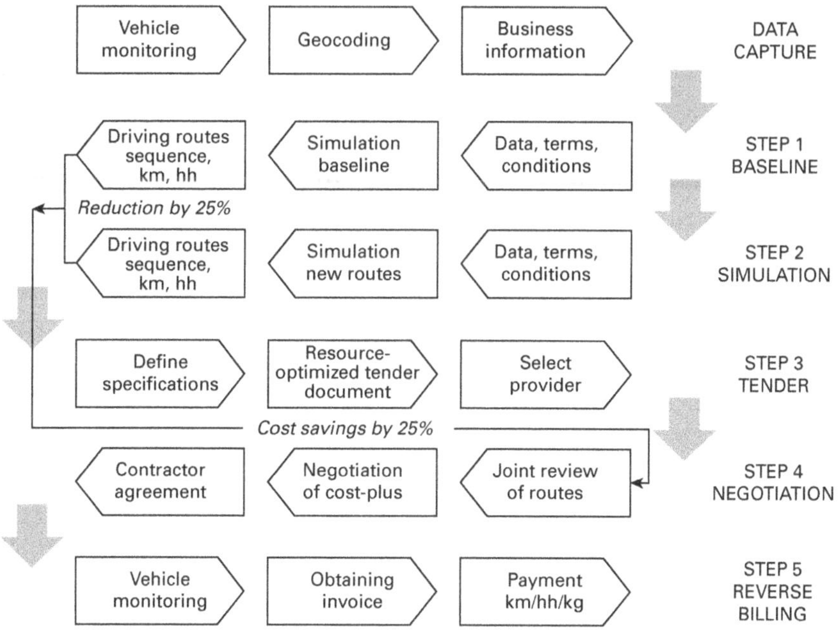

SOURCE Moen, 2016b, p 871

transport planning. Note that the transport buyer has no insights that reveal those changes that, during the contract period, serve as the basis for renegotiation. In the five-step model, however, the changes take place in two stages, through an automated process (the lower circle). First, replanning is carried out, either manually by making minor changes to individual driving routes, or when major changes occur through a completely new simulation with route optimization. In the second step, distance and time are recorded, where the payment is based on fixed tariffs for kilometres and hours based on the transport service provider's quoted price in the tender (ie the reverse billing concept). The five steps of the procurement process are shown as a flowchart (Figure 15.3).

Step 1 – Baseline

Step 1 is based on comprehensive data captured during the preparatory phase to simulate the baseline (situation analysis) of the current transport network that will be procured. A baseline is needed to measure quality aspects (eg delivery precision) and efficiency gains (eg VKT) in a given transport service.

This is done to obtain accurate results in kilometres and working hours and the sequences in each route, in order to transform the cost structure from price per stop, hour or day (the conventional business model) to payment per kilometre driven and hours worked for a defined invoice period.

Step 2 – Simulation

Step 2 involves the simulation of new driving routes in the same way as used to reconstruct the baseline in step 1, while using the same road network, geocoded delivery addresses, stop times and volumes of goods transported. What the computer simulations provide are new partitions (districting) of driving routes with an optimized sequence. The software algorithms strive to minimize VKT (ie deadhead driving) based on the constraints applied, which in route optimization terminology are referred to as 'business rules'.

Step 3 – Tender

Step 3 is similar to the conventional procurement process but features the unconditional demands of digital input from step 2, which define the specifications of the assignment. The actual procurement process then begins, based on a resource-optimized tender document; it is uniformly executed through the procedure used in the municipal co-distribution of goods, in which bids are placed on sequenced routes with specified kilometres and working hours per route (Moen, 2014).

Step 4 – Negotiation

Step 4 takes place at the negotiating table, with open book pricing. Open book pricing, which is also known as open book accounting (OBA), refers to the sharing of facts and cost information with the provider within a contractor–clientrelationship, depending on the purchasing strategy chosen (Agndal and Nilsson, 2010). Unlike a contract negotiation in the conventional business model – which is done through price indicators between parties, but at arm's length – here, the contract is negotiated through collaboration among stakeholders. Negotiation with transparency is the most radical element of the new transport services purchasing model, since it is not customary in the transport sector; as such, it poses a dilemma to transport buyers in terms of enforcement and serves as a general barrier of sorts (Christensen, 1997). R&D has shown that trust is a prerequisite for a long-term OBA perspective, where commitment and cooperation provide the basis for trust building among the negotiating parties (cf Sadeghi and Jokar, 2014).

Step 5 – Reverse billing

Step 5 involves follow-up and control while undertaking quality assurance of the transport service provider's performance; additionally, as a basis for the reverse billing payment method, vehicle monitoring is undertaken in the same manner as in case study 1 (ie the Ystad–Österlen model).

The model application

The case study was executed in two parts. First, a baseline was created for all driving routes; the same parameters were used in a simulation with route optimization, thus providing a basis of comparison between the two business models. The transport network started from the transport buyer's warehouse

Table 15.1 Summary of the baseline (situation analysis) and simulations featuring route optimization, in the five-step model case study

	Baseline	**Optimization 1**	**Optimization 2**
Description	Routes of baseline, the initial planning	Routes based on baseline, optimized sequence	Terms and conditions of baseline, new routes
(%) compared to	–	(Baseline)	(Baseline)
Deliveries	324	324	324
Routes	18	18 (*0%*)	13 (*–28%*)
Tours	28	28 (*0%*)	17 (*–39%*)
Total VKT	2 135 km	1 836 km (*–14%*)	1 251 km (*–41%*)
Total driving time	61 hh 53 min	57 hh 13 min (*–8%*)	47 hh 5 min (*–24%*)
Total working hours	126 hh 23 min	121 hh 42 min (*–4%*)	105 hh 4 min (*–17%*)
Average fill rate	53%	53%	87% (*+34%*)
Deliveries per route	18.00	18.00 (*0%*)	24.92 (*+38%*)
VKT per route	118.61 km	102.00 km	96.23 km
Driving time per route	3 hh 26 min	3 hh 11 min	3 hh 37 min
Working hours per route	7 hh 1 min	6 hh 46 min	8 hh 5 min

SOURCE Moen, 2016b, p 867

and featured distribution to 324 stores in Sweden's capital, the greater Stockholm area. The established baseline was based on existing transport planning. The optimization of the current situation was also done in two steps – namely: 1) optimization of the sequence of each driving route or tour (where there may be two tours in one driving route); and 2) optimization where the algorithms freely select vehicles and sequences in completely new driving routes or tours, with the aim of minimizing VKT.

The case study results are shown in Table 15.1. The transport planning at baseline required 18 vehicles, with a total driving distance of 2,135 kilometres per day and an average per-vehicle working time of 7 hours and 1 minute, including a one-hour break. The results show one hour of slack in an eight-hour workday featuring a time window of 9 am to 5 pm. Note that order collection and packaging takes place until 11 am, and 10 of 18 vehicles will return for a second tour of their driving route. By optimizing the sequence in existing driving routes in Optimization 1, VKT decreases from 2,135 to 1,836 kilometres (14 per cent). Optimization 2 involves total replanning, with the same input, business rules (eg constraints) and recorded stop times as the baseline; the simulation showed that VKT decreased by a total of 41 per cent, from 2,135 kilometres to 1,251 kilometres. What has happened is that the same distribution work was done with fewer vehicles (ie 13 instead of 18), with the VKT decreasing and the fill rate increasing. The number of deliveries per vehicle increased by 7, from 18 to almost 25 (ie 24.92) per route (38 per cent). This is the key to realizing cost and environmental savings.

In the context of the five-step model, OBA implies that the buyer and provider of transport services together define compensation for actual costs incurred and negotiate the margin that can be added to expenditures, in what is also referred to as a cost-plus contract. The case study indicates a remarkable 41 per cent difference between the output of steps 1 and 2. Cost savings are distributed according to OBA, which is performed transparently in step 4 in negotiation rounds between the transport buyer and the transport service provider; there, the contractor agreement determines how the cost reduction will be allocated among stakeholders. However, the margin of 41 per cent should not go solely to the transport buyer or the intermediary company; rather, compensation should also be allocated to subcontractors (transport companies), who constitute the exposed part in the freight transport sector in Sweden and lack the opportunity to take action in the process.

Overall, the innovation is justified by improving the quality of transport services and cutting the transport buyer's cost base; this serves as an incentive in pushing for change towards the new business model. The productivity (ie fill rate) per vehicle increases from 53 to 87 per cent with route optimization; as a point of reference, the average fill rate in Sweden rarely exceeds 50 per cent (Transport Analysis, 2011). There are no official statistics on the load factor in Sweden, but individual studies show that the fill rate is quite lower and, on average, is frequently below 30 per cent (Gebresenbet *et al*, 2011).

In summary, the five-step model does not represent a win–win situation for all stakeholders. There will be an elimination of vehicles; however, the vehicles that remain will become more profitable, with a higher transport workload per route. Moreover, Hassall and Walsh (2014) note that in the e-freight market in Australia, the intermediary company will receive a lower percentage of customer revenue. The intermediary will inevitably cannibalize its own sales, since the freight-forwarding fee represents a percentage of work performed, VKT and the number of vehicles. How the procurement process is carried out and how cost savings will be shared among transport buyers, intermediaries and subcontractors are precisely the elements for which the five-step model provides a framework. What becomes mission critical is not the route optimization; indeed, that is the easy part. It is the legal document for tender, the contract agreement and the project plan for implementation that transport buyers have used in practice when the five-step model is implemented.

Conclusions

The approach taken in both case studies stands in sharp contrast to the conventional business model of the Swedish transport industry, where in general, the intermediary company is solely responsible for logistics and transport planning, and the transport buyer lacks transparency and cannot monitor vehicle kilometres of travel (VKT) or hours worked. On the contrary, in the new business models presented are intermediaries and commissioned transport companies paid only for hours worked and VKT driven. Changes will of course have consequences for stakeholders – that is to say, both transport buyers and transport service providers – where there is a built-in resistance from primarily intermediary companies, which account for 75–80 per cent of the transport services provided in Sweden (Swedish Association of Road Transport Companies, 2013). These stakeholders live in, on, and according to the conventional business model, would inevitably cannibalize on their own turnover and profit.

On the contrary, most R&D in the freight transport sector has been centred on a win–win perspective, with a focus on fuels and efficient engines. The relationship is clearly illustrated by an example within the framework of the 'Klimatneutrala Godstransporter på Väg' (Climate-Neutral Freight Transportation) or KNEG, an association whose membership boasts large companies (Volvo, Scania, Stora Enso, PostNord, DB Schenker and five others), research organizations (Chalmers University of Technology and University of Gothenburg) and public authorities (the Swedish Transport Administration). The members of the KNEG network have joined forces to work towards a shared goal – namely, reducing the climate impact of Sweden's freight transport sector (Hedenus, 2008). In looking at the cumulative transport efficiency made possible by the various actions undertaken by KNEG companies in 2015, one sees that while greener (renewable) fuels and more energy-efficient vehicles accounted for 90.5 and 9.2 per cent of reduced emissions, respectively, behavioural changes (eg more efficient transport systems and new business models) accounted for a mere 0.3 per cent (Ahlbäck and Johansson, 2016).

The procurement processes in the business models (ie case studies) are based on the above-mentioned trends regarding digitalization, consolidation and shifts in power within the transport supply chain. The trigger in these changes has been IT's rapidly increasing computational power, which has improved opportunities for real-world modelling and statistical analysis, highlighted in this chapter, through the use of a commercial software for route optimization based on vehicle routing problem (VRP) algorithms. However, the foci must be on business models and external regulations, rather than stakeholders acting in their own interests and displaying resistance to change. VRP algorithms provide a digital tool that enables change, but no gains can be made without making the same changes in organizational structure (Brynjolfsson and McAffe, 2012).

Furthermore, business model innovation as shown in the case studies will not lead to a win–win situation for all stakeholders, as changes are made to the game plan, relative to the existing business model. Instead, the innovation will 'rock the boat' and in itself become a barrier to change process – and hence, to transport efficiency (Williamsson and Moen, 2017). There has, nonetheless, been a major obstacle to these changes – namely, a negligible amount of research and development (R&D) that, at the system level and when enacted, would otherwise lead to innovation by promoting behavioural changes (Quak *et al*, 2014). This dearth of R&D has been mainly due to a lack of appropriate and challenging questioning, and thus a lack of economic resilience in pushing new business models to 'stand on their own feet'. In the urban logistics context the importance of the procurement process merits much greater attention.

References

Agndal, H and Nilsson, U (2010) Different open book accounting practices for different purchasing strategies, *Management Accounting Research,* **21** (3), pp 147–66

Ahlbäck, A and Johansson, H (2016) KNEG tar sikte på 2030. KNEG Resultatrapport 2016 *(KNEG aims for 2030. KNEG Result Report 2016),* KNEG, Chalmers University of Technology, Swedish Transport Administration

Arvidsson, N, Woxenius, J and Lammgård, C (2013) Review of road hauliers. Measures for increasing transport efficiency and sustainability in urban freight distribution, *Transport Reviews,* **33** (1), pp 107–27

Backman, H, Blinge, M, Hadenius, A and Wettervik, H (2001) Miljöeffekter av samordnad varudistribution i Borlänge, Gagnef och Säter *(Environmental effects of co-distribution of goods in Borlänge, Gagnef and Säter),* Swedish Road Administration Publication 2001:12, Borlänge

Braic, D, Josephson, M, Stavenow, C and Wenström, E (2012) Strategisk offentlig upphandling *(Strategic public procurement),* Jure Förlag, Stockholm

Browne, M, Sweet, M, Woodburn, A and Allen, J. (2005) Urban freight consolidation centres – Final report, University of Westminster, Transport studies group, London

Browne, M and Goodchild, A (2013) Modeling approaches to address urban freight's challenges. A comparison of the US and Europe, in *City Logistics Research. A Transatlantic Perspective*, pp 5–7, Transportation Research Board, Proceedings **50**, Washington DC

Brynjolfsson, E and McAffe, A (2012) *Race Against the Machine. How the digital revolution is accelerating innovation, driving productivity, and irreversibly transforming employment and the economy*, MIT Sloan Management, Cambridge

Carr, W (2006) Philosophy, methodology and action research, *Journal of Philosophy of Education,* **40** (4), pp 421–35

Christensen, C (1997) *The Innovator's Dilemma: When new technologies cause great firms to fail*, Harvard Business Review Press, Cambridge

Coyle, JJ, Langley Jr, CJ, Novack, RA, Gibson, BJ and Bardi, EJ (2008) *Supply Chain Management: A logistics perspective*, 8th edn, Cengage Learning, South-Western

Dubois, A and Hulthén, K (2014) Transport as a loosely coupled system: Implications for research and practice. National Conference in Transport Research, 21–22 October 2014, Linköping University, Campus Norrköping

Engström, R (2004) Competition in the Freight Transport Sector – a Channel Perspective, Dissertation, Doktorsavhandling, The Department of Business

Administration, The School of Business, Economics and Law, University of Gothenburg, Intellecta Docusys

Gebresenbet, G, Nordmark, I, Bosona, T and Ljungberg, D (2011) Potential for optimised food deliveries in and around Uppsala city, Sweden, *Journal of Transport Geography,* **19**, pp 1456–64

Golden, B, Raghaven, S and Wasil, E (2010) *The Vehicle Routing Problem: Latest advances and new challenges*, Springer-Verlag, New York

Hall, R (2006) On the road to integration, *OR/MS Today,* **33** (3), pp 50–57

Hassall, K, Welsh, K and Qi, M (2012) The beginnings of national e-freight portals in Australia, Asia and Europe, *International Journal of E-Business Management,* **5** (1) pp 33–47

Hassall, K and Welsh, K (2014) *Can E-freight Marketplaces Be Successful? Fifteen years of experience from Australia*, Industrial-Logistics Institute, Melbourne

Hedenus, F (2008) *On the Road to Climate Neutral Freight Transportation – a scientific feasibility study*, Swedish Road Administration Publication 2008:92, Borlänge

Hesse, M and Rodrigue, J-P (2004) The transport geography of logistics and freight distribution, *Journal of Transport Geography,* **12**, pp 171–84

Jonsson, P, Rudberg, M and Holmberg, S (2013) Centralized supply chain planning at IKEA, *Supply Chain Management: An International Journal,* **18** (3), pp 337–50

Kant, G, Jacks, M and Aantjes, C (2008) Coca-Cola Enterprises optimizes vehicle routes for efficient product delivery, *Interfaces,* **38** (1), pp 40–50

Kohn, C and Huge-Brodin, M (2008) Centralised distribution systems and the environment: how increased transport work can decrease the environmental impact of logistics, *International Journal of Logistics Research and Applications,* **11** (3), pp 229–45

Lammgård, C, Andersson, D and Sthyre, L (2013) Purchasing of transport services – A survey among major Swedish shippers, NOFOMA Conference, Paper 52001, 3–5 May, Gothenburg

Laporte, G (2009) Fifty years of vehicle routing, *Transportation Science,* **43** (4), pp 408–16

Levin, E, Alsén, Y, Moen, O and Savola, H (2016) Samordnad varudistribution i skånska kommuner. Nulägesanalys och vägen framåt *(Co-distribution of goods in municipalities of Skåne. Analysis of the current situation and the way forward),* Rapport County Administrative Board of Skåne Publication 2016:28, Malmö

Lindholm, M (2012) How local authority decision makers address freight transport in the urban areas, *Procedia – Social and Behavioral Sciences,* Elsevier Ltd, London, **39**, pp 134–45

Lumsden, K (2007) *Fundamentals of Logistics*, Division of Logistics and Transportation, Department of Technology Management and Economics, Chalmers University of Technology, Gothenburg

Marchet, G, Perego, A and Perotti, S (2009) An exploratory study of ICT adoption in the Italian freight transportation industry, *International Journal of Physical Distribution & Logistics Management,* **39** (9), pp 785–812

Mason, SJ, Ribera, PM, Farris, JA and Kirk, RG (2003) Integrating the warehousing and transportation functions of the supply chain, *Transportation Research Part E,* **39**, pp 141–59

Moen, O (2013) Samordnad varudistribution 2.0. Logistik i kommunens varuförsörjnings kedja *(Co-distribution of goods. Logistics in the municipal supply chain),* Studentlitteratur, Lund

Moen, O (2014) Co-distribution of municipal goods in Sweden – procurement from a new standpoint, *Procedia – Social and Behavioral Sciences,* **125**, pp 484–95

Moen, O (2016a) Femstegsmodellen – Affärsmodell med ruttoptimering för ökad transporteffektivitet vid urbana godstransporter *(The five-step model – business model with route optimization to increase transport efficiency in urban distribution of goods),* Swedish Transport Administration Publication 2016:100

Moen, O (2016b) The five-step model – procurement to increase transport efficiency for an urban distribution of goods, *Transportation Research Procedia*, **12**, pp 861–73

Moen, O (2017) Municipal co-distribution of goods. Business models, stakeholders and driving forces for change, in Proceedings of the 10th International Conference on City Logistics, June 2017, pp 245–60, Phuket, Thailand

Nanda Kumar, S and Panneerselvam, R (2012) A survey on the vehicle routing problem and its variants, *Intelligent Information Management,* **4**, pp 66–74

Piecyk, MI and McKinnon, AC (2010) Forecasting the carbon footprint of road freight transport in 2020, *International Journal of Production Economics,* **128** (1), pp 31–42

Quak, HJ (2008) Sustainability of Urban Freight Transport – Retail Distribution and Local Regulations in Cities, ERIM, Management 124, TRAIL Thesis Series T2008/5, Rotterdam

Quak, HJ and DeKoster, MBM (2009) Delivering goods in urban areas: how to deal with urban policy restrictions and the environment, *Transportation Science,* **43** (2), pp 211–27

Quak, HJ, Balm, S and Posthumus, B (2014) Evaluation of city logistics solutions with business model analysis, *Procedia – Social and Behavioral Sciences,* Elsevier, London, **125**, pp 111–124

Rogerson, S, Andersson, D and Johansson, MI (2014) Influence of context on the purchasing process for freight transport services, *International Journal of Logistics: Research and Applications*, **17** (3), pp 232–48

Russo, F and Comi, A (2010) A modelling system to simulate goods movements at an urban scale, *Transportation,* **37**, pp 987–1009

Sadeghi, L and Jokar, I (2014) Identification and classification of open book accounting dimensions, *Management Science Letters,* **4**, pp 931–36
Sandberg, E (2007) Logistics collaboration in supply chains: practice vs theory, *The International Journal of Logistics Management*, **18** (2), pp 274–93
Santén, V (2016) Towards environmentally sustainable freight transport. Shippers' logistics actions to improve load factor performance, Dissertation. Department of Technology Management and Economics, Chalmers University of Technology, Gothenburg
SFTI (2011) Handledning för samordnad varudistribution. Tillägg till SFTI/ ESAP 6, Version 1.1 *(Tutorial for co-distribution of goods. Supplement to SFTI / ESAP 6, Version 1.1),* Swedish Association of Local Authorities and Regions, 2011-07-06, Stockholm
Somekh, B (2006) *Action Research: A methodology for change and development*, Open University Press, Maidenhead
Swahn, M (2013) Företagens logistikanalyser – Åtgärder för bättre resurseffektivitet och mindre miljöpåverkan (*Analysis of corporate logistics – Measures to improve resource efficiency and reduce environmental impact*), Swedish Transport Administration Publication 2013:095, Borlänge
Swedish Association of Road Transport Companies (2013) Fakta om åkerinäringen *(Facts about the haulage industry),* Swedish Association of Road Transport Companies Report, Stockholm
Swedish Competition Authority (2011) Mat och marknad – offentlig upphandling (*Food and market – public procurement*), Swedish Competition Authority Publication 2011:4, Stockholm
Swedish Road Administration (2009) Strategisk hantering av varudistribution i tätort – Exempel på effekter av innovativa åtgärder (*Strategic management of goods distribution in urban areas – Examples of the effects of innovative measures*), Swedish Road Administration Publication 2009:69, Borlänge
Taniguchi, E (2003) Introduction, in *Innovations in Freight Transport 1–14*, ed E Taniguchi and RG Thompson, WIT Press, Southampton
Taniguchi, E, Thompson, RG, Yamada, T and van Duin, R (2001) *City Logistics: Network modelling and intelligent transport systems*, Elsevier, Oxford
Teece, DJ (2010) Business models, business strategy and innovation, *Long Range Planning,* **43**, pp 172–94
Transport Analysis (2011) Statistikunderlag rörande tomtransporter och fyllnadsgrader *(Statistical data on empty running transport and fill rates),* Government Agency for Transport Policy Analysis Report 2011:5, Stockholm
Transport Analysis (2012) Godstransporter i Sverige. Redovisning av ett regeringsuppdrag *(Freight transport in Sweden. Report of a government assignment),* Government Agency for Transport Policy Analysis Report 2012:7, Stockholm

van Duin, JHR, Tavasszy, LA and Taniguchi, E (2007) Real time simulation of auctioning and re-scheduling processes in hybrid freight markets, *Transportation Research Part B*, **41**, pp 1050–66

van Weele, AJ (2010) *Purchasing and Supply Chain Management: Analysis, strategy, planning and practice*, 5th edn, Cengage Learning EMEA, Andover

Vierth, I, Mellin, A, Hylén, B, Karlsson, J, Karlsson, R and Johansson, M (2012) Kartläggning av godstransporterna i Sverige (*Survey of freight transport in Sweden*), VTI Publication 11 May 2012, Linköping

Waller, MA and Fawcett, SE (2013) Data science, predictive analytics, and big data: a revolution that will transform supply chain design and management, *Journal of Business Logistics,* **34** (2), pp 77–84

Weick, KE (1976) Educational organizations as loosely coupled systems, *Administrative Science Quarterly*, **21** (1), pp 1–19

Weigel, D and Cao, B (1999) Applying GIS and OR techniques to solve Sears technician-dispatching and home-delivery problems, *Interfaces,* **29** (1), pp 112–30

Williamsson, J and Moen, O (2017) Barriers to business model innovation in urban freight, Paper presented at the I-NUF conference, 20 October 20 2017, Long Beach

WinRoute (2012) *WinRoute 7.0. User's manual*, Routing International, Brussels

Future developments in modelling and information 16

EIICHI TANIGUCHI AND RUSSELL G THOMPSON

Introduction

City logistics provides innovative solutions for complicated urban freight transport problems to achieve the goals of developing mobile, sustainable and liveable cities. Several city logistics policy measures, including joint delivery systems, off-hour deliveries, truck bans and access control to city centres and the provision of on-street loading/unloading bays have been implemented in various cities of the world. However, evaluation of these policy measures is required before implementing them. Modelling urban freight transport is necessary to understand the benefits and issues of applying these policy measures. This chapter highlights the trends in modelling city logistics and also focuses on data collection and sharing for developing improved models. Since there are a number of stakeholders involved in city logistics, models need to encompass multiple actors with multiple objectives, and the evaluation of policy measures should incorporate multiple criteria.

City logistics is highly dependent upon urban freight transport systems as well as information systems. Recently, new technologies including ITS (intelligent transport systems), ICT (information and communication technology), the IoT (internet of things), big data and AI (artificial intelligence) are available for improving urban freight transport. Smart cities and smart logistics using these advanced information systems will be established in the near future.

This chapter addresses important features of advanced information systems for collecting and sharing data, communicating among stakeholders and making decisions for efficient and environmentally friendly urban freight transport systems within public–private partnerships. An outline of how city logistics models can be enhanced by incorporating more financial and business related concepts is presented. The need for information to improve infrastructure and land use planning for freight and logistics in cities is discussed. An overview is presented of how the management of freight vehicles on urban traffic networks can be improved by implementing sensor and dynamic control systems. A description of how models can be developed and applied to design multimodal and transshipment networks is also provided.

Financial modelling

The main focus of city logistics models to date has been on representing the physical elements such as truck and van movements in contrast to the business processes that motivate them. Better understanding of the information needs of decision-makers within businesses such as shippers, carriers and receivers that affect urban logistics is required to improve the sustainability and efficiency of urban freight systems.

Revenue management

To date, there has been an emphasis on models that aim to minimize the financial costs of freight operations in cities. However, more attention in the future needs to focus on profit maximization and value creation since these motivate the behaviour of shippers and carriers. To help cope with growing uncertainty and dynamic aspects of urban freight, revenue or yield management concepts could be adapted to develop effective decision support systems that incorporate profit. Recently, there are more opportunities for transport companies to access a larger number of jobs (collections and deliveries) due to online freight marketplaces.

Revenue management systems comprise four main components: demand forecasting, dynamic pricing, overbooking capacity and inventory control. They have been used in the aviation industry where information is exchanged between each component. Demand forecasting methods need to consider the trends, seasonality and cycles associated with freight demand. Estimates of future demand patterns of requests are important to match with capacity as well as determining prices and profits. Shippers and receivers can have different requirements in terms of delivery and pickup times. Inventory control involves how capacity is sold and managed, in terms of whether it is sold at a certain price or reserved for a potentially more profitable request later. Dynamic pricing involves how the price of jobs can be varied to account for fluctuations in demand and supply to maximize revenue and profits. This involves consideration of operating costs. Overbooking of capacity can be managed either by cancelling jobs, or postponing or outsourcing them.

There is need for information-based tools for couriers and carriers of general goods in cities that provide guidance on selecting the most profitable set of jobs. These should incorporate marginal and opportunity costs to identify optimal variable prices that can be used in dynamic competitive environments such as reverse online auctions.

Gain sharing

It is important that gain sharing procedures be incorporated within models for designing and evaluating horizontal collaborative transport networks since difficulties in determining and dividing financial gains can be a real impediment for implementing collaboration schemes.

A number of principles and methodologies have been developed for exploring how to share the costs or profits. Fair distribution of expected and unexpected costs among contributors is crucial. Models will be required to ensure transparency and to allow compensation rules so that the gains and risks can be allocated equitably in contrast to equally.

Several gain sharing methods based on compensation or cost allocation rules have been promoted including those based on distributing gains in proportion to a single indicator, marginal costs of entry as well as considering separable and non-separable costs (Guajardo and Ronnqvist, 2016; Cruijssen, *et al*, 2007). Desirable properties include equity (considering contributions) and stability (considering the share of the profits gained by each contributor).

There are major challenges in applying business modelling concepts in multi-stakeholder environments. However, business ecosystems that consider a network of connected businesses and value transfer and creation mechanisms seem to have potential for modelling the dynamics of city logistics schemes (Zenezini *et al*, 2018). This approach can overcome the weakness of business models that focus on only one company and do not explicitly consider decisions and evolution. Agent-based models have potential for representing the financial interactions between stakeholders and how these can change over time.

Toll usage

Carriers often have a choice of whether or not they use toll roads in many cities. Online systems currently exist for estimating travel times between trip origins and destinations (eg GoogleMaps) as well as vehicle operating costs (eg FreightMetrics, 2018). Dynamic path guidance systems incorporating predicted travel times, operating costs considering the type of vehicle and carrier (hire and reward or ancillary) would allow the financial benefits of using toll facilities to be estimated.

ETA prediction

The reliability of arrivals of delivery vehicles at shops and cross-docking facilities are becoming important concerns for retailers in major urban areas. Late arrivals can add considerable delays and resource costs for receivers. Scheduling of unloading equipment, stock checking and unpacking can be negatively impacted. Delays produce numerous challenges for facility managers in terms of the optimal assignment of loading docks as well as checking the quality and quantity of consignments. Management of sorting and temporary storage areas can also be affected.

Travel times between suppliers, warehouses and stores in cities are becoming more variable due to rising congestion levels and the growing number of incidents (including crashes, breakdowns and extreme weather events). Large freight vehicles have limited alternative routes that make it difficult for them to react to changing traffic and network conditions.

Large retail chains often utilize large freight vehicles that make dedicated deliveries to stores from distribution centres. Products from numerous suppliers are consolidated at distribution centres where products are cross-docked and transported to stores. Coordination of processes at both distribution centres as well as the stores is vital to minimize logistics costs. The supply chain is largely controlled by the stores with upstream logistics processes being influenced by the requirements of the stores.

Consequently, there is a need to produce more accurate forecasts of the expected time of arrival (ETA) of trucks at stores and distribution centres by utilizing a range of advanced sensors and traffic modelling procedures. This will allow receivers to more efficiently manage facilities and staff associated with receiving goods. Reduced costs for retailers will also be realized.

Carriers will benefit by quicker turnaround of trucks from fewer delays from accessing loading docks by more efficient allocation of resources at stores.

Recent developments in sensor and communication technologies as well as traffic modelling software has the potential for receivers of goods to improve their service levels in terms of reliability. Predicted arrival times of trucks at stores can be more responsive by being updated to reflect the conditions being experienced within the traffic. Better traceability of vehicles and products will enable improved communication between shippers and receivers that can lead to smoother handling of goods at customers' facilities and depots. Monitoring the location of freight vehicles in the traffic network (real-time vehicle tracking) will improve the transparency about the location of the delivery.

Procedures for designing and evaluating improved ETA estimation systems for trucks to provide dynamic traffic guidance and estimation of arrival times need to be developed. Such systems will utilize existing sensors and communications systems. A range of key technologies will need to be integrated, including:

- traffic simulation and prediction systems that utilize real-time traffic data from signal systems and allow accurate short-term predictions of traffic flows and travel times between specific origins and destinations on urban traffic networks;
- GPS and Bluetooth sensors for detecting the location of trucks travelling in the network in real time;
- linking shippers and receivers to improve dock management systems and unloading/loading scheduling.

ITS, ICT, the IOT, big data and AI

New technologies including ITS (intelligent transport systems), ICT (information and communication technology), the IoT (internet of things), big data and AI (artificial intelligence) are useful for establishing smart city logistics (Taniguchi and Thompson, 2014). These technologies allow an integrated platform for managing urban freight transport systems to be provided and operated in urban areas. The function of ITS and ICT includes:

- collecting data;
- storing data;
- analysing data for improving existing urban freight transport systems.

ITS and ICT are basic systems for collecting precise data about freight vehicle and goods movement. Recently, probe data of urban pickup–delivery trucks are recorded using GPS (global positioning systems) and telecommunications technology. Online data about the location of trucks can be used for improving the real-time operation of trucks. As well as accumulating and storing these data for the long term (a year or more), historical data allow freight carriers to find optimal solutions to their vehicle routing and scheduling problems for delivering commodities to customers.

Recently, the IoT has become popular in production and logistics systems using sensors for measuring the location, acceleration and weight of loads of freight vehicles, the temperature within containers, as well as RFID (radio frequency identification). The IoT can connect a great number of production sites, distribution centres, freight vehicles and commodities. Networks based on ITS, ICT and the IoT provide big data on urban freight transport systems. Big data has five 'V' characteristics: 1) Volume; 2) Velocity; 3) Variety; 4) Value; and 5) Veracity (Fosso-Wamba *et al*, 2015). Big data has a large Volume of data; for example, some in the order of petabytes (1 petabyte = 1,000 terabytes) of information are available on urban freight transport. Velocity is related to the frequency of data acquisition or data delivery. Probe data of truck movements in urban areas at every second are often provided from ITS. Variety indicates that data may have both quantitative and qualitative information including text messages. Big data can generate Value in terms of economic, social and environmental aspects. The Veracity of big data is associated with the inherent unpredictability within big data, which requires data analytics to gain reliable data. For example, some data are scattered in various data marts and filtering processes are needed before performing analyses.

Mehmood *et al* (2017) analysed the effects of big data on city transport providing a new understanding of load sharing and optimization in a smart city context. They demonstrated how big data can be used to improve transport efficiency and lower externalities in a smart city. Bibri (2018) highlighted the IoT and related big data applications for smart sustainable cities, focusing on an analytical framework for data-centric applications enabled by the IoT to advance environmental sustainability. The important point of big data applications in city logistics is the collaborative operation of urban freight transport in sharing the capacity of vehicles, distribution centres and information systems in the sharing economy. Big data related to urban freight transport are typically owned by private companies but the integration with publicly owned traffic and infrastructure data are needed for enhancing the operation of urban freight transport.

Taniguchi *et al* (2018) presented concepts of an integrated platform for innovative city logistics with urban consolidation centres (UCC) and transshipment points (TP). The concepts encompass joint delivery systems with shared use of pickup–delivery trucks, urban consolidation centres and transshipment points based on big data analytics. These systems involve public–private partnerships among shippers, freight carriers, UCC operators, municipalities and regional planning organizations, since the location of UCC and TP are highly related to urban land use plans and infrastructure provision as well as urban traffic management. ITS and ICT based communication systems for stakeholders are also essential for the efficient management of integrated platforms for both real-time and long-term operations. Integrated platforms can provide benefits such as improving the efficiency of urban deliveries and reducing CO_2 footprints.

Infrastructure and land use

Both infrastructure and land use have a profound influence on the efficiency and demand patterns of freight in urban areas. Although there is a vast range of issues and initiatives that will require enhanced data analysis and modelling methods in the future, this section focuses on how new infrastructure such as parcel lockers and transfer facilities can be developed using more shared and integrated networks for improving the sustainability of cities. A brief discussion of land use protection and schemes for safeguarding areas for freight and logistics activities is also presented.

Hyperconnected city logistics

Hyperconnected city logistics (HCL) is an emerging concept based on the physical internet (Crainic and Montreuil, 2016) that involves improved management of goods transfer facilities such as loading docks and parcel lockers. HCL consists of an integrated network of containers, nodes and vehicles using a shared network of nodes, including urban consolidation centres (UCCs) and cross-docking centres (CDCs) as well as joint multi-modal transport services (Taniguchi *et al*, 2018c). UCCs provide both a storage and transfer function while CDCs provide only a transfer service.

Information requirements for designing HCL networks include determining the: location, size and function of nodes; capacity, in terms of types of vehicles servicing nodes; and equipment for transferring containers.

The information requirements for network operations relate to developing schedules (frequency and timing) to coordinate transport services.

Parcel lockers

E-commerce, especially business to consumer (B2C), continues to grow at increasing rates and there is a need to develop more efficient and sustainable processes to cater for the rising levels of demand and provide high levels of service. Parcel lockers provide a flexible option for receivers to pick up goods and they can provide substantial financial savings for carriers as well as social and environmental benefits for residents.

To promote the use of parcel lockers in the future it will be important to improve understanding of the demand patterns and trends (from internet sales) as well as how this interacts with the supply of locker banks. The supply of parcel lockers relates to the location of banks as well as the number and size of lockers within them. Market segmentation involves understanding the convenience that lockers provide for online shoppers. Models are required to predict the best location for locker banks including sites near residences, offices, public transport terminals and shops.

There is a need to improve methods for determining the optimal number and type of lockers at parcel locker banks for maximizing convenience for customers as well as minimizing fixed and operating costs. Providing too many lockers can lead to additional capital and operating costs, while too few can lead to customers not being able to pick up their goods at their nominated location. Procedures for estimating the savings in capital and operating costs for incorporating uncertainty as well as financial benefits of offering incentives for early pickups will be required.

To maximize the potential of parcel locker systems for improving the efficiency and sustainability of last kilometre freight it will be important that open systems are created where lockers can be shared by multiple logistics organizations. Shared parcel locker systems also allow integrated multimodal business-to-business (B2B) logistics networks to be created.

Loading docks

Planning new major activity hubs such as office and residential towers requires the provision of adequate on-site loading/unloading facilities. It is important that designated space and access is provided for freight delivery vehicles. Information relating to the number and type of loading docks within off-street areas is required to ensure efficient and safe deliveries.

However, developers are generally reluctant to provide dedicated on-site space for deliveries at large freight generators. Therefore, given the constraints on the number of loading docks, it will be important that models be developed to identify cost-effective solutions for avoiding unnecessary delays for delivery vehicles as well as queues developing on the streets. Tools for predicting levels of freight trip generation based on initiatives for reducing (joint delivery services) and retiming of deliveries will be required. Other initiatives such as temporary storage including lockers as well as internal delivery services can reduce the time that delivery vehicles require to unload goods at loading docks. Models will also be necessary for identifying the most cost-effective options that could include dedicated off-site urban consolidation centres or dock booking systems that can smooth out the arrival profiles of delivery vehicles.

HCL will involve loading docks within central city areas having a broader precinct role allowing receivers outside the building or hub to be serviced. This will result in fewer freight vehicle movements but longer dwell times.

Logistics sprawl

Logistics sprawl involves the trend for warehousing to be pushed to the fringes of large cities. Before redeveloping logistics and industrial areas in the inner regions of cities, there needs to be an assessment of the freight impacts of relocating them to the outer areas. This will require a detailed understanding of freight and logistics patterns and models for predicting how they will be affected by moving warehousing to the outer metropolitan regions.

Due to logistics sprawl, many central city areas lack logistics facilities and this is adding to the costs of deliveries (Aljohani and Thompson, 2016). There is need to protect logistics spaces near central city areas, but procedures for estimating the financial, social and environmental impacts will need to be developed to ensure that planners can justify the retention of inner city logistics facilities. A recent study of the relocation of the wholesale fruit and vegetable market from an inner area to an outer area in Melbourne found that this added substantial logistics costs (Aljohani and Thompson, 2018).

Improved models and data collection procedures will be required to undertake impact assessments of rezoning existing logistics areas. This will involve estimating the environmental, energy, congestion and transport operating costs associated with changes in land use zoning. It is also important that freight transport impacts are considered when planning the location of new ports and airports servicing urban areas.

Safeguarding

As cities grow spatially it is important that areas for future major freight links and terminals be planned before development takes place so that freight can flow efficiently in and out as well as around urban areas. Future freight corridors and hubs need to be identified well in advance and protected from encroachment, otherwise the costs of providing infrastructure later can be prohibitive. To ensure that areas are adequately safeguarded an integrated set of freight and land use models will need to be developed.

Traffic management

Lane management

Freight vehicles typically share urban traffic networks but this can lead to increased levels of congestion and safety issues. There is a growing need for simulation models to be developed to explore how traffic lanes on urban motorways and main roads can be better managed. This would involve determining the effects of trucks on overall congestion levels and how different types of trucks and technologies such as platooned trucks would improve capacity. Such models could also be used for estimating the benefits of separate or exclusive truck lanes and lane restrictions for freight vehicles. The safety and productivity impacts of lower speed limits for trucks could also be investigated with more realistic simulation models.

Signal priority and speed guidance

Freight vehicles in large cities typically operate on road networks that are experiencing increasing levels of congestion and disruption. Recent developments in sensor and communications systems such as dedicated short range communication (DSRC) allow trucks to communicate in real time with infrastructure as well as other vehicles to improve the efficiency of urban distribution systems.

A substantial proportion of freight in many major cities is transported on arterial road networks that have a high density of signalized intersections. Although adaptive traffic signal systems have been implemented in various cities, they are currently not responsive to freight vehicles in real time.

Current signal timing procedures do not incorporate the operational characteristics of individual trucks such as longer braking distances and low acceleration rates compared with passenger vehicles. Consequently, freight vehicles typically experience significant delays that lead to increased operating costs and poor reliability for receivers.

City logistics schemes involve implementing advanced information systems to minimize social and environmental as well as economic costs. Additional stopping by trucks causes increased noise levels, fuel consumption and emissions. Since freight vehicles have substantially higher values of time compared with cars there are significant economic benefits from being able to adjust traffic signals to minimize delays for trucks.

Recent developments in ICT allow interaction between freight vehicles and traffic signals in real time. Characteristics of freight vehicles such as size, location, goods carried and their destinations can be transmitted to traffic control systems. For example, priority could be provided for freight vehicles carrying high-value goods that have economic importance or have high levels of consolidation.

Such vehicle to infrastructure (V2I) systems could be designed to minimize the total cost of moving freight on arterial roads of cities. Allocations of priority for freight vehicles at different times of the day, considering traffic conditions and impacts on adjacent land use such as noise levels in residential areas could be considered. Signal systems can utilize this information to grant priority or communicate to freight vehicle advisory speeds to minimize stops along key freight routes.

To improve the flow for freight vehicles, signal controllers could also be adjusted by:

- offsets between intersections that can be adjusted to reflect the slower acceleration of trucks from stops or upcoming electric trucks;
- green window stretching, where available green time can be lengthened to enable trucks to clear signals;
- special phases that could be incorporated with priority truck lanes;
- priority phase sequencing, enabling initiation of phases that grant priority to approaching freight vehicles.

Future traffic management systems will allow traffic signal systems to be integrated with freight vehicles in real time using connectivity technology such as DSRC called V2X. A range of roadside units and control systems will need to be designed, developed and evaluated. Such systems will utilize existing sensors and communications systems that have already been installed in the Australian Integrated Multi-modal EcoSystem (AIMES) including the transport network dashboard and large number of V2X roadside units deployed at major intersections on arterial roads in the AIMES area (AIMES, 2018).

Loading zone reservation and guidance systems

Distribution in central city areas is a challenging task that can be resource intensive for carriers and cause congestion. There is a need for improved decision support systems to reduce the driving and walking costs of vans and trucks. Sensor technologies can provide real-time data on the availability of bays in loading zones. This could be used to provide guidance and information for carriers. Reservation systems for on-street loading bays based on delivery schedules would also reduce carrier operating costs.

Routing models that incorporate both driving and walking can reduce the financial and environmental costs of deliveries in inner city areas (Thompson and Zhang, 2018). Such models can be used to predict the effects of changing the supply of on-street loading zones and their duration limits on carrier operating costs as well as emissions and congestion levels.

Optimal toll levels

Trucks typically generate more externalities (environmental and social) than passenger vehicles and this can be exacerbated when trucks divert off urban motorways. When toll charges are increased, more trucks tend to avoid toll roads (quality roads) generating more externalities. This adds substantial negative impacts on residents, the environment and society.

Determining optimum toll charges for freight vehicles is a crucial decision to be made by policymakers considering socio-economic aspects. Therefore, there is a need to develop models for determining optimal toll schemes for multi-class vehicles, including various truck types, considering direct costs and externalities. Procedures are required to identify the trade-offs between various objectives of the scheme considering given constraints.

The toll-setting problem can be considered a hierarchical problem where investors in collaboration with the government set toll prices (on certain links) with the intention of optimizing revenue. Once the prices are set, users react by setting up their itinerary such that their total travel cost, that is standard operating costs (time, distance, etc) plus tolls, are minimized. This hierarchical relationship exists between two autonomous, possibly conflicting decision-makers. This condition is similar to the Stackelberg game (leader–follower) in economics. However, it is important to note that leaders cannot control followers or their decision-making, but they can only influence them by setting the toll price. Therefore, once the toll prices are set, it is the user's decision to choose which route should be taken to a given destination. Thus, models developed would require two levels of decision-making, government at the upper level and users at the lower level.

The upper level would describe the role of policymaker, which is usually the government, who tries to minimize a number of main objectives considering all key stakeholders. Separate objectives could include minimizing total user costs (including toll cost), minimizing social costs and minimizing environmental costs. Constraints could include maximum toll charges for specific types of vehicles as well as maximum toll revenue levels based on reasonable return on investment values.

Models are required for designing road charging schemes for freight vehicles that create incentives for higher levels of consolidation and the production of lower emissions and noise levels.

Vehicle routing and scheduling

There is need to develop vehicle routing and scheduling procedures that avoid sensitive facilities such as schools and hospitals in urban areas. Procedures need to consider the social and environmental impacts adjacent to traffic links between customers. Initial results suggest that reductions in impacts can be achieved with relatively low increases in operating costs (Qureshi *et al*, 2018).

Loading dock booking systems

Unscheduled and unannounced arrivals by freight vehicles at loading docks at large activity centres in urban areas can have many consequences. These relate to the substantial costs that are associated with vehicles queuing at entrances to loading docks due to all loading/unloading bays being occupied during peak periods. This can result in increased traffic congestion on adjacent streets. The time spent coordinating deliveries manually including communication between suppliers, carriers, buyers and receivers can also be substantial.

Loading dock booking systems allow appointments to be made to access loading bays by electronically exchanging information between shippers, carriers, receivers and facility operators (Sanders *et al*, 2016). Booking systems can smooth out delivery patterns throughout the day since facility managers do not like too many drivers in a complex at one time, producing clutter and conflicts with shoppers. Significant safety issues can arise from too many vehicles trying to enter and leave a facility. Security can also be a concern in basement loading docks with some vehicles using the facility without delivering goods to that facility.

Models are required to predict queue lengths and delays as well as the number of loading bays required at facilities based on the number and type of stores, offices and residences. Predictions of revenue from booking systems are also required for budgeting capital and operational costs. Information is required on their potential environmental performance by considering the impacts on fuel consumption and emissions.

Evaluation and multi-agent models

Evaluating city logistics policy measures is important for understanding the benefits and problems of policy measures in advance before implementing them as well as assessing their effects after implementation. At both stages, feedback from evaluation is performed to modify the policy measures or implement other solutions if issues from the results were found.

Evaluation is conducted on multiple criteria in terms of economic, financial, environmental, social, safety and energy savings aspects, since a number of stakeholders are involved in city logistics including shippers, freight carriers, administrators and residents who have different objectives and interests.

In this context multi-agent models are required for evaluating city logistics policy measures based on the multi-actor, multi-criteria concepts. Multi-agent models address the behaviour of multiple agents, namely shippers, freight carriers, administrators and residents and, in addition, other agents of urban consolidation centre operators or urban motorway operators (Taniguchi *et al*, 2007; Tamagawa *et al*, 2010; van Duin *et al*, 2007, 2012; Roorda *et al*, 2010; Teo *et al*, 2012, 2014, 2015; Anand *et al*, 2014, 2016; Pira *et al*, 2017). These models allow city logistics policy measures to be evaluated in a dynamic manner with updated travel times on road networks given by traffic simulation. A reinforcement learning model including Q-learning (Teo *et al*, 2012) was used for replicating the learning behaviour of stakeholders. Adaptive dynamic programming (ADP) has also been used as a reinforcement learning model (Firdausiyah *et al*, 2018) in the dynamically fluctuating environment of customers' demands and travel times on the road network.

Multi-agent models assume decision-making mechanisms within agents. Agents usually make decisions based on their experience in the past and exploration in the future to maximize their expected sum of rewards. The process of agent's learning is sensitive to the fluctuating environment and the interaction among stakeholders. Therefore, agents need to update their policies at any time to adjust to changes in the environment. On-policy learning systems (Sutton and Barto, 1998), such as adaptive dynamic programming, are more suitable for adaptive management of urban freight transport in dynamically changing environments than off-policy learning systems including Q-learning (Firdausiyah *et al*, 2018).

Anand *et al* (2016) presented a validation framework based on a participatory simulation game and discussed how decision-making processes presented in multi-agent models can be validated. Validation of multi-agent models is required to apply them to real cases of urban freight transport. Taniguchi *et al* (2018b) demonstrated how multi-agent simulation can be used for evaluating a combination of city logistics policy measures focusing on consolidation centres, green management and parking management. They pointed out that in public–private partnerships (PPP), multi-agent models will play an important role for evaluating city logistics policy measures based on data. Sharing data from both the public and private sectors is essential and interaction between both sectors is necessary to find better solutions using the results provided by multi-agent simulations. This type of collaboration between public authorities and private companies is a key component of city logistics.

Network design challenges

Network design of urban freight transport systems depicts the comprehensive view of city logistics in terms of the location of terminals, vehicle routing on the road network and consolidation and transshipment points. As urban goods distribution networks are composed of nodes and links, network design encompasses determining the location of depots that provide the origin of travel and intermediate satellites for consolidation and transshipment as well as determining optimal vehicle routing on the road network considering various requests by customers and traffic conditions. As well, the combination of infrastructure and information systems is also an important feature of network design, since the efficient operation of logistics in urban areas greatly depends on how effectively information is used to minimize the costs of goods distribution and reduce negative environmental impacts.

Crainic and Sgalambro (2014) presented a service network design model for two-echelon city logistics. They addressed two-echelon goods delivery systems, which form the first tier from distribution centres on the outskirts of the city to satellites and the second tier from satellites to final customers. Faccio and Gamberi (2015) proposed eco-logistics systems in the last 50 miles using an eco-logistics hub and several local transport hubs. The idea highlights two-echelon city logistics with the consolidation of commodities in an eco-logistics hub. Snoeck *et al* (2018) demonstrated a stochastic mixed integer linear programming model to solve a two-echelon capacitated location-routing problem with uncertain demands in urban goods transport. In real operations two-echelon goods delivery systems are often observed. Taniguchi *et al* (2018a) discussed an urban consolidation centre (UCC) in Tokyo for delivering goods to a multi-tenant building in the heart of Tokyo, which contributed to substantially reducing the total number of small trucks used. These UCCs serve the role of satellites or intermediate depots in two-echelon goods delivery systems.

Munuzuri *et al* (2012) addressed the location of mini-hubs for distributing goods on foot to final customers in congested downtown areas with time windows. Goods delivery on foot or by carts or bicycles is a good option in busy city centres. The use of non-motorized modes for last mile delivery can be incorporated in the network design of city logistics.

Intermodal freight transport plays an important role in city logistics, as intermodal systems can support both economic efficiency and environmentally friendly urban freight transport. Teye *et al* (2017) presented models for optimizing the location of urban intermodal container terminals that interface with both road and rail networks. van Duin *et al* (2014) discussed the possibility of using freight waterborne transport for urban goods delivery in Amsterdam.

Shared transport of passengers and freight in urban areas provides new challenges for using transport modes for carrying both passengers and goods. Fatnassi *et al* (2015) proposed a shared goods and passenger on-demand rapid transit system in urban areas. They investigated the potential of an integrated network designed for passenger rapid transit and freight rapid transit. Ronald *et al* (2016) discussed co-modality using on-demand transport systems for transporting both passengers and freight in urban areas. Advanced information systems using mobile phones and GPS (global positioning systems) allow combined passenger and freight transport systems.

Network design is highly related to land use and infrastructure provision. As discussed in section four, in many urban areas logistics sprawl is common where more logistics facilities including warehouses are being located on the fringe of cities leading to a lack of distribution centres in the inner area of cities. Improving network design using joint delivery systems with urban consolidation centres and transshipment points can help reduce delivery costs and optimize the location of logistics facilities in urban areas (Taniguchi *et al*, 2018a).

Conclusions

As the population in cities continues to grow there are increasing challenges for all city logistics stakeholders to cope with growing levels of congestion and disruption. More integrated and real-time data from sensors provide an opportunity to develop richer information and improved models. New sensor technologies and analysis tools will allow more intelligent management of road freight systems in cities. The IoT and data mining procedures can be used to design more dynamic, shared and open urban freight networks.

An increased emphasis on financial modelling will be required to develop new business models for successfully implementing city logistics solutions. More integrated models are necessary for designing multi-modal freight networks. There is also a need for improved decision-making tools for enhancing land use planning that considers freight and logistics. Modelling and evaluation tools that incorporate multiple actors and multi-criteria are required to provide information for decision-makers for improving the sustainability and efficiency of freight in cities.

References

AIMES (2018) The University of Melbourne [Online] https://industry.eng.unimelb.edu.au/transport#aimes

Aljohani, K and Thompson, RG (2016) Impacts of logistics sprawl on the urban environment and logistics: taxonomy and review of literature, *Journal of Transport Geography*, **57**, pp 255–63

Aljohani, K and Thompson, RG (2018) Impacts of relocating a logistics facility on last food miles – the case of Melbourne's fruit & vegetable wholesale market, *Case Studies on Transport Policy*, **6**, pp 279–88

Anand, N, van Duin, JHR and Tavasszy, L (2014) Ontology-based multi-agent system for urban freight transportation, *International Journal of Urban Sciences*, **18** (2), pp 133–53

Anand, N, Meijer, D, van Duin, JHR, Tavasszy, L and Meijer, S (2016) Validation of an agent based model using a participatory simulation gaming approach: the case of city logistics, *Transportation Research Part C*, **71**, pp 489–99

Bibri, SE (2018) The IoT for smart sustainable cities of the future: an analytical framework for sensor-based big data applications for environmental sustainability, *Sustainable Cities and Society*, **38**, pp 230–53

Crainic, TG and Sgalambro, A (2014) Service network design models for two-tier city logistics, *Optimization Letters*, **8**, pp 1375–87

Crainic, TG and Montreuil, B (2016) Physical internet enabled hyperconnected city logistics, *Transportation Research, Procedia*, **12**, pp 383–98

Cruijssen, F, Dullaert, W and Fleuren, H (2007) Horizontal co-operation in transport and logistics: a literature review, *Transportation Journal*, **46** (3), pp 22–39

Faccio, M and Gamberi, M (2015) New city logistics paradigm: from the 'last mile' to the 'last 50 miles' sustainable distribution, *Sustainability*, 7, pp 14873–94

Fatnassi, E, Chaouachi, J and Klibi, W (2015) Planning and operating a shared goods and passengers on-demand rapid transit system for sustainable city-logistics, *Transportation Research Part B*, **81**, pp 440–60

Firdausiyah, N, Taniguchi, E and Qureshi, AG (2018) Multi-agent simulation using adaptive dynamic programming for evaluation urban consolidation centres, in *City Logistics 2: Modelling and planning initiatives*, ed E Taniguchi and RG Thompson, pp 211–28, ISTE, London

Fosso-Wamba, S, Akter, S, Edwards, A, Chopin, G and Denis Gnanzou, D (2015) How 'big data' can make big impact: findings from a systematic review and a longitudinal case study, *International Journal of Production Economics*, **165**, pp 234–46

FreightMetrics (2018) [Online] www.freightmetrics.com.au

Guajardo, M and Ronnqvist, M (2016) A review on cost allocation methods in collaborative transportation, *International Transactions in Operational Research*, **23**, pp 371–92

Mehmood, R, Meriton, R, Graham, G, Hennelly, P and Kumar, M (2017) Exploring the influence of big data on city transport operations: a Markovian approach, *International Journal of Operations & Production Management*, **37** (1), pp 75–104

Munuzuri, J, Cortes, P, Grosso, R and Guadix, J (2012) Selecting the location of minihubs for freight delivery in congested downtown areas, *Journal of Computational Science*, **3**, pp 228–37

Pira, ML, Marcucci, E, Gatta, V, Ignaccolo, M, Inturri, G and Pluchino, A (2017) Towards a decision-support procedure to foster stakeholder involvement and acceptability of urban freight transport policies, *European Transport Research Review*, **9**, p 54

Qureshi, AG, Taniguchi, E and Iwase, G (2018) Vehicle routing considering the safety and environment near urban facilities, Chapter 18 in *City Logistics 1: New opportunities and challenges*, ed E Taniguchi and RG Thompson, ISTE, Wiley

Ronald, N, Yang, J and Thompson, RG (2016) Exploring co-modality using on-demand transport systems, *Transportation Research Procedia,* **12**, pp 203–12

Roorda, MJ, Cavalcante, R, McCabe, S and Kwan, H (2010) A conceptual framework for agent-based modelling of logistics services, *Transportation Research Part E,* **46**, pp 18–31

Sanders, D, Hancock, S and Thompson, RG (2016) Managing City Logistics with MobileDOCK, Paper AN-CP0324, 23rd ITS World Congress, Melbourne, Australia, 10–14 October 2016

Snoeck, A, Winkenbach, M and Mascariono, EE (2018) Establishing a robust urban logistics network at FEMSA through stochastic multi-echelon location routing, in *City Logistics 2: Modelling and planning initiatives*, ed E Taniguchi and RG Thompson, pp 59–78, ISTE, Wiley, London

Sutton, RS and Barto AG (1998) *Reinforcement Learning: An introduction*, MIT Press, Cambridge

Tamagawa, D, Taniguchi, E and Yamada, T (2010) Evaluating city logistics measures using a multi-agent model, *Procedia – Social and Behavioral Sciences,* **2** (3), pp 6002–12

Taniguchi, E, Yamada, T and Okamoto, M (2007) Multi-agent modelling for evaluating dynamic vehicle routing and scheduling systems, *Journal of Eastern Asia Society, Transportation Studies,* **7**, pp 933–48

Taniguchi, E and Thompson, RG (2014) *City Logistics: Mapping the future*, CRC Press, New York

Taniguchi, E, Dupas, R, Deschanmps, J-C and Qureshi, AG (2018a) Concepts of an integrated platform for innovative city logistics with urban consolidation centers and transshipment points, in *City Logistics 3: Towards Sustainable and Liveable Cities,* ed E Taniguchi and RG Thompson, pp 129–46, ISTE, Wiley, London

Taniguchi, E, Qureshi, AG and Konda, K (2018b) Multi-agent simulation with reinforcement learning for evaluating a combination of city logistics policy measures, In *City Logistics 2: Modelling and planning initiatives*, ed E Taniguchi and RG Thompson, pp 165–78, ISTE, Wiley, London

Taniguchi, E, Thompson, RG and Qureshi, A (2018c) Recent developments and prospects for modelling city logistics, Chapter 1 in *City Logistics 1 – New opportunities and challenges*, ed E Taniguchi and RG Thompson, pp 1–28, ISTE, Wiley, London

Teo, JSE, Taniguchi, E and Qureshi, AG (2012) Evaluation of distance-based and cordon-based urban freight road pricing on e-commerce environment with multi-agent model, *Transportation Research Record: Journal of the Transportation Research Board*, **2269**, pp 127–34

Teo, JSE, Taniguchi, E and Qureshi, AG (2014) Multi-agent systems modelling approach to evaluate urban motorways for city logistics, *International Journal of Urban Sciences*, **18** (2), pp 154–65

Teo, JSE, Taniguchi, E and Qureshi, AG (2015) Evaluation of urban distribution centers using multiagent modeling with geographic information systems, *Transportation Research Record: Journal of the Transportation Research Board*, **2478**, pp 35–47

Teye, C, Bell, MGH and Bliemer, MCJ (2017) Urban intermodal terminals: the entropy maximising facility location problem, *Transportation Research Part B* **100**, pp 64–81

Thompson, RG and Zhang, L (2018) Optimising courier routes in central city areas, *Transportation Research Part C*, **93**, pp 1–12

van Duin, JHR, Kortmann, R and van der Boogaard, SL (2014) City logistics through the canals? A simulation study on fright waterborne transport in the inner-city of Amsterdam, *International Journal of Urban Sciences*, **18** (2), pp 186–200

van Duin, JHR, van Kolck, A, Anand, N, Tavasszy, L and Taniguchi, E (2012) Towards an agent based modelling approach for the dynamic usage of urban distribution centres, *Procedia – Social and Behavioral Sciences,* **39**, pp 333–48

van Duin, JHR, Tavasszy, LA and Taniguchi, E (2007) Real time simulation of auctioning and re-scheduling processes in hybrid freight markets, *Transportation Research, Part B,* **41** (9), pp 1050–66

Zenezini, G, van Duin, R, Tavasszy, L and De Marco, A (2018) Stakeholders' Roles for Business Modeling in a City Logistics Ecosystem: Towards a Conceptual Model, Chapter 3 in *City Logistics 2 – Modeling and Planning Initiative*, ed E Taniguchi and RG Thompson, pp 39–58, ISTE, Wiley, London

INDEX